Parallel Politics

Parallel Politics

Economic Policymaking in the United States and Japan

SAMUEL KERNELL

Editor

JAPAN CENTER FOR
INTERNATIONAL EXCHANGE
Tokyo

BROOKINGS INSTITUTION
Washington

Library of Congress Cataloging-in-Publication data:
   Kernell, Samuel, 1945–
      Parallel politics : economic policymaking in Japan and the United States /
   Samuel Kernell.
          p.   cm.
      Includes bibliographical references and index.
      ISBN 0-8157-4892-2 (alk. paper)—ISBN 0-8157-4891-4
   (pbk. : alk. paper)
      1. Japan—Economic policy—1989– 2. Japan—Politics and government—1945–
   3. Political culture—Japan. 4. United States—Economic policy—1981–
   5. United States—Politics and government—1989– 6. Political culture—United
   States. I. Title.
   HC462.9.K4436 1991
   338.952—dc20   90-21946
                                                                             CIP

9 8 7 6 5 4 3 2 1

Set in Linotron Times Roman
Composition by Monotype Composition Co.
  Baltimore, Maryland
Printed by R.R. Donnelley and Sons Co.
  Harrisonburg, Virginia

℔ THE BROOKINGS INSTITUTION

The Brookings Institution is an independent organization devoted to nonpartisan research, education, and publication in economics, government, foreign policy, and the social sciences generally. Its principal purposes are to aid in the development of sound public policies and to promote public understanding of issues of national importance.

The Institution was founded on December 8, 1927, to merge the activities of the Institute for Government Research, founded in 1916, the Institute of Economics, founded in 1922, and the Robert Brookings Graduate School of Economics and Government, founded in 1924.

The Board of Trustees is responsible for the general administration of the Institution, while the immediate direction of the policies, program, and staff is vested in the President, assisted by an advisory committee of the officers and staff. The by-laws of the Institution state: "It is the function of the Trustees to make possible the conduct of scientific research, and publication, under the most favorable conditions, and to safeguard the independence of the research staff in the pursuit of their studies and in the publication of the results of such studies. It is not a part of their function to determine, control, or influence the conduct of particular investigations or the conclusions reached."

The President bears final responsibility for the decision to publish a manuscript as a Brookings book. In reaching his judgment on the competence, accuracy, and objectivity of each study, the President is advised by the director of the appropriate research program and weighs the views of a panel of expert outside readers who report to him in confidence on the quality of the work. Publication of a work signifies that it is deemed a competent treatment worthy of public consideration but does not imply endorsement of conclusions or recommendations.

The Institution maintains its position of neutrality on issues of public policy in order to safeguard the intellectual freedom of the staff. Hence interpretations or conclusions in Brookings publications should be understood to be solely those of the authors and should not be attributed to the Institution, to its trustees, officers, or other staff members, or to the organizations that support its research.

Foreword

As Japan and the United States pursue their sometimes fitful search for a new partnership in a dramatically changed global environment, both sides occasionally resort to old caricatures of the other. A burgeoning popular literature in this country about Japanese society and politics stresses the many ways in which Japan is different from the United States.

Some observers attribute Japan's economic success to a consensual culture that subordinates private interests to the general welfare. Others locate success more narrowly in the talents of a class of politically insulated bureaucrats who guide the nation's economic policies without regard to partisan or private interests. Still others, adopting a cynical view, find that private interests are well served by economic policy under the guise of national welfare.

This volume instead emphasizes the commonalities in economic policymaking in the two countries. The countries may have dissimilar economic policies, but their leaders are motivated by broadly similar political concerns. Members of the U.S. Congress and the Japanese Diet who have participated in exchange programs and joint seminars have found little difficulty in appreciating the political circumstances of their counterparts in the other country.

This book is the outcome of an eighteen-month seminar of Japanese and American scholars organized to seek a broad understanding of each country's policymaking institutions and processes. Two sessions were held in Tokyo and one in Washington. The enterprise became a search for underlying commonalities that could provide a truly comparative framework.

The editor of the volume, Samuel Kernell, is professor of political science at the University of California at San Diego and a former senior fellow in the Brookings Governmental Studies program. He wishes to thank the many people who assisted in the book's preparation. Nancy D. Davidson, Martha V. Gottron, and Venka Macintyre edited the volume. Secretarial assistance was provided by Renuka D. Deonarain, Ellen Isan, Pamela Kulik, Dierdre Martinez, Vida R. Megahed, Eloise C. Stinger, Susan Thompson, Teresita V. Vitug, and Antoinette T. Williams. Sandra Z. Riegler assisted in managing the project. Todd L. Quinn verified factual statements and citations, Susan L. Woollen prepared the manuscript for typesetting, and Florence Robinson prepared the index.

The Japan Center for International Exchange cohosted the seminar with Brookings and is a copublisher of this volume. Brookings has worked on numerous occasions with the JCIE and its president, Tadashi Yamamato. The seminar was financed by a generous grant from the Henry Luce Foundation, Inc.

The interpretations, conclusions, and recommendations presented here are solely those of the authors and should not be ascribed to the persons whose assistance is acknowledged, to any group that funded research reported herein, or to the trustees, officers, or other staff members of the Brookings Institution.

BRUCE K. MacLAURY
President

February 1991
Washington, D.C.

Contents

Part I: Overview of the Japanese and American Political Systems

Part II: The Politics of Budgeting

Part V: Conclusion

Tables

Figures

The Need for a
Comparative Perspective

Samuel Kernell

THE United States is Japan's largest export market for consumer goods; Japan, in turn, has become the largest foreign consumer of the American debt. Such developments are pulling these two countries' economies into increasing interdependence, yet injecting serious political tensions into their relations. Dissatisfaction is no longer limited to local producer groups—such as Flint, Michigan, auto workers or Japanese rice farmers—that are threatened by the other country's participation in their domestic market. Rather, in both countries their bilateral relations are quickly becoming a thorny political issue.[1]

The fruits of escalated rhetoric are coming to harvest. A 1990 survey in the United States found respondents identifying Japan more frequently than the Soviet Union as the greater threat to U.S. security. And in the July 1989 Japanese elections, candidates calling for resistance to U.S. trade pressure garnered more votes than their parties' past performance gave them a right to expect. If political parties in both countries discover that tough rhetoric wins a receptive audience, can public policy be far behind?

Even the long-standing security pact between the two countries, firmly footed on mutual advantage, has become controversial. During the postwar occupation period, the United States required Japan to dismantle its military and agreed to provide in return for that country's defense needs. In addition to preventing the unacceptable remilitarization of its recent enemy, this arrangement gave the U.S. Seventh Fleet strategically important naval bases and legitimated the American presence in Asia. In return, Japan partially subsidized the costs of these military installations and became one of the United States' staunchest allies in international affairs.

1. Karl Schoenberger, "U.S.-Japan War of Words Grows More Confrontational," *Los Angeles Times,* October 23, 1989, p. D1.

Today each of these features is the subject of negotiations between the two countries. The United States is pressing Japan to shoulder a greater share of security costs, while Japan is insisting on greater participation in the development and manufacture of the weapons systems deployed in its defense. And both recognize that Japan should assume a posture in world affairs commensurate with its economic strength. With these and other important issues on the negotiating table at the same time, each country has undertaken a fundamental reassessment of its relationship with the other. They are engaged in this exercise at a moment when their interests are more tightly, yet more problematically, intertwined than ever before.

At times this reappraisal turns introspective. Leaders on both sides assess the adequacy of their own country's policies and institutions against the other's success. This has led many business and political leaders in the United States to consider adopting as a model Japan's government-sponsored research and development associations, which allow businesses to share the cost of developing new technologies. The Sematech consortium for developing future generations of semiconductor technology is the first important enterprise of this type adopted in the United States. And it in turn has stimulated calls for similar enterprises in other research-intensive fields, including high definition television, biotechnology, and computer software. Imitation of Japanese practices has also occurred in manufacturing. Detroit has incorporated many features of the Japanese team approach on its automobile assembly lines in hopes of achieving comparable levels of worker productivity. In Japan, the government and businesses are being pushed to expand domestic consumption by liberalizing consumer credit and rules governing the distribution of retail goods and services. Advocates point to American practices as examples of success and models for reform.

Political institutions have not been exempt from this reappraisal. American politicians from both political parties have advanced a version of Japan's Ministry of International Trade and Industry (MITI). In October 1989 House Majority Leader Richard Gephardt introduced legislation to reorganize the Commerce Department and the Office of the U.S. Trade Representative into a MITI-styled cabinet-level department. In Japan, conversely, there has been increased interest in strengthening its Fair Trade Commission and making it more aggressive in breaking up collusive practices.

Before either side begins grafting institutions, however, a clearer appreciation of their appropriateness as a model for reform is needed.

Given the interdependencies of governmental institutions, they are not easily uprooted and transplanted from one political system to another. For example, much of MITI's success has come through brokering the formation of hundreds of cartels, which if implemented in the United States would require dismantling a well-established system of antitrust regulations. MITI was developed under a conservative regime trying to restore its war-ravaged industrial base through a strategy of expanding exports, restraining domestic consumption, and encouraging savings. It required state-directed financing to generate the necessary capital for industrial expansion and to induce private industry to accept fixed market shares. Moreover, the governing Liberal Democratic party (LDP) ceded great discretion to the bureaucracy to develop and administer these enterprises. It is hard to envision public or private institutions in the United States accepting such changes.

Each country's most pressing need for information about how the other conducts its business and government is in the area of trade. The United States is pushing for a dramatic liberalization of Japanese trade practices on many fronts—including finished lumber imports, access to the equities markets, participation of American professional services, and opportunities to bid on construction contracts—while Japan is trying to preserve current arrangements and insisting that the United States tackle its budget deficit. Thus these two countries find themselves locked in a fitful search for some new, as yet uncertain, equilibrium in their relations. Given their differing stances on current arrangements, arriving at agreements for change has understandably been arduous. Because trade balances, currency rates, and macroeconomic indexes have dominated current discussions, it is easy to forget that the relationship between Japan and the United States is founded essentially on each side's domestic political imperatives.

When Secretary of Commerce Robert Mosbacher traveled to Japan in September 1989 with the message that opening up Japanese markets is in that country's best economic interest, he enlisted the compelling rationale that subsidies, whatever their form, promote inefficiencies. But his statement was greeted more by derision than by enthusiasm. Macroeconomic considerations were but one concern of the architects who constructed Japan's economic system. The kinds of changes Mosbacher was proposing would entail significant income transfers, either from one group of producers to another or between producers and consumers. The current economic system reflects a long-standing political pact between the LDP and numerous sectors of the economy that have profited handsomely over the years. Perhaps this was the commerce secretary's real message when he reminded Japanese consumers that they pay dearly for their country's current import and retail system.

Whatever the effects of current import and retail practices on the overall economy, their distributional effects are critical to an economic policy's political feasibility. Classic political questions must be addressed. Who wins, who loses, and to what extent? How well mobilized are the affected constituencies? How sympathetic a hearing will they receive from the political parties and government? And as politicians sort through the claims of particular economic interests, to what extent do they lose sight of the broader national interest?

Each country is well advised to anticipate the domestic political reverberations for the other as it fashions proposals for negotiation. Each needs to advance proposals that satisfy its policy objectives while minimizing the costs imposed on the other side. In the end, these are the kinds of policies that will provide the basis for a stable bilateral relation. Such an exercise requires each country to develop a sophisticated appreciation of the other's political dynamics, and this, many critics have concluded, has been missing in current relations.

The protracted dispute over the development of Japan's next-generation fighter aircraft provides numerous examples.[2] The U.S. State and Defense departments naively accepted at face value the Japan Defense Agency's assertion that certain contract provisions were politically mandatory if a joint production agreement were to be accepted by the LDP. Many of these provisions were subsequently dropped without much controversy. And later, during the congressionally mandated renegotiation of what had appeared to be a settled coproduction agreement, Japan's leaders protested with such vehemence as to reveal a lack of understanding of the difference of interests between a Republican administration and a Democratic Congress. Rather than reconciling these long-standing security partners, the final coproduction agreement left both countries deeply suspicious of each other's motives.

James Fallows, who is among the most politically attuned observers

---

2. The most thorough analysis of the FSX negotiation is Gregory W. Noble's "Japan, America and the FSX Jet Fighter Plane: Structural Asymmetries in Bilateral Negotiations," paper prepared for the 1990 meeting of the Association for Asian Studies. Also see the introduction to the paperback edition of Clyde V. Prestowitz, Jr., *Trading Places: How We Are Giving Our Future to Japan and How to Reclaim It* (Basic Books, 1989).

of these countries' relations, contends that Japan's firms and government representatives have enjoyed a competitive edge because they have been more astute politically than their American counterparts. This view is echoed by Dutch journalist Karel van Wolferen, who has written, "The continual frustration of the U.S. expectations with regard to Japanese policies, or their absence, indicates that Washington's understanding of its foremost Asian ally . . . is often so faulty as to appall observers."[3] That this would be true is reasonable, given that Japan's economy has been more conditioned by America's economy and markets over the postwar era than vice versa. And Japan has needed fewer concessions: its export industry found ready access to the U.S. market. But Fallows points to another reason for Japan's political success: "America contains a class of lobbyists who are paid to help bend policy in another country's favor; Japan does not." While "the spectacle of retired politicians promoting Japanese interests has attracted a lot of publicity in the United States," Fallows argues, "the real significance is the imbalance it creates in the two nations' ability to influence each other."[4]

Thus even Japan's success has less to do with a sophisticated appreciation of American politics than in having high-quality surrogates available to represent its interests. And those surrogates may offer only a second-best arrangement. The myopic attention of paid consultants poorly equips them to help a country or firm recognize its broader strategic interests in dealing with the other country's government and market.

What is needed, and is presently conspicuously missing, is a broad understanding of each side's preferences and motives and how these collective positions are arrived at. This book reflects the work of an eighteen-month seminar of Japanese and American scholars organized to correct this deficiency. Because budgets, taxes, and other macroeconomic policies are so central to the activities of these governments and because they dominate discussions about these countries' bilateral relations, the participants in the seminar agreed at the outset to concentrate largely on this important subset of government decisions. We excluded trade policy from formal consideration for two reasons. Unlike these other subjects, trade policy has received substantial comparative treatment in news coverage and scholarly analysis. Moreover, because

3. Karel van Wolferen, *The Enigma of Japanese Power: People and Politics in a Stateless Nation* (Knopf, 1989), p. 4.
4. James Fallows, "Tokyo: The Japan-Handlers," *Atlantic*, August 1989, p. 18.

trade policy is so entwined in bilateral negotiations it provides a less suitable subject for assessing the political logic of each country's posture toward the other.

The seminar convened in both countries' capitals, some of its time devoted to interviewing and being briefed by government officials and politicians, but more in discussion, comparing notes and exchanging impressions. The enterprise soon took the form of a search for underlying commonalities and principles—that is, a framework with which to compare these two countries' political systems.

We began with simple questions: To what extent do politics matter? Is there any reason that elected officials should not be the appropriate subjects of our inquiry? Finally, finding that these politicians merited our consideration, we asked how they might pursue their self-interest in making public policy. These questions may be unobjectionable for those who study American politics, but they are offensive to many who write about Japan. Clyde Prestowitz throws down the gauntlet more earnestly than most when he argues, "There is an obtuse tendency to interpret Japan in terms of the United States and to assume that if there is not an overt legal basis for power, it does not exist. To accept this fallacy is . . . to ignore the subtle, nonlegalistic nature of Japanese society."[5]

A Framework for Comparative Analysis

By definition, politicians' self-interest includes reelection or movement to a higher office. Thus political ambition will direct their actions in ways that enhance their chances for reelection. This will make them *strategically* responsive to public opinion, but may not guarantee that they will follow their constituents' preferences or will champion a broad conception of the public good.

Politicians rely upon their constituents to tell them their preferences. The views that are communicated most frequently and forcefully will weigh most heavily in their decisions. But staying informed about upcoming policy choices and communicating with one's representative are costly for citizens. On any given issue, most will not communicate their preferences to their representative, and those who do can be expected to have a sufficiently large stake in the outcome of the policy to justify the effort. Typically, communication will be at odds with majority preferences when the benefits are highly concentrated and the

5. Prestowitz, *Trading Places*, p. 238.

costs are distributed across a broad population. The standard example of this phenomenon is the differential political involvement that commonly exists between producers and consumers. Japan's medical profession has for years successfully lobbied the government against the import of birth control pills, thereby preserving its lucrative business of abortions as the chief method of birth control. Similarly, American computer chip manufacturers prevailed upon the Reagan administration to negotiate voluntary restraints on Japanese "dumping" practices that drove down the price of computer chips. And in both countries, farmers (that ubiquitous class of politically active producers) effectively press their interests within the government.

Bureaucrats' behavior must also be taken into account in any comparative assessment of national policymaking. Although they occupy a constitutionally subordinate position in both countries and lack the legitimacy of elective officeholders, they enjoy certain assets that allow them to influence public policy. For one, they may have a monopoly on expertise and technical information. And while they do not have constituents in a formal sense, their relations with client groups may provide formidable political allies in their dealings with politicians.

Certainly, many political relations conform to the broad contours of the political explanation sketched above. Indeed, the reader will find a variety of interpretations of Japanese and American politics in the following chapters. Yet this broad emphasis on political institutions and actors disciplined our comparative inquiry in an important way. In subordinating explanations that render each country's politics exceptional in favor of those that find similarities in goal-seeking behavior, it kept our inquiry directed toward their underlying commonalities of public life.

Politics versus Culture

Scholarly, as well as popular, accounts of Japanese policymaking tend to trivialize politicians and instead find explanations for policies in broader cultural and societal forces. Consider how different the following two popular accounts of Japanese policymaking are from the assumptions that guided the seminar.

The first comes from sociologist Ezra F. Vogel in his highly influential 1979 book *Japan as Number One*, the second from journalist Karel van

Wolferen in his 1989 book, *The Enigma of Japanese Power*.[6] Vogel locates decisions in an elite group groomed to preside over the cultural pact, while van Wolferen leaves decisions mostly unmade, floating amorphously within "the System." However serious their disagreement about Japanese society, they concur in denying that public policy arises from strategic politicians engaging one another in the political marketplace.

More than anyone else, Vogel popularized the persistent image of Japan as a consensual society. So different from Americans' critical perceptions of their own country's politics, Vogel's Japan remains for many a model for how public life should be transacted. It also deserves serious attention because his statement conveys a perspective that has long been favored by many Japanese scholars.[7]

The consensus that regulates Vogel's Japan is not hammered out by political exchange and coalition building, but rather arises when members of a community voluntarily subordinate their private interests to a shared view of the common good. In part, Vogel locates this culture of consensus in the nation's racial homogeneity and late emergence from its feudal heritage. Yet some mechanism must be at work manufacturing consensus by reconciling the variety of different interests and, when necessary, fending them off from encroachment on the broader public interest. Clearly, the political system described in this book, with its factionalized political parties, organized economic constituencies, election-driven politicians, and bureaucrats competing for influence, is ill suited for the dispassionate reasoning Vogel's communitarian society requires.

What is needed, instead, are philosopher kings, and Vogel finds them toiling away in the upper echelons of the bureaucracy. Trained for public service at elite institutions, secure in their employment, and inculcated with a "sense of responsibility for overall economic success," these bureaucrats are well able "to concentrate on what is good for the nation as a whole." And there is one more critical attribute: they have the upper hand over those self-interested, partisan politicians. As Vogel says, "Politicians respect the ability of bureaucrats and recognize that they need their good will."[8]

---

6. Ezra F. Vogel, *Japan as Number One: Lessons for America* (Harvard University Press, 1979); and van Wolferen, *Enigma of Japanese Power*.

7. For a recent English-language presentation of this line of argument by a Japanese scholar, see Murakami Yasusuke, "Ie Society as a Pattern of Civilization," *Journal of Japanese Studies*, vol. 10 (Summer 1984), pp. 281–363.

8. Vogel, *Japan as Number One*, pp. 59, 65.

Free of political control, the elite bureaucracy goes about its work of creating consensus by a process known as social "root binding":

> The Japanese bureaucracy provides vigorous direction on many major issues, continuing over a long period of time, and during this process they are in close touch with all relevant groups to make sure they understand the evolving decisions, that their roots are bound. . . . The relevant groups are not expected to agree with all decisions made by the bureaucrats. Sometimes a group's interests are not in keeping with the emerging decision, and this group must be made to understand the necessity of the decision and the well-considered impartiality of the decision. If that group is disadvantaged by this decision, then it is understood that they will be given special consideration now or in the future. The long-term continuity in bureaucratic leadership, unimpaired by changes of politicians, ensures the reliability of bureaucrats in carrying through future commitments.[9]

Elites within the bureaucracy implement a cultural system of shared values, the most important of which is that some transcendent public good should not be compromised by private interests.

Karel van Wolferen finds fault with Vogel's virtues. He sees the cultural system of which consensus is a central feature as merely a mechanism of social control. While van Wolferen's model of Japanese politics, which he calls "the System," is a highly original and suggestive statement, it contains profound contradictions that would go far beyond the scope of this essay to resolve. It deserves consideration, nonetheless, as the most recent effort to explain Japanese public policy while minimizing the role of elected politicians and constitutional offices.[10]

Japan is a society riddled by fragmented authority, he claims, a nation leaderless because no one is able to muster sufficient power. Even within institutions—newspapers and government ministries are two favorite examples—leaders are short on authority, a fact that is reflected in their organizations' inability to act coherently. None of this violates the notion that politics among constitutional actors is what really matters.

---

9. Vogel, *Japan as Number One*, p. 94.

10. The following passage is as close as van Wolferen comes to defining his System: "The term 'system' is . . . very useful in speaking of political Japan, and I will give it the capital 'S' it deserves for denoting something, neither 'state' nor 'society,' that nevertheless determines how Japanese life is lived and who obeys whom." Van Wolferen, *Enigma of Japanese Power*, p. 44.

But van Wolferen also claims that somehow this "System" without a center or core has managed to install extraordinary mechanisms of social control. Hierarchy in social relations, imposed conformity, and Vogel's communal society in which private interests are illegitimate all work to enforce an uneasy equilibrium of the social order. Massive social control, apparently involving the participation of virtually everyone to hold their competitors in check, suppresses claims of self-interest—the same interests our seminar regarded as the driving force behind economic policymaking.

Clearly, some groups in society, such as big business, are better off than others. And van Wolferen describes in great detail how efforts to move policy in a majoritarian direction are subverted. But he says repeatedly there is no conspiracy because there is too little concentration of power.[11] So, like Vogel, he sees some ineffable culture (the System) enveloping political relations and preventing politics from being transacted in the normal manner by political parties, elections, and governmental institutions.

Given the essential fragmentation of authority, the author feels obliged at times to confront directly the tenets of pluralism. He defines pluralism as "the ability of sizeable groups . . . to help choose, via their representatives, the nation's long-term goals," and asserts, "The Japanese people have had no say whatsoever" in the choice of such goals.[12]

As the following chapters will show, the members of the seminar clearly found much more grist to Japan's politics than did Vogel or van Wolferen. While acknowledging that culture plays a part in prescribing how politics is transacted and may alone explain certain dissimilarities between the two countries' politics and priorities, these essays rely little upon that construct. The seminar was engaged, after all, in a search for comparability. By rooting decisions in each country's unique collective experience, cultural explanations return policymaking to the realm of exceptionalism. The goal of comparative analysis led the seminar, without any formal declaration, to save culture as an explanation of last resort.

This does not imply that the seminar searched for understanding in

11. While skirting the issue generally, the following passage is suggestive: "This striking communalism is, however, the result of political arrangements consciously inserted into society by a ruling elite over three centuries ago, and the Japanese are today given little or no choice in accepting arrangements that are still essentially political." Van Wolferen, *Enigma of Japanese Power*, p. 3.

12. Van Wolferen, *Enigma of Japanese Power*, p. 80.

dramatically different phenomena. From the institutional perspective, however, culture is best understood as behavioral expressions of underlying instrumental relations that can be better appreciated by direct examination. Why, students frequently ask, should political adversaries such as Senators Edward Kennedy and Strom Thurmond heap courtesies upon one another on the floor of the U.S. Senate? One explanation is that this is the Senate's culture: the two senators are conforming to the chamber's expectations that govern how colleagues publicly regard one another. But *why* has the modern Congress become this widely acknowledged "cocoon of good feeling"? Certainly, the nineteenth century Congress, where members were known occasionally to carry weapons for good reason, rarely evinced such camaraderie. An answer that focuses upon the strategic circumstances of these two politicians is that any two senators, however distant they may be politically, recognize that there will be many occasions when they will need favors from each other to achieve their goals. Their nineteenth century counterparts, typically transients passing through Congress on their way to political careers elsewhere, had less need to invest in such courtesies, and so rowdyism was the order of the day. The cultural explanation places the two senators' behavior in a broader context, but the institutional analysis, focusing on their strategic predicament, explains why such a normative system should arise and endure. In the case of Japan and the United States, much about each country's political culture that strikes the distant observer as both peculiar and explanatory can be similarly incorporated into a more structured statement of the pursuit of interest within a particular political setting.

The Essays

The members of the seminar were recruited to represent the different intellectual currents and tastes circulating in both countries' scholarly communities. Many of these initial differences of perspective and interpretation are preserved in the following essays. For the most part, the authors limit their attention to the political system they know best.

The first two chapters offer an overview of the aspects of each country's governmental system that are most relevant to economic policymaking. John Chubb and Paul Peterson concentrate on the political evolution of the U.S. governmental system, which has rendered it highly responsive to the particularistic claims of organized constituencies but ill equipped to respond to—much less solve—national problems. Eisuke

Sakakibara describes Japanese political arrangements designed to distribute goods and services in politically efficient ways. While his argument does not deny the role of the Ministry of International Trade and Industry, he maintains that the principal day-to-day business of government has less to do with long-range economic planning than with responding to demands emanating from constituencies.

Both countries have experienced bouts of budgetary deficits. The U.S. budget deficit is of more recent origin than Japan's and smaller in relation to the gross national product. However, the low U.S. savings rate presents this country's deficit as a more severe problem that continues to hamstring the ability of politicians to broach new public policy. The political causes of deficits and the techniques employed to respond to them are described in the next two chapters. After considering various arguments that have been offered to explain the U.S. deficit, Mathew McCubbins suggests persuasively that divided party control of government is more to blame than has been generally recognized. Japan's deficit arose in the 1970s amid dramatic growth in social expenditures and a shortfall of projected revenues. Yukio Noguchi relates how government programs competed in the Ministry of Finance and the Diet for increasingly scarce resources and how the government ultimately gained control over the deficit.

Similarly, both governments have recently passed extensive tax reforms. In the U.S. case, the reform confounded insiders' expectations that the morass of tax breaks covering everything from political contributions to real estate tax shelters would never be removed from the tax code. But in one fell swoop they were, and at the same time many lower-income citizens were removed from the tax rolls and everyone's marginal tax rate was dramatically reduced. Allen Schick probes the details of the legislative process to uncover the particular transactions that yielded this extraordinary legislative outcome. In Japan, tax reform failed to be enacted through the tenures of several prime ministers, and, reflecting the potency of the opposition to reform, its final passage contributed to the early retirement of the prime minister who succeeded in pushing its enactment through the Diet. Michio Muramatsu and Masaru Mabuchi examine the long history of this tax reform and show how the provisions for a national sales tax triggered the political efforts of formidable economic constituencies on both sides of the issue.

The next several chapters consider the relation between political structures and the government's capacity to engage in sectoral policy-making. In a joint introduction, Roger Noll and Haruo Shimada offer a number of persuasive explanations for the stronger efforts of Japan's government in coordinating economic units within sectors and planning overall sectoral economic strategies. These have to do both with characteristics of the governmental system—centralization through unified control of government in a parliamentary system—and with the presence of issues other than economic growth that contribute to sectoral policies.

Shimada's own essay discusses Japan's direct government efforts to guide economic development, while Noll must search for de facto sectoral policymaking in the procurement decisions of the Pentagon and the ebb and flow of regulatory practices during the twentieth century. Despite these differences, both authors find examples of a salutary effect of government participation and instances where it has subsidized inefficiencies.

Although the presidential and parliamentary constitutions of the United States and Japan impose fundamentally different architectures, a comparative institutional analysis also yields some equally fundamental similarities that are consequential for economic policy. In both countries politicians are inspired by similar strategic considerations as they plot their careers and make policy. Drawing upon evidence presented in the preceding chapters, I conclude by comparing the calculated behavior of Japanese and American politicians in their constituencies, in their legislatures, and in their executive offices.

Part I
Overview of the Japanese and
American Political Systems

Political Institutions and the American Economy

John E. Chubb
Paul E. Peterson

AFTER NEARLY a decade of economic expansion, the United States enters a new decade in a precarious economic position. Signs of recession—rising unemployment, fading consumer confidence, a decline in GNP—are everywhere. And there are indications of problems deeper than a temporary economic downturn. Domestic savings is low, foreign indebtedness is high, and dependence on foreign oil is setting new records. The budget deficit keeps climbing despite the 1990 legislative compromise that was supposed to cut it by $500 billion over the next half-decade. In short, there is little confidence that the government has put the U.S. economy on the right track for the decade ahead.

Many observers attribute the economic difficulties that now trouble the United States to questionable behavior in both the public and the private sectors during the 1980s. Consumers went on a consumption binge. Banks invested too heavily in overheated real estate markets. Republican presidents and Democratic Congresses, deadlocked over budget priorities, boosted economic growth with a myopic policy of massive deficit spending. All of this is true. Yet it would be a mistake to view America's current economic difficulties as only the result of errors made during the last decade.

The economic challenges that the United States faces today can be traced back to at least the early 1970s. It was then that the country was introduced to stagflation, sluggish productivity growth, soaring oil prices, intensified international economic competition, and, in short order, mounting trade and budget deficits. During the 1970s as well as the 1980s, the U.S. government attempted to solve these problems. But its performance has fallen short, regardless of which party was in control—the Democrats during the Carter administration, the Republi-

An earlier version of this essay first appeared as "American Political Institutions and the Problems of Governance," in John E. Chubb and Paul E. Peterson, eds., *Can the Government Govern?* (Brookings, 1988), pp. 1–43.

17

cans during the early years of the Reagan administration, or both parties during the Nixon and Ford administrations and more recently.

The economic problems of today do not seem to be rooted, then, in the political or market forces of the 1980s. They seem to go deeper. In our view, they reflect a basic incompatibility between the government institutions that the United States has developed to manage its economic affairs and the new economic challenges that it has come to face over the past two decades.

In carrying out permanent responsibilities such as stabilizing the economy, managing trade, and ensuring energy security, the government works through extensive—and complicated—institutional arrangements that require cooperative efforts among congressional committees, White House offices, and bureaucratic agencies. If these arrangements are not appropriately designed, the government, regardless of its partisan makeup, will have difficulty adapting to new economic conditions and political demands.

The problem, of course, is not simply one of institutional adaptability. The institutions of a democratic government must work with the demands that the public makes of them. Inasmuch as changes in both domestic and global economies have made it more difficult to satisfy pressing political demands without creating larger problems, institutions cannot be assigned all the blame for not responding adequately to all of society's troubles. And it must be said that in recent years the American public has made strikingly inconsistent demands upon its representatives in Washington. During the 1980s Americans told pollsters that they simultaneously opposed tax increases, supported almost all major government programs at existing or higher levels, and insisted upon the elimination of budget deficits. In a no less self-contradictory mood, the public also welcomed the plummeting price of gasoline, opposed a tax on its consumption, and wanted to be free from dependence on oil from the Middle East. If during this same period the government promoted an unsustainable economic expansion with budget deficits, foreign capital, and cheap energy, it was in part simply giving the public what it wanted.

It seems most unlikely, however, that the public has carefully and thoughtfully decided to sacrifice the long-run economic security of the country for temporary prosperity. More likely, it has not made any decisions on a set of difficult issues that cannot be resolved without detailed information, considerable expertise, and an ability to balance conflicting values. Inconsistencies in public opinion may well have made government decisionmaking difficult: choosing between special interests and general ones and between present benefits and future ones is never easy. But if governing institutions are not to lose the confidence of a public frustrated with their performance, they must not simply reflect specialized pressures and every change in public opinion, no matter how short-sighted and inconsistent. They must make whatever adaptations are necessary to govern on behalf of the common good. This essay examines the problem of governing the economy that the collision of new issues and established institutions has created for the United States throughout its history and that stymies the management of the U.S. economy today.

Political Institutions and Government Performance

The problem of governing the economy effectively in the United States is mainly one of creating institutions or governing arrangements that can pursue policies of sufficient coherence, consistency, foresight, and stability that the national welfare is not sacrificed for narrow or temporary gains. The United States has difficulty in arriving at such arrangements because it must fashion them out of three partially autonomous political institutions: Congress, the presidency, and the bureaucracy. Because each institution represents different interests and holds different views of effective government, the development of governing structures, and consequently the management of economic and other problems, must always contend with political tension. This tension is a well-known part of the legislative process, such as in the making of the federal budget. But this tension is also manifest in battles between Congress and the president for control over bureaucratic agencies—how they should be set up, be reorganized, make decisions, and otherwise fulfill their routine responsibilities.

Historically, Congress and the president proved remarkably adept at building decisionmaking structures that could contain the political tensions between them and at the same time manage the major problems of the nation with reasonable effectiveness. During the nineteenth century, for example, the nation's affairs were managed quite effectively through a system of patronage that was shocking to most European observers and quite different from the bureaucratic arrangements in Japan. Yet when changing demands rendered patronage less effective and less politically useful, it was replaced by two very different but still distinctively American institutions: a civil service headed by a full tier of political appointees, and independent regulatory commissions given quasi-judicial status.

Such changes have not occurred easily, however. Most of the time, the vested interests that each of the competing institutions has in existing arrangements, and the differing objectives each would hope to satisfy through institutional change, keep established governing structures in place. When economic or other policy conditions change, Congress, the president, and the bureaucracy usually respond and adapt in ways that represent their respective interests and protect their respective powers. These ad hoc adjustments—recently, for example, the decentralization of Congress and the centralization of the presidency—will often solve immediate political problems for each institution, and they may even amount to effective adjustments for the government as a whole. But in time, piecemeal institutional change can prove inadequate, for politics and for government performance, and conditions become ripe for more creative institutional change.

Perhaps the essence of the problem of economic governance in the United States today is that current administrative structures, erected mostly during the Progressive era (1896–1920) and the New Deal (1932–1940), are so entrenched that their adaptations to new conditions contribute little to overall government effectiveness. Established structures no longer can contain political tensions between Congress, the president, and the bureaucracy, and, riven by conflict, they often do not permit successful management of the nation's problems.

This is the case, we shall suggest, with the administrative arrangements that the United States employs to manage three key economic problems: energy prices, trade relations, and macroeconomic stability. But the difficulties encountered in governing these crucial areas are not unique. The political tensions between Congress, the presidency, and the bureaucracy have shaped governing arrangements in nearly every American policy domain. And despite corrective measures that occur from time to time, the debilitating effects of these tensions are perhaps more evident today than they have ever been. It will come as no surprise, then, that the problem is not subject to a quick fix. Indeed, the problem of governance is such a pervasive part of the American political tradition that one can obtain the best understanding of the current predicament by initially considering its origins in the nation's constitutional history.

The Historical Legacy

Americans have always been better at representing than governing. The American Revolution was itself an attack on effective government. As Harold Laski observed, "Those who made [the government arrangements] were, out of actual and inferred experience, above all afraid of arbitrary power."[1] If the clarion calls of the colonials were "no taxation without representation" and "give me liberty or give me death," then the product of that revolution could hardly give priority to the needs of government.

The revolutionary leadership, as expressed through the Continental Congress, initially left matters of governance largely to the states, as the colonies were now to be called. Only the most urgent questions of mutual defense and foreign policy were to be considered by the Continental Congress, and these could be decided only with the consent of the individual states. Since the national government did not so much govern as represent the will of the states on a limited set of topics, it scarcely needed an executive officer. Policies could be determined by the Continental Congress, and these policies, the product of broad agreement, would be more or less self-enforcing.

The early years of the Republic gave ample testimony to the truth that representation alone was not sufficient for national unity. Under the Articles of Confederation, Congress could not contain the competitive instincts of the states—neither their overlapping claims on western lands nor their attempts to manipulate trade and tariffs for their individual benefit. Influential American leaders soon became aware that European powers had a vested interest in encouraging state rivalries, hoping to divide and weaken this new nation to the ultimate benefit of nations more studied in the art of statecraft.

The Constitutional Framework

To meet these domestic and foreign challenges, a call was issued for a national convention to consider revisions in the Articles of Confederation. The Constitution that emerged from this government, it hardly need be said, was a tour de force, an extraordinary success in grafting

1. Harold J. Laski, *The American Presidency: An Interpretation* (New Brunswick, N.J.: Transaction, 1980), p. 155.

upon a system of representation a governmental mechanism that survived a civil war, an industrial revolution, and the transformation of a fledgling republic into the world's richest and most powerful nation.

But for all its success, the Constitution still betrayed its origins in a revolution against executive power. Congress, the entity that most resembled the Continental Congress and state assemblies that had been the vehicles for revolution, was given pride of place in the new document. Its powers to tax and spend, regulate commerce among the states, and issue copyrights and patents were carefully enumerated; its system of representation was spelled out in detail; its rules for meeting, recording activities, and adjourning were clearly set forth; and the division of responsibility between its upper and lower chambers was quite self-consciously delineated. For example, the power to initiate revenue-raising legislation is specifically reserved to the House of Representatives.

The executive branch, the one that was to administer the new government's policies, was treated summarily. The Constitution devotes less than half as much space to the executive's design as to the legislature's. Most of that space is devoted to the clumsy procedure by which the president is to be chosen, a procedure that was soon modified by the Twelfth Amendment and to this day is the subject of unremitting criticism. The only powers the president is specifically granted by the Constitution are the powers to command the armed forces, to make treaties and appoint officers (with the advice and consent of the Senate), to veto legislation (which, however, can be overridden by a two-thirds vote), to pardon offenses, to receive ambassadors from foreign countries, and to convene Congress. It is often remarked that little attention was given to the presidency because it was generally assumed that General George Washington would be chosen for the job. But reticence was more deeply rooted than that. In a country that had forsworn royalty, the role of executive power was expected to be very limited. As de Tocqueville observed, "the President is placed beside the legislature like an inferior and dependent power."[2]

Some have contended that a more expansive view of the presidency is inherent in certain brief phrases included in the Constitution. Much has been made, for example, of the clause that states "the executive power shall be vested in a president" and the statement that requires that the president "shall take care that the laws be faithfully executed."

2. Alexis de Tocqueville, *Democracy in America,* vol. 1 (Vintage, 1945), p. 128.

As the executive has gained in strength and independence, presidents have drawn upon these phrases to expand their prerogatives and justify actions they have taken. Relying on these provisions, Abraham Lincoln suspended the writ of habeas corpus, recognized rump bodies as state legislatures in seceding states, and freed slaves in rebellious parts of the nation. Harry Truman declared that powers inherent in the executive allowed him to declare a national emergency and seize the steel mills. Richard Nixon said that executive powers enabled him to impound funds that Congress had appropriated and gave him and his close White House aides the right to refuse Congress documents and testimony they regarded as privileged. While some of these and other claims of executive authority have been recognized by courts, most have been denied or subjected to stringent limits. And whatever might have been the intentions of the men who signed the Constitution, these clauses played almost no role in the early years of the American Republic.

The First Century

Both the executive branch and the national government as a whole played a relatively limited part in the nation's economic governance during the Republic's early years. By and large problem solving was simplified by delegating the job to state and local governments. Trade and commerce flourished not so much because Washington nurtured and kept watch over them, but because the Constitution prohibited the barriers to a national market that had existed under the Articles of Confederation. To be sure, the national government provided economic stimuli in the form of protective tariffs, grants for internal improvements, and the sale of cheap federal lands. But economic management was not one of the national government's strengths, and it handled regular booms and busts with frustrated resignation. Twice Congress established national banks to provide such basic minimums for national commerce as a common currency and coordinated credit policies. But these banks lacked the political support to act independently to stabilize the economy. The first bank therefore never really tried to do so, and the second bank became the object of a presidential-congressional battle when it moved to regulate the economy in the 1820s. Both banks failed politically, leaving economic management to the uncoordinated policies of the states until near the end of the nineteenth century.

As the century drew to a close, however, problems of economic governance escalated more rapidly. Industrialization was fast beginning to generate demands—for economic regulation and social amelioration—that only the federal government could fulfill. The government, though, was not well organized to respond to these concerns. Its administrative capacity, revealed most clearly by the collapse of the Second National Bank, was insufficient to handle more than the most rudimentary domestic responsibilities. There was clearly a need for more permanent, professional, and powerful forms of government organization. Yet establishing them was difficult. Congresses and presidents, each responding to different constituencies, had very different ideas about their design and supervision. In time, however, compromises among these divergent interests were reached, and a new administrative structure better suited to the changing requirements of effective governance was created. Although the emerging structure was the culmination of a series of political compromises and not the product of a coherent design, it included institutions that would become vital to government performance for a century to come. Perhaps the most important of these, and surely the most creative, were the civil service and the independent commission.

The Civil Service

Civil service reform pitted the interests of highly competitive, militant, patronage-hungry parties against the rising cadre of professionals eager to ply their trade in the public sector. Members of Congress, especially senators, were typically allied with party interests, particularly because senatorial courtesy gave senior senators great influence over executive appointments within their states. The position of the president was more ambiguous. On the one hand, the president was also the product of a party-controlled nominating process, and he could hardly ignore the forces that had placed him in office. On the other hand, civil service reform promised to give the president and his administrative aides more direct control over the bureaucracy than was possible in a system controlled by senators and the local politicos with whom they were connected. "By freeing the executive branch from the domination of party bosses in Congress, reform would give its leaders an opportunity to assert an independent control over government."[3]

The disjunction of interests between president and Congress was

3. Stephen Skowronek, *Building a New American State: The Expansion of National Administrative Capacities, 1877–1920* (Cambridge University Press, 1982), p. 55.

acknowledged by no less a product of the party system than President Rutherford B. Hayes: "The end I have chiefly aimed at has been to break down . . . Senatorial patronage. . . . It seemed to me that as Executive I could advance the reform of the civil service in no way so effectively as by rescuing the power of appointing to office from Congressional leaders."[4] After the assassination of President James Garfield by a rejected job hunter, pressures for civil service reform mounted, and the Pendleton Act, signed into law in 1883, established a civil service commission that initiated the long and laborious process of separating employment in the federal government from loyal work in the party apparatus.

Civil service reform has so often been cast as a struggle between parties and reformers that the contest between executive and legislative centers of power has been largely overlooked. But the champions of reform were not just Teddy Roosevelt and Woodrow Wilson. They also included Ulysses Grant, Chester Arthur, William Harrison, Grover Cleveland, and William McKinley. Not all of these chief executives were unabashed supporters of reform; loyalty to party and alliances with congressional leaders constrained their enthusiasm. But the steadiness with which an increasing number of federal positions were "blanketed in" to the civil service illustrates how presidents could combine political strategies with reform objectives.

Rearguard opposition to civil service reform was, of course, well entrenched on Capitol Hill. When Theodore Roosevelt's Commission on Department Methods recommended a broad range of sweeping reforms in 1907, "Congress rejected every one. . . . So vehement was the opposition that Congress even refused a public printing of the commission's final reports." Significantly, one Republican senator denounced the schemes as an "executive encroachment on the sphere of Congressional action" that threatened to make Congress "a victim of a bureaucratic advance to power."[5]

The bureaucratic advance continued into the twentieth century. The Civil Service Commission standardized recruitment and promotion procedures, established a uniform pay schedule, and provided a pension fund and retirement system. The Bureau of the Budget provided for centralized direction of agency requests for funding, and the General Accounting Office was created to audit agency expenditures. All of these

4. Skowronek, *Building a New American State*, p. 56.
5. Skowronek, *Building a New American State*, p. 185.

devices gradually rooted out the most blatant forms of graft, corruption, and patronage that had been a by-product of a legislative and party-controlled apparatus. But even though many civil service requirements spread throughout the executive branch, they never culminated in the sort of unified, merit-based, professional administration that Bismarck first created in Prussia.

Japan, Canada, Britain, France, and Sweden were all finding ways of integrating the Germanic administrative model with quite different political systems. President Woodrow Wilson thought Americans could achieve similar results by drawing a sharp distinction between policy and administration. Congress was willing to agree to only a portion of the reform agenda, however, for the very currency of its power base was control of the way in which federal administrative actions affect states and communities. To concede that control to the executive would have granted it control over the local politics that was the congressional lifeblood.

The reform impulse was strong enough to eliminate overt political patronage from lower-level administrative agencies, thus reducing the most politically embarrassing instances of governmental incompetence and abuse of power. But the main policymaking positions of the executive branch remained exempt from civil service requirements. Job retention for the 3,000 or more appointees to these key positions depended upon sensitivity to the needs of political influentials in the White House, on Capitol Hill, or on the Republican and Democratic national committees.

This truncated civil service developed features very different from fully developed counterparts in Japan and most other industrial societies. Lacking access to the highest policymaking positions, the civil service acquired little prestige. Lacking ready transfer and promotion across agencies, the civil service consisted of a host of departments, bureaus, agencies, and commissions, each with its own traditions, areas of expertise, and sources of personnel recruitment. Since entry into the civil service could be achieved by completing any one of a wide range of educational programs and passing a quite general examination, no common set of identifications and commitments developed. Even though each federal agency developed its own professional cadre—health care specialists, welfare workers, urban planners, engineers—the concept of a public administrator, someone who could perform effectively in a wide variety of executive positions, never really took hold. The experts were on tap, not on top. The study of public administration, once the darling child of the Progressive movement, became an orphan, scorned by the best universities as lacking in high academic standards and intellectual rigor.

The fragmentation of the civil service into professional subspecialties—networks of analysts with expertise in a particular domain—was quite consistent with the preservation of congressional prerogatives.[6] Although senators no longer controlled an array of lower-level patronage appointments, they still built close ties to those specialized professionals whose work impinged most directly on the political life of their states. The well-known iron triangle consisting of interest group, executive agency, and congressional committee could operate semiautonomously precisely because the professionals working within the triangle could not move beyond it easily. The bureaucracy could not develop a cross-cutting set of loyalties and identifications that would have tied them together, connected them to their hierarchical superior—the president—and removed them from congressional scrutiny.

Still, civil service reform was an important step forward. Although administration under the new civil service remained fragmented, it was also more expert, experienced, and objective than when bureaucracy was pregnant with patronage. This was vital to the success of the modern presidency, for stable and capable organizations were necessary if presidents were going to discharge effectively the new responsibilities an industrializing society was expecting of them. Managing the macro-economy, regulating industries, and implementing trade policy were technically and administratively demanding tasks requiring professional expertise. Congress was willing to accept, and eventually embraced, this more professional system of administration as long as power remained functionally decentralized along the same lines as the legislature. Civil service reform, then, served the political needs of the president without jeopardizing those of Congress. It also facilitated the management of emerging national problems that, at least at that point, were not too complex and interdependent for a fragmented administration to handle reasonably well.

The Regulatory Commission

The second administrative institution that exemplifies the political bargain struck between Congress and the president during the first part

6. Hugh Heclo, *A Government of Strangers: Executive Politics in Washington* (Brookings, 1977).

of the twentieth century is the independent regulatory commission. Many of the responsibilities that the government was being asked to assume at this time required more than just narrow administrative competence. The government was taking responsibility for the behavior of business, industry, and the economy as a whole. If it was going to do so effectively, it would need to rely more on its power to direct firms and members of the business community to perform their specific tasks in particular ways. This required the exercise of more of the government's power of coercion. Unlike traditional government responsibilities that could be accomplished through the adept provision of information, services, or grants to state and local governments, the responsibility for economic performance could not be fulfilled without strict enforcement of authoritative commands.[7] Standards needed to be set and compliance monitored.

Standard setting had been mostly a legislative function, though, and even if Congress could not hope to set numerous detailed requirements in a wide range of policy arenas for many different industries, it was nonetheless wary of turning its legislative powers over to the executive. Since it was reluctant to delegate this power directly to the president, it therefore established "a headless fourth branch of government," a collection of regulatory commissions that operated semiautonomously of the president.[8] Within several decades these commissions included the Interstate Commerce Commission, Federal Reserve Board, Federal Trade Commission, Federal Power Commission, Federal Communications Commission, Securities and Exchange Commission, the National Labor Relations Board, Atomic Energy Commission, and a host of other regulatory bodies semi-independent in nature.[9]

Although these boards and commissions were established at different times, exercise different responsibilities, and vary in their constitutional

7. Theodore J. Lowi, *The Personal President: Power Invested, Promise Unfulfilled* (Cornell University Press, 1985), chaps. 2, 3.

8. The term was originally used by the President's Commission on Administrative Management, often known as the Brownlow commission. See Harold Seidman and Robert Gilmour, *Politics, Position, and Power: From the Positive to the Regulatory State,* 4th ed. (Oxford University Press, 1986), p. 286.

9. For a more extended listing and classification of government agencies, see Seidman and Gilmour, *Politics, Position, and Power,* chap. 11. Not all regulatory agencies are independent. Although this mode predominated in the early twentieth century, in more recent years Congress has felt more comfortable with departmental exercise of regulatory powers. The Food and Drug Administration, the Federal Aviation Administration, and the Environmental Protection Agency all report to the president either directly or through a cabinet official.

design, most have several characteristics in common. They exercise direct authority over some economic or social activity. They thus can mandate a desired pattern of activity from particular firms or individuals. Ostensibly because this authority is deemed to be "quasi-judicial" in character, the commissions were set up in such a way as to limit executive control of them. The commissions do not have a single executive officer, but rather consist of five, seven, nine, or thirteen members who share responsibility for official action. "Boards and Commissions are unloved by everyone but the Congress," Harold Seidman has observed. "Plural executives may be inefficient administrators, but the Congress is more concerned with responsiveness than efficiency."[10] Members are appointed by the president with the consent of the Senate for fixed terms rather than "at the pleasure" of the president. Often they have to come in more or less equal numbers from both political parties. Once appointed, the commissions can not be directed by the president to decide cases before them in any particular way nor are their decisions subject to anything other than judicial review.

Presidents have nonetheless been able to influence the work of these commissions.[11] The power of appointment can be used gradually to change the philosophical disposition of the commission. A new, politically astute chairman, who has direct access to staff resources, can shape the agenda of the board in ways consistent with a president's larger policy objectives. The commission budget is subject to review and approval by the Office of Management and Budget (OMB). A president can also dramatize issues in ways that constrain commission alternatives.

But Congress also has influence over these commissions. Subcommittees closely monitor their work, amend the statutes under which they operate, appropriate their funds, and influence (through the process of senatorial consent) the appointment of new members. Above all, commission independence legitimates an autonomous capacity for action that enables boards to respond to preferences from sources outside the executive branch. Thus agencies can develop close ties to the industries they regulate as well as to the relevant congressional committees, whose members typically have come from areas of industry concentration.

For several decades independent agencies constituted effective

10. Seidman and Gilmour, *Politics, Position, and Power*, p. 61.
11. See, for example, Terry M. Moe, "Control and Feedback in Economic Regulation: The Case of the NLRB," *American Political Science Review*, vol. 79 (December 1985), pp. 1094–1116.

institutional compromises between Congress and the president. Political problems were solved by delegating issues to bureaucrats who often turned out to have the resources to resolve them in ways that served the nation rather well. In a few cases regulatory commissions continue to perform their functions effectively even today. But in recent years the agencies have been beset by diverse interest group pressures and have become mired in institutional conflicts. By the late 1970s and early 1980s, the move to deregulate many industries that had ossified under regulatory direction had gained broad public support.[12] And in other arenas the weaknesses of the independent regulatory commissions became increasingly apparent as the number of politically effective interests competing for their attention escalated and the number of issues presented for their consideration grew exponentially.

The Contemporary System

It may seem that the congressional reluctance to share power was the only force shaping the development of the government's administrative capacity. But if there had been no pressures countervailing those coming from Congress, the governing structure would have collapsed under the increasing burden of responsibilities assumed by the federal government in the late twentieth century. The countervailing force consisted of a succession of strong, administratively oriented presidents who asked for more mechanisms to help control the proliferating bureaus and agencies for which they were ostensibly responsible. By the 1980s presidents had succeeded in winning enough control over the departments so that the White House became a formidable competitor with the congressional system. Yet each advance in executive power was hedged with caveats and restrictions that left Congress with the continuing capacity to shape administrative actions. And it is precisely the even terms on which Congress and the president now compete for direction of the bureaucracy that raises anew the old question of governability. The tension between the branches, observed at periodic junctures in American history, has been steadily growing, but an institutional compromise that would resolve the tension has not yet been realized.

12. See Martha Derthick and Paul J. Quirk, *The Politics of Deregulation* (Brookings, 1985).

A Strengthened Executive

De Tocqueville recognized that the weak executive he observed in the 1830s was in good part due to the fact that "the United States is a nation without neighbors. Separated from the rest of the world by the ocean, and too weak as yet to aim at the dominion of the seas, it has no enemies, and its interests rarely come into contact with those of any other nation of the globe."[13] As these circumstances changed, the executive grew in strength: it is no accident that Abraham Lincoln, Theodore Roosevelt, Woodrow Wilson, and Franklin Roosevelt are all known both for enhancing the power of the Oval Office and for their wartime or imperial responsibilities. The role of the executive has also been changed by the alteration in public expectations about appropriate governmental responsibility for securing economic progress and domestic welfare. Theodore Roosevelt assumed greater responsibility for managing the public lands, Wilson for maintaining economic competition, and Franklin Roosevelt for establishing the welfare state and managing the national economy. In the postwar era, governmental activities in these areas—and many more—have been expanded and intensified.

The escalation of demands and the expansion of government institutions have both augmented the role of the president and given the presidency a distinctive institutional form. Undoubtedly, the seminal organizational advance for the contemporary presidency was the establishment of the Bureau of the Budget in 1921. Before the bureau's creation, budget making was an anarchical process with each department sending its own budget to Congress, leaving the resolution of competing priorities to the appropriations committees. After 1921 the Bureau of the Budget at least reconciled these departmental requests and submitted a single budget on behalf of the president. During and after World War II, the bureau grew in size, complexity, and responsibility. It acquired the power to approve virtually all agency proposals that had fiscal implications before they were submitted to Congress. It stepped up its scrutiny of departmental programs, calling upon agencies to justify in detail their proposed increases in expenditure. In recent years it has tightly reviewed the regulations agencies have proposed, instituted more uniform personnel policies across departments, and exerted even more stringent fiscal control.

13. de Tocqueville, *Democracy in America*, p. 131.

But as the bureau (renamed the Office of Management and Budget), became increasingly powerful, it also became increasingly politicized.[14] Initially expected to be kept separate from more political concerns, the OMB director has in recent years become a top domestic policy adviser of the president, often superseding in influence any of the cabinet secretaries with operational responsibilities for domestic policy. Although this trend was significantly accelerated by Ronald Reagan, under future presidents the OMB will probably continue to be less neutral, less oriented toward helping the government to control and coordinate its expenditures, and more oriented toward helping presidents achieve programmatic and partisan goals. Consistent with recent trends, Richard Darman, Bush's current OMB director, has emerged as one of the president's most politically shrewd, forceful, and influential advisers on a wide range of domestic policy issues.

Almost as significant as the OMB for the extension of presidential power has been the growth of the White House staff. Since the 1930s there has been a fundamental change in the size and organizational complexity of the group of advisers who work in closest proximity to the president. The existence of the staff was not formally recognized until 1939, when the Brownlow commission proposed that presidents have a small number of special assistants. Roosevelt used these assistants informally by assigning them on an ad hoc basis to pressing issues that did not fall within the domain of a particular department or agency. The staff has since grown to roughly 500 members and contains well-organized units such as the Office of Personnel Appointments and Office of Communications. The growth of these and other offices within the White House staff has in fact been so extensive that a chief of staff, once a controversial position, is now accepted as a virtual necessity.

These changes are not simply due to presidential predilections, although the management styles of particular incumbents certainly affect the character of the staff.[15] The growth in size and complexity has been continuous from one administration to another despite changes in party and personality. Admittedly, its size peaked during the Nixon administration. After the Watergate scandal forced President Nixon to

14. Hugh Heclo, "Executive Budget Making," in Gregory B. Mills and John L. Palmer, eds., *Federal Budget Policy in the 1980s* (Washington: Urban Institute Press, 1984), pp. 255–91; and Terry M. Moe, "The Politicized Presidency," in John E. Chubb and Paul E. Peterson, eds., *The New Direction in American Politics* (Brookings, 1985), pp. 235–71.

15. Samuel Kernell, "The Evolution of the White House Staff," in Chubb and Peterson, eds., *Can the Government Govern?*, pp. 185–237.

resign from office, the White House staff, which had been deeply involved in illegal activities, became so unpopular that presidents Ford and Carter both made a point of reducing its political significance. Both committed themselves to cabinet government, and both made some efforts to carry out that intention. But the realities of governing precluded no more than marginal reductions in staff even in these worst of times. With Reagan's ascension to the presidency, the need for a strong president was boldly reasserted, and the influence of the White House staff reached new heights. The organizational and political aggrandizement of the White House staff, like the OMB, has been something of an inexorable response to the growing tension between Congress and the presidency, especially as manifested in the struggle for control of the administrative machinery of the government. Increases in political demands and decreases in the strength of the institutions that once relieved interbranch tensions, particularly political parties, have driven presidents to augment and institutionalize their own mechanisms of influence and control.

If the growth of the White House staff has been almost inevitable, so too, however, have been its problems. Watergate is not the only scandal that has touched the White House. Indeed, there is no other part of the executive branch so prone to become the object of press, congressional, and criminal investigations. The hint of scandal that always seems to hover about the White House testifies both to its political power and the informality with which individuals gain positions on its staff. What presidents want in their White House staff is loyalty. They can obtain this because few restrictions surround a staff appointment. Civil service requirements do not apply, senatorial advice and consent is unnecessary, and it is conventional practice to fill positions with staff from the presidential campaign. Committed to the president and convinced of the public support for his agenda, presidential staff members are usually eager to make sure the president's wishes (or what they think are his wishes) are fulfilled. Sophisticated about only the electoral side of politics, however, they are often less sensitive to the traditions, norms, procedures, and agendas of the entrenched agencies of the government and those agencies' patrons in Congress.

Prepared for the job or not, the White House staff is now expected to capture control of the government, and for this purpose the staff has fashioned ever more effective instruments. Departmental appointments increasingly are screened to ensure that the officers are loyal to the president—and not necessarily committed to departmental wish lists.

New initiatives are more likely to emerge from discussions within the White House than from agency recommendations. Legislative liaison is a White House function; departments are often as little involved as possible. In the most extreme case (the Iran-contra scandal being the outstanding example), the White House staff is asked to carry out a major operational mission that the departments (State, Defense, CIA) are thought to be too clumsy, rule-bound, or self-protective to attempt. Finally, the management of the president's direct relationship with the public, his ultimate and probably greatest source of political influence, has become something of a science. The president may not always convince the public, but he is routinely assisted by a standing army of pollsters, public relations experts, journalists, and speechwriters that strengthens his power of persuasion.

A Resurgent Congress

Congress has not allowed the centralization and politicization of executive power to progress unchecked. Although aggressive presidents and public emergencies have strengthened the presidency, Congress is too self-conscious of its own prerogatives to permit, for long, presidential intrusion on what it deems appropriate legislative domains. What James Bryce observed in the late nineteenth century is no less true today: "Men come and go, but an assembly goes on forever; it is immortal, because while the members change, the policy, the passion for extending its authority, the tenacity in clinging to what has once been gained, remain persistent."[16]

The techniques of congressional influence over agency activities are virtually infinite in number. Congressional appropriations often contain specific instructions on how—and especially where—monies are to be spent. Congress can also withhold appropriations from uncooperative agencies, though doing so can backfire if constituents are deprived of services. Agency administrators are frequently called upon to testify in oversight hearings on particular actions they have taken. New legislation is regularly accompanied by detailed committee reports that give specific instructions on the meaning of the new law, and courts have accepted these reports as documentary evidence of congressional intent.[17] Con-

16. James Bryce, *The American Commonwealth*, vol. 1 (Chicago: C. H. Sergel, 1891), p. 223.

17. Appropriations committees often earmark appropriations for very specific activities in the reports accompanying their legislation. In the spring of 1988, James Miller, Reagan's OMB director, urged agencies to ignore hundreds of millions of dollars

gress even incorporated into law provisions that allowed committees of either house to veto actions taken by executive agencies. These techniques are not all easy to employ, because except for oversight, they require the assent of the majority of the members of Congress.[18] Still, through the occasional use of these techniques and the continuously implied threat of exercising them again, Congress is well equipped to try to keep agencies within narrow bounds.

Perhaps as important as any technique, though, may be the constitutional conception that executive power does not inhere in the president himself but in subordinate heads of departments and bureaus. What Woodrow Wilson observed a century ago still remains substantially correct: Congress "does not domineer over the president himself, but it makes the secretaries (of the departments) its humble servants. Not that it would hesitate, upon occasion, to deal directly with the chief magistrate himself; but it has few calls to do so, because our latter-day presidents live by proxy; they are executives in theory, but the secretaries are executives in fact."[19] Today one would need to substitute for secretaries of departments bureau chiefs and agency heads, placing the president even more distant from the active agent in the government. As the Hoover commission complained in 1947, the "statutory powers often have been vested in subordinate officers in such a way as to deny authority to the president or a department head."[20] This is additionally significant because the Congress has organized itself so that its system of committees and subcommittees is congruent with a decentralized executive.

Many of these mechanisms of legislative control are now hallowed by long tradition. But Congress has in recent years developed new and sometimes controversial techniques of legislative influence devised to keep an increasingly centralized and politicized executive from

---

of such earmarks. He asserted, correctly, that they were not legally binding. But when members of Congress and agency officials severely criticized this "usurpation" of congressional power by the executive, Miller backed down. On the general question of committee reports, executive decisions, and judicial interpretation of legislative intent, see R. Shep Melnick, *Regulation and the Courts: The Case of the Clean Air Act* (Brookings, 1983); Robert A. Katzmann, *Institutional Disability: The Saga of Transportation Policy for the Disabled* (Brookings, 1986); and Katzmann, *Judges and Legislators: Toward Institutional Comity* (Brookings, 1988).

18. These are detailed and placed in proper perspective in Terry M. Moe, "An Assessment of the Positive Theory of 'Congressional Dominance,'" *Legislative Studies Quarterly*, vol. 12 (November 1987), pp. 475–520.

19. As quoted in Laski, *The American Presidency*, p. 126.

20. As quoted in Seidman and Gilmour, *Politics, Position, and Power*, p. 57.

emasculating congressional power. Perhaps the most important of these is the Congressional Budget and Impoundment Control Act of 1974. Enacted in the aftermath of the Watergate scandal, it modifies an old interbranch practice, codified with legislation in 1950, that gave the president the right to impound funds whenever circumstances made it infeasible for expenditure to occur.[21] President Nixon interpreted this law in such a way as to give him the right to impound funds for practices that he felt were undesirable, unnecessary, or fiscally irresponsible. It was this substitution of the policy judgment of the president for that of Congress that angered congressional critics, who instigated lawsuits against the practice. The 1974 legislation ended the dispute by making it clear that Congress had delegated no such policymaking authority to the president. Of perhaps even greater importance, the act also attempts to make Congress a full and equal partner of the president in fiscal policymaking. It goes so far as to say that Congress will, through its budgetary and tax-writing processes, adopt a fiscal policy and coordinate federal activity, if necessary without the help of the president.

In addition, Congress has enhanced its own capacity to review, revise, and reinstruct the executive agencies. Congress has divided its work load into ever smaller bites by delegating more responsibility to a growing number of subcommittees. These subcommittees have been given bigger budgets, enabling them to hire additional staff. They have also been given more autonomous authority. Oversight of administrative agencies has been enhanced by an increasing number of hearings devoted to the review of agency activities.[22] At the same time, the staff and travel resources of individual members of Congress have been enhanced, facilitating congressional casework that mediates between administrative decisions and local constituents. These resources have also helped to spawn a profusion of special interest caucuses that monitor particular issues and policy domains. Finally, the research and investigative arms of Congress—the General Accounting Office, the Congressional Research Service, the Office of Technology Assessment, and the Congressional Budget Office—have gained new resources and prominence.

These developments have not helped Congress unambiguously, however. They have come at the expense of Congress's ability to act

21. James L. Sundquist, *The Decline and Resurgence of Congress* (Brookings, 1981), pp. 199–215.
22. Joel D. Aberbach, *Keeping a Watchful Eye: The Politics of Congressional Oversight* (Brookings, 1990).

decisively as an institution.[23] Before the 1970s the locus of power in Congress was a level above the subcommittees, centered in the committees and their autocratic chairs. The work of Congress was divided rationally among committees, which although substantially autonomous, acted with the effective assent of the whole Congress. With the decentralization of power in Congress, the body came to speak with many voices on issues where it had once spoken with just one. This not only complicated and slowed the legislative process; it also changed the nature of congressional control of administrative operations. Agencies that once enjoyed the predictable congressional control that went along with the iron triangles found themselves subject to multiple and often conflicting jurisdictions in Congress. An able agency chief might well exploit this arrangement, playing one subcommittee off against another, to get from Congress what his agency wanted or needed. But many agencies have been hampered by the lack of clear direction that has emerged in both inconsistent enabling legislation and conflictual oversight.

Decentralization can also reduce congressional leverage with the president on major administrative matters such as the size of the budget deficit or the growth of the money supply. A president may be less willing to negotiate with congressional leaders when he knows that the institution is not fully behind them. Congress has taken steps to offset this and other consequences of decentralization by increasing the powers of congressional party leaders and by employing binding central decision-making procedures such as budget reconciliation. But these efforts have nevertheless left Congress better able to represent than to govern. Undoubtedly Congress has increased its ability to challenge the president for control of the bureaucracy. Still, the only certain effect of all of this is that during the 1970s and 1980s interbranch tensions grew more intense and the administrative structure of the national government became more unsettled.

The Partisan Dimension

In the first 150 years under the Constitution, the separation of powers was mitigated by the fact that the same political party regularly dominated

23. Kenneth A. Shepsle, "The Changing Textbook Congress," in Chubb and Peterson, eds., *Can the Government Govern?*, pp. 238–66.

both branches of government. As one well-known scholar of the American party system has observed, "From the time the two-party system settled into place in Andrew Jackson's time until the second election of Dwight Eisenhower, only two Presidents—Zachary Taylor, elected in 1848, and Rutherford B. Hayes, in 1876—had to confront immediately upon inauguration a House of Representatives organized by the opposition."[24] The Senate was equally likely to be held by the same party as the presidency—1848 and 1884 being the two exceptions.

Capture of both branches of government did not ensure harmonious cooperation. Civil service disputes between Republican presidents and Republican-controlled Congresses were endemic in the late nineteenth century. And Roosevelt's court-packing plan, reorganization schemes, and late New Deal initiatives went awry in an overwhelmingly Democratic Congress. Yet partisan loyalty, presidential coattails, and executive patronage facilitated concerted action by Congress and the president on such crucial occasions as the Great Depression and the beginning of the New Deal. In recent decades, however, unified government has been replaced by one in which each political party has acquired a distinctive grip on a particular branch of government: the Democrats on Congress and the Republicans on the presidency. As a result, the long-standing institutional contest for power has become intensified by the stake each of the two parties has in the outcome. Animated by both institutional and partisan interests, disputes between president and Congress have become not only a routinized component of American politics but the central issue of governance in the modern era.

The Republican party has called for changes in the Constitution that would strengthen the executive, such as the item veto, a balanced budget amendment, and repeal of the Twenty-second Amendment, which limits the president to two terms. Republican presidents have, moreover, pursued a governing strategy that has emphasized their administrative powers. They have attempted to centralize executive branch authority by assigning to the OMB budgetary and regulatory policymaking tasks once left to the departments. Under Reagan the president's budget was largely prepared within the OMB, only to be modified substantially on Capitol Hill by legislators who found ready, if covert, access to disgruntled agency and department officers. Many new policies were initiated by White House task forces who developed legislative programs

24. James L. Sundquist, "Strengthening the National Parties," in A. James Reichley, ed., *Elections American Style* (Brookings, 1987), pp. 202–03.

quite independently of any input from the departments expected to manage them. New regulations could not even be presented for public consideration until the OMB had given them preliminary approval.

Democratic presidents have, of course, pursued some of their goals administratively as well. Jimmy Carter, for example, appointed outspoken environmentalists and consumer advocates to regulatory posts and tried to reshape agency decisionmaking with zero-based budgeting. Still, the Democrats have been the party more suspicious of executive power and they have led congressional efforts to limit it. They pushed through Congress legislation limiting the power of the executive to impound appropriations. They limited the authority of the OMB to estimate the revenues and outlays of the federal government, asking it to share that responsibility with the Congressional Budget Office under the overall supervision of the quasi-independent General Accounting Office.[25] They subjected the executive to sunshine legislation, freedom of information laws, a new code of ethics, and the inquiries of special prosecutors.[26]

Conflicts between the legislative and executive branches have accelerated in the past two decades as the Democratic party has solidified its hold on Congress and the Republican party has dominated presidential contests. The Democratic party's hold on the House of Representatives has, in fact, become almost ironclad: it has lost control of the House in only four of the past sixty years (1946–47 and 1952–53). Democratic control of the Senate is not quite as predictable: Republicans had a majority for the first six years of the Reagan administration and for six other years in the postwar era. But since it requires control of both houses to run Congress, the competitive position that the Republicans may have established in the Senate can hardly cause them to regard the legislative branch as the one more likely to protect their interests. If Republicans in Congress are going to tilt in one direction or the other on issues involving the balance of power, they will probably still favor the presidency, where they are truly competitive with, if not marginally stronger than, the Democrats.

The Democratic party's capacity to control Congress is due partly to historical accident, partly to its internal diversity, and partly to the fact that its weakness in presidential contests has strengthened its hand in Congress. The accidents of history have been of great benefit to the

25. A provision in the Gramm-Rudman-Hollings deficit-reduction legislation created this novel power-sharing arrangement.

26. Benjamin Ginsberg and Martin Shefter, *Politics by Other Means: The Declining Importance of Elections in America* (Basic Books, 1990).

40   JOHN E. CHUBB AND PAUL E. PETERSON

Democratic party on three occasions: the depression of the 1930s, the 1958 recession, and the Watergate scandal. In each case Republicans were blamed for a major misfortune, and Democrats were elected to both the Senate and House in large numbers. Once in office Democratic incumbents used their name recognition, constituent casework, legislative assistants, power of the frank, and other perquisites of office to solidify their electoral victories. Democratic advantages at particular historical moments thus became an entrenched component of overall governing arrangements.[27]

Apart from (or perhaps because of) these historical accidents, the Democratic party's congressional strength has been enhanced by its appeal for such diverse groups as urban ethics, trade unions, blacks, Jews, Hispanics, southerners, environmentalists, farmers, and feminists. Many of these groups have little in common with each other, but all can find reasons for supporting the Democratic party. Each senator or representative emphasizes that face of the party that is most appealing to his or her constituents. And the very fact that each component of the party finds itself represented in Congress helps to perpetuate each group's identification with the Democrats. Historical accident, incumbency advantage, and party diversity all reinforce one another and help make the Democratic party the majority party among voters nationwide.

Democrats in Congress also prosper because of (and not in spite of) their difficulty in capturing the presidency. Generally speaking, whoever carries the burdens of executive power loses ground in Congress in nonpresidential-year elections. At times—such as 1958 and 1974—congressional losses can be quite substantial. Republicans gain back some of the lost ground in presidential years, when their nominee pulls a number of senators and a few House members into office on his coattails. Eisenhower in 1952 and Reagan in 1980 had long enough coattails to help capture control of the Senate for a portion of their presidential tenure. But presidential coattails have been less efficacious in House elections, and their overall effect has waned over time as more and more voters have acquired the political independence to split their votes between the parties in presidential and congressional races. In the end the congressional Democrats seem to benefit from discontent with incumbent Republican presidents. As one congressional scholar has

27. Thomas E. Mann, "Is the House Unresponsive to Political Change?" in Reichley, ed., *Elections American Style*, pp. 261–82. Mann argues that state legislative gerrymandering of congressional district boundaries seems not to be a major factor in sustaining a Democratic majority.

observed, "House Republicans have been victims of their party's success in presidential elections."[28]

If Congress is a Democratic stronghold, Republicans may have the advantage in presidential contests. By 1992 Republicans will have held the White House for twenty of the twenty-four years since 1968 and twenty-eight of the forty years since 1952. Although more Americans identify with the Democratic party than the Republican party, the large and, until recently, increasing number of voters who call themselves independents have tended to vote Republican in presidential elections. So too have many conservative southern Democrats, who have also begun to vote for Republicans in nonpresidential elections. Perhaps the most important reason for this is that the Republican party, somewhat more homogeneous and less dominated by assorted activists, has been able to unite behind candidates who are closer to the views of election-deciding voters, such as independents and conservative Democrats.

Conversely, Democrats find that the very diversity that helps solidify their hold on Congress undermines party unity in presidential contests. Members of Congress can appeal to different interests while still claiming loyalty to the Democratic party, but presidential candidates cannot follow this strategy without becoming accused of inconsistency, ambiguity, or playing into the hands of special interests. Bringing the diverse and often conflicting components of the party's constituency together into one national coalition has proven to be a formidable, if not impossible, task for Democratic presidential contenders.

Republicans also benefit from the electoral college system, which overrepresents small states (which are disproportionately Republican in orientation).[29] But not too much should be made of this point. History has shown that the Democrats can win the presidency if they nominate a candidate who is not outside the popular mainstream (1976) or is significantly closer to the mainstream than the Republican nominee (1964). And many of the key elections have been too close to conclude that one or the other party is the "natural" holder of the presidency. Still, if Republicans do not quite have a lock on the presidency in the way Democrats have one on the House of Representatives, the logic of the competitive situation in the postwar period is that each party has

28. Mann, "Is the House Unresponsive," p. 277.
29. Rosenstone puts the advantage at 52 percent versus 48 percent of the respective shares of the popular vote that Democrats and Republicans have needed respectively to win an electoral college majority. See Steven J. Rosenstone, "Why Reagan Won," *Brookings Review,* vol. 3 (Winter 1985), pp. 25–32.

come to identify its interests with a particular branch of government. Republicans have a vested interest in strengthening the autonomous capacity of the executive branch, while the Democrats seek to conserve and extend congressional power.

In addition, each party is developing an internal coherence and partisan self-consciousness that makes it a particularly vigorous defender of its interests and priorities. Partisan voting in both the Senate and the House increased steadily during the 1980s. In addition, power shifted from the substantive committees to procedural committees, such as the House Rules and Senate Budget committees, where the party leadership exercises more direct authority. The party leadership is no longer just minding the legislative calendar; it is also mediating and resolving substantive issues. As power has become more partisan, the Republicans in the House, frustrated with their "permanent" minority status, have concentrated their political fire on the House Speaker, who at one time was treated as a figure who stood above petty party disputes. The process began during the term of Thomas P. (Tip) O'Neill and intensified when James Wright became Speaker and Republicans uncovered book sales as a subterfuge for honoraria above the legal limits, as well as numerous other improprieties. The partisan spirit has become a pervasive part of the debate over budget resolutions, fiscal deficits, and automatic deficit-reduction procedures.

Vigorous partisanship on the presidential side once was thought to have reached its apogee during the Nixon administration. Assertion of the constitutional and legislatively delegated powers of the president was vigorous and controversial. Congress was denounced for passing liberal, spendthrift legislation. Congressionally appropriated funds were impounded; White House staff refused to respond to congressional inquiries; wage and price controls were established by presidential decree; the Domestic Council was created within the White House staff to coordinate legislative policy proposals; and covert actions, both legal and illegal, were organized by the White House to ensure the president's reelection.[30]

In the aftermath of the Watergate scandal, the intensity of the partisan debate between the president and Congress temporarily eased. Lacking electoral legitimacy, President Ford used the powers of his office more guardedly and signed congressional legislation for which he had little

---

30. On the aggrandizement of presidential power during this period, see Arthur M. Schlesinger, Jr., *The Imperial Presidency* (Houghton Mifflin, 1973).

enthusiasm.[31] But after a Carter presidency that was similarly deferential to congressional powers, the Reagan administration intensified the partisan conflict between the branches in a systematic way that made the Nixon approach appear uncertain and ad hoc by comparison. The Reagan administration took office with an open call for public support for a strong, independently minded presidency. Loyalty to the Reagan movement was given top priority in selecting appointees not only for the White House staff but also for the OMB, the executive departments, agency heads, and members of regulatory commissions. The OMB drastically cut agency budgets to conform with the presidential commitment to reduced domestic spending. At the same time the president criticized Congress harshly for excessive spending, high deficits, and overregulation of the economy. Negotiations between president and Congress were often marked by mutual recriminations, allegations of malfeasance, and accusations of power usurpation. As the Reagan administration drew to a close, inherent tensions between the legislative and executive branches had been reinforced and heightened by conflict between the parties. President Bush, a longtime veteran of Washington politics and an "insider," began his presidency by preaching bipartisanship, thus winning approval from congressional leaders for the spirit of cooperation he attempted to spread. But by his second year in office, cooperation gave way to conflict as the parties fell into acrimonious and protracted debate over budget priorities. By the mid-term elections of 1990, the differences between the parties and the institutions had hardened.

An Ineffective Bureaucracy

The congressional-presidential struggle for power has distinctively shaped the administrative structure of the national government. Although this influence is perhaps most obvious in the institutional arrangements that the two branches have devised to control how federal money is spent, the scars of the battle between Congress and the president are no less impressive in the bureaucratic institutions that ultimately do most of the nation's actual managing. It has become increasingly clear that Congress, responding to interest group demands, creates bureaucratic agencies and assigns them vital tasks, but then often fails

31. Even though he vetoed sixty-one bills, he still reluctantly signed such landmark pieces of Great Society legislation as the Education for All Handicapped Children Act.

to give them the requisite resources, authority, or autonomy to do their jobs effectively. Indeed, it has been argued that the bureaucracy is really not designed to be effective.[32]

The demands to which Congress must respond are no more concerned with establishing bureaucratic agencies according to principles of rational administration than they are with fashioning public policies consistent with the national interest. Interest groups that want a federal agency created or reorganized by Congress are concerned that the agency not be diverted from serving their interests by presidents or even future Congresses of a different political makeup. They therefore want an agency insulated from day-to-day political control. Interest groups that oppose the agency will favor a different design, one that allows political attacks. Opponents will therefore favor arrangements that permit a legislative veto, place the agency close to the president, or otherwise limit agency autonomy. Meanwhile, Congress has its own structural interests: it wants bureaucratic agencies to resolve political conflicts that it cannot solve itself and tries to ensure that the agencies are as susceptible to congressional influence as to presidential influence.

Arguably, the president's preferences for agency design stem mainly from his responsibility for the execution of policy and the overall performance of the government. The president's potential need to coordinate and control administrative decisionmaking leads him to resist the creation of independent agencies and the imposition of excessive constraints on agencies directly under his authority. The structure of bureaucratic agencies, like the content of national policy, is therefore a compromise, not only among society's interests but between the institutional interests of Congress and the president. The problem with this is that while a policy compromise may be necessary to solve the political conflict temporarily, an agency whose structural integrity is compromised or perhaps even sacrificed in the battle for political control cannot carry out the assigned policy effectively.

Significantly, these points are well illustrated in the three problem areas that plagued the United States during the 1970s and 1980s and continue to trouble the American economy today. The United States still tries to manage energy supply and demand with an administrative structure that predates the twenty-year-old decline of domestic oil production and the consequent development of new energy issues such

32. Terry M. Moe, "The Politics of Bureaucratic Structure," in Chubb and Peterson, eds., *Can the Government Govern?*, pp. 267–329.

as rising prices and increasing threats to the environment.[33] For example, nuclear power development is regulated and thereby impeded by a federal licensing agency that employs slow, ad hoc, unstandardized procedures instituted in the early 1950s when nuclear power plant construction was in its infancy.[34] The development of electricity in the United States more generally is controlled by fifty state public utility commissions, created at the turn of the century, that are free to make decisions about the kind and amount of electricity produced in their states, regardless of the rapidly increasing impact of these decisions on the welfare of other states and the nation as a whole.

Although Congress and a series of presidents have long recognized that the administrative structure of which these agencies are a part is antiquated, they have been unable to agree on how to change it.[35] Meanwhile, the battles for control of this structure and the efforts to keep it from collapsing have produced unsatisfactory results. Ultimately, both conservation and domestic energy production have been discouraged while energy consumption, especially of foreign oil, has been encouraged. Oil remains the dominant fuel in the United States, and record amounts must now be imported. Nearly two decades after the first energy crisis, the United States again faces economic hardship as conflict in the Middle East has destabilized world oil prices.

Similarly, the government has been battling its record trade deficit with weapons forged in the 1930s. Congress and the president recognized in the midst of the Great Depression that the nation's economic welfare had been reduced by protectionist policies that exempted many U.S. industries from foreign competition. To encourage free trade, Congress passed the Reciprocal Trade Agreement Act, which shifted the responsibility for trade policy from the legislative branch, where political pressures for selective protection were most effective, to the executive branch, where institutions more committed to free trade could better resist industry pressure. As in the energy arena, the arrangement worked

33. The relationship between energy institutions and energy policy is examined in John E. Chubb, "U.S. Energy Policy: A Problem of Delegation," in Chubb and Peterson, eds., *Can the Government Govern?*, pp. 47–99.

34. The Nuclear Regulatory Commission—not Congress or the president—finally instituted one-step, standardized licensing in 1989, but it remains to be seen whether these changes have eliminated enough regulatory impediments to raise the rate of nuclear power development.

35. The government did agree to deregulate natural gas in 1989, but only after thirty-five years of debate and twenty years of gas shortages and oil import increases caused by regulation.

well until the issues began to change in the 1970s. As more U.S. industries became threatened by foreign competition and the trade deficit grew, the bargain between Congress and the president became strained by escalating demands for protectionism.

Although the arrangement has not yet collapsed, it is no longer solving the problem. U.S. trade policy has not succeeded in easing out of existence many of the country's least promising industries nor has it worked well to open foreign markets to many of the nation's most dynamic industries.[36]

For most of the twentieth century the conduct of macroeconomic policy has also relied heavily on a fixed set of institutional arrangements. The Federal Reserve Board has long been responsible for monetary policy, and the president—with the steadily increasing assistance of the Bureau of the Budget and its successor, the Office of Management and Budget—has taken charge of fiscal policy since at least 1920. As in the other policy arenas, the arrangements for both monetary and fiscal policy worked reasonably well and kept political pressures, for faster or slower economic growth, contained until the early 1970s. But here the story diverges somewhat from that in energy and trade policy. When economic issues began to change and the established institutions had to manage a decline in productivity, two oil price shocks, and unprecedented stagflation, one set of institutions—that for managing monetary policy— ultimately adjusted successfully.[37] The Federal Reserve Board, after a number of rather unsuccessful experiments between 1978 and 1982, settled upon a conservative, anti-inflation, moderate-growth strategy that supported the longest period of sustained growth in the postwar period. This ability of the central bank to stabilize the economy is testament to the effectiveness a governing institution can achieve when the president and Congress do not weaken its capacity for sustained and concerted action.

The failure of the fiscal policy apparatus to avert record budget deficits is quite another matter and is consistent with governing difficulties encountered in other policy arenas. Institutional adjustments in the budgetary process have taken place, to be sure, but they have served

36. This argument is developed in David B. Yoffie, "American Trade Policy: An Obsolete Bargain?" in Chubb and Peterson, eds., *Can the Government Govern?*, pp. 100–38.

37. This assessment of monetary policy and the assessment of fiscal policy below is developed in Paul E. Peterson and Mark Rom, "Macroeconomic Policymaking: Who Is in Control?" in Chubb and Peterson, eds., *Can the Government Govern?*, pp. 139–82.

more to strengthen the hand of one of the branches than to create an arrangement that will help the government to restore its budget to balance and keep it there. During the fall of 1990 this institutional struggle left the government unfunded and "closed" for days and threatened to close it several times more. The budget agreement that was eventually reached, nearly a month late, promised some deficit reduction but did not resolve the budget impasse that has nearly paralyzed the federal government for more than a decade.

Toward a New Institutional Equilibrium

The subordination of the nation's governing structure to the presidential-congressional struggle is understandable. But it becomes increasingly difficult to defend when it leads to the design and implementation of short-sighted policies in such crucially important areas as energy, trade, and finance. To be sure, the conditions that the government must manage have become more difficult. A number of developments—including increased competition from Europe and Asia, the rise of the Organization of Petroleum Exporting Countries, and the aging of major domestic industries—eventually slowed the nation's economic growth and magnified the problems of governance. It is more difficult for a government to balance budgets, soothe dying industries, and ensure reliable energy supplies when its economy weakens and external threats strengthen simultaneously.

But U.S. policymakers responded to these changes by simply accelerating trends in institutional development that were already well under way. The presidency aggressively politicized the administrative processes of the executive branch. Congress fortified its defenses of the constituencies that it had increasingly taken responsibility to protect, while it searched for ways to defend its view of the national interest. And the two institutions struggled between themselves and with the bureaucracy to manage the nation's macroeconomy, foreign trade, and energy supply—in large part because the administrative arrangements with which they were trying to manage had become obsolete.

One could approach these policy problems with solutions specific to each policy arena.[38] For example, economic welfare could be enhanced by a strategic trade policy that would encourage free trade but would

38. The following policy recommendations are made and defended in pt. 1 of Chubb and Peterson, eds., *Can the Government Govern?*, pp. 47–182.

provide government assistance to domestic industries seeking better access to foreign markets. A balanced budget would benefit the U.S. economy in the long run and leave the stabilization of the economy in the short run to monetary policy, which is now better suited to the task. An increase in the federal gasoline tax, expedited deregulation of electricity production, and reform of the process by which nuclear plants are licensed would help to ensure that energy is produced and consumed as efficiently as possible.

None of these recommendations is new. Each already enjoys backing from many policy analysts. And yet, for reasons that go to the heart of congressional-presidential tension, none of these recommendations stands a good chance of being adopted, at least in a form that is likely to work. Each proposal is justified by its long-run contribution to the nation's welfare. But in the short run each threatens to reduce the welfare of particular groups and perhaps even society as a whole. As a result, each policy places a burden on political institutions. If the policies are to become law, Congress and the president must obviously stand up to the well-organized interests supporting the status quo. But if the policies are going to work, the institutions must also agree to a significant restructuring of their own responsibilities and a new division of political power. By and large, the policies that are often recommended to solve contemporary economic problems will not work under existing institutional arrangements. This may be the crux of the current problem of economic management. The need for institutional reform helps to stalemate congressional-presidential negotiations over policy changes and to hamper the implementation of those policy changes that do get made.

Consider several examples. If existing institutions were asked to put into effect a strategic trade policy, it would likely degenerate into a politically motivated program of protectionism. Congress would demand that a variety of "deserving" industries benefit from strategic assistance. The bureaucracy would be ill equipped to defend itself against a new form of industry claims. And the president would not have the political support to thwart these pressures. Similar problems await a new energy policy. If the nation is to produce, consume, and regulate energy more efficiently, it will need to rely not only more on markets but also more on government authority, specifically the authority of the national government placed behind national standards. Unless administrative arrangements are reformed, however, a new national policy would only have to approve a few nuclear power plants or utility rate increases before political pressures would mount and congressional (and state) efforts to provide special dispensation would prevail. Finally, there is the policy of a balanced budget. Here institutional reform has been tried and tried again. It is true that reforms of the budget process, perhaps especially those stimulated by the Gramm-Rudman-Hollings bill, have marginally reduced the size of the deficits. But presidential-congressional infighting over tax increases, defense spending, and entitlement policy has limited the progress toward a fiscally responsible budget, and, as a result, Congress has given up on specifying a deadline for a balanced budget.

The specific institutional reforms that are needed to adopt and implement more effective economic, trade, and energy policies are varied and well beyond the scope of this essay. But it seems clear that the United States needs institutions that have the responsibility and the authority, the incentives and the power, to pursue long-term national interests. If the problems of the last two decades have one cause in common, it is the growing vulnerability of the United States to economic developments in the rest of the world. Since this vulnerability is only likely to intensify, the country would do well to fashion institutions that can help policymakers give greater consideration to the national interest, a concept that acquires more specific meaning in an increasingly competitive environment.

The Japanese Politico-Economic System and the Public Sector

Eisuke Sakakibara

RECENT DISCUSSIONS of the politics of Japanese economic decisionmaking have revolved around two main issues. One is whether the government bureaucracy or the Liberal Democratic party (LDP) dominates decisionmaking. The other is how much power the government actually has over the private sector, particularly the manufacturing-service segment, which is dominated by large corporations. Opinion is divided on both questions.

In the case of decisionmaking, some analysts argue that leadership resides in the bureaucracy.[1] Others, in both professional and journalistic circles, say the party is playing an increasingly important role in the symbiotic relationship between the two.[2] Chalmers Johnson takes the extreme view that "Japan's elite bureaucrats make almost all the major decisions, effectively draw up all legislation, oversee the national budget and are also the source of all major policies."[3] In contrast, Seizaburo Sato and Tetsuhisa Matsuzaki summarize the system as "compartmentalized pluralism administered by party-bureaucracy coalition" and suggest that the well-established party apparatus plays the crucial role.[4]

The other issue concerns "targeting," "industrial policies," or, more generally, the role of the government in planning and implementing economic policies. Although the argument for a monolithic Japan, Inc., has waned somewhat, many still think of the public sector as the central

---

1. Takashi Inoguchi calls the system "bureaucracy-led mass-inclusionary pluralism." Takashi Inoguchi, *Gendai Nihon Seiji Keizai no Kōzu: Seifu to Shijō* (The structure of contemporary Japanese politics and economics) (Tokyo: Toyo Keizai Shinpōsha, 1983).
2. See, for example, Seizaburo Sato and Tetsuhisa Matsuzaki, *Jimintō Seiken* (The Liberal Democratic party) (Tokyo: Chuo Koronsha, 1986).
3. Chalmers Johnson, *MITI and the Japanese Miracle: The Growth of Industrial Policy, 1925–1975* (Stanford University Press, 1982), p. 20.
4. Sato and Matsuzaki, *Jimintō Seiken*, p. 170.

power in a corporatist framework.[5] More in line with recent analyses that emphasize the Japanese tendency toward pluralism and decentralization, Richard Samuels argues that "the state often tries to order choices in the market, but negotiations between the public and private sectors define not only the market choices, but also those of the state."[6]

Whatever position analysts take, almost all appear to agree that some central policymaking mechanism exists. Many also assume that the state has some important stake and strong leverage in the manufacturing and service-oriented corporate sector of the economy and that individual policies are formulated, negotiated, and implemented as part of a coherent policy toward that sector.

This discussion casts serious doubt on both assumptions. As the following analysis of the structure of public expenditure shows, the Japanese government is heavily involved not in the private sector, but in public works such as the construction of infrastructure in agriculture and fishery, forestry, transportation, and telecommunications. Of course, the government can use regulations, taxes, and finances to influence the private sector. The last two are policy instruments only in a broad sense, however, in that they conform to the general structure of Japanese expenditures and are incorporated in the budget compilation process. And although regulations were important in the 1940s and 1950s and are still significant in some areas (such as energy, finance, and transportation), they are administered independently by separate regulatory bodies and are not normally used in any coherent way to implement overall economic policy.

As direct instigators and financiers of public works, the different levels of government do not engage in overall planning or targeting; rather, they identify and implement individual projects. In other words, government agencies are the players and not the conductors. Owing to the nature of public works, government activities in this area are demand driven and highly cumulative. Also, a great many political forces come into play since public works typically cover wide geographical areas and

---

5. See, for example, T. J. Pempel and Keiichi Tsunekawa, "Corporatism without Labor? The Japanese Anomaly," in Philippe C. Schmitter and Gerhard Lehmbruch, eds., *Trends toward Corporatist Intermediation* (Sage, 1979), pp. 231–70.

6. Richard J. Samuels, "Nihon ni Okeru Kokka no Business," trans. Toshiya Kitayama, *Leviathan 2* (Spring 1988), p. 86. See also Samuels, *The Business of the Japanese State: Energy Markets in Comparative and Historical Perspective* (Cornell University Press, 1987).

52 EISUKE SAKAKIBARA

involve many institutions and people trying to garner support for specific projects.

This profile of the Japanese government is certainly not one of a planner and coordinator of industrial policies. Of course, all governments have different faces depending on the area of activity being considered. The point is that the public works face of the Japanese government, hitherto largely ignored in the analytical literature, dominates the politics of economic policymaking in a pattern that is becoming increasingly institutionalized in the party organization and the bureaucracy. This pattern is only natural since the bread and butter of the members of Japan's political parties, particularly the LDP, is public works. A public works–based coalition of regional semipublic institutions, such as agricultural and land improvement cooperatives, private construction companies, and local governments, often serves in Japan as the political base for both regional and national elections.

By contrast, the large manufacturing-service corporations have remained relatively independent from government and have developed into semiautonomous bodies. These are located mainly in Tokyo, but are sometimes based in regional cities. A prime example of the latter is the Toyota Motor Corporation, based in the city of Toyota.

In other words, thriving side by side in the Japanese economy are two distinctively different sectors: the market-oriented private sector, mainly in manufacturing and services, and the politicized public or semipublic sector, spanning agriculture, fishery, construction, transport, telecommunications, and a part of finance and commerce. In areas where the two overlap, such as finance and commerce, competition between entities in the public sector, such as postal savings, and their private-sector counterparts is indeed intense. The quarrel between postal savings and the large private banks can at times be greater than that between private banks alone. In the politicized public sector, government involvement is extensive and direct; in the market-oriented private sector, it is limited and indirect. The government's regulatory grip on the private sector, which was significant in the 1940s and 1950s primarily because of wartime and postwar emergency measures, loosened substantially as private firms matured and solidified their own independent kingdoms beginning in the 1960s.

One measure of the emphasis on the public sector in the government's policymaking activities is the allocation of central government funds (general account) to the different ministries: in the original budget for fiscal 1988, 6.5 percent went to the Ministry of Construction, 4.5 percent

to the Ministry of Agriculture, Forestry and Fisheries, and 1.4 percent
to the Ministry of Transport, whereas only 1.1 percent went to the
Ministry of International Trade and Industry (MITI). Moreover, about
a fifth of this small fraction for MITI was absorbed by measures
subsidizing small business.

However demand-driven and decentralized economic policymaking
may be, the government needs some coordinating mechanism if it is to
arrive at specific numbers in taxes, expenditure, and finance. The effort
to integrate these fragmented requests and policies is jointly undertaken
by the party and the bureaucracy in the budget compilation procedure.
As explained later in this chapter, most of the government's policy
decisions are made in relation to budget compilation and are packaged
into one giant appropriation bill. Here, economic policymaking is almost synonymous with budget compilation. As such, policy formulation is both a decentralized and cumulative process, with the LDP
and the Ministry of Finance (MOF) in most cases playing no more than
a passive coordinating role; even the sections of the spending ministries
formally responsible for creating policy are usually not policy instigators.
What emerges from each annual political battle is the original budget
for the fiscal year—normally a hodgepodge of various requests from the
bottom layers of the public sector, but with a subtle balancing of vested
interests. It is hardly appropriate to interpret this as a coherent policy
framework.

What is the politician's role in this process? In a sense, it is to
pursue public works programs, as Prime Minister Kakuei Tanaka did so
enthusiastically. As long as large corporations stay based in urban areas
such as Tokyo and Osaka, regional economic activity can be encouraged
only by public-sector projects and the corporate enticement for which
they act as pump primers. Budget appropriations from the central
government are crucial. The role of the politician is to comply with the
wishes of local governments and the agricultural and other cooperatives
that are the major force in his constituency and to request appropriations
from the central bureaucracy. In this system the politician is much like
an executive treasury officer of various regional institutions who happens
to be stationed in Tokyo.

Of course, in a parliamentary and cabinet system politicians also head
the executive branch of government, but there is no doubt that their real
job in Japan is to manage the treasury operations connected with
government projects. The great majority of *zoku* representatives—
members of informal policy groups in the LDP, who are becoming

increasingly powerful and are the subject of much attention from political scientists and journalists these days—are involved in public-sector projects ranging from construction, agriculture, fisheries, and forestry to transportation, telecommunications, and finance.[7]

Historical Overview

In the early Showa period, which began in 1925, Japan was a typical model of classical capitalism.[8] However, a prolonged recession and impoverished agricultural sector had begun to turn popular opinion against the *zaibatsu,* or family-owned business empires, and push the country toward physiocracy. Both of these trends changed the nature of government involvement in the economy.

The backlash against the *zaibatsu* set the stage for the subsequent move to an agricultural system revolving around owner farmers, intended to eliminate the existing polarization of the agricultural community into bourgeoisie and proletariat. This move, coupled with the pre–World War II military buildup and the policy of support for the munitions industry and the new *zaibatsu* that were emerging, led to a gradual increase in the level of government intervention in agriculture and other key industries. The groundwork for postwar land reform was laid by the 1924 Tenant Farmers Act, the 1938 Farm Land Adjustment Act, and the 1942 Food Control Act, all of which greatly reduced landlord powers.

Although the government leaned toward the new *zaibatsu,* it also favored intervention in the financial area. It created the necessary framework for such intervention by expanding the powers of the Industrial Bank of Japan and by promulgating the 1937 Provisional Funding Act and the 1942 Bank of Japan Act.

The *zaibatsu* initially resisted these government policies, but eventually reached a mutual understanding with the government following the about-face by Mitsui's Nariakira Ikeda, formerly a vehement opponent of the government, and a system of cooperation between the two was consolidated. Despite their subsequent cooperation, relations between the military and the *zaibatsu* in early Showa do not seem to have been

7. See, for example, Takashi Inoguchi and Tomoaki Iwai, *"Zokugiin" no Kenkyū: Jimintō Seiken o Gyūjiru Shuyaku-tachi* (A study of "zoku" representatives: main actors controlling Japanese politics) (Tokyo: Nihon Keizai Shinbunsha, 1987).

8. For details, see Takafusa Nakamura, *Showa Keizaishi* (Economic history of the Showa era) (Tokyo: Iwanami Shoten, 1986).

at all smooth, to judge by the assassination in 1932 of Mitsui's Takuma Dan by ultrarightists.

Nonetheless, the large Japanese corporations were able to lay the foundation of what today is known as Japanese-style management. Although it is said that the power of the *zaibatsu* families was never as great as that held by family empires in the United States or Europe, the power of the *zaibatsu's* head clerk-president—men such as Nariakira Ikeda, Ichizo Kobayashi, Sanji Muto, and Ginjiro Fujiwara—was growing at this time, and the organization and institutionalization of *zaibatsu* management forged ahead quickly. In addition, the concept of familial management had started to evolve into lifetime employment and the seniority system. As a result, the situation that developed was not so much a polarization of capital and labor, but a lessening of capitalists' authority, which paved the way for the modernization of management organization and greater employee sovereignty in the large companies. It is not hard to see how these claims evolved amid the rivalry with and acquiescence to the largely military public sector.

The decisive factor in transforming the Showa Japanese political-economic system into its present form was the postwar reforms carried out by the Allied Forces General Headquarters (GHQ), especially the 1946 land reform and the 1947 dissolution of the *zaibatsu,* although these arrangements had already begun to change before World War II. Particularly in the case of land reform, the Ministry of Agriculture, Forestry and Fisheries is said to have played a leading role. The economic system held up as the ideal of the ultranationalist Japanese officers involved in the famous military coup of February 26, 1936, was implemented by U.S. "New Dealers" at GHQ, the only difference being that democracy rather than an imperial system was the catalyst. That these diametrically opposed groups would favor the same kind of economic system and put it into place is perhaps one of history's great ironies. It should be remembered, however, that both groups were strongly opposed to laissez-faire principles, mainly in response to the Great Depression of the 1930s.

Continuity in the immediate postwar period with the prewar regime was provided by the economic bureaucracy—such as the MOF, MITI, and the Ministries of Agriculture, Forestry and Fisheries, Transport, and Construction—which were all virtually untouched by GHQ-led reforms. With national security expenditures more or less taboo after the war, the government concentrated its economic efforts in agriculture and public works, but it also provided some financial support for the manufacturing and service sectors of large corporations. Because dismantling the *zaibatsu* had eradicated almost all the capitalists in Japan, companies seeking funds for their plant and equipment investments were left to rely on a regulated financial system consisting mainly of city banks, long-term credit banks, and public financial institutions. In response to this system, new interlocking shareholdings and fundraising networks began to emerge and gradually evolved into management-controlled corporate groups. The new companies emphasized technology developed through military production and imported from abroad and were organized around professional managers. These companies pinpointed the export market as the area in which to grow. Acting as guarantor or mediator, the state wielded some influence in this process, using mainly finance and regulations as leverage. Nevertheless, the corporate groups remained more or less independent from the government, and the corporations eventually developed into semiautonomous bodies making up the market-oriented private sector.

Meanwhile, as already mentioned, the government bureaucracy conducted its business in such public-sector areas as construction, transport, communications, finance, and agriculture, following a system that had its roots in the Showa period. There were, however, some changes due to land reform. Rural communities, for example, became democratized when agricultural cooperatives (*nōkyō*) were formed to take over from their prewar counterparts, the *nōkai*, which had evolved into a major regional force. Despite being subject to severe fiscal and budgetary controls, local authorities had also grown into an important regional force, alongside the cooperatives, since they had become comparatively independent from the central government after the dismantling of the Ministry of Home Affairs.

Interestingly, the old rivalry between the public and private sectors has started building up again now that the large management-controlled corporations have reestablished their semiautonomous base and public business has been rapidly expanding in such areas as postal savings and agriculture. A notable newcomer in the public sector, however, is the LDP. It emerged amid the political changes after World War II, which, unlike the gradual economic developments rooted in the Showa period, were abrupt and radical. The LDP, formed in 1955, represented the grand consolidation of conservative (or, more precisely, nonsocialist) parties into a single dominant party. With the gradual institutionalization of party functions vis-à-vis the bureaucracy and the Diet, the LDP

Table 1. **Final Government Consumption and Fixed Capital Formation in Selected Countries, by Level of Government**
Percent of GDP

Item	Japan[a]	United States[a]	United Kingdom[a]	Federal Republic of Germany[b]	France[c]
Final government consumption	9.73	18.31	21.13	19.96	16.20
Central government	2.37	8.69	12.89	3.76	11.35
Regional governments	7.28	9.63	8.00	9.74[d]	3.82
Central government transfers to regional governments	7.37	2.83	6.65	3.51	3.63
Government fixed capital formation	4.81	1.60	1.89	2.29	3.06
Central government	0.79	0.36	0.90	0.31	0.63
Regional governments	4.06	1.24	0.99	1.82	2.19
Total	14.54	19.91	23.02	22.25	19.28
Central government	3.16	9.05	13.79	4.07	11.98
Regional governments	11.34	10.87	8.99	11.56	5.99

Source: OECD Department of Economics and Statistics, *National Accounts*, vol. 2: *Detailed Tables, 1975–1987* (Paris: OECD, 1989).
a. 1985.
b. 1984.
c. 1982.
d. Sum of state or provincial governments and local governments.

became the leading force in policymaking, or in the budget compilation process described below.[9]

The Public Sector

Some of the characteristics of the Japanese public sector become clearer when one compares the structure of government expenditure with that in Western nations. In 1985, for example, government final consumption and general fixed capital formation in Japan totaled 14.54 percent of gross domestic product, far below the 20 percent or so for the other major economies (table 1). Although Japan would appear to have the smallest government in this sense, it is actually only final government consumption that is small (some 10 percent, compared with the 20 percent or so of Europe and the United States), since Japan's fixed capital formation is two to three times higher than that in other major economies.

Another salient point is that almost 80 percent of government expendi-

9. See, for example, Sato and Matsuzaki, *Jimintō Seiken*.

Table 2. Components of Final Government Consumption in Selected Countries, 1985
Percent of GDP

Component	Japan	United States	United Kingdom	Federal Republic of Germany	France
Final government consumption	9.73	18.31	21.13	19.96	16.20
Wages and salaries	7.74	10.88	n.a.	n.a.	11.37
Remainder	1.99	7.43	n.a.	n.a.	4.85
Component of consumption[a]					
General services	2.57	1.16	1.08	2.04	2.10
Defense	0.94	6.57	5.12	2.79	3.49
Public security	[b]	1.15	1.64	1.55	0.91
Education	3.58	4.41	4.77	3.98	5.31
Medical	0.41	0.84	3.92	5.94	0.49
Welfare	0.53	0.61	1.45	2.03	1.20
Housing	0.57	0.39	0.69	0.29	0.91
Culture and religion	0.23	0.18	0.47	0.46	0.60
Economic	0.98	2.33	1.31	0.89	1.16

n.a. Not available.
a. Some minor categories not shown.
b. Included under general services.

ture takes place at the regional government level. That proportion is higher than that of West Germany (51.9 percent) and the United States (54.6 percent), and much higher than that of France and other countries with large central government expenditures. As is well known, Japanese taxes make their way to regions largely as local grants and subsidies. Transfers from the central government to local government in 1985 came to 7.37 percent of GDP, which is much higher than the percentage in other major economies.

When final government consumption is broken down by category, it can be seen that the much higher consumption in other major economies is due not only to their greater medical, welfare, and education costs, but especially to their defense expenditures (table 2). In Japan, defense accounts for only one-tenth of final consumption, as opposed to 15–35 percent in the United States and Europe. In addition, the GDP share of final consumption minus wages and salaries is a mere 2 percent in Japan, in comparison with 7.4 percent in the United States or 4.9 percent in France. Although the ratio of wages and salaries in Japan is itself low, final government consumption minus wages and salaries is also low, being equivalent to only 40 percent of government fixed capital formation.

At the same time, Japan's GDP ratio for total fixed capital formation is about 30 percent, which is approximately 10 percentage points higher

Table 3. Government Share of Fixed Capital Formation in Selected Countries, 1975–85
Percent of GDP

Country	1975	1980	1985
Japan			
Total fixed capital formation	32.45	31.57	27.72
Government fixed capital formation	5.29	6.11	4.81
Including public corporations	9.05	9.53	6.83
Government's share of total	27.89	30.19	24.64
United States			
Total fixed capital formation	17.19	19.13	18.64
Government fixed capital formation	2.12	1.76	1.60
Including public corporations	2.98	2.57	2.17
Government's share of total	17.34	13.43	11.64
United Kingdom			
Total fixed capital formation	19.86	18.18	17.15
Government fixed capital formation	4.82	2.39	1.89
Including public corporations	8.42	5.28	3.52
Government's share of total	42.40	29.04	20.52
Federal Republic of Germany			
Total fixed capital formation	20.39	22.71	19.53
Government fixed capital formation[a]	3.87	3.59	2.29
Government's share of total	18.98	15.81	11.73
France			
Total fixed capital formation	23.27	21.90	18.90
Government fixed capital formation[a]	3.56	2.85	2.88
Government's share of total	15.30	13.01	15.24

a. Separate public corporation statistics unavailable.

than the corresponding figure for the other major economies; and the share of government fixed capital formation is 25–30 percent of the total, which is in a class of its own (table 3). If public corporations are included under general government, the Japanese GDP ratio for fixed capital formation climbed to 7 percent in 1985, far above the 2 percent recorded in the United States or the 3.5 percent in the United Kingdom. While these shares have gradually been contracting under the impact of privatization and expenditure cuts, they are not by any means negligible. In particular, the government and public corporation share of total fixed capital formation in the United Kingdom was more than halved to 20 percent by 1985 under the Thatcher government from more than 40 percent in 1975, when many key industries were run by the public sector.

In summary, three characteristics of Japanese government consumption and capital formation are worth noting. First, final expenditure by the Japanese government is markedly less than that of other major economies because of its low defense, medical, and education costs.

Second, the Japanese government's fixed capital formation is far larger than that of the other major economies. When coupled with public corporations, its GDP ratio comes to 7 percent and accounts for one-quarter of total fixed capital formation. This is more than double the U.S. or West German share and is higher than the share in the United Kingdom, where public corporations have gradually been privatized. Moreover, when wages and salaries are excluded from government final consumption, fixed capital formation is 2.4 times the size of final consumption (0.2 times in the United States). Whereas in the United Kingdom the government and public corporations account for almost a fifty-fifty share, in Japan the government accounts for more than twice the share of public corporations.

Finally, almost 80 percent of final government expenditure in Japan takes place at the local government level; the regional share of government fixed capital formation has reached 84 percent. This ratio is higher than that in West Germany and the United States. Moreover, a considerable portion of this local final expenditure is covered by a transfer of treasury resources from the central government in the form of grants and subsidies.

This picture of a concentration of government expenditure in fixed capital formation, largely in public works, contrasts sharply with that painted by foreign analysts, who emphasize the role of MITI or the targeting of industrial policy. To be sure, there are other instruments of economic policy such as taxes, finance, and regulations. However, neither taxes nor finance gives special treatment to the private industrial sector, unlike agriculture, construction, transport, or other parts of the economy closely related to public works. The corporate profit tax rate, currently 42 percent for large corporations, for example, is substantially higher than the rate in other industrial countries. Nor is there evidence that special corporate tax exemptions such as tax investment credits are more pervasive in Japan than elsewhere.

In the area of public finance, the government's key policy instrument is the Fiscal Investment and Loan Program (FILP), the bulk of which is financed by postal savings and government pension funds. FILP investments and loans to public works institutions in fiscal year 1988 totaled ¥4.1217 trillion, or 16 percent of the ¥25.3440 trillion subtotal that excludes the investment trusts. Because virtually all of the funding for regional public bodies as well as a portion of that for financial intermediaries will ultimately find its way into public works or related projects, public works account for close to 50 percent of FILP's direct and indirect investment and loans, excluding the investment trust portion of FILP's portfolio.

It is also noteworthy that regulations are not targeted at the large corporate sector. MITI's regulatory powers are quite restricted, at least at present, except in energy. Regulations are much more stringent and pervasive in transportation, construction, and agriculture, where they are administered by the Ministries of Transport, Construction, and Agriculture, Forestry and Fisheries, respectively. Even in energy, where MITI's influence on the private sector is comparatively strong, Samuels notes that its "long-time dream of creation of a national oil champion continuously producing and refining has not come about."[10]

Also, MITI struggled with and was defeated by the Ministry of Post and Telecommunications in the value-added network area at the time of the passage of the Electricity and Communication Industry Act in 1984.[11] As Takashi Inoguchi and Tomoaki Iwai correctly point out, MITI's influence within the LDP is weak compared with that of other ministries. Accordingly, this reduces leverage with the firms it seeks to regulate.

Regulations covering the private sector are administered by the bureaucracy, but the support of *zoku* representatives in the LDP is essential to sustain or skillfully use these regulations for policy purposes. MITI, lacking well-organized support from the party, has increasingly depended on international crises such as oil shocks or trade quarrels to secure its position. It is certainly true that some of the wartime emergency measures in various industries (the Oil Industry Act of 1934, the Auto Manufacturing Industry Act and Steel Industry Act of 1936, the Industrial Machinery Act of 1938) strengthened the regulatory hand of MITI substantially during the 1940s and 1950s. However, deregulation, starting in 1960 with Japan's liberalization of payments for imports of goods and services (in accordance with the International Monetary Fund Articles of Agreement), had stripped away most of these regulatory powers by the 1970s.

To be sure, MITI has performed important functions in such areas as energy, policy for medium-sized to small corporations, and international trade issues. Even so, the facts do not justify the emphasis many analysts have placed on MITI in order to demonstrate the role of the government in the private sector.

The actual role of the government can best be understood by looking

10. Samuels, "Nihon ni Okeru Kokka no Business," p. 96.
11. Inoguchi and Iwai, *"Zokugiin" no Kenkyū.*

at specific examples, such as a typical land improvement project, where the government is largely a financier, and the Japanese postal savings system, which the government runs directly.

A Land Improvement Project

The structure of a land improvement public works project, one that includes irrigation and drainage, illustrates both the role of the government in the project and the interactions among the national government, the prefecture, and the beneficiary (city, town, village, land improvement cooperative, or individual).[12] The central government provides subsidies for prefectural and collective enterprises apart from government-run ones. Depending upon the specific project, the central government, prefecture, or beneficiary bears the funding burden except in unusual cases. Because land improvement projects often encompass a number of cities, towns, and villages, the financial burden is shared according to the standing of the city, town, village, and co-op members. Every proposal for land improvement is submitted to the Ministry of Agriculture, Forestry and Fisheries through the prefectural governor to determine its suitability; even the works of a co-op member cannot be carried out without prefectural and national approval. In short, although the cooperative at the bottom of the scale can determine needs and initiate proposals, the actual works themselves are tightly controlled by the national government and the prefecture. Of course, the bodies that carry out these works are often the prefecture, the city, town, or village, or the land improvement cooperative. Except in certain national enterprises, the central government functions primarily as a supervisor and bankroller.

Although the amount of interaction among state, local government, cooperatives, and individuals varies from one type of project to another, irrigation and drainage works provide a good idea of how the Japanese system works, which is by and large as follows:

—The central government's role in implementing public works is to oversee and finance, not to instigate.

—While the prefecture often instigates works programs directly, it also acts as bankroller.

—Although a city, town, or village has a strong presence as instigator,

12. The item-by-item share of public works, in order of increasing importance, is roads; sewerage and parks; agriculture, fisheries, and forestry; education and hospitals; and flood control works.

the co-ops (land improvement, agricultural, fisheries, and forestry co-ops and the chamber of commerce) and local small and medium-sized companies are vital to the success of a project. Therefore public works are often joint regional projects that closely involve the local private sector.

This pattern—of local governments acting either as the hub of public-sector enterprises or as the actual instigator of public works, or of cooperatives acting as works coordinator—is an unfamiliar one in the United States and Europe, but in Japan it is the norm. It is not unusual, in fact, for representatives in regional assemblies to be members of a major co-op or to be public works contractors and for the administrative and executive branches of municipal bodies to work as one coherent entity in running public businesses. Nor is there any shortage of examples in which municipalities engage in so-called non-public-sector activities: Tokachi City's Tokachi Wine, Furano City's Furano Wine on Hokkaido, and the Oguni cedar development authority in Kumamoto Prefecture's Oguni Town, to name a few. Rather than being a new trend toward regional decentralization, however, such involvement is more an extension of the role hitherto played by municipalities, as illustrated by some of the activities in Oguni Town.

The core of the rehabilitation project for Oguni cedar is being financed fifty-fifty and jointly managed by Oguni Town and the forestry cooperative. Carpenters under exclusive contract are responsible for everything from lumber production to housing construction; they built the first traditional Japanese farmhouse for export in Fukuoka. Using its position as a public works body, the town is also constructing marketing and forwarding facilities for local products and a local produce hall. The former are for a livestock market managed by the local agricultural co-op, and the construction contractor is the Agricultural Land Development Corporation. This project is being carried out as a subcontract of the larger development project for regional agriculture. The local produce hall, a public facility owned by Oguni Town, is managed and operated by the same agricultural co-op, which will experiment in manufacturing and marketing butter, cheese, ham, and sausages under co-op brands. Both facilities are being constructed with the help of central government and prefectural subsidies as part of a model scheme to stem the flow of young residents to the cities. Among the other new ideas the town has introduced is a design for a municipal gymnasium and traffic center constructed of reinforced steel rods and wood.

The entrepreneur for this series of undertakings, the town mayor,

Yoshitoshi Miyazaki, ordered the wooden gymnasium after reading in a magazine about a similar one produced by a local architect. The governor of Kumamoto Prefecture, Morihiro Hosokawa, is also enthusiastic about these projects and is said to have his mind set on creating a rural cultural zone. Although the prefecture subsidizes such "biggest-best-first in Japan" projects to the tune of ¥20 million per project per year, most central government subsidies come with strings attached, making it difficult for new projects to qualify. Ever-increasing central government red tape is said to be a constant headache.

Oguni Town's progressive mayor and governor have enabled the town to go ahead with more ambitious projects, but it is the current system that provides the framework allowing them to take the initiative and work in conjunction with the co-op. The number of actors involved in public works in this system, however, is large, and enormous energy and political influence are needed, first to create a local consensus with the co-ops and then to pursue the project up the various ladders of the prefectural and central government. In many cases, the services of the Diet representative in the constituency are essential to convince the central bureaucracy that subsidies or permits are merited.

The Postal Savings System

The postal savings system, unlike public works, is directly run by the central government. A measure of its importance in the financial sector is that it has captured one-third of total deposits in Japan and has become a strong rival of commercial banks, as can be seen in table 4.

Although the ratio of postal savings to bank deposits fluctuated wildly in the nineteenth century, when the financial system was by no means fully established, it stabilized in the vicinity of 15 percent in the second decade of the twentieth century. When private financial institutions were rocked by the Great Depression and the Japanese recession in the Showa period, however, postal savings gained a much larger share as many banks folded or were merged. By 1944 postal savings accounted for 49.8 percent of bank deposits.

Although the hyperinflation of the latter half of the 1940s caused the ratio of postal savings to bank deposits to drop to around 15 percent during the 1950s and 1960s, postal savings went up again in the high-growth period of the late 1960s, reaching a ratio of 45.4 percent by 1985. In contrast to the prewar period, the postwar years have been free of bank failures or mergers in the private sector and so there has been no

Table 4. Postal Savings and Commercial Bank Deposits in Japan, Selected Years, 1900–85
¥ 100 million

Year	Postal savings[a]	Bank deposits[b]	Ratio of postal savings to bank deposits	Interest rates Postal[c]	Bank[d]
1900	0.25	4.37	5.7	4.80	7.03
1905	0.56	6.93	8.1	5.04	5.73
1910	1.70	0.12	14.3	4.20	4.43
1915	2.41	0.17	14.2	4.20	5.18
1920	8.85	0.58	15.2	4.80	6.50
1925	11.67	0.87	13.4	4.80	6.00
1930	24.97	0.87	28.6	4.20	4.50
1935	32.33	1.00	32.5	3.00	3.70
1940	79.15	2.47	32.1	3.76	3.30
1945	471.52	10.23	46.1	3.40	3.30
1950	1,547.00	9,286.00	16.7	3.50	4.70
1955	5,383.00	35,801.00	15.0	6.00	6.00
1960	11,231.00	84,995.00	13.2	6.00	6.00
1965	27,025.00	196,449.00	13.8	5.50	5.50
1970	77,439.00	389,248.00	19.9	5.75	5.75
1975	245,626.00	870,398.00	28.3	8.00	8.00
1980	619,498.00	1,470,366.00	42.1	7.25	7.25
1985	1,023,859.00	2,256,053.00	45.4	5.25	5.25

a. Excludes postal transfer deposits. Calculated on a fiscal year-end basis by savings office.
b. Includes bonds and deposits of a transferable nature. Calculated on a fiscal year-end basis.
c. Ordinary deposit rate; after 1941, longest fixed-amount deposit rate.
d. From 1919–47, after-tax interest for fixed deposits, calculated according to regulations covering Tokyo deposit interest; from 1948, long-term fixed-deposit interest, calculated according to the Temporary Rate Adjustment Act.

obvious reason for postal savings to make large inroads into private-sector finance. Nevertheless, the rapid growth in the agricultural and regional economic sectors as well as in middle-class income, as a result of Japan's fast economic growth, probably worked to the postal savings system's advantage, given its nationwide low-cost network.

In the late 1970s and early 1980s, postal savings recorded an accumulating deficit, which was up to ¥500 billion by the end of fiscal 1984. Some analysts have argued that postal savings tried to expand its deposit-taking share with stronger competitiveness by shifting the brunt of its deficit to postal operations, but this is a misperception that derives from a poor understanding of the structure of the postal savings balance sheet.

Postal savings funds received as deposits for six months or longer are redeposited with MOF's Trust Fund. Fund-raising operations take place on a short-term interest basis, while the fund is managed on a long-term basis, the balance fluctuating according to the yield curve formed by interest rate outlooks at the time. The balance sheet goes into the black in periods of low interest and into the red when interest rates are high. A volatile interest rate is particularly unsettling because of the time lag between the receipt and conferral of funds. The low interest rates that have prevailed since 1985 have made it possible to wipe out the accumulated deficit. Postal savings is able to shoulder the risk of such interest rate fluctuation over a long period precisely because it is in the government sector.

As is often pointed out, the jewel in the postal savings crown is the fixed-amount deposit, an extremely competitive instrument in terms of both liquidity and yield. Deposits made in periods of high interest continue to receive the same rate of interest for ten years, making them similar to a long-term government bond, but deposits can be withdrawn any time after six months at no capital loss. Such deposits enjoy considerable advantages over other long-term fixed-interest instruments in times of interest rate volatility or uncertain outlook because they can be deposited on a short-term basis. This is an extremely attractive instrument for the ordinary small depositor, as it offers a choice of fixed or floating interest for a maximum of ten years, according to one's needs, and also has good liquidity. Of course, the more advantageous it is for the depositor, the greater the burden for postal savings, but, at least at present, the fixed-amount deposit has not generated structural deficits for the post office.

Japan's 18,000 special post offices are the backbone of its postal savings operations, and the majority of postmasters see postal savings, not postal or insurance services, as their main area of activity.[13] Postal services themselves are carried out mainly by special collection and delivery post offices in conjunction with ordinary post offices, and postal insurance operations are run by agents at ordinary post offices, so in effect the three areas are managed separately.

The postmasters for special post offices are almost always appointed

13. Although the great number of postal savings branches in residential areas would seem to be inefficient, the rate of postal savings operating costs is only 0.7 percent, a figure that has been falling swiftly with the increase in postal savings deposits in recent years. One reason for this low rate is that in the public sector workers' wages are about half those of staff in private financial institutions. Another is that the postmaster's own residence often serves, at low rental, as a branch office. Postmasters are able to offer their residences at a low rental rate while receiving the low salary of some ¥6 million to ¥7 million precisely because of the official nature of postal operations and the honor associated with the position of postmaster in local communities.

on a hereditary basis and are usually influential figures in the community with formidable deposit collection ability. Postmasters also wield considerable political power because of their ability to deliver votes at election time, and their nationwide organization has considerable influence on the LDP.

To sum up, the sharp increase in postal savings deposits both before and after the war has been due to the government-backed, nationwide network of special post offices and their ability under a system of regulated interest to offer an overwhelmingly competitive instrument, the fixed-amount deposit. All this has been possible only because of the official nature of the postal savings system, which functions as a strong competitor of private financial institutions.

Although some might question whether it is desirable in terms of national economic efficiency for the public sector, with its inherent advantages, to compete with the private sector, in the case of Japanese finance, the answer is a clear yes. In the first place, the private sector enjoys several advantages over the public sector (for example, it is able to offer loans and issue bonds). Moreover, it is not at an overwhelming competitive disadvantage in relation to the public sector. From the point of view of efficiency, competition between organizations with different objectives and functions is extremely desirable. Indeed, the public sector has been particularly useful as a countervailing power to somewhat oligopolistic private financial institutions. The Japanese financial system would have become even more biased toward big financial institutions and even more oriented toward wholesale banking had it not been for the services that postal savings and agricultural co-ops provide for the small depositor. Although there was not much interest rate competition at the retail end, nonprice competition was tough, thanks to postal savings and agricultural co-ops. Their activities in the finance area are a prime illustration of the competition between the public sector and the relatively independent private sector that has become one of the predominant characteristics of the Japanese economy.

The United States would probably counter any tendency toward monopoly or oligopoly in large corporations with antimonopoly legislation, but in Japan's case the countervailing force has been public-sector participation in the same operations. In the financial markets, postal savings, postal insurance, and agricultural co-ops have been the main instruments used for this purpose. In other areas, such as construction and commerce, the local authorities of city, town, village, and interconnected cooperatives have been a force of resistance. The role of the special post office postmaster within the postal savings system is also in the nature of local co-op chief and is another example of public-sector business and countervailing powers centered on local authorities. Apart from this direct involvement in national land improvement and postal savings operations, the central government's main job in the public sector is to oversee and manage, in conjunction with the prefecture, and to make budgetary appropriations. While the actual implementation of public-sector projects is decentralized, the supervisory powers of the prefecture and central government have remained fairly strong, mainly because of their budgetary control and allocation of subsidies.

In some respects this pattern resembles the internal organization of large Japanese corporations, where the dissemination of information and the implementation of activities are decentralized but personnel and financial power remain concentrated at the head office. Both are fundamentally decentralized, bottom-up organizations characterized by exceedingly strict management and supervision. In the case of large private companies, however, the supervisory body is one-dimensional, and this concentration of authority can at times make top-down activity possible, whereas supervision in the public sector is multidimensional and imbued with politics. This makes the top-down approach extremely difficult: negative checks on new projects can interfere at all levels, making it exceedingly difficult to change the status quo. Karel van Wolferen has criticized precisely this state of affairs, pointing out that the Japanese government is besieged by special interest groups, that its complex system of overlapping hierarchies enables it to create a balance but not to make decisions, and that a Japanese prime minister has less power than the head of government of any Western country.[14]

Budget Compilation

"You can't get money out of the government when all you've got are representatives who think they're kingpins. You can't keep everyone happy unless you're prepared to lay your life on the line and go about overturning the desk of the Director General of the Budget Bureau at MOF!" So said a senior LDP leader, Shin Kanemaru, in April 1988

14. Karel G. van Wolferen, "The Japan Problem," *Foreign Affairs*, vol. 65 (Winter 1986–87), pp. 288–303.

Table 5. Diet Enactments, by Type of Session and Budget Relation, 1975–87

| Year | Total enactment | Major session | | |
		Total	Cabinet proposed	Budget related
1975	98	67	48	25
1976	85	69	59	31
1977	91	76	65	34
1978	113	95	83	34
1979	72	53	45	30
1980	115	85	75	33
1981	95	89	72	39
1982	103	98	79	35
1983	81	60	52	29
1984	78	78	70	40
1985	119	100	85	36
1986	110	85	73	33
1987	115	81	72	41

during a speech at Kikuchi City in Kumamoto Prefecture.[15] Kanemaru was not exaggerating: a Diet member must be prepared, should the need arise, to resort to such physical means as overturning desks to build agreement between the demands of the localities and the regulations and budget allocations of the central government.

In this system, the annual budget compilation occupies a central place in policy formulation. Although planning is the first concern in areas directly administered by the government, such as foreign policy and defense, the budget is important in relation to the implementation of this planning process. For public works programs and the like, however, the central government does not often directly plan, but mostly appropriates, so that passive adjustment dictates policy.

The Diet enacts about one hundred public laws each year. They can be divided according to those passed in major, or budget, sessions and all others, and according to budget-related and unrelated bills (table 5). The major session is normally convened in late December and lasts 150 days, or more in the case of extended sittings. Depending upon the year, there may be one or two temporary sessions in which a supplementary

15. Kanemaru's remarks are a succinct description of the politician's role in Kikuchi, a public works "mecca," where agricultural irrigation works are being carried out under a special national land improvement account of the Ministry of Agriculture, Forestry and Fisheries. This project covers 4,740 hectares and is expected to cost ¥20.9 billion. Started in 1979, it is scheduled to be completed in 1992. Also under way in the area are prefecture works covering 4,720 hectares, cooperative works covering 830 hectares, and the construction of the Ryumon Dam by the Ministry of Construction.

budget or another important bill such as a tax reform bill is deliberated, but under normal conditions, Diet proceedings pivot on budget appropriation debates.

As table 5 shows, more than 80 percent of all bills have been enacted in major sessions. Of those bills, 85 percent have been submitted by the cabinet, and about half of those have been budget related. Bills are considered to be budget related if they directly affect budget numbers, but even bills officially classified as budget unrelated are in most cases indirectly related to the budget. Apart from "deadline" bills, such as those involving international treaties, which need to be enacted by a certain date, budget-related bills are given priority over bills that are not budget related.

Thus most bills enacted in the Japanese Diet are related in one way or another to the budget, and the passage of the budget appropriation bill and budget-related bills is given utmost priority. In fact, all cabinet members are expected to be present when the budget package is debated in the Budget Committee, regardless of the specific topic of discussion. Thus other Diet committees cannot be convened when the Budget Committee is in session because the responsible cabinet ministers are not available to attend. It is customary for each committee to hold discussions only twice a week, and although a Diet session is just as long as or longer than its European or U.S. counterparts, the number of hours spent on actual discussion of each bill is relatively short.

Moreover, if any party refuses to debate, discussions can be suspended because convention dictates that the Diet must reach a consensus, not a majority, on procedural matters. Bulldozing legislation through the Diet is deemed an infraction of the rules, even by the news media, and in this respect the opposition parties exercise considerable power.

Because of this consensus rule on procedure, time schedules are of paramount importance in the Diet: is there enough time to discuss the proposed bills? It is precisely these time constraints that have given the Diet House Management Committee and the Diet committees from each party a decisive role in Diet deliberations. For the government, it is of the utmost importance that the budget and related bills be passed in the major session. Since 1955, the government has had the necessary majority to pass bills, so that discussions taking place in the Diet are more often than not a mere formality for the LDP and the government. The real challenge is in sticking to the time schedule. Answers to opposition questions therefore need to be defensive and veiled, and avoiding confrontation on key policy issues is an important strategy for the government. This is the main reason why answers to opposition questions tend to be clearly spoken but ambiguous in meaning.

A Decentralized and Cumulative Process

Behind this budget-oriented "viscosity" of the Diet lie the government bureaucracy and the dominant Liberal Democratic party.[16] In a sense, Diet discussions are merely a last-minute fine-tuning or a somewhat ritualistic confirmation of policy decisions already arrived at by the huge government-party apparatus during the six months before the major session is convened. The ritualistic nature of the process, however, does not make it any less important. In fact, a wrong step at any point can kill a bill. This all-or-nothing situation differs substantially from the approach in the U.S. Congress, for example, where bills are debated and numerous amendments made.

The all-important budget compilation officially starts in late June, with discussions on aggregate figures or "ceilings" for requests in the major functional categories, such as general expenses and public works (figure 1). Each spending ministry as well as the MOF undertakes regular personnel reshuffling from mid- to late May to prepare for the start of the budget season. Often, the cabinet is also reshuffled at this time. The paramount importance of time schedules in the parliamentary sessions has already been mentioned, but the calendar for budget compilation is also a crucial factor in these proceedings. With the presentation of government proposals to the major session as a deadline, the MOF, the spending ministries, and the LDP engage in complex and intricate consultations and negotiations, but because of the sheer number of players involved, sequential and ritualistic formulas are required to keep the process from getting bogged down. Consequently, one of the more important exercises for the participants is deciding at what stage to pass on what information.

The first vital decision, at least from the point of view of economic policy, is made within a relatively short period. In July, the MOF, in close consultation with the spending ministries and leading LDP politicians, prepares a ceiling draft for budget requests. As requests in aggregate numbers are ordinarily sanctioned up to the ceiling, this then constitutes the de facto determination of aggregate budget numbers. The

16. Mike Masato Mochizuki, "Managing and Influencing the Japanese Legislative Process: The Role of Parties and the National Diet," Ph.D. thesis, Harvard University, 1982.

Figure 1. Budget Compilation Calendar (1987 Budget)

	Party	Spending ministries	Ministry of Finance	Cabinet
June				
July	Subcommittees and senior party officials July 31: Executive Council and PARC approval of ceiling	Informal negotiation and coordination of ceiling Formation of policies and budget, tax and FILP requests	Informal negotiation and coordination of ceiling July 31: Determination of ceiling	Cabinet approval of ceiling
Aug.	Preliminary hearing of requests (subcommittees)	Aug. 31: Formal submission of requests	Preliminary hearing of requests	
Sept.		Explanation of policies and requests to MOF at assistant director level	Examination of policies and requests at assistant director level	
Oct.			First high-level examination involving director generals	
Nov.	Various subcommittees Individual influential representatives Senior party officials Consultation and petition Informal negotiation and coordination	Negotiations on policies and requests Informal negotiation and coordination Informal negotiation and coordination	Reexamination at assistant director level Second high-level examination involving director generals	
Dec.	Executive Council PARC Tax Committee Final coordination for MOF draft Dec. 25: Joint meeting of Executive Council and PARC on MOF draft Executive Council and PARC Dec. 29: Final coordination by senior party officials	Final coordination for MOF draft Final coordination on MOF draft Dec. 26–29 Budget restoration negotiations	Final coordination for MOF draft Formal explanation to and final coordination with finance minister Dec. 24: Final ministerial meeting on MOF draft Dec. 25: Presentation of MOF draft to spending ministries Budget restoration negotiations	Formal explanation to and final coordination with Prime Minister's Office Dec. 25: Cabinet meeting on MOF draft Dec. 30: Cabinet meeting on government budget

The Japanese Politico-Economic System and the Public Sector   73

fact that this initial process is usually short and relatively problem-free illustrates how much more important distribution on a micro level is in Japanese politics and administration than the determination of overall volume on a macro plane.

After being advised on the ceiling for each functional spending category, each spending ministry sets about preparing its policy and detailed budget requests. As I have stressed earlier, budget compilation and government policymaking are virtually synonymous. Each spending ministry scoops up requests from its respective regional offices and related government institutions and consults with the policy divisions of the LDP (*bukai*) and other concerned organizations. Although the role of the central government is not insignificant in the sense of conceiving new policy ideas or putting together an overall policy package, the projects themselves are largely instigated at the city, town, village, or regional cooperative level. In this case, the central bureaucracy is not making requests but fielding them, and its job in a broad sense is that of coordinator.

The role of the members of the *bukai* (known as *zoku* representatives) is to lobby the central government on behalf of their local government and organizations and to see their demands successfully incorporated into ministry policy. At another level of the budget compilation process, *zoku* representatives also work closely with each spending ministry, lobbying for them with the Ministry of Finance. The draft budget of the MOF or the government must ultimately be approved by the Executive Council and Policy Affairs Research Council (PARC) of the LDP. Since *zoku* lobbyists have close ties with these committees or are themselves key party officials, they wield considerable lobbying power.

Although the budget process entails complex interaction between the LDP, MOF, and the spending ministries (figure 2), in actual practice it is the will of the party that ultimately prevails over the MOF in key decisions when the party is backed by the prime minister (who is also president of the LDP). And even the prime minister is constrained by factional considerations and cannot go against strong party will. Nor can the bureaucracy meet the party head on. To the extent that the spending ministries and the MOF act as the secretariat for policy and budget compilation, thereby dominating the logistics of the process, the prime minister cannot afford to flaunt the will of the secretariat.

The schema of party versus bureaucracy often put forward in the mass media or academic circles is somewhat misleading, however, in view of the spending ministries' collaboration with the LDP *bukai*.

Figure 2. Interaction between Major Actors in Budget Compilation

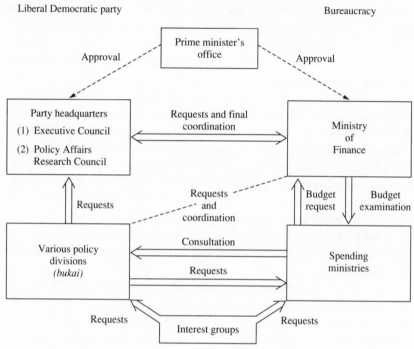

Therefore, it might make more sense to analyze the situation using a schema of MOF and party bosses versus spending ministries and party *bukai*. In fact, the rise of the *zoku* representatives, especially since the mid-1970s, has coincided with a relative decline in the power of the MOF and the party bosses over the past two decades, and the budget compilation process has become much more decentralized and pluralistic since the 1950s and 1960s.

Budget requests are formally submitted to and examined by the Ministry of Finance between September and December. During this time, the major actors conduct various behind-the-scenes consultations and negotiations. The most important channel, on the surface at least, runs between the MOF and the spending ministries, whose assistant directors negotiate detailed policies and numbers between the two. The process is highly decentralized and cumulative. Assistant directors in the spending ministries draw up the policies that come under their own jurisdiction, coordinate these with the policies of the institutions concerned, and submit the resultant budget requests to the MOF either themselves or through their director. All the necessary documentation and explanation of policies must go through this channel. Although the accounting (or budget) division of each spending ministry coordinates and oversees all the detailed requests of its own ministry, each request originates in the section or in the local government or cooperatives for which that section does the coordinating. In other words, policies and budget requests do not flow in a top-down pattern.

Although the assistant directors of spending ministries carry out the budget process, they brief directors when necessary. They also sound out superiors on strategic points or formulate proposals at the suggestion of directors or their superiors. Bureaucrats above the director level consult with each other, with LDP politicians in the *bukai,* or with party headquarters and related institutions to generate a consensus. The role of top officials in both the government and the party, however, is usually passive.

This decentralized, cumulative process can also be found in large, private Japanese organizations, but not in so extreme a form. Private companies have a greater concentration of authority and a larger degree of top-down decisions.

Because the assistant director has a relatively narrow jurisdiction and the section acts as coordinator rather than instigator, policies are often fragmented and devoid of a grand vision. Moreover, since policy proposals have a long path to follow from local body to final adjustment and are scrutinized by many people, they tend to become somewhat conservative and aim at preserving or patchworking the status quo. Any departure from the status quo would make it even more difficult to arrive at a consensus among all the players. In many cases, lobbyists manage to get their interests (or at least, already existing vested interests) woven into budget figures in some form or another, and it requires something really out of the ordinary to change the status quo.

The basic goal of this long and intricate process is to reach a consensus. Given the number of actors who have a say, even the prime minister has difficulty realizing his initiatives. According to van Wolferen, this very fact is the crux of the "Japan problem."

Former Prime Minister Yasuhiro Nakasone, who aimed at a "presidential style" of politics, is said to have bypassed a considerable part of this decisionmaking mechanism in an attempt to implement top-down politics and administration. Nevertheless, the system was largely unchanged by Nakasone's tenure. Indeed, it is probably because he managed the government and executive branches so skillfully without changing existing mechanisms that he was able to carry out several radical policies (privatization of the national railways and Nippon Telegraph and Telephone, for one). No doubt he was also assisted in this regard by the fact that he had an unusually long term as prime minister (five years) and could therefore make an all-out effort at reform.

The Party versus the Bureaucracy

By and large, however, structural adjustment has become increasingly difficult in the four decades since World War II as the political process of decisionmaking has matured and become more institutionalized. The bureaucratization of the country's dominant political party, the LDP, and the institutionalization of its interaction with the government bureaucracy have expedited this maturing process. The establishment of firm career paths and the emergence of *zoku* representatives within the LDP, as well as the institutionalization of support groups in their constituencies, have all contributed to the consolidation of party organizations.

In particular, the ties between *zoku* representatives and government bureaucracies are strong and have become increasingly institutionalized. Early in their careers, politicians elected to the House specialize in the affairs of one ministry or another and become members of the Diet committee and LDP policy research subcommittee related to that ministry. Throughout their careers, these representatives cultivate their relationship with the ministry. Because many representatives act as the Tokyo treasury officer or lobbyist for municipal bodies or public works in their constituencies, a good relationship with the ministry is essential.

Bureaucrats in the ministries welcome this kind of association because such politicians become strong supporters and lobbyists for their policies. Fielding local requests, they also act as buffers between vested interest groups and the ministry and wield strong political clout vis-à-vis the Ministry of Finance. Moreover, the LDP seniority system ensures that all of these policians will rise to the position of parliamentary vice-minister or minister if they are elected the requisite number of times, so it is to the advantage of the ministry itself to court these prospective heads. While the seniority system is a common feature of Japanese organizations, it is strongest within the LDP and not the corporate or bureaucratic sectors. (Strictly speaking, in the party's case it is not the number of years but the number of elections that determines seniority.) Politics and bureaucracy are often juxtaposed as "motion" and "rest," but with regard to personnel, which is the bottom line of any organization, it is the LDP adherence to extremely conservative and impartial rules that gives the party organization its stable and bureaucratic flavor.

Thus, the frequent contacts and interaction between *zoku* representatives and ministry bureaucrats closely resemble those of business partners. *Zoku* representatives essentially chase after votes and political contributions while the ministry seeks more funding and influence. True, both politicians and bureaucrats pursue policies aimed at the national interest, but only in an indirect way. Each ministry puts together its budget requests or policy in consultation with the *zoku* representative who has already fielded requests from the constituency. Whether the coordination is weighted to suit national interests, ministerial interests, or *zoku* interests is not clear.

Budget requests are also examined by the MOF, LDP party headquarters, the Policy Affairs Research Council, and the Prime Minister's Office. Traditionally, the role of coordination has been strong at MOF and party headquarters and is still considerable. With the increase in the political clout of the spending ministries and the institutionalization of *zoku* representatives, however, the MOF's coordinating role has started to weaken, though it has often been boosted by intervention from the prime minister's office, particularly under Nakasone.

This rise in the *zoku* representatives' influence has strengthened the role of LDP headquarters and its key officials vis-à-vis the MOF because of its control over the *zoku*. It is only the party bosses who can keep the *zoku* under a tight rein, which is often politically efficacious in opposing specific policies that have their strong support. The actual coordination of important policies is often carried out by the prime minister, the minister of finance, and senior LDP officials. To the extent that both the prime minister and the minister of finance are key party members, final coordination can be said to be carried out by the LDP. The party's role, however, is passive and often results in a middle-of-the-road approach, or as the Japanese put it, "add, then divide by two." This can be attributed to the fact that in many cases the ultimate policy instigator is the municipal body or local groups, whereas budget requests are drawn up at the central bureaucratic level.

Generally speaking, coordination by the MOF, the prime minister's office, or senior party officials has become increasingly ineffective since the high-growth period, and even more so in the past decade or so. So-called revolts by *zoku* representatives against party bosses often succeed if strongly backed by interest groups. Some examples include the 1985

Table 6. General Public Works Budget, by Category, 1979–87
Percent

Category	1979	1987
Agricultural infrastructure[a]	14.11	14.13
Irrigation[a]	13.55	13.72
Road construction	30.77	28.92
Housing	11.25	12.44
Sewerage	10.71	10.91
Forestry	4.53	4.56
Fishery	2.87	2.95
Port infrastructure	4.20	4.17

a. Both have been especially stable: agricultural infrastructure accounted for 14.1 percent every year from 1979–87 and irrigation for 13.6 percent, except in 1987, when it rose fractionally to 13.7 percent.

rice-price-cut revolt staged by so-called Viet Cong representatives and the 1987 tax reform revolt. Whereas it would be possible to put down such revolts in the corporate or bureaucratic sector by reshuffling personnel, appointments within the LDP have become formalized without an adequate centralization of authority. Representatives represent their respective constituencies and are more like feudal lords—in the sense that they are closely connected to public subsidies and public works in those constituencies—than vassals of the LDP. This is precisely why neither the prime minister nor party headquarters can make them toe the party line unilaterally.

Although this decentralization of power in the Japanese government implies active participation by many parties, the point at issue here is where a leadership base can be established to orchestrate these numerous participants. In the private corporate sector, the distribution of information and the decentralization of business operations aimed at injecting enthusiasm in employees, or "firing them up," is counterbalanced by the centralization of authority over treasury and personnel decisions. In this setting it is possible to respond top-down to environmental changes. In the public sector, however, centralization has never been strong and is gradually becoming weaker. A breakdown of the public works budget provides one example of the various rigidities in the public sector that have resulted from increasingly ineffective coordination (table 6).

The public works budget is parceled out among five ministries (Agriculture, Forestry and Fisheries; Construction; Transport; International Trade and Industry; and Welfare) and three agencies (Hokkaido Development, Okinawa Development, and National Land). Changing their respective allocation ratios is extremely difficult, if not impossible; as table 6 shows, they have remained virtually unchanged for almost ten years. These figures are all the more startling when compared with the rapid pace of change in the private sector during the same period. Enormous political energies must be harnessed to make even the smallest change in these shares. Any significant change is far beyond the capabilities of either senior LDP party officials or the Ministry of Finance unless strong external pressure can be brought to bear on them.

A few general observations emerge from the foregoing discussion:

—Politics at the central level in Japan revolves around the annual budget compilation, and budget logistics dominate the LDP, its interaction with the ministries, and the ministries' interaction with each other.

—Policy formulation is both a decentralized and cumulative process in which the LDP and MOF usually play no more than a passive coordinating role.

—Even the divisions of the spending ministries responsible for policy creation are usually not the instigators of the policy, so that what is said to be creation is often coordination.

—Interdependence between the LDP and the bureaucracy is strong and has been increasing in recent years. Relations between *zoku* representatives and their ministries are both long-term and stable and, as such, closely resemble the relations between large Japanese companies and their business partners.

—The role of politicians in this process is to look after the funding needs of the local business interests in their constituencies and to lobby the central government on behalf of those interests. In this sense, Japanese politicians have a far stronger entrepreneurial role than their European or U.S. counterparts. This is due largely to the fact that the Japanese public sector is dominated by public works.

Part II
The Politics of Budgeting

Party Politics, Divided Government, and Budget Deficits

Mathew D. McCubbins

MEMBERS OF Congress and the president have been grappling with runaway budget deficits for more than a decade. The twelve-digit budget deficits of the 1980s have been blamed for everything from a decline in private investment and personal savings to trade imbalances with Japan. Congress and the president seem unable or unwilling to come to grips with this problem. The budget agreement struck between President Bush and congressional negotiators in the fall of 1990, for example, claimed to slash $500 billion from the deficit over the next five years—while allowing the national debt to almost double to $6 trillion by 1995. Collectively, national policymakers seem akin to credit card junkies, hooked on living beyond their means, borrowing to pay the interest on their debt. But federal budget deficits are not new. Every president since World War II has run on a platform that promised to bring federal spending under control. Indeed, in only ten of the last sixty years have federal revenues exceeded expenditures.

Two explanations for the runaway deficits of the 1980s have received considerable play in both the popular press and the scholarly literature. One argues that they are the by-product of the "Reagan revolution," which combined tax cuts with sizable increases in defense spending. The other school of thought blames Congress, or more specifically, a change in the way Congress sets the budget. The Congressional Budget and Impoundment Control Act of 1974 gave the authority to determine the budget to newly created Budget committees in the House and Senate. The 1974 act, this school argues, broke the traditional role of the House Appropriations Committee as "guardian of the Treasury" and unleashed the spending profligacies of Congress.

These explanations represent two fairly common perceptions of American politics. The first views the twentieth century president as the dominant figure in policymaking, while the second emphasizes the influence of congressional committees. In this essay I attempt to show that neither of these two common perceptions is true, and that the budget deficits of the 1980s and early 1990s are a consequence of divided partisan control of the presidency and Congress.

Presidential Ascendancy

The Framers of the Constitution did not consider the possibility that the president could attain a dominant position in federal policymaking. Although the members of the Constitutional Convention fretted about the powers assigned to Congress, their concern was not that Congress would abdicate its powers, but that, through the power of the purse and other indirect measures, it would encroach upon the powers of the other branches of government. Consequently, the members of the convention sought to restrict the powers of Congress by establishing a system of checks on legislative decisionmaking.[1] The principal check on congressional authority, the veto, was delegated to the president.

The intentions of the Framers notwithstanding, it has become part of the lore of American politics that the president has come to dominate national politics.[2] This thesis is not without merit. The executive branch submits roughly 200 proposals to Congress every year. Among these proposals are budget requests, requests relating to fiscal management and proposals to reorganize the executive branch, and general policy proposals. Congress frequently accepts these proposals without amendment and moreover almost never takes action on an issue until it has received a proposal from the president.[3] Presidents also nominate several thousand people for appointment to federal posts. Rarely are these nominations rejected, and most receive only perfunctory review.

1. Alexander Hamilton, James Madison, and John Jay, *The Federalist Papers* (New American Library, 1961), no. 47.

2. See, for example, Wilfred E. Binkley, *President and Congress,* 3d ed. (Vintage Books, 1962); James Bryce, *The American Commonwealth* (Macmillan, 1924); James MacGregor Burns, *Presidential Government: The Crucible of Leadership* (Houghton Mifflin, 1965); Harold J. Laski, *The American Presidency* (Harper and Brothers, 1940); George F. Milton, *The Use of Presidential Power, 1789–1943* (Octagon Books, 1965); Richard E. Neustadt, *Presidential Power: The Politics of Leadership from FDR to Carter* (Wiley, 1980); Arthur M. Schlesinger, Jr., *The Imperial Presidency* (Houghton Mifflin, 1973); and James L. Sundquist, *The Decline and Resurgence of Congress* (Brookings, 1981).

3. See James P. Pfiffner, *The President, the Budget, and Congress: Impoundment and the 1974 Budget Act* (Westview Press, 1979); Paul E. Peterson and Mark Rom, "Macroeconomic Policymaking: Who Is in Control?" in John E. Chubb and Paul E. Peterson, eds., *Can the Government Govern?* (Brookings, 1989), pp. 139–82; and George C. Edwards III, *Presidential Influence in Congress* (Freeman, 1980).

How did this alleged transformation of national politics come about? While it is true that modern presidents exercise more authority than did nineteenth century presidents, most of this increase in authority has been the result not of executive encroachment, but rather of congressional delegation.[4] For example, in the 1921 Budget and Accounting Act Congress redelegated the authority to compile, revise, and transmit budget estimates for executive functions from the various departments to the Bureau of the Budget and the president.[5]

Delegation or Abdication?

In delegating such powers to the executive, did Congress actually abdicate its authority to make decisions? The distinction between delegation and abdication is more than just a semantic dispute.[6] In delegating, members of Congress retain their authority over policymaking, even if they do not directly make the policy decisions. If Congress as a body has abdicated its authority, then not only does it no longer make the policy choices, but it no longer affects the choices being made.

Many have argued, given the facts summarized above, that Congress no longer affects decisionmaking on those issues, such as the budget, that it has delegated to the executive branch and the president. The evidence for this proposition is that policy decisions made by the president are rarely if ever challenged in Congress, and that policy recommendations made by the president to Congress "are not seriously reviewed."[7] The complaints of members of Congress about apparent executive usurpations of legislative authority have also been cited as evidence for this interpretation.

But what can one actually infer from these stylized facts? These observations are entirely consistent with an interpretation that Congress, in delegating, actually has retained all of its authority over policymaking.

4. D. Roderick Kiewiet and Mathew D. McCubbins, *The Logic of Delegation*: *Congressional Parties and the Appropriations Process* (University of Chicago Press, 1991), chaps. 7, 9.

5. See D. Roderick Kiewiet and Mathew D. McCubbins, "Congress and the Budget Bureau: Delegation or Abdication?" paper prepared for the 1989 annual meeting of the American Political Science Association. See also *U.S. Bureau of the Budget, Communication from the President of the United States, Transmitting Laws Relating to the Estimates of Appropriations, the Appropriations, and Reports of Receipts and Expenditures*, H. Doc. 67-129 (Government Printing Office, 1921).

6. For a discussion of the difference between delegation and abdication, see Sundquist, *Decline and Resurgence*, p. 12.

7. Sundquist, *Decline and Resurgence*, p. 12.

The argument is as follows: Congress delegates its authority to make public policy to the executive. Members of Congress agree to do so because it is a more efficient way for them to make policy, and delegation therefore allows members to make policy in many more areas than they otherwise could. Congress then uses direct and indirect means to discipline those in the executive branch charged with carrying out this delegated authority.[8] Through these means Congress retains control of policymaking. Members indirectly shape executive decisions as they are being made, thus largely relieving themselves of the need to intervene directly or to challenge executive decisions at a later point.

Because Congress holds the power to veto or amend executive recommendations—such as the president's budget—the executive in his proposals likely will anticipate members' reactions and accommodate their demands before submitting his recommendations. Thus members are rarely seen to "seriously" review presidential proposals, for their demands have already been met in the proposals sent to them. The absence of evidence of congressional influence, therefore, should not be mistaken for the evidence of the absence of congressional influence.

Lastly, as James Sundquist noted, forebodings on Capitol Hill about executive ascendency are most marked when the president comes from a different party than the one that controls Congress. Complaints of executive usurpation, then, may reflect a wish for decreased delegation in the face of partisan conflict. Indeed, delegations to the executive seem to expand when both branches are controlled by the same party and to contract when control is divided.[9]

So has Congress, in delegating, retained control over policymaking? In addressing this question, students of American politics have examined

8. Michael W. Kirst, *Government Without Passing Laws: Congress's Nonstatutory Techniques for Appropriations Control* (University of North Carolina Press, 1969); Mathew D. McCubbins and Thomas Schwartz, "Congressional Oversight Overlooked: Police Patrols versus Fire Alarms," *American Journal of Political Science*, vol. 28 (February 1984), pp. 165–79; Mathew D. McCubbins, Roger G. Noll, and Barry R. Weingast, "Administrative Procedures as Instruments of Political Control," *Journal of Law, Economics and Organizations*, vol. 3 (Fall 1987), pp. 243–77; Mathew D. McCubbins, Roger G. Noll, and Barry R. Weingast, "Structure and Process, Politics and Policy: Administrative Arrangements and the Political Control of Agencies," *Virginia Law Review*, vol. 75 (March 1989), pp. 431–82; and Barry R. Weingast and Mark J. Moran, "Bureaucratic Discretion or Congressional Control? Regulatory Policymaking by the Federal Trade Commission," *Journal of Political Economy*, vol. 91 (October 1983), pp. 765–800.
9. See Kiewiet and McCubbins, *Logic of Delegation*, chaps. 7, 9.

the links between congressional committees and the agencies they oversee.[10] They describe federal policy as the product not of presidential direction, but of policy subgovernments, made up of the committees (or subcommittees) in the House and Senate with jurisdiction over the policy, the executive agency charged with executing the policy, and the constituents to whom the agency caters.[11] These studies have amassed a tremendous amount of evidence on particular policy decisions that clearly demonstrates that members of Congress take a much more active role in the day-to-day decisionmaking in the executive branch than is attributed to them by the presidential dominance thesis.

Further evidence of congressional efforts to control delegations to the president is exhibited by the ways Congress structures these delegations. The Budget and Accounting Act of 1921, for example, contains many provisions to control the revision, compilation, and transmittal of agency budget requests by the president.[12] These provisions have been amended and expanded many times in the intervening years.[13] Those who have argued that Congress has abdicated its responsibilities over policymaking have not ignored these facts, but they have missed their significance.

Congress therefore has the capability, through the structural details of delegation and through budgetary and legislative means, to control its delegations. But the effort required to restructure a delegation or sanction an errant agent may make the costs of control, for any specific instance

10. Weingast and Moran, "Bureaucratic Discretion."

11. Douglass Cater, *Power in Washington: A Critical Look at Today's Struggle to Govern in the Nation's Capital* (Random House, 1964); J. Leiper Freeman, *The Political Process: Executive Bureau-Legislative Committee Relations,* rev. ed. (Random House, 1965); Theodore J. Lowi, *The End of Liberalism: The Second Republic of the United States,* 2d ed. (Norton, 1979); and Randall B. Ripley and Grace A. Franklin, *Congress, the Bureaucracy, and Public Policy,* 3d ed. (Homewood, Ill.: Dorsey Press, 1984).

12. See Kiewiet and McCubbins, *Logic of Delegation,* chap. 9. In granting authority to the president under the 1921 act, Congress required that the estimates submitted conform to existing law. The earlier legislation, for example, required that estimates be made only for those items authorized by law and that large deviations in estimates from the previous year's appropriations be explained in detail. Further, the form and content of the estimates were closely prescribed, as was the information required to justify each request. For details on the requirements of the 1921 act, see *Communication from the President,* H. Doc. 67-129.

13. The requirements have been expanded in the Budget and Accounting Procedures Act of 1950, the Government Accounting and Procedures Act of 1956, the Budget and Accounting Act of 1958, the Legislative Reorganization Act of 1970, and numerous other acts. See Kiewiet and McCubbins, *Logic of Delegation,* chap. 7, for a complete discussion.

of agency slippage, exceed the benefits. Put another way, although Congress has the ability to exercise control over policymaking, do its members lack the will to do so?[14]

Members of Congress do seem more willing to exercise control at some times than at others. The efforts by Congress to restructure presidential discretion in the 1970s—for example, through the War Powers Act of 1973 and the 1974 budget act—are prominent examples. The mantle of responsibility, it seems, is delegated only when the president and the majorities in Congress share the same party label.

Although Congress may not have abdicated its authority to the president, its delegations have indisputably expanded the president's authority. Many analysts contend that the delegation of policy initiation to the president, such as the budget, has tilted the balance between the branches to favor the president.[15] Although the president has a vague constitutional mandate to present proposals to Congress, most success-ful proposals arise out of congressional delegation.[16] And it was the establishment of legislative clearance at the Budget Bureau, created under the 1921 budget act, that has been heralded as the principal source of presidential dominance in this century.[17]

What must be remembered, however, and has not been forgotten by the Budget Bureau and its directors, is that Congress created the Budget Bureau (now the Office of Management and Budget), Congress funds the OMB, and Congress regulates the activities of the OMB.[18] As a former general counsel to the clerk of the House remarked, "Congress created OMB. Congress can uncreate it—or change it."[19] To this effect,

14. Morris P. Fiorina, "Congressional Control of the Bureaucracy: A Mismatch of Incentives and Capabilities," in Lawrence C. Dodd and Bruce I. Oppenheimer, eds., *Congress Reconsidered,* 2d ed. (Washington: Congressional Quarterly Press, 1981), pp. 332–48.

15. Why members of Congress have delegated to the president the authority to propose legislation is explored by D. Roderick Kiewiet and Mathew D. McCubbins, "Presidential Influence on Congressional Appropriations Decisions," *American Journal of Political Science,* vol. 32 (August 1988), pp. 713–36.

16. For example, proposals for executive reorganization, which are not requested by Congress, are almost never approved, while Congress almost always passes a bill for spending or tax proposals.

17. See Sundquist, *Decline and Resurgence,* especially p. 155, for this argument.

18. See Kiewiet and McCubbins, *Logic of Delegation;* and Lucius Wilmerding, Jr., *The Spending Power: A History of the Efforts of Congress to Control Expenditures* (Yale University Press, 1943).

19. Stanley Brand, quoted in Joseph A. Davis, "Growth in Legislative Role Sparks Concern in Congress," *Congressional Quarterly Weekly Report,* September 14, 1985, p. 1815.

Chet Holifield, then chairman of the House Committee on Government Operations, remarked to then OMB Director Roy Ash at a subcommittee hearing, "The budget director serves the President only because the President serves the Congress in making budget recommendations. And the budget director himself serves the Congress."[20]

But even with an explicit delegation of authority to the president, as Ronald Reagan witnessed, Congress need not even consider the president's proposal. Referring to his troubled budgets at a press conference on October 22, 1987, Reagan observed that "I submitted a budget program early in the year, and as they've done every year I've been here, they've simply put it on the shelf and have refused to even consider it."[21] "When the delegation is not a power to act but only responsibility to recommend," Sundquist observed, "—the executive budget, for instance—the Congress explicitly retains not only its full authority but also its responsibility to act."[22]

Nonetheless, presidents do gain some influence over outcomes through the recommendations they make. The president and members of his party in Congress run for reelection based, in part, on how well the party does at implementing its platform. Because their electoral fates are partially linked, the president and his party in Congress will find it in their best interest to cooperate on passing the party's platform. Policy initiation, then, is a cooperative process. How much influence is shared by the president in this process is open to debate, particularly when his party is in the minority in both houses of Congress.

Presidential Power and the Veto

In contrast to the powers delegated to the president by Congress, the veto conveys to the president a property right in the legislative process. The president's proposal may matter on some occasions and not on others, but the veto power applies to all acts of Congress. Moreover, coming last in the sequence of legislation, the president's veto power will affect decisions at all the previous stages.

Some people, in analyzing presidential vetoes, have inferred that the veto power is ineffective because it is rarely used. Again, as in the thesis

20. "OMB Director," *Congressional Quarterly Weekly Report,* March 10, 1973, p. 544.
21. "President Faces Questions on Budget, Persian Gulf Policies," *Congressional Quarterly Weekly Report,* October 24, 1987, p. 2626.
22. Sundquist, *Decline and Resurgence,* p. 12.

of presidential dominance, this is a mistaken inference. Members of Congress logically anticipate the president's reaction to their proposals. Their proposals, then, usually accommodate the president's demands to avoid a veto. Indeed, if members of Congress have good information as to what is and what is not acceptable to the president, there should never be any vetoes.

The influence that the veto gives the president is, however, asymmetrical. The president can use the veto to restrain Congress when he prefers to spend less than its members do, but he can not use it to extract more appropriations from Congress when he prefers to spend more than its members do.[23] This asymmetry derives from inherent limitations in the veto power. The veto provides the president with only the power to reject acts of Congress; it does not provide him with the power to modify these acts. Thus Congress submits take-it-or-leave-it offers to the president, who is then faced with choosing between the bill passed by Congress and, at best, some future legislation that he may or may not prefer to the current offer.

On spending bills, the president's position is even more precarious: on receiving the bill from Congress, the president can either accept the appropriations contained therein or veto it and let Congress write a continuing resolution.[24] Because of the emergency nature of continuing resolutions, they are virtually veto proof. Also, because continuing resolutions almost always contain less spending than that contained in the corresponding appropriations bills, the president is able to reduce spending (to the level contained in the continuing resolution) through the use or threat of the veto, but he cannot get increased spending from a Congress that does not favor it.

The limited and asymmetric influence conveyed to the president by the veto is illustrated by the budget debates in Reagan's second term. In his budget request for fiscal year 1985, Reagan proposed a large increase in defense spending for fiscal year 1986, coupled with a proposal to slash social security and domestic spending and eliminate cost of living

23. For a theoretical development and some empirical validation of this point, see Kiewiet and McCubbins, "Presidential Influence on Congressional Appropriations Decisions."

24. Continuing resolutions are joint resolutions that may provide temporary funding for affected agencies when Congress fails to complete action on one or more regular appropriations bills before the start of a fiscal year. See Walter J. Oleszek, *Congressional Procedures and the Policy Process,* 3d ed. (Washington: Congressional Quarterly Press, 1989), pp. 74–76.

adjustments for federal pension payments (including social security). The new political reality on Capitol Hill, however, did not favor a package of defense increases and domestic spending cuts. Senate Budget Committee Chairman Pete Domenici stated his expectation that defense spending would be held to less than a 6 percent inflation-adjusted increase for 1986.

Reagan buckled to the pressure and reduced his defense request to a 5.9 percent real (inflation-adjusted) increase. The package of domestic spending cuts and defense increases was still unacceptable to Democrats and liberal Republicans. In March 1985, the Senate Budget Committee voted to recommend an inflation-adjusted "freeze" on defense spending and a freeze on social security. Trying to unite a fractured party, the Senate Republican leadership negotiated with Reagan a 3 percent real increase in defense spending, combined with domestic spending cuts. In announcing this new deal, Reagan stated it was the "rock-bottom level" he would accept.[25] But Reagan was holding the wrong veto stick. The veto does not offer the president a means to get increased funding out of a recalcitrant Congress. Despite Reagan's veto threat, the Senate rejected the Republican leadership's package. Ultimately, the Senate approved a budget resolution that reduced, but did not eliminate, cost of living adjustments and provided an increase in defense spending just large enough to offset the projected rate of inflation for fiscal year 1986.

On the other side of the Capitol, the House Budget Committee, on a party line vote, recommended more spending for domestic programs and less for defense than the budget passed by the Senate. The House, also on a party line vote, passed the resolution. Reagan pronounced the House budget resolution "unacceptable."[26] In conference the House and Senate compromised on defense, while accepting much of the domestic spending increases advocated by the House. As expected, Reagan accepted the bills passed under this resolution.

When Congress again slashed his requests for defense increases in favor of increases in domestic expenditures in 1986, Reagan again threatened to veto any bill that contained less than the increase in defense spending he had requested. In response to a query on this veto threat,

25. Elizabeth Wehr, " '86 Budget Hung Up in Senate Floor Squabble," *Congressional Quarterly Weekly Report*, April 27, 1985, p. 771.

26. Jacqueline Calmes, "House, with Little Difficulty, Passes '86 Budget Resolution," *Congressional Quarterly Weekly Report*, May 25, 1985, p. 971.

William H. Gray III, chairman of the House Budget Committee, recognizing the asymmetry of influence offered by the veto, countered, "What's
he going to do, veto the defense bill because it's too low?"[27] Ultimately,
again, the answer was no.

In the final analysis, presidents do make numerous proposals to
Congress. Congress generally takes no independent action on an issue
before the president's request. And on budget, tax, and economic policy,
Congress typically enacts legislation that, in its broad outlines at least,
is similar to the president's proposal. This does not, however, imply
congressional abdication or presidential ascendency. If his proposals
are to succeed, the president must anticipate the reaction of members
of the House and Senate to his proposals and accommodate their
demands and interests. Presidents know this, so they rarely submit
proposals that are likely to fail. Those who ignore this lesson have their
proposals ignored in lieu of congressional proposals, as happened to
Reagan's budgets. Further, if Congress has delegated authority to initiate
legislation to the president and thus has requested a proposal from him,
and the president accommodates congressional interests in his proposal,
then members of Congress should be expected to wait for his proposal
and to enact something once they get it.

The Reagan "Revolution"

Perhaps the strongest evidence in favor of the presidential ascendancy
model came in Reagan's first year. The budget for fiscal year 1982,
passed in May 1981, was heralded (or decried) as a victory by a powerful
president over an institutionally weakened Congress. But what sort of
victory was this for Reagan? In the first place, the much-ballyhooed
budget "cuts" of $36.6 billion did not actually cut spending. These cuts
were measured not against the spending totals in the fiscal 1981 budget,
but against Jimmy Carter's proposed budget for fiscal 1982.[28] Congress

27. Stephen Gettinger, "Spending Panels Confront Life after Gramm-Rudman,"
Congressional Quarterly Weekly Report, June 7, 1986, p. 1261.
28. Indeed, due to the recession of 1981–82, spending for fiscal 1982 actually
exceeded Reagan's budget by $35 billion, wiping out his "cuts." Unless otherwise
indicated in the text, budgetary data were collected from the following government
publications: budget by function data are reported in *The Budget of the United States
Government,* prepared and submitted annually by the president; line item and agency
estimates are reported in the annual Senate document, *Appropriations, Budget
Estimates, Etc.*; and comparisons of House, Senate, and presidential spending proposals
for line items and agencies are collected from various House and Senate appropriations

had actually slashed a larger percentage from Carter's previous four budgets than it cut from the 1982 budget.

Second, over 90 percent of the programs and agencies that suffered cuts in Reagan's budget had previously suffered cuts by the Democrats and Jimmy Carter. Almost half of these agencies' budgets were cut not only by Reagan and Carter, but also by Democratic Congresses when Gerald Ford was president. Further, those items that were expanded under Reagan's budget, such as defense, had been expanded in Carter's previous two budgets. Thus, although the 1982 budget may have accelerated the spending reallocation, it was not a radical change. The 1982 budget merely continued trends of the previous two Democratic budgets.

Third, when Reagan did try to depart from the budgetary consensus of the previous administration, he was rebuffed. In the reconciliation legislation, Senate Minority Leader Robert Byrd successfully offered amendments to keep alive many programs scheduled for termination under the president's budget. Indeed, almost all of the programs Reagan tried to terminate survived his tenure in office.[29] Fourth, the "revolution" wrought by this victory was short-lived: in May 1981, for example, Reagan proposed a decrease in social security benefits, which was withdrawn without a hearing; he also proposed an additional $16 billion in spending cuts (relative to the levels authorized for fiscal 1982), which Congress rejected. Congress chipped away at Reagan's "cuts," passing a $4.5 billion supplemental spending bill to fund programs for the Environmental Protection Agency cut in the earlier reconciliation legislation and a $14.2 billion supplemental funding bill that included a $6.2 billion pay raise for government employees, $5 billion for agricultural programs, and $1 billion for social programs. Congress, in fact, overrode Reagan's veto to enact this second supplemental bill.

What responsibility, then, does Reagan bear for the runaway deficits of the 1980s? Table 1 compares changes in budget requests, relative to

---

bills and associated committee reports. For a complete discussion, see Kiewiet and McCubbins, *Logic of Delegation*, chap. 8.

29. In each of his budget requests, Reagan sought to terminate several dozen programs. In 1985, for example, he sought to end twenty-six programs, including the Job Corps, Amtrak, the Small Business Administration, urban mass transit subsidies, and rural water and waste disposal grants. But such cuts were not part of the Democratic-Republican compromise on spending: Congress voted only to terminate the U.S. Travel and Tourism Agency and to sell Conrail. Indeed, of the programs Reagan sought to terminate, only half even had their budgets reduced.

Table 1. Average Change in Budget Requests and Congressional Appropriations,
by Administration, for Domestic Agencies, 1948–85
Percent

Administration	Change in president's requests[a]	Change in appropriations[b]	n[c]
Truman	17.4	8.2	260
Eisenhower	11.5	8.2	373
Kennedy/Johnson	11.8	8.0	401
Nixon/Ford	11.1	11.5	386
Carter	10.7	10.3	214
Reagan	−7.7	0.6	215

Source: Data collected from annual Senate document, *Appropriations, Budget Estimates, Etc.*
a. Mean percentage change in president's budget requests for sixty-three agencies relative to previous year's appropriation, averaged over president's term.
b. Mean percentage change in congressional appropriations for sixty-three agencies relative to previous year's appropriations, averaged over president's term.
c. Number of items in author's sample of agency spending decisions.

the preceding year's appropriation, averaged over a sample of sixty-three domestic agencies, for each president from Truman to Reagan.[30] The table shows that, on average, most presidents (other than Reagan) requested more than a 10 percent increase for these programs. Reagan, in his first three budgets, requested on average, almost an 8 percent decrease. Reagan, in fact, requested spending cuts for nearly half the agencies in this sample. Nixon, by contrast, requested cuts for only 16 percent, while Eisenhower requested cuts for 19 percent.[31]

Table 1 also shows that spending growth, for this sample of programs, was slower during Reagan's administration than during any other presidential administration since World War II. Whereas spending grew, on average, between 8 percent and 11 percent for each president from Truman to Carter, spending growth for the 63 domestic agencies in this sample was held to less than 1 percent under Reagan. Thus there is some reason to believe that Ronald Reagan blazed a new direction in American politics in his first term in office.

But Reagan had one major advantage over his Republican predecessors: he did not have to contend with large Democratic majorities in both chambers of Congress. The Republicans held a majority of seats in the Senate for the first time in over two decades during Reagan's first six

30. The sample expands from Fenno's sample of thirty-six agencies in Richard F. Fenno, Jr., *The Power of the Purse: Appropriations Politics in Congress* (Little, Brown, 1966). See Kiewiet and McCubbins, *Logic of Delegation*, chap. 6.
31. Kiewiet and McCubbins, *Logic of Delegation*, chap. 8.

years in office. In comparison, when the Republicans controlled both houses of Congress in 1947–48 and again in 1953–54, they cut over 42 percent of the items in a sample of sixty-nine agencies (sixty-three domestic and six defense agencies). In fact, the Republican Congress of 1953–54 cut spending for almost two-thirds of the programs in this sample. When Reagan was elected and control was split, with the Republicans controlling the Senate and the Democrats controlling the House, spending was cut, on average, for only 30 percent of these sixty-nine agencies. When the Democrats controlled both chambers (1949–52, 1955–80), they cut the budgets of only 17 percent of these agencies, on average.

Should Reagan have done better? Because most of the federal programs in the postwar era were instituted and supported by the Democratic party,[32] it is reasonable to expect that Republican control of Congress would bring about reductions in many of these programs. Further, it seems reasonable to expect that a divided Congress would reduce spending for more budget items than would one controlled by the Democrats, but not as many as would a Republican-controlled Congress. Reagan and the Republicans in the Senate, then, did about as expected: the 30 percent rate of reductions for 1982–85 falls almost dead center between the 17 percent rate for Democratic Congresses and the 42 percent rate for Republican Congresses.

A roughly similar pattern is evident for presidential success in Congress generally. Democratic presidents facing Democratic Congresses have won roughly 81 percent of their key votes; Republicans facing Republican Congresses have had an 86 percent success rate (on average); Reagan, facing a Democratic House and a Republican Senate (1981–87), won roughly two-thirds of the key votes; but Republican administrations facing Democratic Congresses have won, on average, 58 percent of these key votes.[33] During his first year in office, with a Republican majority in the Senate, Reagan won an impressive 82 percent of the votes on which he took a stand. His success dropped to a postwar low of 44 percent in 1987, the first time he faced Democratic majorities in both chambers of Congress.[34]

32. See Robert X. Browning, *Politics and Social Welfare Policy in the United States* (University of Tennessee Press, 1986).

33. The figures are based on the number of votes on which the president announced a position. See Harold W. Stanley and Richard G. Niemi, *Vital Statistics on American Politics* (Washington: CQ Press, 1988), pp. 220–21.

34. In his last year in office his success rate climbed to roughly 47 percent.

Table 2. Congressional Responses to Presidents' Requests for Cuts or Increases
in Spending, by Administration, 1948–85
Percent

	President requested cut		President requested increase	
Administration	Congress ap-propriated more than previous year	Congress ap-propriated less than previous year	Congress ap-propriated more than previous year	Congress ap-propriated less than previous year
Truman	0	100.0	86.7	13.3
Eisenhower	16.4	83.6	90.0	10.0
Kennedy/Johnson	3.3	96.7	91.3	8.7
Nixon/Ford	26.8	73.2	96.1	3.9
Carter	31.6	68.4	96.9	3.1
Reagan	40.4	59.6	91.2	8.8

Source: See table 1.

Thus the question becomes, what was Reagan's net effect on spending? Certainly, Reagan was no more successful than expected, given the
circumstances in Congress. He actually was less successful than any
other postwar president at pushing his spending cuts through Congress
(see table 2). Truman succeeded in getting Congress to enact all of the
relatively few cuts he requested. Eisenhower succeeded 84 percent of
the time. Reagan, by contrast, succeeded less than 60 percent of the
time. Also, his batting average at getting spending increases out of
Congress was less than any recent president. More generally, Reagan's
success rate in influencing congressional votes for each of his eight years
in office was less than that of Dwight Eisenhower in each corresponding
year.[35] Indeed, Reagan's success rate against a Democratic Congress
was less than Richard Nixon's success rate, even during the period of
the Watergate scandal (Nixon won roughly 60 percent of his key votes
that year). By this comparison Reagan was a weaker president than his
predecessors.

What does account for the spending pattern of the 1980s? In the first
place, though there has been much talk of budget "cuts" in the 1980s,
nominal spending nearly doubled from fiscal years 1981 to 1989.[36]

35. Stanley and Niemi, *Vital Statistics*, pp. 220–21.
36. The federal government has an unusual way of defining a cut. Although claims
that tens of billions had been cut from the budget were made during the Reagan
presidency, the budget actually increased from $600 billion in fiscal 1981 to $1.2 trillion
in fiscal 1989. Indeed, rarely was spending actually reduced; "cuts" referred to changes

Similarly, while gross national product (valued in 1972 dollars) grew only 15 percent from 1981 to 1987, spending grew 40 percent. Defense spending, which grew by less than 30 percent (in 1972 dollars), accounted for roughly one-quarter of the increase during the 1981–87 period. Social security spending roughly matched the growth rate of defense. Another large chunk of the increase resulted from a near doubling (in real terms) of interest payments on the national debt. The remaining 30 percent of the total growth in the budget was in other domestic programs.

Second, the agencies and programs chosen for spending reductions in the 1980s were largely those whose budgets also declined throughout the latter part of the 1970s. The decline of the Great Society programs and the regulatory activities of the federal government started under Gerald Ford and accelerated under Jimmy Carter. Therefore the cuts in these programs began under a Congress in which both chambers were in Democratic hands and accelerated when both branches were controlled by the Democrats.

The budget story of the 1980s, then, is not the fiscal contractions so often advertised by Congress and the president. But several questions remain unanswered. Why should spending have grown during the administration of a fiscally conservative president? Should not Republican control of the Senate have brought about a reduction in federal spending?

Party Governance in Congress

To some analysts of American politics, the runaway deficits of the 1980s are not the unintended result of the Reagan revolution, but rather a consequence of a change in congressional procedure. This perception is based on a well-accepted view that Congress is not so much a democratic institution as a pluralistic leviathan.[37] Central to this view is the thesis, more than a century old, that congressional politics is committee politics.[38] As Kenneth Shepsle writes, speaking of the 1940s and 1950s:

---

in authorization so that spending was less than it would have been had the law not been changed. This was true even if spending ultimately was greater than it had been the year before. For example, "cuts" in medicare were said to exceed $50 billion for the 1980s. Yet medicare outlays actually grew from $32 billion to $94 billion. Timothy Muris, "The Uses and Abuses of Budget Baselines," Working Papers in Political Science, P-89-3 (Hoover Institution, January 1989).

37. Freeman, *The Political Process*, p. 2.

38. Woodrow Wilson first said it in *Congressional Government* (Houghton Mifflin, 1885).

In terms of making policy, committee politics provided fertile soil for interest group liberalism, policy whirlpools, cozy little triangles, and unholy trinities. Policy was incubated and crafted by interested members who monopolized the berths on committees important to their constituents' concerns. Proposed legislation attracted few amendments on the floor because political conflicts were resolved inside committees, the legislators most interested were already on them, and those not on a given committee had little expertise and few resources to mobilize against committee recommendations. For all these reasons, deference to the committees' positions became the norm. Thus a gigantic logroll sanctified the division of labor that permitted policymaking by subgovernments—congressional committees, interest groups, and governmental agencies.[39]

Shepsle and others argue that "geography, jurisdiction, and party hang together in a sort of equilibrium," but that the balance that had held in the 1940s and 1950s, described above, has shifted further away from centralized party—or committee—control of Congress. Parties, by the 1970s, had become "considerably more submissive holding companies for member enterprises than had earlier been the case."[40] But this shift has not altered their interpretation that "subgovernments" play a central role in policymaking. The "interest group liberalism" that purportedly dominates congressional politics,[41] if true, has profound implications for budgeting as well. As Shepsle and Barry Weingast argue:

The omnipresent electoral imperative induces members of Congress to target expenditures to their electoral constituents or to those who can provide electorally relevant resources. This implies that legislators invent programs, seek funding, and are especially attentive to policy areas that create or maintain jobs within their electoral constituency. . . . Expenditure programs are, as a consequence, biased away from least-cost methods of production so as to favor those methods that yield greater electoral support.[42]

39. Kenneth A. Shepsle, "The Changing Textbook Congress," in John E. Chubb and Paul E. Peterson, eds., *Can the Government Govern?* pp. 246–47.

40. Shepsle, "Changing Textbook Congress," pp. 245–46.

41. Lowi, *End of Liberalism*.

42. Kenneth A. Shepsle and Barry R. Weingast, "Legislative Politics and Budget Outcomes," in Gregory B. Mills and John L. Palmer, eds., *Federal Budget Policy in the 1980s* (Washington: Urban Institute Press, 1984), p. 355.

As each subgovernment pursues its policies in the way Shepsle and Weingast describe, the end results could be that the government outspends its receipts.

To mitigate the effects of interest group liberalism, members of Congress traditionally were said to rely on the members of the House Appropriations Committee to guard the federal treasury, to make the hard choices between supporting their colleagues' programs and the need to economize on spending.[43] As David Mayhew concluded in 1974, "By cutting budgets they work against the diffuse and primal danger that Congress will spend more money than it takes in. They lean against particularism and also against servicing of the organized."[44] This system was supported by rules and procedures in Congress that separated authorization from appropriations. And the system appeared to work reasonably well, producing small but manageable deficits through the 1950s and 1960s.

This all changed with the Congressional Budget and Impoundment Control Act of 1974. Many viewed the new budget process established by the act as a way to coordinate spending and revenue decisions between the various congressional subsystems in order to cut the deficit. However, by transferring authority for establishing overall spending limits to the Budget committees, the budget process so weakened the House Appropriations Committee that it could no longer act to guard the treasury. Instead, its members seemingly became claimants on the federal treasury rather than its protector.[45] The budget process itself, this school argues, has failed to work and there has been no restraint on spending in Congress.

Two assumptions underlie this explanation of the deficit crisis. The first is that "power in Congress has rested in the committees or, increasingly, in the subcommittees," and thus as a consequence, "throughout most of the postwar years, political parties in Congress have been weak, ineffectual organizations."[46] The second is that the House Appropriations Committee was once the "guardian of the federal treasury" and now is only a subdued guardian. I examine these assumptions in turn, arguing that congressional parties and party leaders

43. Fenno, *Power of the Purse.*

44. David R. Mayhew, *Congress: The Electoral Connection* (Yale University Press, 1974), p. 153.

45. Allen Schick, *Congress and Money: Budgeting, Spending, and Taxing* (Washington: Urban Institute, 1980), especially pp. 441–81.

46. Lawrence C. Dodd and Bruce I. Oppenheimer, "The House in Transition," in Dodd and Oppenheimer, eds., *Congress Reconsidered,* p. 50.

exercised more control and greater influence in congressional politics, and in budgeting in particular, than commonly has been perceived. I then seek to explain the budgetary decisions of the 1980s in light of this new understanding.

The Institutions of Agency: Parties and Committees

The common view of weak parties and autonomous committees in Congress, in its logical form, is identical to the view of presidential dominance presented above. The membership of each house has delegated to its committees wide-ranging authority to write legislation, hold hearings, and oversee the executive branch. This delegation, like congressional delegation to the executive, has been mistaken for abdication.

Two factors underpin the alleged importance and autonomy of committees and subcommittees.

First, committees and their subcommittees originate legislation. Although there is some built-in overlap in committee and subcommittee jurisdictions, these units typically have jurisdictional monopoly over specific public policies. As a result, changes in statutory policy require the assent of relevant committee and subcommittee majorities. In other words, changes in policy may be vetoed by committees and subcommittees if their preferences are not reflected in the new policy.[47]

And second,

In order for [committees and subcommittees] to maintain this control and influence, as well as to take even more affirmative steps in representing the interests of the policy constituencies, it must be the case that legislative majorities or other power centers in the legislature cannot or will not frustrate their designs. We maintain that this circumstance is achieved by the honoring of subcommittee veto power and other forms of reciprocity. Each subcommittee has its own turf, both to protect and to cultivate. The current arrangement among the

47. Shepsle and Weingast, "Legislative Politics and Budget Outcomes," p. 351.

committees of Congress embodies the bargain, "You can retain veto power and influence in your area if I can retain it in mine." The important consequence of this bargain . . . is that people on the relevant subcommittees hold the power to protect and enhance the flow of public benefits to their constituents.[48]

This view of committee and subcommittee power has been developed to explain a set of generalized observations about congressional behavior. It explains, for example, why coalitions within Congress are seemingly universal and nonpartisan: all members face the same need to bring home particularistic benefits, and the institutions are geared toward establishing and enforcing vote trades across projects and benefits. It also follows, for the same reason, that party discipline will be very lax—the vote trades cross party lines. Committees also use their powers, particularly their ex post veto, to ensure that amendments rarely get offered to their bills, and when they are offered, few, if any, are successful. Further, committees can withhold legislation from consideration even in opposition to concerted floor majorities. Lastly, because committees are central to the policymaking process, committee members spend most of their time and effort in their committee work.

But these observations are not inconsistent with party control of committees. If congressional party organizations controlled committee decisionmaking, one would still expect to observe all of the phenomena typically recounted in support of the subgovernment model of congressional politics. Indeed, none of these observations discriminates between the two views.[49] However, obvious violations of this cozy view of subcommittee autonomy are easily observable. For example, multiple referrals, where legislation is sent to several subcommittees, are increasingly common in the House.

The influence of congressional parties and their leadership may be indirect rather than direct and overt. It is important to consider how congressional majorities retain their authority to make decisions. Members of Congress design their institutions to fit their purposes. Studies of congressional behavior have focused largely on how members secure

48. Shepsle and Weingast, "Legislative Politics and Budget Outcomes, " p. 353.

49. For some critical tests see Kiewiet and McCubbins, *Logic of Delegation*; and Gary W. Cox and Mathew D. McCubbins, "Political Parties and the Appointment of Committees," paper prepared for the Conference on Congressional Structure and Elections, University of California, San Diego, February 11, 1989.

water projects, military bases, roads, and post offices for their districts, and the consequences of these activities for their political survival. These studies, of course, assume that voters appreciate projects in their district and that members can build reputations as good providers of federal pork.

But party affiliations are also an important ingredient in voters' decisions: party labels signal information that is otherwise very expensive for voters to obtain about the policy positions of candidates. As a result, politicians, in seeking office, also establish reputations as partisans and, moreover, have an incentive to enhance the collective reputation of their party. Thus politicians adopt a mixture of collective (partisan) and individual (district-oriented) activities in seeking reelection.

It follows that members will seek to structure Congress in a way that facilitates both of these activities. Party organizations, their leadership, and the committees that serve them provide the institutional means for pursuing the collective goals of party members. This leads to the enactment and implementation of policies that affect a large proportion of congressional districts and for which the members of the majority party can claim credit. But it is also in the interest of all members of the majority party to establish a system that enables them to secure the individual district-oriented benefits they need to enhance their individual reputations. Thus the majority party leadership uses its agenda powers, in concert with the agenda powers assigned to committees, to secure the omnibus pork barrel legislation so familiar to congressional scholars.

The congressional parties, of course, delegate much of the authority to make these kinds of decisions to the leadership and to committees, although the Democratic caucus has at times met to make policy for the Democratic majority. In delegating, the congressional parties encounter an unavoidable problem: for a variety of reasons, intentional or not, the persons to whom authority is delegated may not act in the best interests of those doing the delegating. Many scholars, in recognition of this problem, have concluded that the congressional parties have in fact abdicated their authority to the standing committees and subcommittees of Congress.

This conclusion, however, ignores the efforts on the part of the congressional parties to mitigate this delegation problem and the effects their efforts have on structuring choices and outcomes. Both authorizing and appropriating committees, as well as the party leadership, have a say in the passage of legislation. In essence, like the separation of powers in the structure of the federal government, party organizations—in particular the party leadership—and the system of standing committees form a separation of powers, a system of checks and balances, that protects the majority party caucus from opportunistic behavior on the part of its agents.

Another important check parties have on standing committees is exercised through appointments. Indeed, appointments to the major committees—Appropriations, Rules, and Ways and Means—and transfers from the lesser committees to the major committees are strongly affected by the leadership's desires and are determined, to an extent, by past party loyalty.[50]

Committee activities are also constrained by procedural restrictions.[51] Procedures can make it difficult for committees to hide information relevant to the evaluation of their recommendations. For example, the Government in the Sunshine Act opened up committee hearings so that committee members could no longer have exclusive access to information. Committees are also required to report their findings in submitting major legislation to the floor. Procedures also establish access points for selected representatives and constituencies to have input into committee decisions.

Some standing committees, of course, will receive greater scrutiny over their activities than will others. A few committees have jurisdiction over issues that are encompassed, at least implicitly, in the meaning of the party label. Because the party's label is a collective good for its members, the actions of these committees affect everyone in the party; the party and its leaders have a greater stake in making sure these committees serve their collective interests. Social security, for example,

50. David W. Rhode and Kenneth A. Shepsle, "Democratic Committee Assignments in the House of Representatives: Strategic Aspects of a Social Choice Process," *American Political Science Review*, vol. 67 (September 1973), pp. 889–905; Shepsle, "Changing Textbook Congress"; and Gary W. Cox and Mathew D. McCubbins, *Party Government in the House of Representatives* (University of California Press, forthcoming), chap. 6.

51. McCubbins and Schwartz, "Congressional Oversight Overlooked"; Mathew D. McCubbins, "The Legislative Design of Regulatory Structure," *American Journal of Political Science*, vol. 29 (November 1985), pp. 721–48; Mathew D. McCubbins and Talbot Page, "A Theory of Congressional Delegation," in Mathew D. McCubbins and Terry Sullivan, eds., *Congress: Structure and Policy* (Cambridge University Press, 1987), pp. 409–25; and McCubbins, Noll, and Weingast, "Administrative Procedures as Instruments of Political Control," and "Structure and Process, Politics and Policy."

has been a core Democratic program since the New Deal; thus the Committee on Ways and Means, which was delegated jurisdiction over this program, has been an important committee for the Democrats. Other standing committees (for example, Post Office, Interior, and Merchant Marine and Fisheries), have jurisdiction over issues unrelated, or only minimally related, to the issues that voters identify with the party. The majority party caucus will treat these committees differently. Those committees whose policy jurisdictions have the greatest external effects (such as Ways and Means, Appropriations, Rules, and Budget) will be the target of the greatest attention and party control: the appointment committee will seek to ensure, through the appointments it makes, that these standing committees pursue the majority party's agenda. On the other hand, committees like Agriculture (since 1960 at least) or Merchant Marine and Fisheries may escape serious efforts to "stack" their assignments.

Committees and their chairmen do of course have extensive discretion. But this range of discretion is not infinite, as the removal of Wright Patman, W.R. Poage, Edward Hebert, and Mel Price and the threatened removal of Les Aspin demonstrate. Party caucuses do take measures to ensure that committees act in a manner responsive to the will of the party.

Again, the conventional view has mistaken delegation—in this case from the majority party caucus to the standing committees of Congress—for abdication.[52] Observers have recognized the transfer of authority and the actions of the agents (the committees). However, they have not recognized the mechanisms used by the majority party to direct the actions and choices of the committees and the effect these mechanisms have had on committee actions.

If committees are agents of party caucuses, then one would expect that most the decisions in Congress could be made in committee, and that committee members would acquire expertise in the committee's jurisdiction. One would not expect these activities to be uncontrolled, however, and indeed there are many and varied attempts by majority party caucuses and their leadership to control committees. Further, committees will anticipate the reaction of the majority party to their proposals and thus can expect that few of their bills will be amended or rejected on the floor. The absence of amendments to committee bills by

52. See Kiewiet and McCubbins, *Logic of Delegation*; and Cox and McCubbins, *Party Government*.

floor majorities is, in fact, equally good evidence that committees are good and responsible agents of the majority party.[53]

The Role of the House Appropriations Committee

In Richard Fenno's classic account, the House Appropriations Committee was depicted as a budget-slashing guardian of the federal treasury, protecting the House from the budgetary excesses of its own committees and from budget-maximizing bureaucrats. This model of the committee was based upon Fenno's interviews of members of Congress and on a comparison of committee decisions and presidential requests for the period from 1947 to 1962. Fenno reported, for the thirty-six bureaus on which he collected data, that the amount recommended by the House Appropriations Committee for a bureau was less than the amount requested by the president in 73.6 percent of the 575 cases in his data set.[54] I extended Fenno's work to a set of sixty-nine agencies and programs, including almost all of Fenno's thirty-six bureaus, for a period extending from 1948 to 1985. I found that the House Appropriations Committee cut the president's requests for 70.4 percent of the 1,983 cases in my data set.[55]

But do these statistics constitute evidence that the "dominant pattern" for the House Appropriations Committee is to guard the treasury? What would the committee recommend if it were not guarding the federal treasury? If the procedural restrictions on the Office of Management and Budget work to constrain its ability to revise agency budget estimates, and agencies compile estimates in accordance with the legislation that authorized their activities, then presidential requests will reflect, to a large extent, the level of funding preferred by the authorizing committees

53. Smith too challenges this stylized fact, pointing out that the frequency of amending activity has increased over the last decade. See Steven S. Smith, *Call to Order: Floor Politics in the House and Senate* (Brookings, 1989). However, his counting has been challenged by Weingast. See Barry Weingast, "Fighting Fire with Fire: Amending Activity and Institutional Change in the Postreform Congress," in Roger H. Davidson, ed., *The Postreform Congress* (St. Martin's, forthcoming).

54. Fenno, *Power of the Purse*, table 8.1, p. 353.

55. The obverse, of course, is that the committee increased spending for more than 19 percent of the budget items that came before it, and they granted an amount equal to the president's request in almost 10 percent of the cases. The proportion of times the committee recommended an increase for one of these items over the president's request ranged from zero in fiscal year 1947, to more than 13 percent in fiscal years 1959–61, to a high of 51 percent in 1984.

in Congress.[56] These figures, of course, are often revised according to the president's policy guidelines. If many committees prefer more spending on items within their jurisdiction than would be preferred by the House as a whole or by the majority party as a whole, and if the House Appropriations Committee is relatively representative of the House and the majority party, then the members of the House Appropriations Committee will prefer to spend less for most items than the members of the committee that authorized the items.[57] Consequently, the House Appropriations Committee will cut the president's spending requests for most agencies. Thus, even if they are not guarding the federal treasury, the members of the House Appropriations Committee can be expected in most years to cut most executive budget requests.

In Fenno's account of the House Appropriations Committee, party politics plays essentially no role. I have argued here and elsewhere that the partisan contingents on the committee are agents of their parties,[58] and that as a result the committee functions as an agent of the majority party, pursuing the collective policy goals of the party's membership. These goals may sometimes be to cut the budget, but not necessarily so. Consequently, the varying goals of the parties controlling the White House and the House of Representatives determine the treatment afforded the president's budget requests by the House Committee on Appropriations. Democratic majorities favor higher spending on domestic programs than do Republican majorities. How often the committee cuts the president's requests is determined by partisan factors (see table 3).

Between 1948 and 1985, the House Appropriations Committee was most likely to cut the president's requests when the president was a Democrat and the House was controlled by the Republicans (cuts amount to 93 percent of actions taken). The committee was somewhat less likely to cut the executive's requests when the same party controlled both branches (roughly 80 percent of the requests). But a Democratic commit-

---

56. This, of course, is implicitly Mayhew's model of agency estimates (*Congress: The Electoral Connection*). If it is true that the committee is protecting members from themselves, the estimates the committee deals with must be a reflection of members' own desires. If they were not, then the committee would be protecting members from the executive branch, not from themselves.

57. On the unrepresentativeness of many House committees, see Cox and McCubbins, *Party Government*. On the representativeness of the House Appropriations Committee, see Kiewiet and McCubbins, *Logic of Delegation*.

58. Cox and McCubbins, *Party Government*; and Kiewiet and McCubbins, *Logic of Delegation*.

Table 3. House Appropriations Committee Treatment of Presidential Budget Requests, by Partisan Control of Presidency and Congress, 1948–85
Percent

Committee action	Republican president, Republican Congress	Republican president, Democratic Congress	Republican president, Democratic House, Republican Senate	Democratic president, Republican Congress	Democratic Congress, Democratic president
Cut president's requests	80.2	67.1	38.5	93.0	78.7
Recommended same amount as president	13.2	14.4	6.0	4.7	8.3
Recommended more than president	6.0	18.5	55.6	2.3	13.1

Source: See table 1.

tee was far less likely to cut a Republican president's requests (only 67 percent). Further, when the Democrats held a majority in the House, but the president and a majority of the Senate were Republicans, the committee cut only 38 percent of the president's requests and actually proposed increases for 56 percent of the items. Fenno described such changes as "mood" swings: the committee would shift from an "economy mood" to a "spending mood." The pattern shown in table 3 suggests that the mood toward executive budget requests by the House Appropriations Committee is determined by partisan differences between the House, the Senate, and the executive.

Further, if the guardianship hypothesis is correct, I would expect no House floor amendments that decrease the committee's recommendations. The committee, after all, is supposedly doing a job the House is incapable of doing, holding back spending. I find, however, that of the spending recommendations made by the Appropriations Committee for individual agencies and programs and amended on the floor, more than 58 percent were decreased and only 42 percent were increased. Of the appropriations bills amended by the House that I examined, 106, or 43 percent of the amendments, reduced the totals recommended by the Appropriations Committee.

Has the budget act of 1974 changed the House Appropriations Committee from the Treasury guardian it once was to subdued guardians who now seek their own claims on the federal treasury? There is no evidence that it was a guardian or that its function has in fact changed.

It has been, and still is, a check upon the authority of the other standing committees in the House, a check used by the majority party leadership to ensure that the policies pursued by the other standing committees in the House reflect the collective goals of the membership of the majority party.[59] This suggests that it is not a change in the behavior of members of the House Appropriations Committee, nor is it a change in the spending process, that wrought the deficits of the 1980s.

The Congressional Budget Process in the 1980s

The budget process created by the 1974 act has two key components. First, the newly created Budget committees are responsible for drafting a budget policy that sets guidelines for all aspects of federal spending and revenue. These guidelines are to be set out in the first budget resolution passed each year. Second, if these guidelines affect programs within a committee's jurisdiction, that committee is required to draft legislation reconciling spending on those programs with the guidelines in the first budget resolution. The 1974 budget act established a scorekeeping system to keep track of each committee's progress at reconciling its programs with the budget guidelines. If a committee fails to recommend legislation providing satisfactory reconciliation, then the Budget committees can write the reconciliation legislation for them. This procedure provides the Budget committees with an effective means of coordinating the activities of the other standing committees.

An important provision of the act ensures that the Budget committees are responsible to the majority party caucus and its leadership by establishing a special relationship between the committees and the party leadership. For example, although the House Budget Committee has standing jurisdiction, it does not have a standing membership. Members cannot attain seniority on the committee, tenure on the committee is limited, and the selection of members is largely controlled by the House leadership. The majority party leadership, through these procedures, has relatively greater control, year in and year out, over the composition of the Budget Committee than it does over the composition of any other committee. If greater control of the committee translates into greater control of the budget process, and if the budget process provides an effective means for coordinating the activities of the standing commit-

59. Kiewiet and McCubbins, *Logic of Delegation*, chap. 3.

tees, then the majority party leadership can use the budget process to inject the party's priorities into all committees' decisions.

Indeed, from the perspective of floor majorities in the House and Senate, the budget process was strikingly effective in the early 1980s. In 1981 the Republicans in the House and Senate, together with some conservative Democrats, used the budget and reconciliation process to "cut" some $36.6 billion in spending for fiscal year 1982. In the House, a majority, consisting of Republicans and conservative Democrats, worked to defeat the House Democratic leadership. This coalition demonstrated how effectively the budget process could used to submit congressional committees to the will of floor majorities. The first budget resolution included instructions for the House Committee on Agriculture to cut $2.18 billion; the House Committee on Banking and Urban Affairs, $12.91 billion; the Committee on Education and Labor, $13.54 billion; the Committee on Energy and Commerce, $6.40 billion; and the Committee on Public Works and Transportation, $6.61 billion.

The first budget resolution in 1982 for fiscal 1983 required cuts of $2.18 billion in budget authority. This time, as the amount indicates, the House Democratic party used inventive procedures, such as the "king-of-the-mountain" rule, to exert some influence over the course of the budget process.[60] The resolution required that the House Committee on Ways and Means and the Senate Finance Committee recommend legislation to raise $20.9 billion in revenue. The budget resolution also required savings of $7.8 billion in defense spending.

In 1983 the House Democrats used the budget process to draft their own budget blueprint, contrived by the entire Democratic membership, as an alternative to the Republican budget submitted by Reagan. The Democrats' budget added $33 billion in domestic spending to Reagan's proposal, requested $30 billion in new revenues, and cut Reagan's defense request by $16 billion. The final conference agreement added $5 billion to the House's defense proposal and reduced, mostly by small amounts, most of the House's domestic spending recommendations.

60. Under this rule, seven budget alternatives (and sixty-eight perfecting amendments) were considered, with the House Budget Committee's recommendation being voted on last. The rule requires that the last alternative to win a majority is the plan that prevails. This is just one example of the extraordinary rule changes used by the Democrats to control the budget process and the conservative "Boll Weevil" faction. In 1982 none of the alternatives won a majority. It was used again in 1983, when the Democratic House Budget Committee's plan prevailed. See Stanley Bach and Steven S. Smith, *Managing Uncertainty in the House of Representatives: Adaptation and Innovation in Special Rules* (Brookings, 1988), pp. 74–78.

The Republicans, who controlled the Senate in the early 1980s, and the Democrats, who controlled the House, chose alternative strategies in using the budget process to further their programs. The Republican leadership used the budget process to give direction to Senate committees. The Democrats used the budget process as a means to unite the party behind a common program; the House Budget Committee held hearings with the entire Democratic caucus.

Ultimately, the result of efforts on the part of party caucuses to control the product and actions of committees is that spending policy reflects the desires of the majority party in each chamber. The evidence also suggests that spending policy is highly partisan: Republican presidents and Republican Congresses budget far less on domestic programs and more on defense than do their Democratic counterparts. Indeed, the single best predictor of changes in spending policy for almost the whole range of federal programs and agencies is party control of Congress and the White House.[61] This analysis suggests that policy is influenced, to a far greater extent than commonly believed, by party politics. Further, the history of the budget process in the 1980s, contrary to the received wisdom, suggests that American political parties, though not as disciplined or cohesive as European political parties, do nonetheless govern.

The Partisan Roots of Deficits

If the two most common explanations of the runaway deficits of the 1980s are incorrect, how can these deficits be explained? Before offering an explanation, however, it is useful to reexamine the problem. The federal budget deficits in constant (1972) dollars are shown in the top panel of figure 1. The figure clearly shows the budget deficits resulting from the war effort from 1943 to 1946. It also shows remarkable stability (at least from the perspective of the 1980s) for the first two decades following World War II. In the late 1960s, however, imbalances in the federal accounts began to oscillate widely, with a constant trend toward increasing deficits. The trend steepened in the late 1970s, producing large, but apparently not unprecedented, peacetime deficits.

This picture of the deficit problem might be misleading, however. The borrowing entailed by these deficits may or may not pose a problem, depending upon the size of the income base against which it is leveraged. The deficits as a percentage of GNP are shown in the bottom panel of

61. See Kiewiet and McCubbins, *Logic of Delegation*, chap. 8.

Figure 1. Federal Surplus and Deficit, Fiscal Years 1929–88

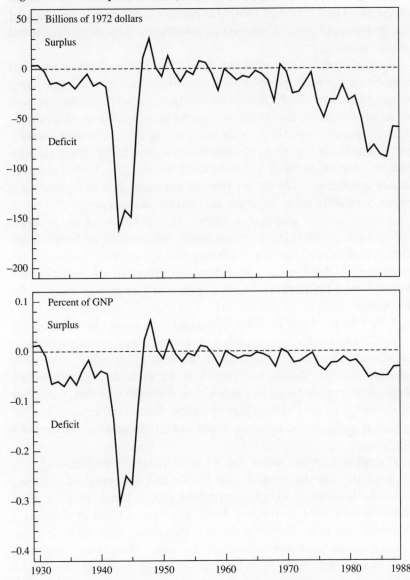

figure 1. (I use constant-dollar figures for both deficits and GNP since the price deflators for government purchases and GNP are different.) This is a dramatically different picture. Although there is a general trend downward during the postwar era (toward larger deficits as a percentage of GNP), the deficits of the 1980s are roughly the same proportion

of GNP as the deficits of the 1970s. The record deficits of 1984-86 are of the same proportion as those during the Great Depression (without the depression), but for the rest of the decade they do not seem out of the ordinary.

To explain deficits, however measured, I need to explain both federal spending and revenue policies. With regard to federal spending decisions, it has been adequately demonstrated that the state of the national economy—in particular, changes in unemployment and inflation rates—affects spending decisions, with increases in the unemployment rate pushing spending up; that spending increases at a faster rate in election years than in off-years; and that the involvement of the United States in armed conflict leads to slower rates of spending growth for domestic programs and, of course, steeper growth rates for defense.

Further, federal spending decisions, at every stage of the process, reflect party politics. Domestic agencies, for example, do better under Democratic administrations and Democratic Congresses than under Republicans. Defense and high-technology programs do better under Republican administrations and Republican Congresses than under Democrats.

When the president is a Republican and both houses of Congress are controlled by Democrats, spending on domestic and social programs is somewhat restrained but is close to the levels that would have been adopted under a Democratic president. In such instances, although Republican presidents act as a restraint on domestic spending, the ability of Congress to package various spending items into an omnibus bill makes it difficult for even the most ardent Republicans to restrain spending.[62]

But what happens when control of Congress is divided—when a Democratic majority controls the House and a Republican majority controls the Senate? This has happened several times, most recently from January 1981 to January 1987. The Constitution established a bilateral veto game between the two chambers, with each chamber holding a check on the actions of the other. The cooperation and coordination necessary to overcome these constitutional checks and balances is frequently inadequate.[63] Budget deficits present members of Congress with a collective dilemma: everyone would be better off if

62. Kiewiet and McCubbins, *Logic of Delegation,* chap. 8.
63. John E. Chubb and Paul E. Peterson, "American Political Institutions and the Problems of Governance," in Chubb and Peterson, eds., *Can the Government Govern?* pp. 1–43.

deficits could be reduced, but individually members are not willing to reduce spending on their preferred programs or to raise taxes for their constituents. Neither congressional party is likely to go along with a solution to a problem, such as the deficit, for which the other party can claim credit, and each will use its institutional position, and the veto granted it by its control of one house of Congress, to defeat the other party's attempts to solve the problem. Under divided control, then, cooperation to solve collective problems, like the deficit, will largely be nonexistent.

What, then, will be the equilibrium in this bilateral veto game? I make a simplifying assumption about the preferences of the members of each party: I assume that there are two types of programs: domestic programs favored by the Democrats and defense programs favored by the Republicans. I assume that the Democrats most prefer that spending on their programs be increased and spending on the Republicans' programs decreased. If this is not possible, they next prefer that spending on all programs be increased. Their next choice would be decreases in both their own programs and the Republicans' programs, with their least preferred choice a decrease in their programs and an increase in the Republicans' programs. I assume that Republican preferences are similar with respect to their own programs.

In bilateral veto games, if no solution is adopted, the equilibrium would be to return to the reversion point, which for most federal programs is zero. That is, Congress must enact annual appropriations for most of these activities if they are to continue. Typically, however, if no appropriations bill is enacted Congress will pass a continuing resolution that pegs spending at some low baseline level (often at the spending rate for the previous fiscal year). Continuing resolutions typically yield little or no growth in spending and may even entail a modest decrease (adjusting for inflation). Thus, the reversion point, if no spending policy is agreed to by the two parties, is to decrease appropriations for all programs. The only alternative that is preferred by both parties, and thus will not be vetoed by one or the other, is for spending for both parties' programs to increase. Thus under conditions of divided control I expect overall spending to increase.

In 1983, for example, reconciliation legislation for fiscal 1984 did not cut budget authority in any area. In 1985 reconciliation legislation for fiscal year 1986 passed by Congress and signed by the president required cuts in agriculture, defense, energy, medicare, and ten other programs, but increased spending for the EPA's Superfund, income and social

Table 4. Budget Authority, by Function, in Concurrent Budget Resolution, Fiscal Years 1962–86
Billions of current dollars

Fiscal year	Communications and transportation	Defense	Community, regional development	Education	Energy and environment	Foreign affairs	Health and income security[a]	Justice[b]	Science	Veterans
1962	3.10	52.40	0.60	1.30	2.20	3.40	5.00	...	1.80	5.50
1963	4.00	54.30	0.60	1.40	2.40	5.70	5.40	...	3.70	5.50
1964	3.00	53.80	0.70	1.50	2.50	4.50	5.70	...	5.10	5.60
1965	3.30	53.20	1.30	2.40	3.00	6.70	7.50	...	5.20	5.80
1966	3.90	67.40	1.80	4.30	3.40	5.50	9.30	...	5.20	6.00
1967	9.59	75.28	6.92	5.33	3.28	5.10	48.41	...	4.97	6.96
1968	9.32	79.23	4.36	9.14	1.88	4.77	49.22	...	4.59	7.84
1969	10.17	80.06	3.35	7.32	2.25	2.84	56.94	...	3.99	7.70
1970	12.26	76.69	6.72	7.31	3.19	3.57	66.02	...	3.75	8.78
1971	27.42	75.22	4.29	8.74	6.46	3.39	75.30	...	3.31	10.25
1972	12.73	80.31	4.92	10.73	5.61	5.01	87.46	...	3.31	11.33
1973	10.54	82.79	6.09	12.05	7.18	3.63	102.05	...	3.41	12.78
1974	23.55	89.29	3.70	13.22	10.65	5.29	121.61	2.62	3.87	13.96
1975	32.43	91.93	5.39	15.53	16.48	4.42	189.22	3.03	4.02	16.75
1976	20.89	103.81	5.71	21.22	19.28	6.56	173.67	3.30	4.26	19.68
1977	15.84	110.43	12.79	30.38	14.44	6.59	208.94	3.60	4.58	19.10
1978	20.35	117.93	10.31	22.37	21.83	9.80	226.55	3.88	4.90	19.04
1979	25.13	127.81	9.97	32.56	20.59	8.69	245.79	4.23	5.38	20.50
1980	30.71	145.76	10.11	30.62	49.50	15.52	284.04	4.39	6.14	21.21
1981	31.46	182.40	8.41	30.55	17.90	24.81	318.86	4.34	6.53	23.17
1982	27.70	218.70	6.60	25.90	14.50	15.30	333.10	4.70	7.10	25.00
1983	32.30	245.00	8.70	28.20	17.40	7.20	206.30	5.40	8.00	25.40
1984	42.50	265.20	8.90	31.60	20.20	24.60	412.10	6.00	8.80	26.50
1985	41.70	294.70	8.20	32.40	22.10	26.50	468.90	6.70	9.20	27.40
1986	39.90	289.10	6.90	30.30	17.70	16.70	483.40	6.80	9.30	27.20

a. Includes social security, medicare, and other health and welfare programs.
b. Functions were listed elsewhere until 1974.

security programs, veterans' affairs, and three other programs. The following year, there again were no significant cuts in any area.

Throughout most of the decade, the Democrats in the House and the Republicans in the Senate forged a union that enacted policies contrary to the basic tenets of Reagan's budget policy. In his second term, this "coalition" enacted increases in social and education programs and cuts in defense spending, despite Reagan's strenuous opposition.

I have already noted that spending increased during Reagan's two terms in office, nearly doubling in current dollars. The Democratic-Republican spending compromise can be seen in an examination of the budget by function (see table 4). Although some areas of domestic spending were reduced (largely those that were under pressure in earlier decades), other areas increased tremendously. Defense spending was the area of the greatest increase during Reagan's first term. As expected, this spending compromise was abrogated once the Democrats regained control of the Senate. With unified party control of Congress, the Democrats could cut back on programs favored by the Republicans, namely defense.

With regard to federal revenues, the story is much simpler. The 1981 tax cut reduced revenues for each succeeding year by over $100 billion. Once Reagan proposed the tax cut and the Senate Republicans endorsed it, the Democrats felt they could not oppose it. Once the tax reduction was enacted, however, income tax increases could not be passed, even in the face of mounting budget deficits. Reagan (and later, Bush) promised to veto any tax increase, and with a large Republican minority in the House and Republican control of the Senate, such vetoes were certain to be sustained. Again, divided party control within the setting of a bilateral veto game led to a form of stalemate in which the deficit problem was allowed to fester.

Federal spending and revenue policy from 1976 to 1986 can be seen in figure 2. The deficit in real terms is the annual difference between these two lines. What is clear at this level of aggregation is, first, that spending continued to climb at the same constant rate throughout Reagan's administration as it did during the previous two administrations. Second, revenues were climbing at almost exactly the same rate as expenditures before 1982, with a relatively small difference between the two lines. As a result of the 1981 tax cut, revenue declined for three years from 1982 to 1984. After 1984, revenues again paralleled expenditures, but the distance between the two lines was three times as large.

Figure 2. Federal Expenditures and Revenues, Fiscal Years 1976–88

Billions of 1972 dollars

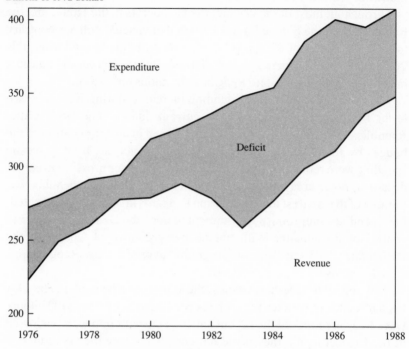

Further, a simple regression employing only three variables—U.S. involvement in armed conflict (World War II, Korea, and Vietnam), the civilian unemployment rate, and the partisan control of the House, Senate, and presidency—can explain over 80 percent of the variation in deficits from 1929 to 1988. The estimated values of the deficit from this model are plotted against the actual values of the deficit in figure 3. A slightly more complicated regression model with these and a few other variables accounts for almost 95 percent of the variation in federal deficits over the same period.[64] Moreover, this more complex model, emphasizing the party control of each of the policymaking branches, yields highly accurate predictions of the level of federal deficits: it predicts deficits $1 billion too small in 1984; $9 billion, $11 billion, and $11 billion too small in 1985, 1986, and 1987 respectively; and $20 billion

64. For details see Mathew D. McCubbins, "Party Governance and U.S. Budget Deficits: Divided Government and Fiscal Stalemate," in Alberto Alesina and Geoffrey Carliner, eds., *Politics and Economics in the Eighties* (University of Chicago Press for National Bureau of Economic Research, forthcoming).

Figure 3. Actual versus Predicted Deficits, Fiscal Years 1929–88

Billions of 1972 dollars

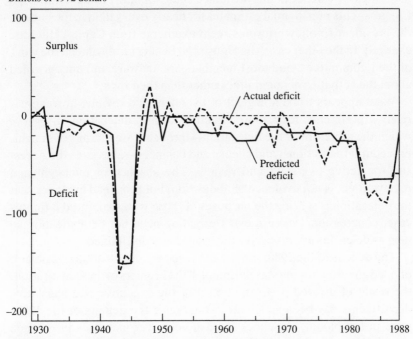

too small in 1988 (the only year the predictions differed significantly from the actual deficit).

Conclusion

Two explanations for the runaway deficits of the 1980s have received widespread comment. The first is that the president did it—that Ronald Reagan, on his way to forging a revolution in American politics, put into place policies that pushed the United States over the deficit precipice. The second has its roots in Congress—that the Congressional Budget and Impoundment Control Act of 1974 led to the unraveling of fiscal restraints in Congress and the unleashing of the spendthrift, committee-centered, policy subgovernments. At the core of both these explanations is a perception that congressional parties are merely shells within which policy is bartered and which have no control over policy. Partisan congressional majorities are said to have abdicated their collective responsibilities over national policy either to the president or to congressional committees and subcommittees.

The apparent neglect of oversight and policy review by congressional majorities is evidence of this presumed abdication. In one case, although Congress cuts presidential estimates for nearly every item in the budget, the president's policy priorities seem to emerge from Capitol Hill little changed. In the other case, the House and Senate rarely amend the work of their committees, and most members are unaware and unconcerned about the activities of committees other than their own.

What appears to be a neglect of oversight and review, however, is really a preference for a more effective form of delegation, a form in which the structure of the delegation—through "fire alarm" oversight, procedural restrictions, and checks and balances—alleviates the necessity for active oversight and review. The absence of oversight and review, then, is not evidence of abdication, but is instead evidence that the delegation is serving the purposes of those who structured it (in this case, congressional majorities). Delegation need not be abdication so long as delegates are properly constrained and disciplined.

The deficits of the 1980s are the consequence of a structural problem: divided government. As was the intent of the Framers of the Constitution, the result of divided partisan control of the executive and legislative departments has been stalemate. Thus, once the deficits of the 1980s were in full bloom, the check Reagan held over increases in revenue was sufficient to prevent Congress from enacting a tax increase. The compromise required to overcome the mutual checks held by the House Democrats and the Senate Republicans over each other's spending programs led to increased spending on nearly every function of government. The arrival of George Bush's lips in the Oval Office has done little to change this stalemate. The budget agreement reached in the fall of 1990 ushered in modest tax increases at the upper end of the income spectrum, no real dollar cuts in spending, and a "deficit reduction" dependent on interest rates declining to a nominal rate of 4 percent in the next five years. The national debt is slated to almost double in that time. Although spending growth has been held in check since the Democrats took control of both houses of Congress in 1986, especially for Republican programs such as defense, continued Republican opposition to tax increases will keep budget deficits in the headlines for years to come.

Budget Policymaking in Japan

Yukio Noguchi

THE PURPOSE of this essay is to examine budgetary policymaking in Japan during the 1980s.[1] The most important budgetary objective of these years was reduction of the budget deficit, or fiscal reconstruction, caused by the large deficit in the national account from the mid-1970s onward.[2] Another important objective was to stimulate domestic demand in response to the record growth of Japan's external surplus and to the criticism this generated among other countries. I discuss the extent to which these contradictory tasks were accomplished and the means employed to deal with them. I also identify the principal actors in the budgetary process and explain how their roles changed in this period.

For many years after World War II, Japan's national budget was managed according to the balanced budget principle, which meant that all expenditures, including capital expenditures, were financed by tax and other current revenues. Although this principle was abandoned in fiscal year 1965, the reliance on bond revenue remained marginal in the

---

1. For discussions of earlier periods, see Gardner Ackley and Hiromitsu Ishi, "Fiscal, Monetary, and Related Policies," in Hugh Patrick and Henry Rosovsky, eds., *Asia's New Giant: How the Japanese Economy Works* (Brookings, 1976), pp. 1–61; Yukio Noguchi, "The Government-Business Relationship in Japan: The Changing Role of Fiscal Resources," in Kozo Yamamura, ed., *Policy and Trade Issues of the Japanese Economy: American and Japanese Perspectives* (University of Washington Press, 1982), pp. 123–42; and Yukio Noguchi, "Public Finance," in Kozo Yamamura and Yasukichi Yasuba, eds., *The Political Economy of Japan*, vol. 1: *The Domestic Transformation* (Stanford University Press, 1987), pp. 186–222.

2. Revenue from long-term bonds is included in the general account revenues. Thus, at the budget stage, the total amount of expenditures must be equal to that of revenues. (In the settlement, there could be a difference between the two.) In spite of this, the amount of bond revenues is usually called the "deficit." This paper uses the word "deficit" in this sense. This usage must not be confused with "deficit-financing bonds," mentioned in note 6.

Table 1. Trends in National Bond Dependence, Fiscal Years 1975–88
Percent

Year	Bond dependence ratio			Outstanding debt–GNP ratio	Ratio of bond-related expenditures to total expenditures[a]
	Initial budget	Revised budget	Actual amount		
1975	9.4	26.3	25.3	9.8	4.9
1976	29.9	29.9	29.4	12.9	6.9
1977	29.7	34.0	32.9	16.8	8.2
1978	32.0	32.8	31.3	20.4	9.4
1979	39.6	35.4	34.7	25.0	10.6
1980	33.5	32.7	32.6	28.8	12.5
1981	26.2	27.4	27.5	31.7	14.2
1982	21.0	30.2	29.7	35.4	15.8
1983	26.5	27.1	26.6	38.6	16.3
1984	25.0	25.0	24.8	40.2	18.1
1985	22.2	23.4	23.2	41.9	19.5
1986	20.2	21.4	21.0	43.4	20.9
1987	19.4	18.1	16.3	43.9	20.9
1988	15.6	12.9	11.6	43.5	20.3

Source: Ministry of Finance, *Zaisei Kinyū Tōkei Geppo* (Monetary and fiscal statistics), 1988.
a. Bond-related expenditures include interest payments and amortization; total expenditures are of general account budget.

next decade, with the dependence ratio hovering at around 10 percent.[3] In 1975, however, tax revenue dropped sharply in the wake of the recession caused by the first oil crisis, and the bond dependence ratio rose to 26.3 percent in the revised budget (see table 1).

Although the government made plans to reduce the deficit, no immediate measures were taken, and the deficit increased further as Japan found itself under pressure to expand domestic demand. Thus in the initial budget for fiscal year 1979 the bond dependence ratio jumped to nearly 40 percent.

The government's first strategy for reducing the deficit was to introduce a new tax. This was a broadly based consumption tax modeled on the value-added tax in European countries, called the general consumption tax (*ippan shōhi zei*). The Ohira administration, which took office in December 1978, declared that it would introduce the new tax in fiscal year 1980. In the fall of 1979, however, the ruling Liberal Democratic party (LDP) suffered a serious setback in the general election, and the

3. The bond dependence ratio is the ratio of revenue from long-term bonds to the total revenue of the general account budget.

Table 2. Growth Rate of General Account Budget, Fiscal Years 1975–88
Percent

Year	Total expenditures	General expenditures[a]	Year	Total expenditures	General expenditures[a]
1975	24.5	23.2	1982	6.2	1.8
1976	14.1	18.8	1983	1.4	0.0
1977	17.4	14.5	1984	0.5	−0.1
1978	20.3	19.2	1985	3.7	0.0
1979	12.6	13.9	1986	3.0	0.0
1980	10.3	5.1	1987	0.0	0.0
1981	9.9	4.3	1988	4.8	1.2

Source: Ministry of Finance, *Zaisei Kinyū Tōkei Geppo*, 1988.
a. Total expenditures less bond-related expenditures and local allocation tax (grants in aid to local governments).

proposed tax became a political taboo. The government was thus forced to change its deficit reduction strategy from increasing tax revenues to reducing expenditures.

Several measures were adopted for this purpose, and during the 1980s expenditure growth declined significantly.[4] The rate of increase in general expenditures fell to 1.8 percent in fiscal 1982, 0 in 1983, and − 0.1 percent in 1984 (see table 2). In response, the budget deficit shrank considerably (table 1).[5] The bond dependence ratio fell from 32.6 percent in 1980 to 15.6 percent in the initial budget for fiscal 1988. In terms of the ratio to GNP, the revenue from long-term bonds declined by 4.1 percentage points (from 7.2 percent to 3.1 percent) during the same period.

The deficit reduction achieved in these years is remarkable, especially in comparison with the United States, where deficit reduction seems slow. Japan's success in this regard raises several questions. Were there

4. The budgetary behavior of the government in this instance resembled a household consumption decision: scarcity of current revenue led to austerity. James M. Buchanan and Richard E. Wagner argue that people feel little or no fiscal burden if expenditures are financed by borrowing rather than by taxes, and hence increased bond dependency leads to fiscal irresponsibility and an increase in expenditures. *Democracy in Deficit: The Political Legacy of Lord Keynes* (Academic Press, 1977). This argument cannot be supported by what happened in Japan. Although it is true that the bond dependence ratio correlates positively with the ratio of general account expenditures to GNP, the causality is that an increase in the deficit forced fiscal authorities to adopt a tight budget policy, which in turn caused the bond dependence ratio to fall.

5. The reduction in the government deficit is more evident if one looks at another index, the saving-investment gap of the general government. The gap was reduced from − ¥ 9,919 billion in fiscal 1980 to − ¥ 2,590 billion in fiscal 1985. It has become positive since fiscal 1987.

any significant changes in the policy formation process that made such a reduction possible? Or was this merely the result of an increase in tax revenues? How were the international pressures to expand domestic demand compromised with the deficit reduction objective? These are the central questions discussed in this essay.

After briefly describing the formal features of the Japanese budgetary process, which have been in place since the 1960s, I review the four major changes in this process over the past decade and consider their implications for deficit reduction. I argue that simple rules were more important in reducing the deficit than political innovation. Contrary to the general perception, expenditure cuts were to a large extent superficial, except for public works, and it was basically increases in tax revenue and social security contributions that reduced the budget deficit. I also discuss fiscal policies for the expansion of domestic demand, especially the ¥6 trillion program of 1987. I point out, again contrary to the general perception, that an increase in public works and a tax cut were passive reactions to an unexpected increase in tax revenue. Despite the deficit reduction, the true objective of Japan's budget policy—adapting to the changing needs of society—remains unachieved.

The Budget Process in Japan

The annual budget cycle in Japan begins with the preparation of budget requests by ministries at the start of the fiscal year (in April). Requests from various sections are coordinated within each ministry, and a consolidated request is submitted to the Budget Bureau of the Ministry of Finance (MOF) by the end of August.

The Liberal Democratic party enters into the process when the ministries prepare their requests. During this preparation the ministries consult frequently with related divisions in the Policy Affairs Research Council (PARC) of the LDP. The Ministry of Finance also exchanges opinions frequently with the board and key persons in the LDP.

The Budget Bureau begins hearing and examining requests from the ministries in September. It also reviews recommendations for next year's budget policy from such advisory bodies as the Tax Council, the Fiscal System Council, and the Bond Issue Advisory Commission. The cabinet establishes the basic principles of next year's budget at this time.

After examining each ministry's requests, the Ministry of Finance drafts a preliminary budget, which is released to the ministries around

December 20. Since this draft does not accommodate all requests, negotiations with ministries begin immediately after its release. These negotiations are conducted first at the bureaucratic level and then at the ministerial level.

Matters that were not settled during the ministerial negotiations are submitted to a meeting of the top three officials of the LDP: the secretary-general, the chairman of the Executive Council, and the chairman of PARC. The minister of finance, the director-general of the Budget Bureau, and the ministers concerned also attend the meeting. After this meeting, the cabinet decides on the final government draft in late December.

The Ministry of Finance then prepares the budget and submits it to the Diet, usually at the end of January. Diet discussion starts in the Budget Committee of the House of Representatives, where the crucial debate is held. After being approved by this committee, the budget is voted on by the House of Representatives and then passed on to the House of Councillors, usually at the beginning of March. In a procedure similar to that followed in the House of Representatives, the budget is approved by the House of Councillors around the beginning of the fiscal year. The government budget is seldom amended during the Diet deliberation, partly because this is the nature of the parliamentary cabinet system and partly because the LDP holds a permanent majority. The prior consultations between the government and the LDP have such sway that Diet deliberation is no more than a formal procedure.

Changes in the Budget Process

After abandoning the proposal to introduce a new tax in 1979, the government introduced several changes in the budgetary process and in the participants.

Adoption of the Deficit Reduction Objective

The first measure the government introduced to reduce expenditures was to establish a deficit reduction objective. The Suzuki administration, which took office in July 1980, decided that the issuance of deficit-financing bonds (*akaji kokusai*) should be terminated by fiscal 1984.[6] Although insufficient growth of tax revenues in fiscal 1981–82 prevented achievement of this objective, it was subsequently adopted by the Nakasone administration with a revised target year of fiscal 1989, and became one of the major policy goals of the five-year economic plan formulated in March 1983.

Given the target year, the government could almost automatically determine the amount of deficit-financing bonds to be issued each fiscal year. This is explicitly described in the MOF's "medium-term fiscal outlook," which was presented to the Diet in January 1981. The outlook has been revised each year up to the present. Although it is formally explained as nothing but "an estimate based on several assumptions," it has in fact been used to set an absolute limit on each year's budget. In this way, the Ministry of Finance has succeeded in making the amount of the bond issue a predetermined variable rather than a policy variable that must be decided upon each year in the budget process.

A Strengthened Ceiling

The second measure was to lower the budget ceiling, which is the upper limit imposed on the rate of increase in budget requests from the previous year's budget. Although a ceiling existed as early as the 1960s, it became considerably more strict in fiscal 1978.

Until fiscal 1981, however, the strict ceiling applied only to general administrative expenditures and not to policy expenditures. In fiscal 1982 the principle of zero increases was applied to all expenditures, except special programs such as defense, energy, and official development assistance. The ceiling was made increasingly tight in subsequent years.

Establishment of the Rinchō

Third, in October 1980 the government enacted a special law establishing a formal organization to review all aspects of its activities and

6. The Fiscal Act limits bond issues to the amount of public works expenditures. However, because deficits have continued to exceed this ceiling since fiscal 1975, a special law is passed every year in order to legalize the issuance of bonds exceeding the limit. These bonds are usually called deficit-financing bonds, even though they finance only a part (about half in recent years) of the total deficit defined in note 2. It is possible to regard these bonds as financing deficits in the "current subaccount," although no such subaccount is actually distinguished in the general account.

to recommend to the prime minister ways to rationalize them. This organization was known as the Second Ad Hoc Council for Administrative Reform (*Dai Niji Rinji Gyōsei Chōsakai,* usually referred to as the Rinchō).[7] It consisted of nine members, including the chairman: three business leaders, two labor union leaders, two ex-bureaucrats, an ex-journalist, and a scholar. There were also twenty-one special members, five advisers, and fifty-five related members. A new division was established in the government to serve as the council's secretariat; it was staffed by about eighty bureaucrats from the various ministries.

In its first recommendation, in June 1981, the Rinchō supported the strategy of reducing expenditures by strengthening the budget ceiling. The zero ceiling for the fiscal 1982 budget was approved at the cabinet meeting in June 1981. The Rinchō also proposed "fiscal reconstruction without a tax increase"; that is, it recommended that the deficit be reduced through expenditure reduction rather than a tax increase.

There are two important points to note about the Rinchō. First, it was an entirely new actor in the budget process. Earlier, the key actors had been the MOF, the requesting ministries, and the LDP. Although several advisory councils were involved in the process, most of them played only a nominal role since their activities were under the direction of bureaucrats. The Rinchō differed significantly from the traditional councils in that it did not hesitate to recommend reforms even if they conflicted with certain bureaucrats' interests.[8] Second, Rinchō policy was supported by the business community, as was clearly demonstrated when Toshio Doko, the chairman of the Japanese Federation of Economic Organizations (Keidanren), became the chairman of the Rinchō.[9] During the era of rapid growth, it was the business community that pressed for an expansionary fiscal policy, and the labor unions and the opposition parties that insisted on administrative simplicity and fiscal austerity. After the second oil shock, however, the business community came to support a tight budget policy. One reason for this change was that business leaders had become disenchanted with the results of the expansionary policy of 1977–78. Another reason was that they believed future tax increases would be directed at corporate income, while the

7. "Ad hoc" means that the council was not a permanent organization. The First Ad Hoc Administrative Reform Council was established in 1962 and dissolved in 1964.

8. It is therefore quite interesting to study the source of the initial thrust for such a new organization. It is said that business leaders pushed Yasuhiro Nakasone, who was then the chief of the Administrative Management Agency, to take action.

9. In contrast, the chairman of the First Ad Hoc Administrative Reform Council was a labor union leader.

benefits of such increases would go to such groups as farmers and small entrepreneurs.

At first, the MOF was reluctant to accept the Rinchō because it feared the new organization would encroach on its sacred territory of budget making. Once the Rinchō was established, however, the MOF changed its attitude quickly and tried to steer the Rinchō's proposals in the direction of expenditure reduction. The Rinchō, too, saw that cooperation was necessary since its proposals would be of little value if opposed by the MOF. This explains the emergence of the first zero ceiling proposal in June 1981. At first glance, the principle of "fiscal reconstruction without a tax increase" might seem to be at odds with the MOF's strategy, but this was not the case. In the first place, it would have been politically impossible to introduce a new tax for several years after 1979 even without this restriction. In the second place, the MOF succeeded in attaching a footnote to the 1981 proposal stating that "tax increase" meant "tax increase by way of introducing a new tax." This footnote may appear to be only a technical detail, but it was extremely important, as will be explained below.

The Rinchō released five sets of proposals before it was dissolved in March 1983. The most important proposals in addition to the first set were those concerning the revision of the social security system and the privatization of three public corporations: the Japanese National Railways, the Nippon Telegraph and Telephone Corporation (NTT), and the Japan Tobacco and Salt Corporation.

The New Role of LDP Politicians

The fourth change that occurred in the budgetary process was the way LDP politicians were allowed to participate in the process through the divisions (*bukai*) of the Policy Affairs Research Council of the LDP. These divisions correspond almost one-to-one to the ministries in the government. The administrative branch is vertically segmented, and the LDP politicians are grouped into cliques (*zoku*) according to the *bukai*. These are different from factions.

Each ministry explains its budget request to the corresponding *bukai*. The role of the *zoku* used to be to assist bureaucrats by exerting pressure on the MOF so that the *zoku*'s ministry would succeed in obtaining its budget. In return the *zoku* would obtain various benefits from the ministry it championed. That is, the major policy decisions used to be made by the bureaucrats, and the politicians' role was to act as a pressure group or "cheering party."

During recent years, however, the situation has changed, at least as far as the elite members of the zoku are concerned.[10] They now coordinate the policy formation process in place of the bureaucrats. Specifically, they have begun to play a central role in adjusting the conflicting interests of various groups, rather than simply being one of the participants.

Their power can be illustrated by the activities surrounding the introduction of the elderly insurance program, which aimed at reducing the government subsidy to the national health insurance program by shifting the burden to the insurance programs of large corporations. The reform bill was prepared by the Ministry of Health and Welfare and was submitted to the Diet in May 1981. After it was approved in the House of Representatives in October, strong opposition arose from business leaders, who realized that the reform would substantially increase corporate burdens, and deliberation in the House of Councillors became bogged down. The "four welfare bosses" (Kunikichi Saito, Tatsuo Ozawa, Masami Tanaka, and Ryutaro Hashimoto—all ex-ministers of welfare) then began some political maneuvering. After many negotiations with business leaders, they finally elicited a compromise, and the bill passed the Diet in July 1982. It is said that without the activities of the four bosses, the Ministry of Health and Welfare could not have pushed the bill through.

Another example of zoku influence can be seen in the determination of the price of rice. During the 1950s and 1960s, the LDP politicians did nothing more than exert pressure on the Ministry of Agriculture, Forestry and Fisheries and the Ministry of Finance to raise the government purchase price of rice as high as possible for the benefit of farmers. In the 1970s, however, when excess production of rice and the deficit of the Food Control Special Account became serious problems, some of the Nōrin-zoku (agriculture clan) politicians formed the Sōgō-Nosei-ha (comprehensive agricultural policy group). The concerns of this group quickly expanded beyond rice to agriculture in general. During recent years, major agricultural policy decisions have been influenced by this group. In the determination of the price of rice, they not only fight with

10. The leaders of respective zoku are usually ex-ministers of related ministries. Takashi Inoguchi and Tomoaki Iwai, "Zokugiin" no Kenkyū: Jimintō Seiken o Gyūjiru Shuyaku-tachi (A study of "zoku" representatives: main actors controlling Japanese politics) (Tokyo: Nihon Keizai Shinbunsha, 1987).

the MOF on behalf of the farmers but also persuade farmers and related groups to moderate their demands.

Importance of the Changes in Reducing Expenditures

The deficit reduction objective has been a highly effective measure, because no one can object to such a general and abstract goal and yet it sets an absolute limit on the size of each year's budget. The ceiling has also been quite effective. In principle, the ceiling is applied equally to all expenditures, and the ministries and the interest groups as well as the politicians must uphold this principle. Simple rules, such as this one, that apply equally to all expenditures have been indispensable in the struggle to discourage expenditure growth. The balanced budget principle that was in effect until the mid-1960s was another example of such a rule. The setting of the deficit reduction objective performed a similar role.

The Rinchō, however, was not as effective as is generally believed. The only recommendation it made that directly resulted in expenditure reduction was the strengthening of the ceiling. But this policy was initiated by the MOF, and the Rinchō simply endorsed and authorized it. It is true that the privatization of public corporations contributed to fiscal reconstruction. In particular, the sale of the NTT shares produced a huge amount of revenue for the government, but this might have been achieved without the Rinchō's recommendation. Probably the most important contribution of the Rinchō was that it helped the government reach a consensus on the overarching objective of fiscal reconstruction.

The change in the LDP politicians' role is more difficult to evaluate. It is true that many measures, including the deficit reduction objective and the ceiling, would not have been introduced without their cooperation. Generally speaking, however, a relative increase in the power of politicians tends to increase expenditures because politicians are interested in the benefits of the individual ministries and their political constituencies. Unlike the MOF in the bureaucratic system, which takes responsibility for the entire budget, politicians are not concerned with the total size of the budget or the deficit level. In fact, the LDP voices strong opposition to the strict ceiling from time to time. It was only because of the pressure of the deficit that politicians' demands to expand expenditures were ignored.

Table 3. Ratio of General Account Budget Items to National Income, Fiscal Years 1975–88[a]
Percent

Year	Bond-related expenditures	Social security expenditures	General expenditures	Total[b]	Tax revenue	Bond revenue
1975	0.9	3.2	13.2	16.8	10.9	4.4
1976	1.3	3.5	13.6	17.6	11.1	5.3
1977	1.5	3.7	14.4	18.8	11.0	6.4
1978	1.9	3.9	15.1	20.0	12.3	6.6
1979	2.4	4.2	16.1	21.8	12.9	7.7
1980	2.8	4.1	15.6	21.9	13.6	7.2
1981	3.2	4.3	15.6	22.6	15.3	6.2
1982	3.2	4.2	15.2	21.9	14.0	6.6
1983	3.6	4.0	14.5	22.3	14.0	6.1
1984	3.9	4.0	13.8	21.5	14.5	5.4
1985	4.0	3.9	13.1	20.9	15.0	4.9
1986	4.0	3.8	12.6	20.3	14.9	4.3
1987	4.3	3.7	12.6	21.1	15.6	3.8
1988	4.0	3.6	11.4	19.7	15.6	3.1

Source: Ministry of Finance, *Zaisei Kinyū Tōkei Geppo*, 1988.
a. Revised budget base.
b. Totals include items not shown in table.

Anatomy of the Deficit Reduction

I have mentioned that both the rate of increase of expenditures and the budget deficit dropped greatly during the 1980s. However, I have carefully avoided drawing a causal relationship between the two. It is generally believed that the deficit shrank mainly because of the expenditure reduction. I now consider whether this view is valid.

If one looks at only the general account figures, this argument is difficult to refute. The ratio of the general account budget to national income fell by 2.2 percentage points during 1980–88 (see table 3). Since the reduction in the ratio of bond revenue to national income was 4.1 percentage points, more than half the deficit reduction appears to have been achieved by expenditure reduction.

It must be noted, however, that the general account of the national budget is only a part of the entire public finance system. Like other industrialized countries, Japan has a fairly complicated finance system. For one thing, it includes the budgets of local governments in addition to the national budget. For another, the national budget is divided into the general account budget, special account budgets, and the budgets of government-affiliated agencies. In addition, the fiscal investment and loan program performs a function similar to that of the budgets. Since

Table 4. Changes in Revenue and Expenditures of the General Government
as a Share of GNP, Fiscal Years 1980–86
Percent

Revenue and expenditure	1980	1986	Change
Current expenditures	25.21	27.43	2.22
Final consumption	9.83	9.79	−0.04
Interest payment	3.26	4.53	1.27
Social security payment	7.98	9.74	1.76
Public assistance	2.17	1.82	−0.35
Subsidies	1.49	1.04	−0.45
Others	0.48	0.51	0.03
Capital expenditures	7.11	5.67	−1.44
Investment	6.09	4.83	−1.26
Purchase of land	1.02	0.84	−0.18
Current revenue	28.15	31.94	3.79
Taxes	18.51	20.37	1.86
Social security contribution	7.41	8.55	1.14
Others	2.23	3.02	0.79
Saving-investment gap[a]	−4.04	−0.52	3.52

Source: Economic Planning Agency, *Kokumin Keizai Keisan Nenpō* (Yearbook of national account statistics), 1988.

a. Equals current revenue minus current expenditures minus capital expenditures plus depreciation and capital transfer from the private sector (neither shown in table).

there are complicated flows of funds between these subsectors, the general account figures do not necessarily reflect the true condition of the entire public finance system. For example, it is possible to reduce general account expenditures by shifting the burden to other sectors of the government. This is in fact what happened during the 1980s, which can be verified by looking at figures from the standard national account (SNA).

The General Government

The SNA statistics on the revenues and expenditures of the general government (which include the general account and some of the special accounts of the national budget, such as the social security special accounts and the corresponding accounts of local governments) are shown in table 4. In this table, the saving-investment gap represents the deficit. (In what follows, the terms "increase" and "decrease" refer to changes in the share of GNP rather than changes in the absolute amount.)

The change in the saving-investment gap (3.52 percent) is almost equal to the increase in current revenue (3.79 percent). Although capital

**Table 5. Ratio of Tax and Social Security Burdens to National Income,
Fiscal Years 1975–88**
Percent

Year[a]	National taxes[b]	Local taxes	Total tax revenue	Social security contributions	Total
1975	11.7	6.6	18.3	7.5	25.8
1976	12.0	6.8	18.8	7.8	26.6
1977	11.8	7.1	18.9	8.3	27.2
1978[c]	13.5	7.1	20.6	8.5	29.1
1979	13.7	7.7	21.4	8.8	30.2
1980	14.2	8.0	22.2	9.1	31.3
1981	14.6	8.3	23.0	9.8	32.7
1982	14.8	8.6	23.3	10.1	33.5
1983	15.0	8.7	23.7	10.2	33.9
1984	15.3	9.0	24.3	10.3	34.6
1985	15.4	9.2	24.5	10.7	35.3
1986	16.2	9.3	25.5	10.8	36.3
1987	16.0	9.8	25.8	11.1	36.9
1988	16.1	9.4	25.5	11.1	36.6

Source: Ministry of Finance, *Zaisei Kinyū Tōkei Geppo*, 1988.
a. All years are actual, except 1988 (initial budget base) and 1987 (revised budget base).
b. Revenue from Japan Tobacco and Salt Corporation included until 1984.
c. There was a change with regard to the allocation of tax revenue between fiscal years in 1978.

expenditures declined, the reduction was more than offset by the increase in current expenditures, so the deficit reduction was smaller than the increase in current revenue. This is considerably different from the impression given by the data in table 3.

Note that social security payments increased. This contrasts sharply with the figures in table 3, which show a decline in social security expenditures. Note also that final consumption remained almost unchanged. Since the general government figures, not the general account figures, represent the true relationship with the private sector, one can conjecture that as far as current expenditures are concerned, fiscal austerity was to a large extent superficial since the underlying systems were not changed and benefits were not reduced.

Furthermore, the increase in the social security burden was substantial, as was the tax increase. The ratio of the total burden to national income increased by 5.3 percentage points during 1980–88 (3.3 percentage points in tax and 2.0 percentage points in social security contributions; see table 5). If one compares 1975 and 1988, the increase in the ratio jumps to 10.8 percentage points. Thus the tax burden increased significantly in spite of the restriction thought to be imposed by "fiscal

Table 6. **Changes in Revenue and Expenditures of the Local General Government as a Share of GNP, Fiscal Years 1980–86**
Percent

Revenue and expenditure	1980	1986	Change
Current expenditures	10.36	10.27	−0.09
Final consumption	7.38	7.18	−0.20
Interest payments	0.88	1.07	0.19
Public assistance	1.46	1.23	−0.23
Subsidies	1.32	0.26	−1.06
Others	0.32	0.53	0.21
Capital expenditures	6.00	4.77	−1.23
Investment	5.14	4.02	−1.12
Purchase of land	0.86	0.75	−0.11
Revenue	14.89	14.26	−0.63
Taxes and other current revenues	7.02	7.86	0.84
Current transfer from the central government	5.47	4.87	−0.60
Capital transfer from the central government	2.40	1.53	−0.87
Saving-investment gap[a]	−1.28	−0.40	0.88

Source: Economic Planning Agency, *Kokumin Keizai Keisan Nenpō*, 1988.
a. Equals current revenue minus current expenditures minus capital expenditures plus depreciation and capital transfer from the private sector (neither shown in table).

reconstruction without a tax increase." The increase was achieved mainly by bracket creep in the income tax.[11] In other words, a significant part of fiscal reconstruction was achieved by an automatic tax increase, which implies that the restriction imposed by the Rinchō was ineffective.

Local Governments

The ineffectiveness of the restriction becomes clearer when the general government is separated into its components. Many of Japan's public services are provided by local governments but are subsidized by the national government. These include public assistance programs, the national health insurance program, compulsory education, and some public works. Altogether, the subsidies from the national government account for about one-third of the total general account expenditures of the national budget. (These subsidies are represented by current and capital transfers from the central government in table 6.)

In the fiscal 1985 budget, a substantial change was made in the system:

11. In this respect, the condition is fundamentally different from that in the United States, where indexation has been introduced in the income tax system.

wherever the subsidization rate exceeded one-half, the subsidy was reduced by about 10 percent. Thus the absolute amount of subsidies was reduced by about 1 percent from the previous year. This measure was further strengthened in the 1986 budget.

The slowing effect of this and other measures on the capital transfer to local governments is confirmed by the figures in table 6. Since capital transfer is determined by the percentage of capital expenditures, the 1986 figure would have been 1.91 percent of GNP (2.40 x 4.77/6.00) if the subsidization rate had been unchanged. The actual figure was 1.53 percent, which implies that the rate was reduced by about 19 percent (0.37/1.91). By the same calculation, the current transfer for 1986 would have been 5.42 percent (5.47 x 10.27/10.36) if the system had been unchanged. Since the actual figure was 4.87 percent, the rate of subsidy must have been reduced by 10.6 percent (0.55/5.20). It follows that if no changes had been made, the 1986 revenues would have been 15.19 percent (7.86 + 5.42 + 1.91) and the saving-investment gap would have been 0.52 percent (− 0.40 + 0.92).

Although the measure to cut the subsidies reduced the level of the national government's expenditures, the amount of public services provided by the local governments remained almost unchanged. Hence it proved to be nothing but a reallocation of the fiscal burden between the national and the local governments. In this sense, the expenditure "cut" was superficial.

The Social Security Fund

Many items in Japan's social security budget increase automatically as the number of eligible people, mainly the elderly, increases. Automatic adjustments account for an estimated 6 percent of the social security budget, which is to say that the social security budget increases by about 6 percent each year even when no improvement is made within the system. Thus, in order to achieve the zero-growth ceiling, a corresponding amount must be cut elsewhere in the social security budget.

Several important changes have been made within the system. For example, a radical reform of the public pension program was introduced in 1987. This will have no immediate effect on the fiscal burden, however, since the reform affects only payments in the distant future.

The most important measure that reduced social security expenditures in the general account budget was the reduction of transfers (subsidies) to the social security fund. First, subsidies to public pension programs

134   YUKIO NOGUCHI

Table 7. Changes in Revenue and Expenditures of the Social Security Fund
as a Share of GNP, Fiscal Years 1980–86
Percent

Revenue and expenditure	1980	1986	Change
Current expenditure	8.24	10.02	1.78
Social security transfer	7.98	9.74	1.76
Others	0.26	0.28	0.02
Revenue	10.97	13.07	2.10
Social security contributions	7.41	8.55	1.14
Interest receipts	1.20	1.92	0.72
Transfer from the central government	2.33	2.57	0.24
Saving-investment gap[a]	2.64	2.94	0.30

Source: Economic Planning Agency, *Kokumin Keizai Keisan Nenpō*, 1988.
a. Equals current revenue minus current expenditures minus capital expenditures (not shown in table), plus depreciation and capital transfer from the private sector (neither shown in table).

have been cut by one-quarter since fiscal 1982. Second, the subsidy to the government-operated health insurance program has been cut since fiscal 1985. The amount saved by these measures was close to ¥360 billion in FY 1988, or about 5 percent of the social security budget. These cuts have had no direct effect on either benefits or contributions, however.[12] The only effect has been a reduction in the surplus in the social security fund and hence the amount available for the fiscal investment and loan program. Other reforms, such as the introduction of the elderly insurance program mentioned above, shifted the burden to the private sector.

The effect of these measures can be evaluated by examining the figures shown in table 7. Since the transfer from the general account is determined as a percentage of social security payments, the 1986 figure would have been 2.84 percent (2.33 x 9.74/7.98) if the system had remained unchanged. The actual figure of 2.57 percent implies that the average subsidization rate was cut by 9.5 percent (0.27/2.84). If the system had remained unchanged, the saving-investment gap would have been 3.21 percent (2.94 + 0.27) instead of 2.94 percent.

12. Social security contributions do not become part of general account revenues. On the expenditure side, only subsidies for social security programs appear in the general account. Thus, in order to find the total revenues and outlays of social security programs, one must include those of the related special accounts. As a consequence of this treatment, the nature of the deficit in the general account is different from that in the United States, where entire revenues and outlays of social security programs are included in the federal budget. Since public pension programs in Japan yield surpluses at present, the magnitude of the deficit would be considerably smaller if a definition similar to the one used in the United States were adopted.

Table 8. Changes in Revenue and Expenditures of the Central General Government as a Share of GNP, Fiscal Years 1980–86
Percent

Revenue and expenditure	1980	1986	Change
Current expenditures	14.48	14.60	0.12
Final consumption	2.31	2.43	0.12
Interest payments	2.38	3.45	1.07
Public assistance	0.71	0.58	−0.13
Subsidies	1.16	0.77	−0.39
Transfers to other general government	7.70	7.15	−0.55
Others	0.22	0.22	0.00
Capital expenditures	3.47	2.39	−1.08
Investment	0.92	0.79	−0.13
Purchase of land	0.15	0.09	−0.06
Transfer to other general government	2.40	1.51	−0.89
Taxes and other current revenues	12.58	13.61	1.03
Saving-investment gap[a]	−5.40	−3.06	2.34

Source: Economic Planning Agency, *Kokumin Keizai Keisan Nenpō*, 1988.
a. Equals current revenue minus current expenditures minus capital expenditures plus depreciation and capital transfer from the private sector (neither shown in table).

The Central Government

The changes in revenues and expenditures of the central general government, which correspond more or less to the general account plus public works special accounts of the national budget, are shown in table 8. The improvement in the saving-investment gap is 2.34 percentage points; the increase in taxes and other current revenue accounts is 1.03 percentage points; and the reduction in expenditures (current and capital) is 0.96 percentage point. This is roughly consistent with the figures in table 3, in that about half the deficit reduction was achieved by expenditure reduction.

However, if the above-mentioned reductions in transfers had not been made, the change in the saving-investment gap would have been only about 1.15 percentage points (2.34 − 0.37 − 0.55 − 0.27), or about the same magnitude as the increase in current revenues. This is roughly the same as that of the general government. In other words, the reduction of the deficit over and above the increase in revenue was made possible by shifting the burden to other sectors of the general government.

Two other items in the central government expenditures show significant reductions: subsidies and public investment (capital expenditures).

Table 9. Trends in GNP and Government Investment, Fiscal Years 1976–88
Percent

Year	Real growth rate		Nominal growth rate		Ratio of government investment to GNP (real)
	GNP	Government investment[a]	GNP	Government investment[a]	
1976	4.6	0.3	12.4	5.7	9.3
1977	5.3	14.7	11.0	19.6	10.1
1978	5.2	13.4	9.9	17.9	10.9
1979	5.3	−2.4	8.0	6.0	10.1
1980	4.0	−1.5	8.7	6.1	9.6
1981	3.3	0.8	5.9	2.6	9.3
1982	3.2	0.1	4.9	0.0	9.0
1983	3.7	−2.2	4.3	−2.8	8.5
1984	5.1	−2.9	6.7	−1.9	7.9
1985	4.5	−6.3	6.0	−6.5	7.1
1986	2.7	7.0	4.1	5.0	7.4
1987	5.4	9.4	5.0	8.9	7.7
1988	5.3	1.2	6.0	1.3	7.4

Source: Economic Planning Agency, *Kokumin Keizai Keisan Nenpō*, 1988.
a. Includes public enterprises.

One of the major items included in "subsidies" is the agriculture-related budget, which was cut significantly during the 1980s, particularly the transfer to the food control special account, which was reduced from ¥955 billion in fiscal 1980 to ¥448 billion in fiscal 1988. As a result, the food control account's share of the general account budget fell from 2.2 percent to 0.8 percent. Reducing the rate of increase of the government purchase price of rice did contribute to the reduction in the transfer, but the reduction was achieved mainly by increasing the consumer price of rice by about 52 percent during 1976–86. The rate of increase in the government purchase price was 13 percent during the same period. This implies that the reduction in the agriculture-related budget was achieved more by increasing the consumers' burden than by reducing farmers' benefits.

The trend in government investment is shown in table 9 (which includes investments by the general government and public corporations). The growth rate of real government investment became negative in fiscal 1979 and has remained at low levels since then. Even in nominal terms, the growth rate of government investment was negative for three years. This implies a substantial cut in the budget for public works. How was this possible when politicians were pressing for an increase? The answer seems to be that politicians are more interested in the geographical allocation of the public works budget than in its total size.[13] Even though the rate of growth was cut, a certain amount of works were funded every year, which provided room for politicians to exercise their political influence. Such influence may even become more valuable as the total allocation decreases (the law of diminishing marginal utility).

One more factor played an important role in reducing general account expenditures: the enormous reductions in the transfer to the Bond Amortization Fund since fiscal 1982. In fiscal 1988, the reduction amounted to 4.4 percent of total general account expenditures. This measure did not affect the actual amortization of national bonds, however. It only reduced the fund for future amortization and the fund for the fiscal investment and loan program.

In conclusion, except for public works, most expenditure cuts were superficial in the sense that there were no reductions in fiscal benefits (transfer payments in the social security budget, public services in the budget for other expenditures, and the producer price of rice in the agriculture budget).

Reactions to External Pressures

With the growing interdependence among countries, international considerations are receiving increasing attention in economic policies. Budgetary policy also has come to be heavily influenced by external pressures in recent years, as is demonstrated by the events of the mid-1970s. When Japan's surplus in the external current account grew from $3.7 billion in 1976 to $10.9 billion in 1977 and $16.5 billion in 1978 and the yen appreciated from 290 to the dollar in January 1977 to 176 in October 1978, international policymakers began to favor the "locomotive theory." Thus, at the London economic summit in May 1977, it was decided that the countries with strong currencies should expand their domestic demand to rectify international imbalances.

In response, Japan approved a comprehensive economic plan in September 1977, followed up by a revised budget in October 1977 that included an increase of ¥300 billion in public works expenditures. The second revised budget of January 1978 increased public works expenditures by another ¥370 billion. As a result, the rate of increase in public works over the previous year was close to 31.4 percent. The

13. The geographical allocation is determined by the Ministry of Construction. The Policy Affairs Research Council of the LDP does not intervene in this decision because it is regarded as a matter of budget execution.

rate of growth in government investment, including that by public enterprises, was 19.6 percent (table 9). The initial fiscal 1978 budget included an "exceptional expansionary policy," in which the amount for public works was increased by 31.7 percent from the previous year. The bond dependence ratio climbed to 32.8 percent, while government investment grew by 17.9 percent.

In spite of these policies, the real economic growth rate remained at about 5 percent (table 9). Thus the locomotive theory and Keynesian demand management policy in general began to generate a degree of skepticism. At the same time, the second oil crisis turned Japan's external current balance into a deficit. Hence the pressure for expansion dwindled during the late 1970s.

In the 1980s the pressure built up again as Japan's external surplus increased. The balance turned positive in 1981, increased to $24 billion in 1983, and reached a record level of $94 billion, or 4.5 percent of GNP, in 1986. The consensus among economists was that although a significant part of the international imbalance could be attributed to U.S. macroeconomic policy, Japan should expand its domestic demand, not to raise the economic growth rate but to reduce its external surplus. Nonetheless, budget policymakers did not yield to this pressure because the Ministry of Finance strongly opposed increasing the budget deficit. Although the government launched "surplus reduction programs" almost every year, no substantial increase in public spending was included (see tables 2 and 9).

The first sign that the Japanese government might respond to international pressure came when it established the Mayekawa committee, which submitted its report to the prime minister in April 1986. In April 1987 a new version of the Mayekawa report was produced under the auspices of the Economic Council. The basic message in both cases was that Japan needed to reduce the huge external surplus in the current account for the sake of international harmony, and that in order to achieve this goal it had to shift the emphasis in its industrial structure from exports to domestic demand. The reports did not explicitly mention the necessity of changing the basic stance of fiscal policy, because of objections from the MOF.

At the Group of Seven's Venice summit in June 1987, member countries agreed to strengthen multilateral surveillance of macroeconomic indicators. To respond to this movement, Japan adopted the ¥6 trillion emergency economic measure just before the summit, in May

1987. The measure included an increase in spending on public works amounting to ¥5 trillion and a tax reduction of at least ¥1 trillion. Was this a basic policy change, as many have suggested?

The first point to note here is that ¥6 trillion, which was 2 percent of GNP in 1987, refers to the size of the entire program, including expenditures by local governments and by government-affiliated agencies that are financed by the fiscal investment and loan program. Also included are expenditures such as those for disaster reconstruction, which would have been disbursed even in the absence of the emergency measure. If they are excluded, the increase in national public works expenditures would have been only ¥1.8 trillion, or about 0.5 percent of GNP. This was financed by the increased issuance of national bonds and the sale of the NTT shares in the first budget revision in July 1987.

In the second budget revision in February 1988, measures were taken to finance an income tax reduction totaling ¥1.8 trillion. At this time, however, it became clear that tax revenues would exceed the estimate in the initial budget. The difference was so large that an upward revision of estimated tax revenues was possible even after the income tax reduction and a reduction in bond issuance were undertaken. Since the amount of the bond issuance reduction was about the same as the increase in the first budget revision, the increased deficit was reversed back to its original level. In other words, if the two budget revisions were combined, there was no increase in the budget deficit: the basic factor that made it possible to increase public works and also achieve a tax reduction was an "unexpected" increase in tax revenues.

An additional astonishing fact became clear in the fiscal 1987 settlement, which was released in June 1988: tax revenues exceeded the revised estimate by ¥3.7 trillion. (Compared with the initial budget estimate, this was an increase of ¥5.6 trillion. Including the income tax reduction, the underestimation in the initial budget was on the order of ¥7.4 trillion, or 18 percent of the initial estimate.) A significant portion of the increase was used to reduce bond issuance: the revised budget was cut by ¥1.1 trillion in fiscal 1987 and by about ¥0.9 trillion in fiscal 1988. This implies that the fiscal 1987 budget had a contractionary, rather than an expansionary, effect on aggregate demand.

It is not clear at what stage the MOF realized the possibility of an enormous tax revenue increase. Although there is no definite evidence, the MOF may have intentionally underestimated tax revenues in order to prevent the increased revenues from being used exclusively for expenditure expansion or tax cuts. At least in retrospect, the underestimation made it possible to use most of the surplus revenues to reduce bond issuance, the MOF's most important objective.

Conclusion

One of the questions raised at the beginning of this discussion was, to what extent and by what means did Japan achieve fiscal reconstruction and expand domestic demand? The Japanese government apparently attached high priority to the objective of fiscal reconstruction. Its reactions to international pressures were designed solely to appease foreign governments, most of which believed that fiscal expansion was undertaken in the 1987 revised budget in the form of increased public works and a tax cut. A closer look, however, reveals that both were financed by an unexpected surplus of tax revenues over the original estimate, rather than by an increase in the budget deficit. It follows, then, that fiscal expansion was only superficial. It is important to note that the government's reluctance to adopt an expansionary policy was not due to a conflict between its domestic and international objectives. In fact, the domestic construction industry would have welcomed an expansion in public works. Rather, the basic reason was that budget authorities had strong reservations about increasing the budget deficit.

Many observers believe that Japan achieved the objective of fiscal reconstruction in recent years. However, a significant part of the reduction in general account expenditures has been nothing more than a shifting of the burden to other sectors of the government. The apparent deficit reduction has been achieved largely by increasing the burden on the general public, mainly through an automatic tax increase, rather than by denying the vested interests of particular groups.

The second question raised at the outset was, who are the key actors in the budget-making process and how have their roles changed in recent years? An important new actor, the Rinchō, appeared during the early 1980s. Also, the elite LDP politicians have been transformed from mere pressure groups to budget coordinators. However, the MOF still controls the essential part of the budget by various technocratic measures, including (1) across-the-board restrictions, such as the deficit reduction objective and the ceiling; (2) complicated transactions between subsectors of public finance, such as the transfer from the general account to social security's special accounts; and (3) manipulation of tax revenue estimates. Consequently, political factors still play a minor role in budget making in Japan.

Needless to say, neither fiscal reconstruction nor expansion of domestic demand is an ultimate goal of public finance. The true task of the budget system is to react to the changing needs of society. The public sector must play a leading role in this in order to orient the economy toward domestic demand, especially in urban areas where improvements in social overhead capital are concerned. The present budget allocation system is quite rigid, however, particularly in the allocation of public works, and hence does not respond adequately to the needs of the society. Because of incrementalism in the budget-making process, bureaucratic sectionalism, and the tendency to avoid explicit political confrontations among various interest groups, it is extremely difficult to change the way the budget is allocated among the different areas of public works and among the different regions. Thus agriculture-related public works still retain a significant share while investment in urban areas remains at an unsatisfactory level.

It is not certain whether the government would consider making fundamental changes in the system to bring about a radical reallocation of public resources. Bureaucrats are apparently incapable of performing this task, which requires powerful coordinating capabilities. Although the LDP politicians have taken on the role of coordination, they have had to deal only with intraministerial affairs. Whether they will be able to handle interministerial conflicts of interest remains to be seen and will not be known for at least several more years.

Part III
Tax Reform

The Surprising Enactment of Tax Reform in the United States

Allen Schick

NEAR THE END of his comprehensive study of the federal income tax published in 1985, political scientist John Witte reviewed several pending reforms, including one to set up a three-rate tax structure, and concluded: *"There is nothing, absolutely nothing in the history or the . . . politics of the income tax that indicates that any of these schemes have the slightest hope of being enacted in the forms proposed."*[1] Barely one year after this prognosis appeared, Congress enacted the Tax Reform Act of 1986, arguably the most sweeping change in federal tax policy since the income tax was broadened during World War II. In what is probably a widely held view, journalists Jeffrey Birnbaum and Alan Murray characterized this law as a "legislative miracle that defied all the lessons of political science, logic, and history."[2]

In terms of the changes made in the tax laws and the loopholes it eliminated, the 1986 legislation certainly was extraordinary. The act (1) reduced individual income taxes from fourteen rates to three and lowered the maximum rate from 50 percent to 33 percent;[3] (2) shifted an estimated $120 billion in taxation over a five-year period from individuals to corporations, while lowering the top corporate tax rate from 46 percent to 34 percent; (3) eliminated the preferential tax rate on capital gains,

Elizabeth Wharton assisted in the preparation of this paper.

1. John F. Witte, *The Politics and Development of the Federal Income Tax* (University of Wisconsin Press, 1985), p. 380 (italics in original).

2. Jeffrey H. Birnbaum and Alan S. Murray, *Showdown at Gucci Gulch: Lawmakers, Lobbyists, and the Unlikely Triumph of Tax Reform* (Random House, 1987), p. 285.

3. The new tax structure's highest marginal rate was 28 percent, but because of a phaseout of certain deductions, taxpayers within a prescribed income range had an effective marginal rate of 33 percent. Above this income range, the effective marginal rate dropped back to 28 percent. In 1990 Congress lowered the effective marginal rate of taxpayers in the 33 percent range to 31 percent, and it also raised the marginal rate for certain high-income taxpayers to this level. However, because of the interaction of various provisions of the tax code, some taxpayers still pay effective marginal rates above the 31 percent level.

146   ALLEN SCHICK

taxing them at the same rate as ordinary income; (4) repealed or curtailed numerous tax preferences such as the investment tax credit, most tax shelters, deduction of state and local sales taxes, individual retirement accounts, and tax-exempt bonds; and (5) eliminated income taxes for an estimated 5 million–6 million low-income people.[4]

Tax reform might have been a miracle, but it was not a preordained one. If tax reform had been stymied at any one of the critical points in its passage through the Treasury Department, the White House, the House, the Senate, or the conference committee, explanations as to why it did not become law would abound. These would undoubtedly be centered on the reform's overambitious attempt to revamp the tax code and redistribute tax burdens. Because tax reform was enacted, political scientists generally treat it as a deviant case that fails to conform to the incremental model of American politics, which holds that policy changes tend to be small and predictable. Incremental change builds on previous developments; tax reform reversed them.[5] But even if the 1986 law is regarded as a deviant case, one can learn a great deal about the politics of taxation by studying its enactment. Like the scientists who studied a rare solar eclipse in 1919 to test Einstein's theory of relativity, observers can enhance their understanding of ordinary events by examining the extraordinary Tax Reform Act.

This chapter places the 1986 law in the context of previous tax legislation, revealing that tax reform was a direct outgrowth of heightened activity and conflict over tax policy in the preceding decade. The historical analysis suggests that were it not for the earlier legislation, there might have been no reform in 1986. An examination of the tactics used to advance the legislation in 1985 and 1986 concentrates on the House and the Senate, though a fuller account would have to cover activity in the Treasury and the White House as well. The legislative history demonstrates that a retreat from some of the legislative reforms

4. The 1986 reform was not the final word on tax legislation. In the few years since that law was enacted, additional changes have been made in tax laws. Some of the changes have modified important parts of the 1986 legislation (such as the marginal tax rates); others (such as those pertaining to deductions) have introduced new complexities into the tax code. Because of pressures to generate additional revenues or to reallocate the tax burden, it is likely that Congress will make further modifications in the coming years. Despite these changes, however, the basic structure of the 1986 reform has survived thus far.

5. In the field of budgeting, the theory of incrementalism is associated with the works of Aaron Wildavsky, especially, *The Politics of the Budgetary Process*, 4th ed. (Little, Brown, 1984).

introduced in the 1970s facilitated the movement of tax reform through Congress, and that some political adjustments eased the path to enactment. The disparity between the legislation's far-reaching changes in tax policy and its claims of neutrality are discussed, and the paper concludes with some reflections on the role of American political institutions in implementing major policy changes. The questions addresssed include: How did the division of political control between the Democratic and Republican parties and between the president and Congress advance the cause of reform? Are the strategies used in tax reform applicable to other issues and circumstances? What lessons and conclusions can be drawn from this case about the governability of the United States?

Hyperactive Tax Legislation

Before the mid-1970s, tax policy was often made by nondecision or inertia.[6] Major tax action was infrequent, as evidenced by the long intervals between the 1939, 1954, and 1969 overhauls of the internal revenue code. In the quarter-century after World War II, Congress tinkered with the tax laws and passed miscellaneous revenue bills each year, but these usually were narrow in scope.

Several factors discouraged frequent revision of the tax laws, including control of the tax-legislating process by the House Ways and Means Committee. Ways and Means, which initiated virtually all tax legislation in Congress, had no subcommittees, and its small staff was controlled by a powerful chairman. Members of the committee were typically recruited from safe seats so they could be relied upon to resist demands to revise the tax laws.[7] The steady rise in federal revenue due to sustained economic growth and inflation also inhibited frequent action in the postwar era. The government could finance its expanding activities without having to make major alterations in the tax laws.[8]

6. The concept of "nondecision" is discussed in Matthew A. Crenson, *The Un-Politics of Air Pollution: A Study of Non-Decisionmaking in the Cities* (Johns Hopkins University Press, 1971). It is applied to tax legislation in Allen Schick, *Congress and Money: Budgeting, Spending, and Taxing* (Washington: Urban Institute, 1980), chap. 12.

7. The role of the House Ways and Means Committee and its reform in the 1970s is discussed in Catherine E. Rudder, "Tax Policy: Structure and Choice," in Allen Schick, ed., *Making Economic Policy in Congress* (Washington: American Enterprise Institute for Public Policy Research, 1983), pp. 196–220.

8. Politics by inertia characterizes taxation in other countries as well. Rose and Karran write that tax policy is shaped by inertia: "Political inertia is the force that makes it possible for politicians to raise the minimum of tax revenue with the minimum

Since the mid-1970s, inertia has been an inadequate theory of tax politics. While it accounts for the bulk of growth in income tax revenue, inertia does not fit well with the extraordinary volume of tax legislation enacted in the dozen years between the Congressional Budget and Impoundment Control Act of 1974 and the Tax Reform Act of 1986. Leaving aside specialized legislation, such as measures pertaining to social security and energy policy, Congress enacted major changes in the tax laws in 1975, 1976, 1978, 1981, 1982, 1984, and 1986.[9] It is from the perspective of this series of laws that Richard Doernberg and Fred McChesney view the tax reform act as "hardly different from its predecessors except for the size of the legislation."[10]

This surge in legislative activity is reflected in the number of provisions of the internal revenue code affected by recent tax legislation. As might be expected, the 1986 law has had the broadest impact, revising all or part of 2,704 subsections of the code. But other laws have also had extremely wide scope.[11]

Increased legislative activity has been associated with the establishment of new tax expenditures.[12] Numerous tax expenditures were initiated during the early years of the income tax (1909-39) and in the period from World War II through the 1954 recodification of the internal

---

of political costs. . . . As long as tax revenue can be collected through the force of inertia, then no decisions are required of politicians." Although the authors wrote specifically of behavior in Britain, their analysis applies as well to other mature economies. Richard Rose and Terence Karran, *Taxation by Political Inertia: Financing the Growth of Government in Britain* (London: Allen and Unwin, 1987), p. 6.

9. These measures are discussed in Schick, *Congress and Money*, chap. 13.

10. Richard L. Doernberg and Fred S. McChesney, "Doing Good or Doing Well? Congress and the Tax Reform Act of 1986," *New York University Law Review*, vol. 62 (October 1987), p. 926.

11. In addition to the 2,704 subsections affected by the 1986 Tax Reform Act, 1,849 were affected by the Tax Reform Act of 1976; 664 by the Revenue Act of 1978; 483 by the Economic Recovery Tax Act of 1981; 530 by the Tax Equity and Fiscal Responsibility Act of 1982; 2,345 by the Deficit Reduction Act of 1984; and 231 by the Omnibus Budget Reconciliation Act of 1987. Harold Apolinsky, "The Changes Just Cost Money," *Washington Post*, April 6, 1986, p. C8; and correspondence with the author, July 20, 1988.

12. Tax expenditures are preferences that reduce federal revenue below the amounts that would be taken in by a "normal" tax system and provide benefits to recipients similar to those provided by direct expenditures. Credits and deductions are among the main forms of tax expenditures. Section 3(3) of the Congressional Budget Act defines tax expenditures as "revenue losses attributable to provisions of the Federal tax laws which allow special exclusion, exemption, or deduction from gross income or which provide a special credit, a preferential rate of tax, or a deferral of tax liability." *Congressional Budget Act Annotated*, Committee Print, Senate Committee on the Budget, 101 Cong. 2 sess. (Government Printing Office, 1990), p. 11.

revenue code. Many of these old provisions remain in effect. Only ten
tax expenditures were inaugurated between 1955 and 1974. Between
1975 and 1981, however, twenty-nine tax expenditures were added, and
many older ones were modified. According to Witte, more than half the
modifications made over the years to the tax expenditures in effect
before the tax reform occurred during 1970–81.[13]

Frequent action generated great volatility in tax policy. The investment tax credit, for example, was initiated in 1962, repealed in 1969,
reintroduced in 1971, expanded in 1975, 1977, and 1981, and repealed in
1986.[14] The capital gains tax has also followed a zigzag course in the
seventy years since a preferential rate was set for it in 1921. The
maximum tax on capital gains was lowered to 20 percent in 1981 (it had
once been about 50 percent), but the preferential rate for this type of
income was abolished in 1986, and the maximum was set as high as 33
percent.

Why has Congress been so active in tax matters, and why has tax
policy been so inconstant? To put the question another way: why did
inertia become unacceptable policy? Inertia is unacceptable under either
of two conditions: when it leads to more or less revenue than is wanted,
or when it results in an unsatisfactory distribution of the tax burden.
Both factors were at work in the decade before the 1986 tax reform.

Revenue Production

Major shortages or excesses of revenue are usually associated with
war and its aftermath. Throughout U.S. history, the federal government
has rarely raised income taxes in peacetime, yet it did so in 1982 and
again in 1984. These increases followed a series of equally unusual
measures that reduced the income tax yield during a period of historically
high deficits. It also is rare for the federal government to make revenue-
neutral changes in the tax laws, as it did in 1986.[15]

To explain these extraordinary enactments, recent tax legislation must be divided into three time periods: the late 1970s, 1981, and
1982-86. Differences in tax policy during these periods are apparent in

13. Witte, *Politics and Development,* table 15.2, p. 315.
14. Doernberg and McChesney, "Doing Good or Doing Well," p. 904.
15. Revenue neutrality refers to the estimates made at the time the tax reform
legislation was considered in Congress. Actual revenues might be higher or lower than
the estimated amounts.

Table 1. Estimated Revenue Effects Of Major Tax Acts, 1975–87[a]
Billions of dollars

	Estimated revenue effects				
Tax act	1st year	2nd year	3rd year	4th year	5th year
Tax Reduction Act, 1975	−22.8	...	...	...	...
Tax Reform Act, 1976	−15.7	−12.8	−6.8	−7.4	−6.2
Tax Reduction and Simplification Act, 1977	−2.6	−17.8	−13.8	...	...
Revenue Act, 1978	−19.3	−37.5	−44.2	−52.1	−58.0
Omnibus Reconciliation Act, 1980	3.6	2.5	4.2	7.0	11.1
Crude Oil Windfall Profit Tax Act, 1980	6.1	12.2	16.3	19.2	20.0
Economic Recovery Tax Act, 1981	−37.7	−92.7	−150.0	−199.2	−267.7
Tax Equity and Fiscal Responsibility Act, 1982[b]	18.0	37.7	42.7	51.8	63.9
Deficit Reduction Act, 1984	1.1	10.6	16.5	22.5	25.2
Consolidated Omnibus Budget Reconciliation Act, 1985	0.8	2.5	2.8	2.9	3.1
Tax Reform Act, 1986	11.5	−16.7	−15.1	8.0	12.0

Source: Joint Committee on Taxation.
a. The table covers general revenue; it does not include legislation earmarking revenue to the social security trust fund or other programs. These estimates were made by the Joint Committee on Taxation at the time the particular legislation was enacted. The estimates may vary from the actual effects of the tax measures.
b. Includes the revenue effect of compliance provisions.

table 1, which shows modest reductions in federal revenue enacted in the late 1970s, a gargantuan revenue cut voted in 1981, and substantial increases adopted in subsequent years. Despite its projected revenue neutrality, the 1986 legislation is included in the table because it is politically linked to the earlier tax laws.

By the late 1970s, high inflation had pushed millions of taxpayers into higher tax brackets. With annual inflation, as measured by the consumer price index, averaging close to 10 percent from 1974 through 1980, the average and marginal tax rates rose sharply for taxpayers at all income levels. Taxpayers earning half the median family income saw their average tax rate escalate from 2.2 percent in 1965 to 4.1 percent in 1975 and 6.5 percent in 1980. Similarly, families earning the median income saw their average tax rates rise from 7.1 percent in 1965 to 9.6 percent in 1975 and 11.7 percent in 1980. The trend in marginal rates also was sharply upward.

This spiral in tax rates raised individual income tax receipts from 9.8 percent of personal income in 1975 to 11.6 percent in 1981.[16] During

16. Tax Foundation, *Facts and Figures on Government Finance: 1988–1989 Edition* (Johns Hopkins University Press, 1988), table C42, p. 131.

these years, individual income tax receipts also climbed from 8.0 percent of the gross national product to a record high of 9.6 percent.[17]

In the face of these escalating tax burdens, Congress could no longer remain inactive. It reduced taxes in 1975, 1976, 1977, and 1978. The reductions were quite modest, however, and they did not fully offset the effects of inflation on high-income taxpayers. Budget deficits averaging about $60 billion a year evidently constrained Congress in the amount of relief it could provide. Small from the perspective of the 1980s, these deficits were considered to be dangerously high by the previous decade's budget makers. Trapped between pressure for tax reduction and deficit reduction, Congress tried to provide a little bit of each but failed to produce a satisfactory amount of either.

Ronald Reagan broke out of this trap by advocating policies that made tax and deficit reduction compatible, rather than antagonistic, objectives. Reagan ran on a platform that decried the upturn in tax burdens and embraced a supply-side view of the economy that saw tax reduction as a means of stimulating economic growth. The new president won enactment of massive tax cuts that slashed federal revenue by almost $40 billion in their first year and by an estimated $750 billion over a five-year period. Because future inflation was overestimated, the 1981 cuts overcompensated for inflation.[18] That was a welcome development for those conservatives who expected a reduction in federal revenue to exert downward pressure on federal spending.

As things turned out, taxes were cut much more than spending, resulting in enormous deficits after 1981. The deficit peaked at $221 billion in fiscal 1986, the year that tax reform was enacted. Regardless of its cause, the deficit required corrective action; a retreat to the policy of inertia was no longer appropriate. In any event, by indexing future individual income tax rates (beginning in 1985) to price changes, the 1981 law took away the government's "inflation dividend." Thereafter, under a policy of inertia, revenue would rise in real terms only to the extent that the economy grew in real terms.

Congress responded to high deficits by enacting tax increases in 1982 and 1984, but because it is generally harder to raise taxes than to lower

17. *Historical Tables, Budget of the United States Government: Fiscal Year 1989,* table 2.3, p. 29.
18. The 25 percent tax cut was spread over four calendar years, after which taxes were to be indexed to changes in the consumer price index. The CPI rose 12.5 percent in 1980 and 8.9 percent in 1981; it rose by 4 percent or less in each of the next three years. *Economic Report of the President, January 1989,* table B-61.

them, the additional money did not come close to replacing the lost revenue. Deepening conflict between the president and Congress over budget policies also impeded efforts to generate more funds. After 1981, congressional Democrats were able to block most of Reagan's cutback proposals, but they could not dislodge his opposition to tax increases. Relenting a bit in 1982, the president agreed to a "three-for-one" deal in which every dollar of revenue increase would be matched by three dollars of spending reductions. When the cuts fell short of this standard, Reagan stiffened his resistance to further tax increases.

Conflict over the appropriate fiscal response to massive deficits also stymied tax policy. With some experts and officials insisting that sizable tax increases were necessary to curtail the chronic budget deficit and others arguing that tax increases would only aggravate future deficits by damaging the economy, meaningful legislative action proved impossible to obtain.

This policy division was etched into the revenue-neutrality principle of the 1986 tax reform. Conservatives embraced revenue neutrality to prevent tax reform from being used to raise taxes. This rule thwarted many members of Congress who believed that first priority should be given to reducing the deficit.[19] Some liberals also favored revenue neutrality, seeing it as a way to encourage redistribution of the tax burden.

Distribution of the Tax Burden

First inertia and then legislative action made the distribution of the tax burden less acceptable in the decade before tax reform. During the stagflation of the late 1970s and early 1980s, tax burdens for many Americans rose even as their real income declined. But in responding to stagnant economic conditions and high inflation, Congress redistributed the tax burden in ways that deepened the perception that the income tax was unfair. To trace this development, it is again useful to divide tax legislation into the pre-1981, 1981, and 1982–86 time periods.

19. On March 4, 1986, fifty senators (half the total membership of the Senate) sent President Reagan a letter declaring that "until a firm, definite budget agreement has been reached between the Congress and the White House, we do not believe that tax reform should be considered or debated by the United States Senate." This letter was followed on April 10, 1986, with a "sense of the Senate" resolution, adopted by a 72–24 vote, that tax reform legislation should not be considered until a budget agreement had been reached by the president and Congress.

High inflation during the late 1970s coincided with weak economic growth and relatively small improvements in personal income. The rising income tax burden, which occurred when inflation pushed taxpayers into higher marginal tax brackets, combined with increases in social security taxes to leave one-earner families with declining real disposable income. In inflation-adjusted (1967) dollars, the median income of these families, after federal taxes, dropped from $7,743 in 1972 to $6,523 in 1981.[20] Congress sought to ease the burden when it reduced taxes in the late 1970s, but because deficits constrained the total tax reduction Congress could provide, the relief it distributed was limited.

Congress also faced escalating demands for tax relief to stimulate investment and capital formation. Within a fixed budget for tax reduction, every dollar returned to low- and middle-income taxpayers takes a dollar away from easing the burden for high-income investors and businesses. The demands to counter economic malaise by spurring investment were effective. In 1975 and 1976 Congress allocated a major portion of the reductions to lower-income taxpayers; it also closed some loopholes and established an earned income tax credit.[21] In 1978, however, Congress partly reversed course, approving legislation that favored investment by lowering capital gains taxes and the minimum tax on people claiming high deductions and exclusions. Because the 1978 tax reduction was proportional, taxpayers earning $100,000 a year received approximately three times the relief provided those earning only $25,000.[22]

These distributive choices resulted from the forced trade-off among competing tax reduction objectives, but they left taxpayers feeling unfairly burdened and business leaders complaining that the tax code was robbing the country of incentives for investment. Striking evidence of taxpayer discontent is available in public opinion trends. When the Advisory Commission on Intergovernmental Relations (ACIR) first surveyed Americans about taxes in 1972, only 19 percent of those interviewed rated the federal income tax as the worst tax; by 1980, that number had reached 36 percent.[23] Obviously, tax relief in the 1970s did not ease discontent over distribution of the federal tax burden.

20. Tax Foundation, *Facts and Figures*, table C45, p. 134.
21. See *Congressional Quarterly Almanac, 1975*, vol. 31 (1976), p. 95, and *Congressional Quarterly Almanac, 1976*, vol. 32 (1977), pp. 41–43.
22. See *Congressional Quarterly Almanac, 1978*, vol. 34 (1979), p. 223.
23. Respondents were asked to compare the federal income tax, the state income tax, the state sales tax, and the local property tax. See Advisory Commission on Intergovernmental Relations, *Changing Public Attitudes on Governments and Taxes, 1987* (GPO, 1987), tables 5–8, pp. 16–21.

With help from supply-side logic, the Reagan administration and Congress wriggled out of the policy dilemma by cutting taxes so deeply in 1981 that substantial relief could be distributed to all income classes and to business. But because so many tax breaks were given to high-income persons and corporations, many Americans still saw the federal tax system as unfair. Despite the 25 percent across-the-board reduction in individual income taxes phased in by the 1981 legislation, 38 percent of those responding to the 1985 ACIR survey rated the federal income tax as the worst tax. (Other polls, such as those conducted by the Gallup Poll and the Roper Organization, showed some moderation in taxpayer discontent in the mid-1980s, compared with the high levels recorded in the late 1970s.)[24]

Public opinion did not play a prominent role in producing tax reform. There was no ground swell of support for reform, nor strong confidence that changing the rules would lead to a fairer, simpler tax system. When Ronald Reagan beat the drums for reform in 1985, he found Americans generally inattentive to his message. Members of Congress were not besieged by volumes of mail demanding tax reform.

Nonetheless, public opinion shaped tax policy in two important ways. Americans did not want to pay higher taxes; most also thought that businesses and upper-income individuals were not paying their fair share. The first attitude precluded use of tax reform to generate additional revenue; the second opened the door to using reform to redistribute the tax burden from individuals to corporations. The 1981 tax cuts were followed by oversized budget deficits averaging close to $200 billion a year in the 1982–86 period. These deficits concerned many Americans but, paradoxically, as the deficit grew larger (from $128 billion in fiscal 1982 to $221 billion in fiscal 1986), taxpayers were less willing to have their taxes raised to ease the budget problem. Table 2 indicates that the percentage of those who thought that the government should increase taxes to reduce the deficit dropped from 31 percent in 1983 to 19 percent in 1985.

Americans felt quite differently, however, about the taxes paid by corporations. In 1981 business obtained accelerated depreciation, a new research and development credit, the opportunity to make money by selling tax credits, and numerous other tax benefits. High-income taxpayers won reductions in the capital gains tax and in the maximum

24. James M. Verdier, "The Prospects for Tax Stability," in *Tax Notes*, vol. 35 (April 13, 1987), pp. 171–78; and H&R Block, Inc., *The American Public and the Federal Income Tax System*, June 1986.

Table 2. Public Attitudes about Tax Increases as a Means of Reducing the Deficit, Selected Opinion Poll Questions, 1982–85

Question	Agree/yes (percent)
Should an increase in corporate income taxes be very seriously considered to reduce the deficit? (Roper, 1984)	78
Should an increase in personal income taxes be very seriously considered to reduce the deficit? (Roper, 1984)	24
To cut the size of the deficit, would you favor putting a minimum tax on corporate income? (Harris, 1985)	73
Do you think the government should increase taxes to reduce the budget deficit? (ABC/*Post*)	
February 1982	23
January 1983	31
January 1984	25
January 1985	19
Are you worried enough about the federal budget deficit to be willing to have your income taxes increased to reduce it? (NBC News, 1985)	
September 1984	43
October 1984	40
January 1985	35

Source: "Opinion Roundup," *Public Opinion*, vol. 8 (February–March 1985), pp. 26–27.

tax on unearned income, as well as new opportunities to shelter income from taxation.[25] A few years after these preferences took effect, reformers produced a series of widely publicized studies showing that some major corporations had paid little or no taxes.[26] Still other data showed that the yield from the corporate income tax had declined sharply relative to individual income taxes and the gross national product.[27]

25. The provisions of the 1981 tax legislation are detailed in *Congressional Quarterly Almanac, 1981*, vol. 37 (1982), pp. 91–103.

26. The most prominent of these, issued by Citizens for Tax Justice, showed that in at least one year between 1981 and 1983, 128 out of 250 large and profitable companies paid no federal income taxes whatsoever. See Robert S. McIntyre, *Corporate Income Taxes in the Reagan Years: A Study of Three Years of Legalized Corporate Tax Avoidance* (Washington: Citizens for Tax Justice, 1984).

27. In 1950, the corporate tax yielded two-thirds of the revenue produced by the tax on individual incomes. By 1980 the relative yield had dropped to only one-quarter of the individual income tax, and by 1985 it had declined (partly because of the 1981 legislation) to less than one-fifth. The ratio to GNP showed a similar trend, with corporate income tax revenue falling from 3.9 percent of GNP in 1950 to 2.4 percent in 1980 and to 1.6 percent in 1985. According to some studies, reduced profitability of corporations, not changes in the tax laws, is the principal cause of declining corporate taxes. See Alan J. Auerbach and James M. Poterba, "Why Have Corporate Tax Revenues Declined?" in Lawrence H. Summers, ed., *Tax Policy and the Economy*, vol. 1 (MIT Press, 1987), pp. 1–28.

These trends in corporate taxation affected public opinion, as the data in table 3 reveal. By the mid-1980s, 59 percent felt that the federal tax system was basically unfair, an equal percentage felt that people whose income came from salaries paid too much in taxes, and 75 percent thought that the tax system was unfair to ordinary working men and women. These attitudes undercut support for increasing personal income taxes to reduce the deficit. But while most Americans were unwilling to be taxed more, they did favor additional taxes on business. More than three-quarters of those polled felt that serious consideration should be given to an increase in corporate taxes, and 73 percent favored a minimum tax on corporate income.

The boomerang effect of the 1981 tax legislation on the deficit and public opinion led to modest tax increases on corporations in 1982 and 1984, including repeal of some of the recently established tax breaks.[28] The 1986 tax reform took an even bigger step in this direction, shifting an estimated $120 billion in tax burdens (over a five-year period) from individuals to corporations. Viewed from this perspective, the 1986 law was enacted not because it reformed the tax system but because it redistributed the tax burden.

While the 1986 legislation deviated from previous tax policy, it exemplified one of the key features of incrementalism—the capacity to make remedial adjustments in policy. The series of tax laws enacted in 1975–84 created the economic and political conditions that spurred adoption of tax reform.

Tax Reform versus Political Reform

Tax reform depended not only on past legislation but on institutions and procedures that enabled Congress to act on such a far-reaching measure. As noted at the outset, the tax-legislating process was once engineered to discourage action in both the House and the Senate (by virtue of the constitutional requirement that revenue measures be initiated in the House). The surge in legislative activity in 1975–86 was at least partly due to changes in House rules that opened up the process

28. The Tax Equity and Fiscal Responsibility Act of 1982 (TEFRA) repealed or trimmed back some provisions of the 1981 tax law, including the "safe harbor leasing" rule, which allowed businesses to sell unused tax breaks, and the provision that allowed corporations to take advantage of both accelerated depreciation and tax credits. The Deficit Reduction Act of 1984 delayed rules liberalizing the taxation of leased equipment, raised taxes on the insurance industry, and curtailed many other preferences.

Table 3. Public Attitudes toward Federal Income Taxes, Selected Opinion Poll Questions, 1972–87

Question	Agree/yes (percent)
Do you think federal income taxes are the worst tax—the least fair?[a]	
March 1972	19
May 1980	36
May 1985	38
June 1987	30
Do you think our system of federal taxes is basically unfair? (*Los Angeles Times*, 1985)	59
Is it your impression that you pay about the right amount of taxes compared to other taxpayers? (*Los Angeles Times*, 1985)	59
What I really object to about the federal income tax system is that I have to pay more than my fair share. (Yankelovich/IRS, 1984)	43
The present tax system benefits the rich and is unfair to the ordinary working man and woman. (ABC/*Post*, 1985)	75
Do you feel corporations are undertaxed? (Yankelovich/*Time*, 1984)	52
Middle income families pay too much in income taxes. (Roper, 1985)	69
People whose income all comes from salary or wages pay too much in income taxes. (Roper, 1985)	59
Lower income families pay too much. (Roper, 1985)	57

Source: "Opinion Roundup," *Public Opinion*, vol. 8 (February–March 1985), pp. 22–23.
a. Responses to the question: Which do you think is the worst tax—that is, the least fair?" Response choices: federal income tax, state income tax, state sales tax, local property tax, and "don't know." Source: *Changing Public Attitudes on Governments and Taxes*, Advisory Commission on Intergovernmental Relations, 1987.

to greater outside influence. These political reforms weakened the Ways and Means Committee as a "control committee" by requiring it to establish subcommittees,[29] divesting it of its role in appointing Democratic members of House committees, requiring committee meetings to be open (except when committee members formally voted to close them), modifying the closed rule (no amendments) under which tax legislation was brought to the House, establishing procedures for unseating committee chairmen, enlarging committee and member staffs, and expanding the Ways and Means Committee from twenty-five to thirty-seven members.

These reforms were part of a series of moves in the late 1960s and early 1970s to democratize the House and give rank-and-file members a greater voice in its operations. Opening up the tax-legislating system

29. The concept of "control committee" was introduced by David R. Mayhew in *Congress: The Electoral Connection* (Yale University Press, 1974).

was a prominent objective of reformers who chafed at the power of the Ways and Means Committee to keep certain matters, such as the oil depletion allowance, off the floor. Many of the young Democrats who entered the House after Watergate were wary of the comfortable bipartisanship practiced by senior Democrats and Republicans on Ways and Means, and they wanted the committee to resemble the House more closely in its makeup and to reflect the views of House Democrats in its actions.[30]

The reforms shifted power from the committee to the floor and from senior Democrats to the party caucus. There was some enhancement of the role of the party leadership, especially in making committee appointments, and some potential for leaders to have a greater voice in substantive policy. But at the time the reforms were implemented, junior Democrats were the winners, and they were in no mood to depose one set of bosses only to have another set emerge.

Few changes were made in the Senate, but its tax-legislating process was already quite open. The Senate Finance Committee frequently turned House-passed tax measures into "Christmas trees," providing benefits to voters by adding revenue-losing provisions. This practice continued on the floor where, unhindered by a closed rule, senators vied to add tax breaks.

With the House reformed and the Senate behaving as usual, the prospect of genuine tax reform was bleak. "The requirements for making responsible tax policy," political scientist Catherine Rudder concluded, "seem to run counter to open, decentralized legislative procedures, especially when organizing forces, such as strong political parties, that can facilitate cohesion are lacking."[31] Political reform was thought to hinder tax reform by opening the process to the influence of lobbyists and others who vigilantly promoted tax benefits for their clients. Where the Ways and Means Committee once considered tax legislation in private, with only members and a few staff aides (including key Treasury officials) present, the process was now open to numerous "Washington representatives" who kept close watch on the proceedings and often prepared amendments considered in markup. Rank-and-file committee members were also more active and independent by virtue of a steep increase in staff resources. The Ways and Means staff ballooned from

30. The 1970s reforms are discussed in Randall Strahan, *New Ways and Means: Reform and Change in a Congressional Committee* (University of North Carolina Press, 1990).

31. Rudder, "Tax Policy," p. 196.

twenty-four in 1970 to ninety-nine in 1979; Senate Finance staff grew from sixteen to sixty-seven.[32] There also were steep increases in the staffs of individual members, some of whom assigned legislative aides to work on tax matters.

To make matters worse, legislative reform was accompanied by a huge influx of political action committees—conduits for money and influence—into the political process. The number of PACs soared from 600 in 1974 to more than 2,500 in 1980 and more than 4,000 in 1986, while their contributions to congressional candidates escalated from $12.5 million at the start of this period to more than $132 million a decade later.[33] Members of the Ways and Means and Finance committees were among the leading recipients of PAC money.[34]

The implication of political reform for tax legislation was evident in 1981, when a bidding war between the Republican White House and the Democratic majority on Ways and Means led to the enactment of tax benefits far more generous than the beneficiaries had expected to obtain. Operating in a legislative fishbowl and buffeted by incessant pressure from tax lobbyists, the Ways and Means Committee could not perform its historic role of protecting the Treasury against revenue losses. Instead, it joined the bidding and produced legislation that drained the government of hundreds of billions of dollars over the next five years. To deflect pressure on it and to minimize its culpability for raising taxes, the committee refused to act on tax legislation in 1982 until after the Senate had passed its own measure. The House thus went to conference without having considered a tax bill of its own. This approach eased the political problem, but it was no model for legislating tax reform.

If political conditions were not favorable, how did Congress manage to revamp the tax code in 1986? Part of the answer is that long before the reform legislation was considered, the House had already retreated from some of the institutional reforms adopted in the 1970s. While the Ways and Means Committee was compelled to establish subcommittees, it never used them for major tax legislation. Moreover, after using permissive rules for floor consideration of some tax measures, the House returned to restrictive practices that permitted only a few floor amendments, typically a substitute offered by the minority and one or two amendments on politically sensitive matters.

32. Norman J. Ornstein, Thomas E. Mann, and Michael J. Malbin, *Vital Statistics on Congress: 1987–1988* (Washington: Congressional Quarterly, 1987), pp. 147–48.

33. Ornstein and others, *Vital Statistics,* pp. 103–04.

34. Birnbaum and Murray, *Showdown at Gucci Gulch,* p. 180.

Another part of the answer is that political reform was at work in 1985 and 1986, but after its damaging effects became apparent, the Ways and Means and Finance committees reverted to prereform behavior. Both committees began markup of the tax legislation in a manner that permitted rank-and-file members full opportunity to shape the measure. The results of this permissive approach clearly demonstrated that, left to their own wills, the two committees would retain or add loopholes and might create an even more unfair tax system than the one already in place. In the Ways and Means Committee, the turning point came after approval of a provision, opposed by the chairman, that would have granted tax breaks to banks. The turning point in the Finance Committee came after a series of votes adding billions of dollars in tax preferences. After these anti-tax reform votes, the chairmen took charge of their committees, cast aside some of the constraints of political reform, and embarked on a course of action that eventuated in tax reform.

When the chairmen intervened, tax reform was transformed from "the bill that nobody wanted" into "the bill that wouldn't die." It might have died, however, if it had not been insulated from political pressure, if the chairmen had not vigorously pushed the legislation through their committees, if the Senate had not changed its behavior on tax legislation, or if the Democratic and Republican leaders had not coalesced in support of the measure. These developments amount to what might be termed the new politics of taxation.

Closing Up the Process

At key points in the process, the Ways and Means Committee suspended markups and relied on small, less formal, groups to make decisions. The full committee was usually convened to get a status report on developments or to ratify the decisions made in private. The private sessions not only insulated members from outside pressure; they also significantly reduced the number of participants.

Although Ways and Means began with closed markups, hordes of lobbyists camped outside the committee room still put heavy pressure on members. Birnbaum and Murray portray the political linkage of the members inside and the lobbyists outside:

> Although they were closed out of the markup, these denizens of the hallway still made their presence felt. Many of the committee members worked hand-in-hand with certain favored lobbyists. . . . Sometimes,

a representative would walk out of the hearing room, crook a finger in the direction of a lobbyist in the hallway, and then disappear for a few minutes into a back room for a strategy session. Many of the committee members, in fact, eagerly became the standard bearers for issues that lobbyists pushed.[35]

Not only were the lobbyists too close, but attention by the media was so sustained and intense that the closed sessions held no secrets. It did not take long for votes on controversial matters to be reported to waiting journalists and lobbyists. To diffuse the pressure and attention, Democratic Chairman Dan Rostenkowski divided the committee into small working groups and assigned each group a revenue target for the items it was to deal with. The working groups operated by consensus, in contrast to the full committee, which relied on formal votes to settle matters. The chairman also took care to stack the working groups with loyal members who could be counted on to support his objectives. These small groups received much less attention than the formal markups; though their deliberations were hardly a secret to affected interests, their informality made it possible to work out compromises while avoiding direct confrontation between the reformers and those who wanted to protect particular tax breaks. The working groups transformed the markup into a procedure for endorsing or fine-tuning the previously decided matters.

Secrecy also became the practice in the Senate Finance Committee, but only after an abortive start that nearly torpedoed tax reform altogether. At the outset, the sessions were public, and the proceedings were piped into a large Senate auditorium where the overflow audience was seated. But after a series of markups during which about $30 billion in tax breaks were added to the draft measure, Republican Chairman Bob Packwood suspended these meetings. Within a few days, however, he was meeting privately with a small group of senators who were willing to close loopholes in order to get substantially lower tax rates. It was at these meetings that tax reform was revived and the basic shape of the legislation that would pass the Senate hammered out. The secrecy of these negotiations—other members of the Finance Committee were unaware of the progress being made—united the small band of reformers with a common mission that sheltered them from outside influence. Deals were hatched in private that could not have been made in public,

35. Birnbaum and Murray, *Showdown at Gucci Gulch*, pp. 121–22.

but when the work was done, the media and tax experts were so captivated by the dramatic turnaround and the starkly lower tax rates that the details mattered less than the whole.

When the full committee was reconvened, it spent less than two days ratifying the package. One of its first items of business was to adopt a revenue-neutrality rule that made it exceedingly difficult for the twenty members of the committee to change what the small group had agreed to in private. With this rule in place, the committee quickly completed its work, though it did make a few adjustments to accommodate oil and gas interests and a few other concerns.

The most important point at which the process was shut off from public view occurred in conference. After the House and Senate conferees had reached a bill-threatening impasse, veteran Senator Russell Long urged the two chairmen to "get together by themselves and come up with a proposal that we all can then consider."[36] The ploy worked, though not without some moments during which the whole enterprise seemed doomed to failure. When Rostenkowski and Packwood presented a summary of their agreement—the actual text of the bill would not be available until some weeks later—one of the Senate conferees sought to postpone final action on the ground that the measure had been written in secrecy. Treasury Secretary James A. Baker III, who participated in this meeting of Senate conferees as well as in many other legislative discussions on the bill, defended the extraordinary procedures used to work out the tax legislation. "We saw what happened in this committee when we tried to markup a tax bill in public. If we hadn't gone into back-room sessions, you wouldn't have ever gotten a bill."[37]

The closed doors kept more than reporters and lobbyists out; they also excluded most members of the Ways and Means and Finance committees. In the course of producing passable legislation, the number of participants steadily narrowed. Both committees began by marking up the bill in plenary session; when this failed, both turned to small groups to achieve consensus. In conference, both delegated authority to their chairmen to negotiate a final agreement.

The Unreformed Chairmen

It was not only at the conference stage that the chairmen dominated the process. After a hesitant start in which Rostenkowski and Packwood

36. Birnbaum and Murray, *Showdown at Gucci Gulch*, p. 268.
37. Birnbaum and Murray, *Showdown at Gucci Gulch*, p. 278.

lost control of their committees, the two chairmen took the initiative to salvage the legislation and assemble a winning coalition. The early markups in the House seemed to confirm Rudder's observation that in the postreform era "the chairman no longer has the tools to control Ways and Means. . . . The chairman now has little to offer members as inducements to cooperate."[38] Ways and Means was splintered into subcommittees, staff resources were amply available to individual members, the chairman was deposable by vote of House Democrats, and committee members came from more varied backgrounds and valued their independence. Rostenkowski could not command the committee the way Wilbur Mills did in his time. But he—and Packwood in Senate Finance—could still lead by using the resources at their command.

When Rostenkowski and Packwood lost in committee, they made effective use of one of their few remaining powers—the power to decide when the committee would meet. The time between meetings was used to corral support for tax reform, with each chairman using the tax benefits of the legislation as inducements to wavering committee colleagues. The two men behaved very much as chairmen did in prereform times, except that the favors they doled out were much bigger this time around. They had to up the ante both because the stakes were so large and because independent-minded members could demand quite a lot in return for their support.

Each chairman leveraged his power in his own way. Though their personal deportment was quite different, their actions were remarkably alike. Rostenkowski was the friendly bully, storming into colleagues' offices, demanding or pleading for their support, and making no bones about his willingness to pay for it. He treated tax reform, Birnbaum and Murray observe, just "like any other tax bill. Deals had to be cut to keep the special interests from overwhelming the effort; votes had to be paid for with favors and special tax breaks."[39] Schooled in the rough-and-tumble of Chicago politics, Rostenkowski was unabashed about trafficking for votes. If he asked for and got a colleague's support, that person would be remembered when the final details of the tax bill were settled; if he asked and was turned down, that person would know that the chairman kept score.

To make a deal, Rostenkowski typically did the work himself. He understood that votes had to be obtained one at a time. By dint of

38. Rudder, "Tax Policy," p. 204.
39. Birnbaum and Murray, *Showdown at Gucci Gulch*, p. 136.

personal contact, Rostenkowski won the loyalty of committee members and the control he sought. This loyalty paid off when Ways and Means Democrats voted with the chairman even when they disagreed with his position.[40]

Packwood was less comfortable about trading for votes, but he was willing to make concessions to keep Finance Committee members happy. Before the committee began markup, he met each member individually to "find out what they needed in the way of tax breaks to win their support for a bill. . . . He wanted to buy tax reform by pleasing his members with giveaways."[41] But because he was not sufficiently specific about what he wanted from them in return, the more concessions Packwood made, the more his colleagues wanted. When markup started, Packwood found that most committee members were not yet committed to genuine reform.

After he discarded the draft legislation used in markup and came up with an option that traded tax breaks for steeply lower rates, Packwood shifted from an individual to a group approach to build support for the measure. The dynamics of group reinforcement encouraged the small band of reformers to give up some of their tax preferences, though they held on to others that they cared about. The enthusiasm of the small group carried over to the full committee and enabled Packwood to steer tax reform through it.

In pushing for reform, Rostenkowski and Packwood had a lot to work with. Their prime assets were general rules (such as the deduction of state and local taxes), which apply to a broad class of taxpayers, and "transition rules," which are narrowly drawn to benefit a few taxpayers, in some cases even a single person or corporation. The general rules were the big concessions made at all stages of the process, beginning with the White House's reworking of the recommendations issued by Treasury and continuing through House and Senate action. There were many of these concessions, and they are reflected in the numerous preferences contained in the reformed code.

One need only compare the politicized version enacted into law with Treasury's original politics-free proposal to measure the high price of

40. Near the end of the markup, a contentious issue arose in which the chairman appeared to be on the losing side. Representative Charles Rangel, a ranking Democrat on Ways and Means, backed Rostenkowski, saying: "Mr. Chairman, we've got the votes but you're our leader—what do you want us to do?" Rostenkowski won. Quoted in Birnbaum and Murray, *Showdown at Gucci Gulch,* p. 150.
    41. Birnbaum and Murray, *Showdown at Gucci Gulch,* p. 192.

reform.[42] For example, the original Treasury proposal would have taxed some fringe benefits (such as a portion of the health insurance premiums paid by employers), while the enacted version made no significant changes in this area. Similarly, a Treasury proposal to limit deduction of charitable contributions was deleted during congressional action. The surviving (and new) tax breaks violated tax reform's emphasis on fairness and simplicity, but the legislation would not have become law without them. The trade-off between rates and breaks limited the dollar value of the general concessions that could be offered. As a consequence, not all members could protect their preferences, and some coveted provisions fell by the wayside. The bill devised by the Ways and Means Committee and passed by the House would have continued the deduction of all state and local taxes. However, the conference committee decided to eliminate this deduction in order to generate sufficient revenues.

The chairmen had another means of rewarding supporters of tax reform: they inserted transition rules into the legislation, usually after the measure had been approved by their committees or the conference. These rules originated as a protection for certain taxpayers who had acted on the basis of provisions in old tax laws from changes made in new ones. In recent practice, however, transition rules have provided preferential treatment to influential taxpayers, including some who have not been harmed by revisions in the tax laws. According to official estimates, $10.6 billion of transition rules were written into the 1986 Tax Reform Act. Most reformers considered these concessions a small price to pay for the major changes that were enacted.[43]

The favors dispensed in transition rules are similar to those granted in prereform days by "members' bills." In the past, numerous members' bills, each one benefiting a particular taxpayer, were enacted each year. Separate bills all but disappeared in the 1980s, but the practice of providing relief to particular taxpayers has been institutionalized in the transition rules. These rules have several political advantages that account for their extensive use in the tax reform legislation. First, by consolidating them with tax reform, a direct relationship was established between supporting the measure and obtaining the relief. Second,

42. See Charles E. McLure, Jr., and George R. Zodrow, "Treasury and the Tax Reform Act of 1986: The Economics and Politics of Tax Reform," *Journal of Economic Perspectives*, vol. 1 (Summer 1987), pp. 37–58.

43. Some estimates of the revenue loss from these rules range up to $30 billion. See a lengthy series of articles on the transition rules: Donald J. Bartlett and James B. Steele, "The Great Tax Giveaway," *Philadelphia Inquirer*, April 10–16, 1988.

transition rules were controlled by the chairmen; they usually decided who got them and who did not. Third, because of the vast scope of the tax reform legislation, many more benefits could be distributed through transition rules than would have been possible through separate members' bills.

The chairmen put most of the transition rules into the legislation on the basis of requests from committee colleagues and others in Congress. Birnbaum and Murray report that after Rostenkowski warned colleagues at a critical meeting that, "as chairman, he would decide who got—and who didn't get—transition rules," he and staff aide "Rob Leonard sat with a stack of papers and a telephone . . . dispensing more than $5 billion in special transition-rule favors. 'What do you need?' the chairman asked each member."[44] The practice was similar in the Senate, where the "Finance Committee chairman . . . [came] to the floor with a kind of slush fund under his control for the purpose of dispensing transition rules. . . . Every time Packwood ventured onto the Senate floor, his colleagues stuffed pieces of paper into his jacket pocket, with additional requests for transition rules."[45]

Transition rules, broad concessions in the tax legislation, and control of committee meetings gave Rostenkowski and Packwood the capacity to push reform through Congress. The process was not what political reformers had in mind in the 1970s when they weakened committee chairmen. In the contest with political reform, tax reform won.

The Reformed Senate

While it was necessary to roll back some political reforms, reverting to old legislative patterns probably would have doomed the legislation. In the past, even if the House had tried to reform the tax code, the effort would have been compromised by the Senate's proclivity to load the measure with additional tax breaks. Behaving in this manner "throughout the postwar period, the Senate . . . consistently increased the net tax reduction of House revenue bills."[46] The Senate's revenue losers often were in the form of loopholes that made the tax code less fair and more complex.

Almost ten years to the day before the Senate passed the Tax Reform Act of 1986, it had taken up another measure to reform the tax system.

44. Birnbaum and Murray, *Showdown at Gucci Gulch*, p. 146.
45. Birnbaum and Murray, *Showdown at Gucci Gulch*, p. 240.
46. Witte, *Politics and Development*, p. 209.

What emerged in the Tax Reform Act of 1976 was a code even more rife with special provisions. The measure was shepherded through the Senate by the legendary Russell Long, then the chairman of the Finance Committee, who expressed his disdain for tax reform: "I have always felt that tax reform is a change in the tax law that I favor, or if it is the other man defining tax reform, it is a change in the tax law that he favors."[47] Through more than six weeks of floor debate (interrupted by some other business) and more than 125 roll call votes, Senate reformers battled to purge the 1976 legislation of many special interest provisions. They lost most of the key votes, including the very last one, which would have deleted the word "reform" from the title of the bill on the grounds that the legislation "retain[s] some of the most notorious features of an unpopular Tax Code."[48]

The outcome was different in 1986 because in the preceding decade the Senate had gradually altered its behavior toward tax legislation. From a body willing to approve just about any tax break proposed by members of the Finance Committee, as well as many offered on the floor by other senators, it had transformed into one concerned about the effect of lost revenue on the budget deficit. An early sign of this reversal appeared in 1978 when the Senate, on a procedural motion, voted to eliminate the federal deduction for state and local gasoline taxes. In 1981, however, the Senate generally reverted to its old habit of approving tax breaks, adopting fifteen floor amendments that would have reduced federal revenue and only one that would have increased it. But the Senate also rejected a dozen proposed decreases in what often were party line votes.

The real turnaround came in 1982 when the Senate took the lead in devising a package of revenue increases and spending cutbacks to lower the burgeoning budget deficit. As reported earlier, the House Ways and Means Committee refused to even consider any tax increase until the Senate had acted. Casting aside its traditional role as a grantor of tax reductions, the Senate Finance Committee recommended $98 billion in tax increases over a three-year period. The bill occasioned many fewer floor amendments than had been the case in other recent tax legislation, and more than three-quarters of those offered were rejected. The Senate did not position itself for the conference with the House by loading the tax bill with numerous revenue-losing provisions.

47. *Congressional Record,* June 16, 1976, p. 18553.
48. *Congressional Record,* August 6, 1976, p. 26193.

The Senate continued to act with restraint in 1984 when it approved tax increases of $47 billion over three years. The Senate version would have added almost as much revenue as the House bill had. Though it did trim about $1 billion from the new revenue recommended by the Finance Committee, once again the Senate considered relatively few floor amendments. Senators were caught in a dilemma: if they proposed revenue increases, they would be attacked for raising taxes; if they proposed revenue losses, they would be criticized for adding to the budget deficit. In what proved to be a harbinger of 1986 action on tax legislation, a few senators tried to escape this predicament by proposing tax increases and deductions that offset each other.

With the 1982 and 1984 precedents, the Senate considered the 1986 tax reform under procedures that made it exceedingly difficult to amend the measure on the floor. Not only did the principle of revenue neutrality rule out amendments that would have cut taxes, but a bloc of senators backed Chairman Packwood's opposition to floor changes. While Packwood did retreat from this posture in the end, no tax reductions he opposed were approved. In fact, at least a half-dozen of the floor amendments had offsetting revenue gains and losses, and another three settled for "sense of the Senate" declarations in lieu of lower taxes.

Senate restraint has been partly institutionalized in the congressional budget process and in the Gramm-Rudman-Hollings deficit reduction law. The former has a procedure, known as reconciliation, for directing congressional committees to report legislation adjusting federal revenue or spending to meet budget targets; the latter has a deficit-neutral rule that bars Senate action that would cause the deficit to increase above the budgeted level.[49] Significantly, this provision does not apply to the House. While these institutional arrangements have undoubtedly influenced Senate behavior, concern about massive budget deficits has also narrowed the Senate's options. If deficits were to abate, or if the Senate were to become less concerned about them, it might revert to its traditional behavior and take an active role in undoing tax reform.

Taking the Parties Out by Putting Them In

The Republican and Democratic parties did not have formal roles in tax reform, but party identifications and positions were essential to the

49. The Senate can waive this Gramm-Rudman-Hollings constraint by a three-fifths vote, but it has proved difficult to obtain this extraordinary majority on controversial matters.

success of this legislation. Tax reform would not have been enacted if Republican and Democrat leaders had withdrawn to the sidelines or if they had fought over the basic shape of the policy. The parties had to be involved in tax reform, but in ways that did not allow partisanship to block progress.

When Ronald Reagan embraced the idea of tax reform in 1984, Democrats had a majority in the House while Republicans controlled the Senate and the White House. Although party lines were not always clear, the Democrats generally gave priority to reducing the burden on low-income taxpayers, while the Republicans sought lower marginal tax rates. The Republicans tended to favor tax subsidies that would stimulate investment and capital formation; the Democrats were concerned that the bulk of these advantages went to the wealthy.

Despite these differences, the parties made tax reform a bipartisan issue. In its early stages, tax reform was embodied in two remarkably similar measures: a bill sponsored by Democrats Bill Bradley and Richard Gephardt, and one introduced by Republicans Jack Kemp and Robert Kasten. The sponsors of these bills were relatively junior members of Congress; hence Republican and Democratic support for tax reform emerged without the matter becoming a party issue.

Because of their junior rank, these legislators could not do much to advance tax reform beyond the introductory stage. President Reagan, however, elevated tax reform to political prominence by announcing a high-level review in his 1984 State of the Union message. At the time, the president's commitment to tax reform was derided by those who noted that the report of the review was to be filed after that year's presidential and congressional elections. As things turned out, the delay protected tax reform from election-year partisanship.

Reform got a vital bipartisan boost on May 28, 1985, the day President Reagan unveiled his plan in a prime-time television address. Following the president's speech, Rostenkowski presented the Democratic response. As one whose career had long revolved around party politics, Rostenkowski might have been expected to lambaste the Republican position or sharpen party differences by offering a Democratic alternative. Instead, his televised speech promised

a great deal of Democratic support. . . . A Republican President has joined the Democrats in Congress to try to redeem this long-standing commitment to a tax system that's simple and fair. If we work together with good faith and determination, this time the people may win. This time I really think we can get tax reform.[50]

Bipartisan cooperation did temporarily break down in the House when most Republicans voted against the measure reported by the Ways and Means Committee. But a sufficient number of Republicans were whipped back into line by President Reagan, who made a rare appearance on Capitol Hill to persuade party colleagues to keep the measure alive. The bipartisan spirit persisted through Senate Finance Committee consideration of the bill, with Republican chairman Packwood working closely with Democratic members to fashion a consensus.

In retrospect, the fact that the House and Senate were controlled by opposite parties gave the measure an advantage. Tax reform avoided being too closely identified with one or the other party. Although the party division between the two houses complicated matters in conference, when Rostenkowski and Packwood announced agreement on a final measure, not only had the House and Senate resolved their differences, but Democrats and Republicans had done so as well.

Bipartisanship was one contribution the parties made to the cause; another was endorsement by party leaders of positions long associated with the opposing parties. James Verdier has pointed out that the prospect of substantial change is enhanced when the leaders of one party accept key political and ideological views of the other party.[51] Some of the policy reversals in the tax reform legislation were truly astounding:

—A Republican president embraced increases of more than $20 billion a year in taxes levied on corporations; congressional Democrats accepted a neutrality rule that precluded the use of tax reform to generate additional revenue.

—Democratic leaders came out in favor of steep reductions in marginal tax rates on high-income people; the Republican plan proposed to make the tax code more progressive and to remove millions of low-income people from the tax rolls.

—President Reagan proposed repeal of the investment tax credit and numerous other tax breaks for business and wealthy individuals; the Democratic Bradley-Gephardt bill was "distributively neutral," retaining the existing shares of tax burden for each income class.

50. Quoted in Birnbaum and Murray, *Showdown at Gucci Gulch*, p. 99.
51. This idea is presented in an insightful paper by James M. Verdier, "The Tax Reform Act of 1986: An Unnatural Leap Over Gucci Gulch," Harvard University, Kennedy School of Government, June 1988.

These reversals took much of the traditional controversy out of tax reform. The legislation that emerged from Congress was an amalgam of policy concessions. Democrats in Congress took what the president offered: an increase in corporate taxes, the elimination of federal income taxes for millions of low-income Americans, and cancellation or curtailment of tax breaks. The Republicans accepted what the Democrats offered: low marginal rates, no tax increase, and rate cuts for all income classes. Rostenkowski made the interplay between the bilateral concessions clear shortly after the Senate approved its tax reform bill. "I would be willing to shoot for the Senate's top rate as long as we approach the House's after-tax income distribution," he said.[52] The Ways and Means chairman was signaling that, despite the bipartisan spirit, the Democrats were still holding on to their core position and he expected Republicans to do likewise. The parties had been taken out of tax reform, but they remained very much in it.

That they continued to be a factor in tax legislation was reflected in the twenty-two Senate roll call votes on the measure. On exactly half of these, a majority of Democrats were opposed by a majority of Republicans. Two of these votes suggest that partisanship might affect the future course of tax policy. One roll call was on a motion to table an amendment to add a 35 percent tax rate. Republicans voted 49–4 to table, Democrats were split 22–25 against.[53] Democratic support for the higher rate would have been greater had not Finance Committee members agreed to band together against all floor changes. The second vote was on a "sense of the Congress" motion that the tax code not be changed for five years. Republicans endorsed this motion 38–14, Democrats opposed it by a 33–12 margin.[54] The two votes indicate that the 1986 tax reform was only a pause in the political war between the two parties. By 1990 the Republicans were demanding that capital gains be once again taxed at a preferential rate, and the Democrats were trying to raise the tax rate imposed on upper-income people.

The Cloak of Neutrality

Bipartisanship depended on more than the goodwill and cooperation of party leaders. It also required legislation that would not let either party claim undue credit for the accomplishment or risk being seen as a

52. Birnbaum and Murray, *Showdown at Gucci Gulch*, p. 258.
53. *Congressional Quarterly Almanac, 1986*, vol. 42 (1987), vote no. 137, p. 25–S.
54. *Congressional Quarterly Almanac, 1986*, vote no. 147, p. 27-S.

loser. This condition was satisfied by the 1986 act's ostensible commitment to neutrality. One aspect of neutrality has been frequently noted in this essay: the legislation was to be "revenue neutral," neither adding nor taking away federal revenue. In addition, the legislation would make the tax code "economically neutral," no longer using tax laws to encourage one or another economic activity. Finally, tax reform was to be "distributively neutral," not significantly altering the relative burden of each class of taxpayers. These objectives were intended to forge a politically neutral tax law. Democrats and Republicans, liberals and conservatives could unite behind tax reform because of its claim to neutrality.

On its face, neutrality is an anomaly, for it purports to depoliticize tax policy. Politics would no longer determine who gets what through the tax system. But why have a political process if economic benefits and costs are not distributed through it? Russell Long cut to the heart of the matter in the last hours of the Senate Finance markup. The issue was protection of certain preferences for the oil and gas industry, the most powerful interest in his home state of Louisiana. After noting that justice is supposed to be impartial, Long defended the taking of sides by legislators:

> We fellas are lawmakers. We're supposed to know who we're helpin' and do it deliberately, and know who we're hurtin' and do that deliberately. Now the people in the oil and gas b'ness are the most depressed industry in the United States.[55]

Not only did Long prevail on the oil and gas issue, he identified a key feature in the success of tax reform. Politicians were not indifferent to the distributive and political characteristics of the tax legislation. If they had been, they could have accepted the apolitical version assembled by the Treasury Department's tax experts. In putting together a bill that could be enacted, legislators abided by the principle of revenue neutrality and made substantial progress toward fairness, but they also departed from the strict demands of economic and distributional neutrality. The legislation probably would not have made it into law if they had not.

Even when neutrality was set aside, it served a useful political purpose. By professing neutrality and behaving otherwise, politicians

---

55. Birnbaum and Murray, *Showdown at Gucci Gulch,* p. 232.

had the best of both political worlds. They marshaled support for the legislation while achieving their distributive objectives.

Revenue Neutrality

Revenue neutrality was the most consistent and powerful decision rule throughout the process, and legislators largely adhered to it for all five years covered by the revenue projections. Revenue neutrality facilitated tax reform in several ways, a few of which have already been alluded to. First, it divorced tax reform from deficit reduction. If the two issues had been entangled, reform might have been stymied by stalemate over the deficit. Second, it took off the table proposals to increase federal revenue, whether made by those concerned about the deficit or by those who wanted more funds to finance federal programs. Third, as it was applied, revenue neutrality ruled out entirely new sources of income, such as a consumption-based tax. In addition to fomenting political controversy, a proposed new tax source would have enabled politicians to avoid genuine reform. They would have been able to pay for lower rates by levying new taxes rather than by broadening the base and eliminating preferences.

The rigors of revenue neutrality made the concept of tax expenditures a potent instrument of reform, though not quite in the manner envisioned by Stanley Surrey when he coined the term some two decades ago.[56] Surrey devised the phrase to emphasize the interchangeability of costs incurred (or benefits provided) through program expenditures and those channeled through the tax system, and to encourage trade-offs between direct expenditures and tax expenditures. However, the forced competition between those who want tax relief and those who want program benefits has not materialized. One possible reason is that the trade is not assured: closing tax preferences would not necessarily provide more funds for related programs.

The revenue-neutrality rule set up a different trade-off: rates versus breaks. At any given revenue target, the more exceptions and preferences written into the code, the higher the marginal tax rates would have to be. This trade was simpler to make than the one involving program expenditures, for it was confined to matters in the jurisdiction of a single set of congressional committees. Moreover, this trade-off spurred those

56. Stanley S. Surrey, *Pathways to Tax Reform: The Concept of Tax Expenditures* (Harvard University Press, 1973); and Stanley S. Surrey and Paul R. McDaniel, *Tax Expenditures* (Harvard University Press, 1985), especially chap. 4.

who wanted lower rates and those who wanted fewer breaks to unite in behalf of reform.

There were quite a few times during the two years that tax legislation was being developed when it would have been expedient for the committees to abandon revenue neutrality, especially when Treasury or congressional tax experts rushed in with fresh computations showing that the package being considered would lose revenue. But because revenue neutrality served a broad coalition of interests, it was upheld in the march toward tax reform.

Economic Neutrality

The political process was less supportive of economic neutrality, despite its endorsement at the highest levels of government. By closing most tax shelters, eliminating numerous deductions and exclusions, and strengthening the minimum tax on those using certain preferences, the new law made the tax structure much more equitable than it had been in the past. But the reformed tax code still falls short of the principle enunciated by President Reagan shortly after he took office in 1981: "The taxing power of government must be used to provide revenues for legitimate government purposes. It must not be used to regulate the economy or bring about social change."[57]

The Treasury's original plan (known as Treasury I) was animated by the pursuit of economic neutrality. While some features violated this standard (such as continuing the deductibility of mortgage interest payments), most preferences would have been eliminated if it had been enacted. But it was not, nor could it be. For example, Treasury's proposal to tax fringe benefits, such as employer-paid health insurance, as if they were ordinary income was politically infeasible. Although economists view these benefits as income, workers do not, because the benefits do not show up in their take-home pay. Even though it was compromised, economic neutrality was useful to the cause of reform. With most Americans believing that the tax system was unfair, this principle helped sell the notion that taxpayers would now be treated in a more evenhanded manner.

57. "President Reagan's Economic Proposals Text," February 18, 1981, reprinted in Congressional Quarterly Almanac, 1981, p. 18-E.

Table 4. Estimated Redistribution of the Individual Income Tax
by the Tax Reform Act of 1986[a]

Income class (in dollars)	Returns showing a tax increase (percent)	Change in share of total tax collections (percent)	Average tax cut (dollars)	Reduction in taxes (percent)
0–10,000	12.0	−0.4	39	65.0
10,000–20,000	15.7	−1.1	200	22.3
20,000–30,000	22.0	−0.5	220	9.8
30,000–40,000	25.0	−0.2	273	7.7
40,000–50,000	20.0	−0.3	486	9.1
50,000–75,000	37.4	0.7	150	1.8
75,000–100,000	37.8	0.4	176	1.2
100,000–200,000	36.8	0.5	612	2.2
200,000 and over	44.2	0.9	3,362	2.4
All classes	21.1	0.0	194	6.1

Source: Joint Committee on Taxation, October 1986.
a. These projections, made shortly after the Tax Reform Act was enacted, estimated the effect of the act on taxes for calendar year 1988.

Distributive Neutrality

Revenue neutrality promised that total taxes would not be increased; distributive neutrality seemed to make the same commitment to individual taxpayers. Yet tension between these objectives was unavoidable. If total revenue and the distribution of tax burdens were both left unchanged, how could reform make taxpayers better off? Economists might answer that everyone would gain from a more efficient and productive economy, but taxpayers needed more immediate and direct benefits, especially because tax reform took away some visible breaks, such as the deduction of state and local sales taxes and the two-income earner deduction.

Under pressure to provide tangible tax relief to individuals, Congress defined distributive neutrality to be equal percentage reductions in individual tax liabilities at all income levels. These reductions were financed by increasing the corporate tax burden. Moreover, as table 4 indicates, the individual income tax burden was also substantially redistributed. According to official projections released shortly after tax reform was enacted, more than 20 percent of all taxpayers had to pay more under the new system than under the old one. Approximately two out of every five taxpayers above the $50,000 income level faced increased payments.

Perversely, a reform that promised to be distributionally neutral was possibly the most redistributive tax law in America history. It made millions of earners better off and millions worse off. Perhaps the redistribution forced reformers to claim that they were not altering relative tax burdens. A tax bill without losers would not have been a reform, but a reform that did not claim there would be no losers certainly would not have passed. Given the promise of distributional neutrality, who lost and why?

As table 4 indicates, a significant portion of the taxpaying population was projected to experience rising tax burdens as a consequence of reform. It was also estimated at the time of enactment that there would be a shift in the relative burden borne by each income class. The five classes of taxpayers with incomes of $50,000 and below would have a smaller share of the burden than they had before reform; each of the four high-income groups would pay a bigger share. This increased progressivity was to be achieved by cutting taxes for all classes, not by raising them for some. The last two columns in the table show that the average taxpayer in each income class obtained some tax reduction. Of course, averages mask the fact that there were losers at each income level, but the veiling of the effect on actual taxpayers served useful political ends. Because each category had both winners and losers, tax reform was not redistributive in the sense of taking from one group to give to another. Most of those disadvantaged by reform did not know they were losers until they filed returns in later years, long after the legislation was enacted.

The pattern was much the same in corporate taxation, except for the sharp increase in this sector's share of the total income tax burden. This outcome was foreordained by Reagan's surprising endorsement of the shift from individual to corporate taxpayers. Significantly, however, many corporations emerged as winners in the redistribution of the tax burden. In their informative account of tax reform, Birnbaum and Murray wonder "why the many powerful interest groups lined up in opposition to reform never joined forces to defeat it."[58] Part of the answer is that approximately two-fifths of the industry groups faced lower effective rates after reform than before.[59] With many corporations paying less tax as a consequence of reform, it is not surprising that so many came out in support of the legislation.

The selective use of transition rules also encouraged corporate support. The $10.6 billion of such rules provided at least 650 exceptions

58. Birnbaum and Murray, *Showdown at Gucci Gulch*, p. 287.
59. Mark L. Starcher, *Quantifying the Impact of the Tax Reform Act of 1986 on Effective Corporate Tax Rates* (Arlington, Va.: Tax Analysts, 1986).

and preferences, many to politically active companies. Because they were narrowly drawn, these rules could be targeted to firms supporting reform, while providing no relief to those that opposed the legislation. A company having the choice of campaigning for an overall reduction in corporate taxes or for relief that it alone would receive could reason that it would be better off getting the special treatment. It would obtain the entire benefit of special treatment, but the benefits of lower corporate taxes would be shared with many "free riders."[60]

The redistribution from individual to corporate taxes offers some support to the old Berle-Means theory concerning the split between the ownership and control of American corporations.[61] The managers of corporations are also individual taxpayers, and many of them benefited greatly from the reduction in marginal rates. It is conceivable that their concern about the rise in corporate taxes was diluted by awareness of the benefits they would receive as individual taxpayers.

Much of the legislative battle was fought over particular preferences in the code. Some valuable preferences fell by the wayside while others survived the brunt of reform. Wide use of a preference appeared to be insufficient protection against repeal. A high number of beneficiaries meant that a preference was likely to be a big revenue loser and therefore an inviting target for reformers who were scouring the code for tax expenditures that could be traded off for lower rates. In 1985, the year that Congress began working on the tax legislation, some 36 million taxpayers claimed deductions for charitable contributions, 38 million deducted taxes paid to other governments, and 36 million deducted interest charges.[62] All three of these preferences survived, but in narrowed form. Congress restricted the tax expenditure for charitable contributions to those who itemize deductions, it took away the deductions for sales taxes, and it restricted the deduction of certain interest payments.

Congress seemingly applied a second criterion: the longevity of the provision. Relatively recent additions to the code were more likely to be curtailed than older ones. In 1985, 16 million taxpayers sheltered some $35 billion in individual retirement accounts (IRAs) and 25 million

60. See Mancur Olson, Jr., *The Logic of Collective Action: Public Goods and the Theory of Groups* (Harvard University Press, 1965), for an explanation of why groups have an economic incentive to seek narrowly drawn benefits.

61. Adolf A. Berle, Jr., and Gardiner C. Means, *The Modern Corporation and Private Property* (New York: Commerce Clearing House, 1932).

62. These data are taken from *Statistics of Income,* vol. 6 (Winter 1986–87), pp. 7–10.

couples claimed the two-earner deduction. The former survived tax reform in greatly shrunken form; the latter was terminated. Both were fairly recent insertions in the code. The IRA deduction was established in 1974, the two-earner deduction in 1981.[63] In fact, most of the preferences introduced in the early 1980s (at least sixteen were enacted in 1980 and 1981) were removed from the code.[64]

Longevity indicates that a preference is perceived to be a normal part of the tax structure rather than a benefit to a particular group. Fringe benefits are a case in point. Although they have long been a target of reformers concerned about the unequal treatment of different types of income, taxpayers generally see them as something different from ordinary income. The exclusion of employer-paid medical insurance dates back to 1943. Many of the biggest revenue losers, such as the deduction of home mortgage interest, have been in the code from the start, and reformers have found it difficult, if not impossible, to take them out. More than half of the $300 billion in existing tax expenditures derives from provisions that were added to the tax code before 1970.[65] Trying to eliminate many long-standing preferences might have jeopardized tax reform.

The Political Process Worked

Tax reform was an extraordinary accomplishment, but it was neither a miracle nor an aberration. During the more than two years that the measure was shaped and debated in the executive and legislative branches, several factors and actions contributed to the success of the enterprise. As Dan Rostenkowski said as he adjourned the conference, "Ladies and gentlemen, the political process worked."[66]

What worked was the capacity of American politicians to adopt tactics that kept the legislation alive and moved it toward enactment. Tax reform succeeded for five reasons. First, politicians decided against paying for

63. Data on the year in which various tax expenditure provisions were established are presented in Congressional Budget Office, *Tax Expenditures: Budget Control Options and Five-Year Budget Projections for Fiscal Years 1983–1987* (November 1982), table C-1.

64. Congressional Budget Office, *Tax Expenditures*, table C-1; and Pearl Richardson, Congressional Budget Office, *The Effects of Tax Reform on Tax Expenditures* (March 1988).

65. CBO, *Effects of Tax Reform*. See also Allen Schick, "Tax Expenditures: Myths and Realities," in Tax Foundation, *Tax Features* (Washington, June 1988).

66. Birnbaum and Murray, *Showdown at Gucci Gulch*, p. 283.

reform with a new tax source and against using reform to augment federal revenues. Second, politicians recast the "pure" proposal fashioned by the Treasury Department's tax experts into a politically driven compromise highly sensitive to the interests that would be aided or harmed by terminating or retaining various preferences. Third, committee leaders took charge of the legislation in Congress, made private deals to secure votes, and abandoned public markups until after the necessary votes were obtained. Fourth, Democrats and Republicans gave tax reform bipartisan support and took active roles in advancing the legislation. And fifth, reformers who professed neutrality actively redistributed the tax burden while reducing tax liabilities for every income class.

Tax reform was, however, more than a matter of sound tactics. It succeeded because the basic institutions of American pluralism fashioned a consensus on reform. In so doing, they reconciled the demands of particular interests with the collective objective of low marginal rates and a fair tax structure. American politics is noted for compromise, not consensus. The government is fractured by competing interests, and the best it can do is to give most of the interests a portion of what they want. But forging a consensus in which the various interests subordinate their aims to a larger public good is a difficult task in this country. There were plenty of compromises in the long march to tax reform, but these would not have sufficed to achieve far-reaching changes. There also had to be consensus about the right thing to do. In explaining tax reform, therefore, it is necessary to know not only the bargains that were struck but also the consensual values that kept this enterprise on course.

Consensual Reform

Competition, not consensus, is the dominant feature of American politics. Interests vie against one another, and the side that has the most votes wins. The national government lacks, according to a theme of contemporary political science literature, consensus-building institutions found in other democracies. It does not bond public and private interests through corporatist institutions, such as some European countries rely upon, nor does it emphasize consensual values, as Japan and some other traditional societies do.

Tax reform demonstrates that the United States can achieve consensus on potentially divisive issues. Each session, Congress settles numerous legislative matters by majority rule. Sometimes the votes are close, sometimes voting is divided along party lines. In the case of tax reform, the final product had to be something that top policy leaders and major groups supported or were willing to go along with. It was too far-reaching and too redistributive to be left to whip counts, roll calls, or interparty conflict. Tax reform took away tax subsidies, added to the tax liabilities of millions of Americans, and shifted a sizable tax burden to the corporate sector. These could not be achieved by close calls. The legislation needed overwhelming support approaching a national consensus.

The major political parties played a critical role in forging a consensus. Tax reform was not captured by the Republicans or the Democrats but was promoted by both. Republican Ronald Reagan was impelled by the need for Democratic support to downplay partisanship and permit congressional Democrats to exercise considerable influence over the substance of reform. Consensus building in Congress was spurred by the fact that one chamber was controlled by the Democrats and the other by the Republicans. Significantly, however, formal party leaders in Congress had only minor parts in advancing tax legislation. Speaker of the House Thomas P. (Tip) O'Neill had little interest in the measure, was skeptical of the fairness of the steep reduction in rates on upper-income taxpayers, and was wary of a Republican trap. Nevertheless, O'Neill allowed the legislation to proceed under the aegis of his close associate, Rostenkowski. The Speaker's most important contribution to consensus was one that derived from party conflict. By insisting that the Republicans supply a minimum quota of votes for the measure, O'Neill ensured that tax reform would carry the label of both parties.

Robert Dole, the Senate Republican leader, had previously chaired the Finance Committee, and he was quite knowledgeable on tax matters. Nevertheless, he had little to do with the legislation, possibly because of other demands on his time or because he did not want to appear to be intruding on Packwood, who had succeeded him as Finance chairman. The task of putting together a consensus bill fell to Packwood, who, as recounted earlier, worked with a bipartisan group in committee to hammer out a measure that was reported by a 20–0 vote.

Why the limited involvement of formal party leaders? The sufficient answer is that Congress is a fragmented, committee-centered institution. Committees do not always respond positively to orders from leaders on substantive—in contrast to procedural—matters. A clear example of the limited power of leaders to compel action occurred in 1987, shortly after tax reform was enacted, when the new Speaker of the House, Jim Wright, openly called for a tax increase. Rostenkowski, who did not want to consider any legislation that would undo tax reform, rejected the proposal.

Party leaders might not matter much, but party labels do. The labels signal whether the issue will divide Congress along party lines or be decided by consensus. Consensus protects both parties against blame and enables both to claim any credit that might accrue from their action.

Key committee chairmen were the main consensus builders. They marshaled support both inside Congress and outside. Consensus building proceeded on two tracks. One was the association of tax reform with broad national values, such as fairness and simplification; the other was the purchase of support through private deals. Both chairmen benefited from restrictions on floor challenges, but approval of the final version by lopsided margins in both the House and Senate indicates that it was a consensus product. In the end, Rostenkowski and Packwood carried the day because the legislation represented the will of Congress, not because expression of that will was thwarted by restrictive floor rules.

The chairmen had to reckon with demands from interest groups. Bargaining was complicated by the extraordinary diversity and number of groups that had high stakes in the outcome. There were no peak associations that could speak for an entire sector, no "wise men" whose counsel would suffice to persuade a wide spectrum of interests to line up in support of tax reform. Consensus had to be assembled in a most nonconsensual manner, bit by bit in ex parte negotiations with particular groups or members of Congress. The bargains had to be struck with subgroups, not with manufacturing companies as a whole, but with those concentrated in a particular product or region. In the end, negotiations often were narrowed to a single company whose tax problems were unique to it.

Acting Collectively and Satisfying
Particular Interests

Bargaining with affected interests is quite common in American politics, and perhaps nowhere more than on Capitol Hill, where the fragmentation of Congress mirrors the pluralism of the political system. The outcome is often policy—or legislation—that is sprawling, lacking in focus, and (sometimes) inconsistent. The collective decision emerging from the interplay of group bargaining is a montage of loosely connected parts. In seeking consensus, the most expeditious route is to give everyone a portion of what they want. The whole then becomes the assemblage of the parts.

Tax reform had to be different if only because the very idea of reform ran counter to the particularistic preferences embedded over the years in the tax code. If Congress had responded to particular demands by "giving away the store," there would have been no reform. The overall coherence of the tax legislation was maintained by the two rules that governed the outcome. Rates had to be lowered substantially and the measure could not surrender additional revenue. Policy coherence was a function of statistical coherence. The parts had to add up to the whole.

Statistical consistency was enforced through corps of experts in Treasury and Congress. The United States is not a government by experts, but because of its complexity the tax code is one policy area where specialists have unusual scope. The experts did not make the big deals on tax reform, but they played a vital role in identifying policy options and estimating their revenue effects. Their estimates were deemed to be so authoritative that when experts produced new numbers at several key points, the politicians immediately took them into account. Without the deference accorded tax experts (who also were blamed from time to time for bearing bad news), reform might have devolved into an opportunity for cross-pressured legislators to fabricate buoyant revenue estimates or to manipulate the timing of provisions.

Of course, statistical coherence is a weaker test than substantive coherence. The pieces were welded together not so much to accomplish a planned objective but to fit the amount of money added to or taken from the treasury into the overall account. Yet out of statistical coherence there emerged reasonably coherent tax reform. One can say of the 1986 law what cannot often be said of federal legislation: it had a clear-cut purpose and came close to fulfilling it.

It is an anomaly of tax reform that the striving for a satisfactory collective product drove the architects of that legislation to more particularistic behavior. The narrower the group they had to bargain with and the smaller the concession they had to make, the less it violated the basic terms of tax reform. One can surmise that the extreme specialization of interest groups complicated negotiations but made striking a deal easier. Perhaps this feature of American pluralism explains why tax reform has been more far-reaching—in terms of lowering marginal rates and terminating preferences—than in most other democratic countries that have sought similar objectives.

Passage of the 1986 tax reform was a special case but one that nevertheless has some lessons for the broader play of American politics. It demonstrated that conventional views have underestimated the capacity of American government for broad consensus and coherent policy. Tax reform also called into question the notion that politicians seeking change would do well to settle for adjustments at the margins, where the prospect of opposition is less and the need for broad support not so urgent. When done right, big moves may be more successful than smaller ones, precisely because they induce politicians to seek consensus and coherence.

Introducing a New Tax in Japan

Michio Muramatsu
Masaru Mabuchi

BETWEEN 1979, when Prime Minister Masayoshi Ohira first proposed a large-scale indirect tax, and 1989, when a consumption tax was finally enacted, Japan's dominant political party, the Liberal Democratic party (LDP), found that majority rule alone was not enough to overcome unified opposition in the short run. However, under a dominant-party system, party leaders can use unique long-term strategies and tactics that are extremely effective. This proved to be the case with the introduction of a consumption tax in Japan.

When Ohira first introduced the idea of a large-scale indirect tax, the issue hurt the LDP in the 1979 general election, even though he withdrew the plan in the early stages of the campaign. Ohira's competitors and followers in the LDP held him responsible for the party's defeat, and rivalry among them plunged the party into turmoil. This intraparty dispute caused the dissolution of the Diet, and during the 1980 general election that ensued, Ohira died.

As a result, tax reform was taboo for some years to come. Approaching the problem of the nation's large deficits from a different perspective, Ohira's successor, Zenko Suzuki, sought to cut government expenditures. This policy was also followed by his successor, Yasuhiro Nakasone, for several years. But once he pared the budget sufficiently to satisfy the public and the business community, Nakasone again looked to tax reform.

Buoyed by massive electoral gains in the Diet in early 1986, Nakasone stood by a tax reform package that would have cut direct taxes and introduced an indirect tax. But Nakasone encountered stiff opposition from the public, the business community, and many of his own LDP Diet members. He was ultimately forced to withdraw the indirect tax plan from Diet consideration in April 1987, although direct tax cuts were enacted in September.

Figure 1. Public Support for Nakasone and Takeshita Cabinets, December 1982–April 1989

Percent

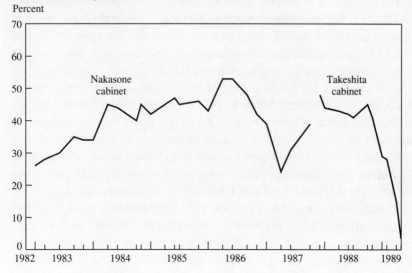

Under the Nakasone administration, the LDP risked the loss of electoral support and a split in its ranks by pursuing passage of the indirect tax. The level of public support for the Nakasone cabinet shows a clear correlation with the course of tax reform politics: Nakasone's popularity dropped steadily from the fall of 1986, when the details of the plan began to be publicized, until the plan was finally killed in April 1987, and then began to rise again in May 1987 (see figure 1).

Noboru Takeshita, Nakasone's successor as prime minister, successfully steered a modified version of the indirect consumption tax plan through the Diet the following year. However, he had to pay a high price: his accomplishment clearly shortened the life of his administration. After opinion polls showed an extremely low level of popularity among voters, he resigned in April 1989, only a year and a half after his inauguration. On the surface, Takeshita's resignation seemed to be more closely related to his involvement in the Recruit scandal than to tax reform. According to political observers, however, his low level of support was attributable primarily to tax reform. Public support for the Takeshita administration started at a high of 50 percent and rapidly dropped to 3.6 percent in April 1989, after the tax law was passed (figure 1).

This brief explanation of tax politics in the 1980s raises two theoretical issues. First, the LDP-centered party system in Japan does not seem to fit the model of a dominant-party system, as developed by Alan Arian and Samuel Barnes.[1] Nakasone, backed by an overwhelming number of seats in the Diet, failed to pass the tax law, yet under the same conditions the Takeshita administration succeeded. The dominant party is not always dominant in the ways Arian and Barnes suggest. There has to be a more effective explanation for Nakasone's failure to win tax reform. Second, and conversely, there has to be an explanation for the success of the Takeshita administration. Although there are differences in the laws proposed by the two administrations, in our judgment the differences are not significant enough to explain Takeshita's success. Therefore the question remains: why and how did the LDP overcome the barriers that had constrained the Nakasone administration?

In addressing these questions, we will apply Mike Mochizuki's theory of viscosity to explain the sources of opposition strength in the Diet.[2] Several factors permit the opposition to play an influential role in government decisions: the relative brevity of the Diet session, the bicameral and committee systems, and precedence and practice, including the rule of unanimity.

To fully explain the story of tax politics in the 1980s, we also have to consider politics outside the Diet. That is, laws and policies must cross important hurdles before reaching the stage of Diet deliberations. These include approval by related interest groups, the bureaucracy, advisory commissions, internal processes of the LDP, and public opinion. Yasunori Sone and Tomoaki Iwai see these barriers as a steeplechase.[3]

The Arian-Barnes dominant-party model fails to consider the time element and ignores contentious activities and negotiations that take place both inside and outside the Diet, often intermediated by the mass media. Our investigation suggests that the strength of the dominant party

1. Alan Arian and Samuel H. Barnes, "The Dominant Party System: A Neglected Model of Democratic Stability," *Journal of Politics,* vol. 36 (August 1974), pp. 592–614. See also Michio Muramatsu and Ellis S. Krauss, "The Dominant Party and Social Coalitions in Japan," in T. J. Pempel, ed., *Uncommon Democracies: The One-Party Dominant Regimes* (Cornell University Press, 1990), pp. 282–305.
2. Mike Masato Mochizuki, "Managing and Influencing the Japanese Legislative Process: The Role of Parties and the National Diet," Ph.D. thesis, Harvard University, 1982.
3. Yasunori Sone and Tomoaki Iwai, "Seisaku Katei niokeru Gikai no Yakuwari" (Role of the Diet in the policy process), *Seijigaku Nenpō* (Annual Journal of Japanese Political Science Association) (1988), pp. 160–61.

resides in its ability to control the agenda, in other words, the power to control the time dimension of the political process. The Mochizuki viscosity model and the Sone-Iwai steeplechase model are sensitive to the issue of time management. However, even these two models consider only the time confined by a single session of the Diet and tend to ignore the dominant party's capacity to develop a strategy that extends over several administrations as well as several Diet sessions under a single administration. As long as it represents a clear decision by the party, the same proposal will be introduced repeatedly by successive administrations until it passes.

The advantageous position of the dominant party with respect to time management does not ensure that it will rule the agenda throughout several administrations. The cohesiveness of the dominant party, the strength of the opposition parties' coalition, and the political climate, as shown through public opinion, all determine in combination the degree of dominance. Through an intensive study of tax politics we will show how a law that concerned many influential actors traversed the political processes inherent in the dominant-party system.

Ohira's Proposal

Tax reform first became a dominant political issue in Japan in 1979, when Prime Minister Ohira proposed the imposition of a large-scale indirect tax as a way to eliminate budget deficits. Balancing the general account of the national budget had been a long-established practice, but in 1965 the government for the first time issued long-term national bonds to finance government operations. For the next ten years, the bonds accounted for an average of only 10 percent of total government revenues annually. However, the oil crisis of 1973–74 caused a recession, which led to a sharp decline in corporate tax revenues. From 9.4 percent of the total initial budget in 1976, national bonds quickly rose to account for fully 40 percent of the initial budget in 1979.

To remedy this situation, the Tax Commission in October 1977 and again in September 1978 recommended the introduction of a general consumption tax. The Tax Commission is an advisory commission of the Ministry of Finance (MOF) attached to the prime minister's office. When the government proposes a major bill, the ministry responsible for the policy and the related advisory commission (*shingikai*) analyze the details of the policy before deliberations begin in the Diet. The recommendations of the *shingikai* are submitted to the cabinet, which then decides whether proposals should become policy and be introduced in the Diet.

Acceptance of the Tax Commission's annual reform proposals concerning income and corporate taxes is routine. However, that was not the case in September 1988 when it announced the details of the indirect tax proposal. The announcement sparked antitax campaigns among various interest groups, especially the Japan Retailers' Association, the National Federation of Small and Medium-sized Companies, the National Federation of Blue-form Return Companies, and the National Organization of Cooperative Associations. Within the ruling Liberal Democratic party, city-based groups formed in opposition to the tax.

Despite this opposition, Ohira made the Tax Commission's report the basis of his plan to introduce a new tax in 1980. Faced with the immediate problem of a huge budget deficit, the prime minister had only a limited number of options. He could have chosen to do nothing, if he had followed the advice of some Keynesians, who asserted that heavy dependence on national bonds was not itself a major problem.[4] But he could not choose a "do-nothing" policy because he was keenly aware that Japan's rate of dependence on bonds in proportion to the general account was the highest among the advanced industralized nations.

Ohira could also have tried to lower the budget deficit by cutting the budget itself. He did not opt for that choice because he firmly believed that spending could not be cut enough to eliminate the deficit. His third option was to raise income, corporate, and commodity taxes without changing the existing tax system. However, such direct taxes accounted for a growing proportion of total government tax revenues. Therefore an increase in the income tax was discarded at an early stage of planning, while an increase in indirect taxes was considered to be worthy of serious discussion.

Ohira thus decided to go ahead with the indirect consumption tax because he had no real alternative. As a result, the proposed tax became the central issue in the general election of October 1979, and the LDP lost seats in the Diet, when it had been expected to regain a comfortable majority. Although the LDP continued in power because several indepen-

4. Tadao Uchida, "Gyou-zaisei Kaikaku no Hihan to Hyouka," (Criticism and critiques of administrative reform), *Kikan Gendai Keizai* (Quarterly Journal of Modern Economics), no. 44 (Autumn 1981).

dent Diet members joined it after the elections, tax reform, and the indirect tax in particular, were no longer matters for discussion.

Nakasone's Struggle

Ohira's successor, Zenko Suzuki, decided to attack the budget deficits by cutting expenditures and carrying out administrative reform. He established the Second Ad Hoc Council for Administrative Reform (Rinchō) to guide the budget cuts. Nakasone was a member of Suzuki's cabinet, and thus oversaw the administration's policy of "financial reconstruction without increased taxes." He also accumulated influence toward his own rise to power. When he succeeded Suzuki as prime minister in November 1982, he followed Suzuki's policy.[5] Under his strong leadership, administrative reform produced major results and stopped the trend of increasing expenditures. He concentrated his attention on administrative reform during his first term as prime minister (1982–84).

Nakasone started showing a strong interest in tax reform in December 1984, when he was reelected as LDP president and prime minister. Announcing his intentions concerning the 1985 budget and the ordinary Diet sessions at a press conference in December, he said that "although it is too late for the 1985 budget, we must review the overall tax system to make it fairer . . . and simpler. I would like to discuss how the tax system should be improved to fit present-day society, including the relationships between direct and indirect taxes and between national and regional taxes."[6] This comment showed that Nakasone intended to shift his emphasis from trimming expenditures to tax reform. The LDP victory in the simultaneous elections for the lower and upper houses of the Diet in June 1986 allowed the prime minister to build interest in tax reform and gave him confidence in its success.

Nakasone's political strategy for achieving tax reform was to appeal to urban dwellers by addressing the widespread perception of unfairness in tax collection among various occupational categories. A famous phrase, the "9-6-4 problem," refers to the relative efficiency of tax collection among the three major occupational groups: the government is able to ascertain and fully tax 90 percent of the actual earned income

5. Masaru Kanbara, *Tenkanki no Seiji Katei: Rinchō no kiseki to Sono Kinō* (The political process at a crossroads) (Tokyo: Sogo Rodo Kenkyujo, 1986), pp. 205–07.

6. *Nihon Keizai Shimbun*, December 4, 1984.

of salaried employees, 60 percent of that of small and medium-sized businesses, and only 40 percent of that of farmers. As a result, the urban salaried workers, who constitute a majority of the population, pay a disproportionate share of the income tax. The rise of the "salaried-men" party in the 1979 and 1983 elections was one symptom of their dissatisfaction, and the LDP defeat in the 1979 election was another. Decreasing the income tax was the most visible method of gaining support among salaried employees.

The LDP also had to make a serious response to Supreme Court decisions on the reapportionment issue. Since 1975 the Supreme Court has ruled that the government has to meet the court's criteria for equalizing the value of a vote across electoral districts. Reapportionment would increase the number of Diet seats allocated to urban districts and thereby decrease the share controlled by the LDP. Nakasone concluded that in order to stay in power after reapportionment, the LDP would have to cultivate urban supporters.

In sum, Nakasone thought he could both expand support for the LDP among the urban middle class and comply with the Supreme Court edicts by reexamining the ratio of direct to indirect taxes and introducing a new indirect tax. He hoped that a package that combined income tax cuts with a new indirect tax would lead to a review of the national tax system, which since its establishment in 1949 had been biased toward direct taxes. Changing the balance between the two sets of taxes could alleviate the 9-6-4 problem.

However, he faced a delicate problem that restricted his policy options. In the February 1985 Diet session, he promised "not to introduce a large-scale indirect tax that the people and the LDP membership oppose." This promise remained arguable because it could be interpreted to mean that the government might introduce a large-scale indirect tax if it obtained support from the LDP. But any resort to such an interpretation would run the risk of confrontation with the public and the opposition parties who opposed any kind of large-scale indirect tax. Therefore he had to lead the deliberations on tax reform in such a way as to not break his word.

There was another reason Nakasone insisted on having his own way on tax reform: he did not trust the Ministry of Finance. This mistrust was rooted in a personal rivalry with the ministry during his days as a minor government functionary and in negative feelings toward bureaucrats that he had acquired from his mentor, Ichiro Kono. Nakasone's mistrust of the MOF, on tax reform specifically, had been heightened by

Ohira's failure. Nakasone laid the blame for the fiasco in the general elections of 1979 and the days of confusion within the LDP that followed squarely on the politically naive MOF.

The Tax Commission Deliberations

Both his strategy of realignment in mobilizing urban dwellers and his public promise made Nakasone take the lead in guiding the discussions on tax reform. The target to be overtaken was the Tax Commission, where drafts of tax reform bills would be written.

One of his first moves was to send his personal "brain trust" to participate as special members in the Tax Commission. He intended to snatch the leadership of the commission from the Ministry of Finance, which had insisted on introducing a large-scale indirect tax.

Second, Nakasone requested that the commission deliberations follow a specific agenda, insisting in September 1985 that "details of tax cuts be discussed first, and those of tax increase later." Mindful of the impending 1986 general elections, Nakasone's intention was to call voters' attention to the attractive points of the tax package.

During the early stages of the Tax Commission deliberations, Nakasone developed his plan into a manufacturers' sales tax. It was a flat-rate sales tax to be levied on manufacturers at the time the goods were delivered to the wholesalers. Because the tax was applied only to manufacturers, it was considered to be medium-scale rather than large-scale in terms of the number of people taxed. He believed a manufacturers' sales tax would not contradict his promise.

After the subcommittee of the Tax Commission proposed several types of indirect taxes in July 1986, plenary sessions of the commission began to examine them. The majority of the regular members were inclined toward the opinion that "the taxpayer base should be expanded with the introduction of a new indirect tax, and a . . . value-added tax was most desirable."[7] Nakasone's brain trust, who supported a manufacturers' sales tax, was a minor force in the commission. Tax specialists noted difficulties with a manufacturers' sales tax, such as the exemption of service companies. These specialists also noted that Canada was planning to abandon its manufacturers' sales tax because of its many inconsistencies and to move to a general value-added tax.

7. Kenzo Uchida, Masao Kanazashi, and Masayuki Fukuoka, *Zeisei Kaikaku o Meguru Seiji Rikigaku: Jimin Yuika no Seiji Katei* (Politics of tax reform) (Tokyo: Chuo Koronsha, 1988), pp. 104–06.

The Ministry of Finance was also critical of Nakasone's plan. The ministry's Budget Bureau found it unsatisfactory because it would not yield enough money to cover both the income tax reduction that Nakasone insisted on and future expenditure increases. The Tax Bureau thought the manufacturers' sales tax was irrelevant in Japan's postindustrial society, where the service industry was predominant. Recognizing, however, that Nakasone was restricted by his own promise, the MOF decided to modify its multi-layered value-added tax proposal to minimize its image as a large-scale tax and thus to characterize it as a medium-scale tax. The ministry emphasized that "if the range of non-taxable transactions is expanded and the exemption ceiling is set higher, it won't be a large-scale indirect tax."

The Japan Federation of Economic Organizations (Keidanren) was also critical of Nakasone's plan, even though it acknowledged a need for some kind of indirect tax. The Keidanren, consisting of all the major manufacturers in Japan, considered the plan unfair and tried to persuade Nakasone to drop his proposal. To obtain the same amount of revenue that would be obtained by a 5 percent multi-layered comprehensive value-added tax, the tax rate for a manufacturers' sales tax would have to be set at 7–8 percent. "I think the . . . value-added tax is the best of all the alternatives discussed by the commission," said Eiji Suzuki, chairman of the tax policy committee of the Keidanren, when invited to the Tax Commission hearings. Keidanren Chairman Eishiro Saito visited Nakasone in his official residence to ask him to change his mind.

These efforts seemed to have some effect on Nakasone. First, he understood his plan was defective in excluding the service industry, which accounted for the greater part of GNP. Second, the MOF's suggestion to modify the general income tax looked attractive. Third, as prime minister he wanted to avoid an all-out confrontation with the Keidanren, one of the country's most influential interest groups. As a result, Nakasone agreed to introduce a multi-layered value-added tax, which was called the consumption tax.[8] It took the entire 1986 session of the Tax Commission to persuade the prime minister to give up his proposal for a manufacturers' sales tax.

Party Deliberations

Since Nakasone, the Tax Commission, and the MOF had come together on the matter, and the commission had issued its final report

8. Yoshimitsu Kuribayashi, *Ōkurashō Shuzeikyoku* (The Tax Bureau of the Ministry of Finance) (Tokyo: Kodansha, 1988), pp. 45–48.

recommending a consumption tax on October 30, the success of the proposal depended on convincing LDP members to approve. The LDP's Research Commission on the Tax System was the arena for this effort.

Nakasone had appointed Sadanori Yamanaka as chairman of the LDP Research Commission when he decided to reform the tax system. Yamanaka was a member of the Nakasone faction and one of the most prominent tax specialists in the LDP.[9] His expertise, Nakasone expected, would enable the chairman to lead the discussion in the Research Commission and to negotiate with the MOF under the prime minister's instructions. However, Nakasone and the MOF had reached a compromise by the time the issue came to the Research Commission, and so Yamanaka's role was to convince LDP members to approve a consumption tax rather than Nakasone's pet program, a manufacturers' sales tax.

The party Research Commission had 244 members and was one of the largest policymaking organizations in the LDP; almost half the LDP members belonged to this committee. Research Commission deliberations are typically held in three stages. The first is a meeting of top members, including the chairman and vice-chairman, to decide the agenda. The second is a subcommittee meeting where every LDP member is allowed to participate. The third is a general meeting where a final decision is made. For consideration of the proposal, Yamanaka initially intended to restrict the subcommittee meeting to official commission members. In the end, complaints from the rank and file, especially from the Miyazawa and Abe factions, forced him to include any interested LDP members. In this way, the interested or *zoku* Diet members got an opportunity to voice their opinions.

Among the top Research Commission members there was a consensus about the outline for the tax reform. First, a manufacturers' sales tax would not raise enough revenue to offset a ¥4 trillion tax cut. Second, there were several types of value-added taxes, from which the Research Commission selected the most suitable one. Third, if the commission were to endorse one of them, the selection should be based on the opinions of LDP members. Most of the top Research Commission members judged that even a large-scale tax, if based on consensus among the LDP members, would not break Nakasone's election promise.

At the subcommittee hearing in November 1986 the majority agreed that the introduction of a new indirect tax in some form was inevitable,

9. Kuribayashi, *Ōkurashō Shuzeikyoku*, pp. 67–74.

and most participants agreed that the value-added tax was more appropriate than the manufacturers' sales tax. The top members of the Research Commission were relieved by the smoothness of the proceedings despite expected dissent. In November the leadership of the Research Commission tentatively agreed on a tax cut proposed by the Ministry of Finance and the Ministry of Home Affairs. They also decided on a policy of "revenue neutrality," which meant that the amount of the direct tax decrease was to be the same as that of the indirect tax increase.

In December a final official decision was made on the LDP Research Commission tax reform proposal. The process had taken about one month since the commission opened deliberations on October 30. But the decision was made without the approval of many of the Diet members who participated in the subcommittee meeting. That meeting was thrown into confusion at the beginning when a young Diet member challenged Yamanaka, saying, "We won't discuss a tax cut without deciding on a new revenue source." Even among the top members, who energetically pushed the value-added tax, there was an opinion that "whatever the limitations, a multilayered . . . value-added tax cannot help becoming a large-scale indirect tax, which means a breach of the prime minister's election promise." But the chairman ended deliberations when every kind of opinion against it seemed to have been voiced, announcing that the proposal had been approved. Yamanaka was responsible for this approach. After all, the Research Commission's deliberations were led by him alone.[10]

After the general shape of the new tax was decided, the next issue was the selection of the tax-exempt items. It further divided the Diet members because Yamanaka intended to reduce the number of such items; there was inevitably a zero-sum relationship among the industries and the Diet members who represented each interest. The industry-backed Diet members were too busy protecting the industries they represented to have much time to think of their common interest.

Electoral Opposition

Diet members who returned to their constituencies during the New Year holidays faced a barrage of criticism from their supporters on the tax reform proposal the LDP Research Commission had approved.

10. *Asahi Shimbun,* May 9, 1988.

Many of those Diet members who were unhappy both with the way the commission's deliberations were conducted and with the outcome joined their supporters to oppose the tax reform. Regional LDP assemblymen also protested the proposed reform. Their apprehensions and complaints, including their concerns that they might be unseated at the simultaneous regional elections scheduled for early 1987, erupted at the national meeting of secretary-generals of the Association of Local Assemblymen on January 19, 1987.

The Association of Tokyo Assemblymen was in the vanguard of the antitax movement. With many small companies doing business in its territory, it had led the opposition to a large-scale indirect tax in October 1986. According to a survey conducted by a wholesaler in Tokyo in January 1987, six LDP Diet members stated their opposition to the indirect tax. Kunio Hatoyama, in particular, often openly criticized it in the media. LDP executives restrained some Diet members from declaring their opposition, but within the LDP itself opposition to the tax reform and suggestions for modifications of the proposal were continuously voiced.

The antitax movement within the LDP gained momentum on March 8, 1987, when an LDP-authorized candidate lost a special by-election for the upper house in the Iwate constituency. This election was the first since the double election of 1986 to be viewed as demonstrating the extent of popular support for the government, and its central issue was the hottest topic in politics—the tax reform proposal. Each party therefore paid special attention to the election. The LDP's Secretary-General Takeshita, Transport Minister Ryutaro Hashimoto, and Finance Minister Kiichi Miyazawa traveled to the constituency to campaign for the LDP candidate, while Chairman Takako Doi of the Japan Socialist party (JSP) appeared on behalf of her party's candidate.

The result was an overwhelming victory for the JSP candidate, Jinichi Ogawa, who was his party's first successful candidate in the "conservative kingdom" of Iwate in thirty-seven years. During his campaign, Ogawa openly stated his opposition to the tax reform plan. He drew support from regular LDP voters and won the largest vote total ever for a JSP candidate in that constituency, 421,432 votes to 197,863 for the LDP candidate.

The "Iwate shock" had a major influence on the political atmosphere surrounding the tax reform proposal. The Association of Iwate Assemblymen, which had supported the proposal during the campaign, turned around to oppose it unanimously. Other regional assemblies also approved resolutions opposing the tax reform plan, and many candidates authorized or recommended by the LDP in the simultaneous regional elections announced antitax positions.

The attitudes of local LDP assemblymen was most clearly shown when they broke with precedent and not only failed to invite Nakasone to speak in their behalf during the regional election campaign, but even declined his offer to do so. The opposition, which designated the simultaneous regional elections as a "national plebiscite" on the tax reform, coordinated election campaigns across the nation calling for the death of the plan. As a result, incumbent non-LDP governors in Hokkaido and Fukuoka, initially thought to be vulnerable, were reelected, defeating LDP-recommended challengers. The LDP lost over 1,200 of 2,000 seats in the prefectural assemblies.

Paradoxically, the fact that the LDP won 304 Diet seats in the double elections of 1986 hurt, rather than helped, the party's cause on tax reform. The saying that "seats equal power" is often correct, but this case was the exception that proves the rule. Most of the new seats were gained by newcomers or very junior members of the Diet, who had not yet established stable bases of support or strong ties with their constituencies and industry and were therefore particularly sensitive to trends in public opinion. Because many industries and ordinary voters opposed the consumption tax, many of these new Diet members also opposed it.

Death in the Diet

Nakasone introduced his consumption tax bill in the Diet in March 1987. He felt little need to offer the opposition any compromises. He maintained his position despite resistance to his plan in local assemblies and the "betrayal" by younger Diet members. "It is the responsibility of the Nakasone administration to pass this bill through the Diet. I will face that responsibility with indomitable resolve," Nakasone said at his New Year press conference in 1987. He was confident that he could handle the Diet despite expected difficulties during deliberations.

The opposition, meanwhile, gathered strength with victories in the regional elections and used that strength to keep the tax bill from passing the Diet. The opposition challenged every LDP attempt to steamroll the measure through the Diet, including refusing to participate in Diet sessions. Three rejections were made, and thirty-one days were wasted.

The confrontation between the government and the opposition reached its peak on April 16, when the LDP steamrolled the bill through the Budget Commission and Diet deliberations were suspended. The LDP, at a loss as to what to do with the budget bill, forcibly tried to convene a plenary session of the House of Councillors on April 21. The opposition again used delaying tactics, and the bill was effectively killed for that session of the Diet.

Nakasone's failure to get his tax reform proposal through the Diet could be explained by his assumption that managing the LDP-dominated parliament would be simple. Under one-party dominance, there is very little possibility that other parties or associations can form a majority. Government by a party other than the LDP seems impossible. Nonetheless, one-party dominance is maintained not by party strategy, but rather by absorbing the varied interests and opinions of society effectively, which means the dominant party must pay careful attention to minority views. It is therefore important for the LDP to bring the opposition to the discussion table and keep it there. To this end, the LDP needs to respond to the opposition's concerns in some way and give the opposition opportunities to take credit for influencing policy.

If instead the LDP tries to pass legislation using only its own majority, it forces the opposition parties to play a game they have no chance to win. In that situation, the opposition naturally tries to change the rules of the game. In extreme cases the minority parties can withdraw from both committee deliberations and plenary sessions of the Diet. Nonparticipation in the Diet deliberations is most effective when the opposition has the support of public opinion and the media. Public opinion is often split between criticism of the LDP for driving the opposition to take extreme measures and of the opposition for adopting the extreme behavior. In the case of the tax reform proposal, however, public criticism landed primarily on the LDP. The opposition strategy to oppose the tax plan on the grounds that it reneged on a campaign pledge was effective in winning public support.

Takeshita's Strategy

When Noboru Takeshita was named prime minister, the tax issue was already an established part of the political agenda, and it was expected that the new prime minister would take charge of passing a tax reform law. Indeed, Takeshita's political career was staked on his success in passing tax reform. It is alleged that Nakasone nominated Takeshita to succeed him with this goal in mind, and within the LDP there was broad consensus that he would not be returned to office if tax reform failed. This mechanism helped to guarantee "goal succession" under the dominant-party system.

The Takeshita administration was conscious of the need for time management in the deliberations. It took care to devise a strategy that would see the tax reform plan through the government Tax Commission and LDP Reseach Commission deliberations and then through debate in the Diet. Two plans of action were considered for the purpose of passing the bill in the fall of 1988. The first was to submit the reform bill to the Diet in April or May, at the end of the ordinary session. In line with this schedule, Finance Minister Miyazawa proposed to proceed with the deliberations in the Tax Commission, coordinating there with the Research Commission.[11] Because there were many other bills to be submitted, however, it was impossible to submit the tax reform plan to the ordinary session without extending the session substantially. The deliberations could be carried over to the next session, but the reform plan could be killed accidentally, as a result of political struggles in the coming Diet session. Once a bill is killed, its revival at the next session is extremely difficult. That plan was therefore risky for the LDP.

The second plan was to convene an extraordinary session in August to allow some months for complete discussion of the bill. This plan seemed sounder, but the recommendation for it would have to be made by both the government and party commissions. Takeshita recognized that lack of full discussion was believed to be a main reason that the Nakasone reform plan failed.[12] This strategy, however, required detailed plans to ensure the eventual support of the opposition, beginning with a decision on the date the proposal would be submitted and including plans for handling each phase of action on the bill leading up to adoption by the Diet. Several contingencies, such as the possible need to dissolve the Diet, and outside factors, including a double election, were also taken into consideration. Takeshita finally chose the second plan. He completed the first two preparation stages, resolutions by the Tax Commission and the Research Commission, and succeeded in overcoming the third obstacle—opposition in the Diet—despite the Recruit scandal.

11. *Sentaku* (Choice), vol. 13 (December 1987), p. 52.
12. Mamoru Ozaki, "Uriagezei Hitorigatari 1" (A tale of sales tax), in *Fainansu* (September 1987), pp. 43–44.

Learning from Past Experience

In developing his strategy on tax reform, Takeshita clearly learned several lessons from Nakasone's experience. The new prime minister's first task was to try to alleviate the popular concerns that the Nakasone plan had raised about an indirect tax. Soon after he entered office, Takeshita announced that he had six concerns about the large-scale indirect tax in an effort to show people that he knew there was some validity to the opposition to the tax and that he was on their side.

These concerns, announced at a plenary session of the House of Representatives in March 1988, were, first, that the indirect tax might be regressive and therefore ineffective in redistributing income; second, that it might nurture feelings of unfairness among middle-income people; third, that it might weigh heavily on people with no taxable income; fourth, that it might be easy to raise the tax because people would not feel its effect as directly as they feel the effect of an income tax; fifth, that it might create an unwieldy amount of clerical work for corporations; and, sixth, that it might raise commodity prices, resulting in inflation.[13] Takeshita promised that his proposal would assuage these concerns. It is notable that three of the six points touched on the regressive nature of an indirect tax, the feature most often cited as the tax's major defect.

Takeshita drew a second lesson from Nakasone's experience and made it a personal responsibility to remove the various obstacles to tax reform that Nakasone had encountered. His main strategy was to respond to suggestions from ordinary LDP Diet members and those with influence through strong ties to interest groups or government organizations. In an unusual public relations effort, for example, the government Tax Commission held regional hearings in eight locations on the Takeshita tax plan, while the LDP Research Commission took testimony from more than 300 organizations. Rather than closing out the opposing forces, Takeshita sought to bring them into his fold. Takeshita's efforts proved successful. Public and special interest opposition to tax reform decreased, and the LDP did not split apart over the issue.

The third effort was to revise the tax plan itself to soften opposition to tax reform. Five major modifications were made to make the 1988 tax plan more acceptable to the industrial and business associations than the Nakasone plan had been.

First, the basis for calculating the tax was changed from the invoice

13. *Nihon Keizai Shimbun,* March 10, 1988.

system to the account bookkeeping system. This change resolved many of the issues that had made the Nakasone plan unpopular, in particular, criticisms that it was too complicated, that it placed companies in a disadvantageous position compared with the existing tax system, and that the details of transactions at each stage were transparent. The invoice system would have levied heavier taxes than the account bookkeeping system, which benefits small enterprises by allowing each company to subtract expenses for purchases from total income, thus leaving room for tax evasion.

Second, the tax rate was lowered from 5 percent to 3 percent. Third, tax cartels were permitted by introducing an exemption in the application of the antimonopoly law. This ensured that all sellers, including competitively weak elements such as small retailers, could pass on the tax to the next seller or to the consumer, the final buyer.

Fourth, the number of companies able to use simplified procedures was expanded from those with taxable sales of less than ¥100 million in the Nakasone plan to companies with sales under ¥500 million. The simplified procedure offers advantages to companies where added value accounts for more than 20 percent of sales; it also allows opportunity for tax evasion.

Fifth, in principle the tax was levied on all items. The Nakasone bill would have exempted fifty-one items from the tax, but the line between taxable and nontaxable items was vague, drawing criticisms that the demarcation between the two was arbitrary and therefore unfair.[14]

In addition to these modifications in the tax plan, the MOF and LDP efforts were crucial in diluting opposition to tax reform. The chief of the MOF's Tax Bureau said, "The Tax Bureau was the center of activities when promoting the Nakasone tax reform. But this time, the entire ministry concentrated efforts to one end: asking all its bureaus to cooperate. We even asked the Ministry of International Trade and Industry to contact concerned industries." MOF officials told representatives of the Association of Department Stores, who were to speak at the first hearing of the government Tax Commission, that "we will do our best, so please be cooperative."[15] A representative of the National Tax Administration Agency in Kumamoto personally contacted the chairman of the Kumamoto city Chamber of Commerce and Industry. The chamber had sent a letter reminding Takeshita of its decision in 1986 to oppose

14. *Nihon Keizai Shimbun,* May 25, 1988.
15. *Aera,* May 24, 1988, p. 22.

the introduction of a new indirect tax, and the MOF now felt it was strategically important to persuade the chamber's chairman to change his mind.

The LDP also tried to persuade antitax business leaders to drop or ease their opposition. One telling event occurred at the end of 1987, when Shinji Shimizu was forced to resign as chairman of the Association of Chain Stores by former Prime Minister Nakasone. Shimizu had spoken against the Nakasone tax reform proposal on behalf of the association, and his resignation was a sign to the business community that the LDP was serious about passing a tax reform law. Nakasone was so angry with Shimizu that he is reported to have said, "I don't care about anybody else, but don't let Shimizu have his way."[16]

The LDP Research Commission, which the Takeshita administration held responsible for the failure of the Nakasone tax plan, also changed its attitude.[17] Where it had acted arbitrarily under Nakasone, refusing to respond to objections raised to the tax plan, under Takeshita it welcomed the opinions of various industry organizations. Research Commission Chairman Yamanaka, who understood Takeshita's intentions, "learned" from the earlier failed reform and maintained a "low-key attitude, begging to hear important opinions" from industry throughout the process. The commission sent questions to industry representatives in advance of the hearings, asking their views on such major points of the new tax plan as the need for tax-exempt items, the range of tax-exempt companies, the inclusion of the tax in the retail price of goods, the cost of tax-related clerical work, and the favored form for the new indirect tax.

During four days of hearings starting on April 5, 1988, it became clear that many organizations that had opposed the earlier tax plan had come to accept the inevitability of a new indirect tax, and the general mood of industry became one of acceptance. Department stores, which had been the center of opposition to the earlier plan, took a neutral stance, and the Japan Association of Chain Stores did not actively oppose the measure.

Although the modifications to the tax plan were targeted to satisfy small and medium-sized businesses—the marginals who are extremely strong politically—not all small companies and family businesses supported tax reform. Although the Japan Chamber of Commerce and

16. *Aera*, May 24, 1988, p. 22.
17. Nagaharu Hayabusa, *Zeisei Koso Kokka no Sebone* (Tax system as the backbone of the state) (Tokyo: Tokuma Shoten, 1989), pp. 64–67.

Industry was not as adamantly opposed to the Takeshita reform as it had been to the earlier plan, it still opposed its enactment. The National Conference on Tax Policy, which mainly represented smaller textile companies, and the distribution industry were neutral.

Strategy for the Diet

The opposition parties can kill a bill in the Diet only if they act in concert and if public opinion supports them. When the proposed tax reform reached the Diet, the opposition could satisfy neither of these conditions. The Japan Socialist party was set squarely against the reform, but the positions of the other two major parties vis-à-vis a sales tax changed when Takeshita became prime minister.

The response of the Democratic Socialist party (DSP) was guided by its long-term plan to form a coalition with the LDP and by the immediate problems over the Recruit scandal, in which so many influential LDP Diet members seemed to be involved. If, after passage of the tax reform bill and elections for the Diet, the LDP no longer had a majority in the Diet, it would have to form a coalition with the DSP. Given that possibility, the DSP decided its wisest course would be let the bill pass and simply criticize it. In terms of tax reform, the DSP insisted (although unofficially) on continuing tax breaks for physicians and treating certain company owners as salaried workers for tax purposes. The party also advocated revision of the inheritance tax. This gave the impression that the party was fighting for certain conditions while accepting the tax reform itself.

The Clean Government party, Komeito, had its own way of interpreting the situation according to its interests and submitted specific modifications it wanted in the tax reform plan, giving the impression that it might agree to the plan itself. From the statements of Chairman Junya Yano, it was easy to guess what the party wanted: a bigger portion of the government budget allocated to public welfare expenditures.

Taking a lesson again from the Nakasone experience, the Takeshita administration exerted a great deal of effort to correct what public opinion deemed to be unfairness in the earlier bill. The efforts had some success. The effect of the tax reform on the middle-income bracket, which was a major issue in 1987, was barely discussed in 1988. Public opinion polls also showed a substantial drop in the public's opposition to the overall plan. According to a survey released by *Asahi Shimbun* on March 14, 1987, as the Nakasone plan was being readied for Diet consideration, only 7 percent of the respondents supported the plan, while 82 percent opposed it. The question was written without bias and even pointed out that the reform would include "income and other tax cuts." Yet the results were clear. As many as 74 percent of the people agreed that the introduction of an indirect tax would represent a breach of Nakasone's election promise. Asked which party they would support in the election after the indirect tax was introduced, 25 percent said the LDP and 27 percent said the JSP. Fully 87 percent said they thought the tax reform issue would influence the results of the simultaneous regional elections in April.

A year later, in March 1988, when the indirect tax again became a political issue, the percentages changed to 25 percent in favor of the tax and 57 percent against it—a significant increase in support and decrease in opposition, which clearly showed the positive effects of the government's attempts to "educate" the public. As one politician noted, the political environment in 1986 and 1987 gave the government a good opportunity to convince the people of its case for tax reform. With their own forces divided and without solid support from the public, the opposition parties were unable to stop the measure in its passage through the Diet.

A year later, Takeshita was forced to resign because of his involvement in the Recruit scandal. The scandal, one of the worst in Japanese postwar politics, broke when it was revealed that the Recruit company had distributed large amounts of money to nearly every influential conservative leader without registering the gifts as political contributions. Because it followed on the heels of enactment of the consumption tax and the partial commitment to liberalize the Japanese market for American agricultural products, the scandal was particularly damaging to Takeshita and his administration. Shrewd political writers said that although the Recruit issue provided an excuse for the opposition to criticize the administration, opponents were really more upset about the consumption tax.

Conclusion

This look at the politics of tax reform shows clearly that the interplay of several factors accounted for the first two failures and the final success. These factors include goal succession in the LDP administrations, the accumulated effects of campaigning for reform, weak cohesiveness of the opposition, the limits of party dominance, and time management of Diet procedures.

Goal Succession

The opposition can formulate strategy for only one Diet session, but the government party can develop strategy that plays out over several administrations and Diet sessions, in a process we call "goal succession." If one administration fails to get the bill through the Diet, the next one can try.

That is what happened with tax reform. Prime Minister Ohira proposed a new tax as a means of eliminating serious financial deficits. His successor, Prime Minister Suzuki, established the Second Ad Hoc Council for Administrative Reform to reduce those deficits by cutting expenses. When Nakasone became prime minister, he was obliged to continue Suzuki's strategy in some way. After accomplishing several major administrative reforms (privatization of the national railway and telecommunications systems), Nakasone revitalized a proposal for a general indirect tax, but failed to win Diet approval for his proposal. Nakasone nominated Takeshita as his successor on the condition that Takeshita would carry through on tax reform.

It is evident that "goal succession" was adopted in the transfer of power from Suzuki to Nakasone and from Nakasone to Takeshita. Takeshita's favorite phrase, "one administration, one task," is based on his confidence that the LDP's dominance would continue for the foreseeable future.

Accumulated Effects

Related to "goal succession" are "accumulated effects." By that, we mean that previous experience may increase accumulated knowledge about an issue by the public as well as by their political leaders. In 1986 the opposition to tax reform was united and strong. Eiichi Nagasue said it was "the most intense opposition since the Treaty of Mutual Cooperation and Security between Japan and the U.S. in 1960." Opposition was not as intense in 1988, however. We interpret this drop in opposition as a sign that the debates on the tax system, through the mass media and widespread informal discussions, had an educational effect on public attitudes in favor of reform.

Ohira's proposal pointed out the basic revenue problem. Nakasone's sales tax incited the anger of the opposition, but at the same time created forums to discuss the issues and problems of tax reform. Additionally, the 1986 political process provided the LDP leaders with information about which key persons and organizations opposed the tax reform and about the various alternatives they would support. Takeshita used this information in defusing the opposition in 1988.

Weak Cohesiveness of the Opposition

The opposition can gather force against a government bill within a single Diet session as long as the opposition parties have the support of public opinion and they form a united front.

Passing a law in the Diet usually involves sending a bill to the Diet, explaining its purpose, referring the bill to a standing (or special) committee, holding committee hearings, settling on the final committee version, and debating and passing the bill at the plenary session. A bill passed in the House of Representatives is sent to the House of Councillors, where it goes through the same procedures. If the versions passed by the two houses differ in any way, there are complicated procedures for resolving those differences and settling on a final bill.

The dominant LDP needs some kind of cooperation from the opposition parties at each stage for the bill to move smoothly from introduction to final passage. The LDP may be able to pass a bill by mobilizing all its members. It can pass bills with the opposition parties absent from the deliberations on the bill. But it is considered politically undesirable for the LDP to pass a law without the presence of the opposition parties in the committees or plenary sessions. If the opposition parties are united, it is to their advantage to block a bill by absenting themselves from the committees and plenary sessions. Such a move usually forces the LDP to offer a compromise to the opposition to persuade it to at least participate in the resolution. Refraining from offending the opposition is therefore an important tactic in this context. During consideration of the Takeshita tax reform in 1988, the Recruit scandal became a major issue, offering the opposition opportunities to disturb the Diet deliberations. Using every measure at his disposal, however, Takeshita succeeded in keeping the two issues separate during the 1988 Diet sessions.

Just as the LDP cannot afford to exclude the opposition, the opposition cannot always use the strategy of nonparticipation. The decision not to participate often leads to public criticism that the opposition is undemocratic. Clear public support made it possible for the opposition to use the strategy of nonparticipation for the tax reform issue in 1986 and 1987.

The opposition parties probably would have liked to put together a longer-term strategy, but divisions among them made that difficult. Opposition parties have to form alliances whenever a government bill that they want to kill is submitted to the Diet, Sometimes they even have to create different forms of alliances at different stages of the deliberations. Conflicting interests within the opposition parties prevented them from adopting a united position over several Diet sessions. The LDP took advantage of these shifting alliances and was able to coax some members to support it. As Arian and Barnes point out, the government party, which had an advantage in using government organizations and public resources, can use "divide-and-conquer" tactics against the opposition.

With regard to tax reform, the form and strength of the opposition alliance differed at each stage of decisionmaking in the Diet. Opposition parties that had stood together in 1986 and 1987 were divided by policy differences in 1988. The alliance lasted only a year, even though the tax issue continued to evoke strong opposition.

Limits of Dominance

The dominant party can determine the final outcome as well as set the agenda, as can be seen in the enactment of the tax reform law in 1988. But we find that at least three factors affect whether the LDP is able to enact its policy preferences.

The first is the ability of the leadership to coordinate different opinions within the party. Because party members who compete to head the government have policy differences, the LDP does not always take consistent policy positions. It is well known, for example, that the Miki administration reversed many of the policies of the preceding Tanaka administration.

Second, the government party may be able to form a long-term strategy at the leadership level, depending on the difficulty of the issue, but it may be much more difficult to pull together its rank-and-file members and maintain their loyalty. Party loyalty is even more difficult to maintain when public opinion on the issue in question is running against the party.

Third, time is not unlimited. Issues must be ranked by priority and time allotted to each in order of its importance. While the tax law was on the agenda, for example, several other laws died on the floor of the Diet.

Time Management

Consequently, even the dominant party, able to do anything it wants in the long run, has to develop a time-management strategy for a single session. Time management weighs heavily on the Japanese political mind.[18] Scheduling strategies of politicians are always a major topic in Japanese newspapers. The opposition's tactic of refusing to participate is effective in persuading the LDP to work out compromises with the opposition, because Japanese Diet sessions usually are not long, and other issues must be placed on hold if the opposition holds up deliberations on any one issue.

After nearly ten years, the Japanese government and the LDP settled the revenue issue by approving a new consumption tax. That, however, represents only the end of the first act. As experience in other countries demonstrates, the drama of the value-added tax has at least one following act in which raising the tax rate will become a major issue. What type of consumption tax will ultimately emerge in Japan remains to be seen.

18. Tomoaki Iwai, *Rippō Katei* (The legislative process) (Tokyo: Tokyo Daigaku Shuppankai, 1988), pp. 126–32.

Part IV
Political Responses
to Economic Dislocations

Comparative Structural Policies

Roger G. Noll
Haruo Shimada

POSTWAR WORLD economic history has many success stories, but none more dramatic than the chronicle of the two countries that outdistance all others in economic strength: Japan and the United States. An interesting aspect of these twin economic miracles is that, while each country intensely studies the other for new ideas about technology, business management, and government policy, and while citizens in each often proclaim that their nation should be more like the other, governmental institutions and approaches to economic policy are very different in the two countries. In Japan, the national government is far more interventionist in controlling the path of national economic development. Japan's industrial combines and their supporting financial institutions stand in contrast to the more fragmented and uncoordinated U.S. industrial structure. Finally, the role of national defense in industrial development is radically different in the two countries.

That the two countries are similar in economic strength, yet different in institutions and policies, raises two important questions. The first is whether government actually matters in promoting long-term economic growth in an advanced industrialized society. If Japan and the United States differ in their institutions, culture, and public policies, yet for several decades do battle as the world's two most important economic forces, perhaps their differences do not matter very much in their overall economic performance. The second question is why policy differences emerge, and whether either country's policies are likely to change substantially in the next decade or two. The second question is interesting only if government does matter in a nation's economic growth, so that a change in institutions and policies would presage a change in the pattern of economic development.

In this chapter, we answer these questions. Our purpose is to explain why structural policies emerge and what factors are likely to influence their effectiveness. We hope thereby to provide a useful analytical framework for our separate chapters on structural policies in each country.

Before proceeding, a definition is in order. The term *structural policies* is vague and broad and can encompass far more than we will attempt to analyze. As used here, the term applies to policies that assist in the development of a nation's basic economic infrastructure and that are consciously designed to allocate economic activity among industries and regions. Thus we include housing policies and infrastructural investments such as roads, airports, and harbors; regulatory programs to set prices, control entry, and establish the ground rules for competition, especially for utilities; policies targeted to assist specific firms, industries, and communities; and research and development (R&D) programs that seek to keep a nation at the forefront of commercial technology. We explicitly exclude several areas of policy that overlap significantly with structural policies: education, taxation, and international trade.

As defined here, structural policies may be coherent and consistent. A nation may have a broad, long-range view of its overall pattern of development and derive its specific structural policies from this vision. Alternatively, a nation may have no coherent long-term economic plan, but still pursue numerous structural policies.

Rationales for Structural Policies

Because all governments seek to promote national economic development, to dwell on why they might choose to do so may appear pointless. Obviously, all nations are likely to prefer rising income. But the underlying rationale for structural policies is more complex than this. Citizens and governments have objectives other than maximizing long-term economic growth, and they face trade-offs among these objectives. Moreover, even if the primary objective is economic growth, crafting effective policies requires understanding why government must intervene and how policies promote growth.

The purpose of structural policies is to alter the rate and pattern of national economic development. Hence the justification for these policies is a failure of private decisions about investment, R&D, and employment to take into account all the values that ought to govern these decisions. Two kinds of market failure are relevant: inefficiencies in producing the right quantity and quality of products, and the inability to deal adequately with issues pertaining to income distribution and noneconomic values.

Efficiency Rationales

The research literature provides a rich analysis of why market-driven private decisions might produce an inefficiently low rate of economic growth. In advanced economies, the sources of long-term growth have been technological progress, increases in capital investment per worker, and increases in the skills of the work force.[1] While estimates of the relative importance of these factors differ, all agree that each plays an important role. Technical progress and greater labor skills account for most of the growth in output per worker; however, fully exploiting advances in either normally requires changes in the design of machines, facilities, and other fixed capital investments.

In advanced, high-income economies, sustaining growth in per capita income requires maintaining international competitiveness in industries in which technology is advancing rapidly. High per capita income goes hand in hand with high labor costs. In industries that have relatively stable technology and are not based on unique resources, low-wage countries eventually will copy the technology and capture a substantial share of the industry from high-wage competitors. In industries such as consumer electronics, steel, textiles, and automobiles, this began to happen to the United States around 1960 and to Japan about 1980.

To offset these inevitable losses, high-income countries must develop new products and production technologies that, for a while, are not likely to be copied by countries with lower labor costs.[2] To succeed at this strategy requires two types of national capabilities. The first is a large, effective effort in research and development that both invents and brings to commercial practice new technical advances. The second is sufficient institutional flexibility to permit major shifts in the structure of the economy, including the skill composition and geographic distribution of the labor force. A rationale for structural policies is to overcome a nation's shortcomings in both capabilities.

One reason that private-market economies may grow too slowly is that advances in knowledge that produce technical progress are not fully appropriable. That is, part of the benefit of technological progress is

1. See Edward F. Denison assisted by Jean-Pierre Poullier, *Why Growth Rates Differ: Postwar Experience in Nine Western Countries* (Brookings, 1967); and Edward F. Denison, *Accounting for United States Economic Growth, 1929–1969* (Brookings, 1974).

2. See Raymond Vernon, ed., *The Technology Factor in International Trade* (Columbia University Press, 1970).

passed on to consumers as rising real income, itself a desirable feature of economic development. But if private investments in new knowledge are based on the quest for profits, investors, by ignoring consumer benefits, will underinvest in technological progress and productivity growth will be slower than if all economic benefits were taken into account.

A second reason growth may be too slow is that capital markets may not be efficient. They may not be structurally competitive and so may have inefficiencies due to monopolization or manipulation arising from imperfect information. But even if capital markets are competitive, other problems may cause funds to be inadequate for some useful purposes. For example, people who otherwise could make productive investments in education or research may be unable to borrow funds because they lack collateral. In addition, to assess investment risks, an investor must have information about the contemplated investment, which requires that the person with the novel idea reveal its nature and thereby risk losing control of it. For these and other reasons, capital markets may not deliver sufficient funds to fuel all the investment required to produce a high rate of growth.

The preceding analysis explains why advanced capitalistic economies may grow more slowly than is desirable, but it does not necessarily justify structural policies. One can attack problems of underinvestments in capital facilities, research and development, and education simply by subsidizing them. Such a policy would not require programs that are targeted at specific industries, technologies, or regions. The implicit presumption of a general policy encouraging investment is that the importance of market failures is more or less the same across all types of investments. In practice, this is unlikely to be the case.[3]

Technologies differ in the extent to which new technical ideas can be copied and hence their benefits not appropriated by the innovating firm. In addition, the ease of entry in an industry can also affect the appropriability of technical advances. In an industry with high entry barriers and few firms, an innovator is likely to capture more of the economic benefits of an innovation than in an industry with easy entry and numerous firms.

Industries also differ in the extent to which their efficiency is important

3. For an excellent analysis of why government might target programs for the energy sector, see Richard Schmalensee, "Appropriate Government Policy toward Commercialization of New Energy Supply Technologies," *Energy Journal*, vol. 1 (April 1980), pp. 1–40.

to the overall economy. Industries that produce important inputs to many other economic activities can affect the entire structure of a nation's comparative advantage. For example, transportation, energy, and communications are important inputs throughout the economy. Thus a poorly performing telecommunications sector can reduce the demand for, and capabilities of, the information services industry, and an inefficient transportation sector can hurt the international competitive position of a resource-based industry located far from international ports. Although eliminating inefficiencies is always economically beneficial, it can be especially valuable in infrastructural industries. Consequently, a nation is more likely to be concerned about market failures in these industries than elsewhere.

Conflicts with efficiency objectives other than growth can cause further differences among industries in the desirability of promoting their growth. For example, short-term pricing efficiency in monopolies, such as public utilities, requires preventing them from setting prices that maximize profits. Keeping a monopoly's prices low also reduces costs in industries that are intensive users of monopolized goods and services, thereby enhancing their competitiveness. Usually utility prices are based on costs so as to prevent the utility from earning excess profits; however, cost-based prices also prevent the utility from appropriating the gains from innovation. Hence pricing policies in public enterprises or regulated industries may cause prices to be more efficient in the short run but blunt the incentive for cost-reducing technological progress, leading to higher prices in the long run.

Other Policy Objectives

Structural policies can arise for numerous reasons other than to promote economic efficiency. One example is income distribution policy. In part, citizens may prefer to serve distributional objectives by providing employment opportunities rather than transfer payments, but even if they do not, structural policies may have a lower immediate net cost. For example, in the short run shoring up a geographically concentrated dying industry may be less expensive than letting it expire and then providing income support to former employees or developing a new industry (and new job skills in the old industry's labor force) to replace it. The former can be achieved by subsidizing the industry. In the long run, however, these policies conflict with economic growth by slowing the transfer of labor, capital, and other resources to industries where they can be used more productively.

Economic efficiency also can conflict with noneconomic policies, such as national security, international political objectives, and aspects of the quality of life that are not conventionally measured in economic terms. High rates of productivity advance in hallucinogenic drugs are unlikely to be a persuasive reason for eliminating restrictions on their use. Or, perhaps more realistically, an important rationale for government support of R&D in some industries—such as nuclear power, aerospace, and microelectronics—is their relationship to international objectives. For example, the United States strongly adheres to a policy of nonprolifer-ation of nuclear weapons. To be effective in preventing nuclear prolifera-tion, the United States must be a major player in the world market for commercial uses of nuclear power in order to retain some control over the use of nuclear technology. Hence, even if commercial nuclear power is not economically attractive for American industry, the U.S. government still pursues R&D and provides other subsidies as long as other nations want to build nuclear power plants. One price of this policy is that it redirects scarce technical personnel and facilities that, if employed elsewhere, would be likely to produce technological advances with a greater economic payoff.

The preceding analysis provides some reasons governments might want to treat industries differently. Industries are likely to differ in the extent to which growth rates fall short of the economic optimum and in the extent to which they pose conflicts between economic efficiency and other public policy objectives. Likewise, the applicability of these rationales is likely to differ among countries. Nations may not share the same policy objectives. For example, Japan and the United States have very different national security policies. Consequently, in Japan "strategic industries" are more likely to be selected on the basis of economic criteria, such as potential for growth in the world market, or domestic political considerations. The United States is more prone to adopt structural policies that favor industries with strong links to international security. A consequence of its greater concern for noneco-nomic international objectives is that, in order to pursue them effectively, the United States must expect to sacrifice some economic growth in comparison with Japan.[4]

4. The Japanese government has become increasingly interested in defense and international relations during the 1980s. To the extent this is manifest in structural policies, it will likewise be likely to detract from economic growth.

Thus neither the overall importance of structural policies nor their role in any specific industry need be consistent among countries—even countries that have similar political ideologies. The array of political rationales is sufficiently rich that they could explain almost any pattern of policies. The main value of these rationales is not that they predict international policy differences, but that they highlight the array of rational arguments for justifying structural policies.

Politics and Structural Policies

The preceding discussion takes the perspective that political officials undertake policies to pursue national objectives concerning economic efficiency, distributional equity, and international relations. In actual political processes, policymaking is more complicated than this for two reasons.[5] First, citizens and political officials may seek to use government to achieve personal objectives that are not in accord with these public purposes. Second, the structure of government may give governmental officials false signals about the relative merits of policy alternatives. In either case, just as private decisions may suffer from market failures, public decisions may fail by leading public officials to pursue policies that do not advance national objectives.

Organized Interests

Both popular and scholarly discourse focuses on the vulnerability of large democracies to excessive influence by organized interests.[6] The problem begins with two principles of democracy: the periodic ratification of governments through elections, and the requirement for a rational, evidentiary basis for coercive policies. Because voting is an almost completely powerless action, a citizen has no incentive to become fully informed on all public issues and almost no incentive even to vote for the preferred candidate. But large groups of citizens, by coordinating their votes and other forms of political participation, can have a real effect on the electoral process. Hence citizens have an incentive to organize for the pursuit of common political objectives.

5. For further elaboration, see Linda R. Cohen and Roger G. Noll, *The Technology Pork Barrel* (Brookings, forthcoming).
6. See Terry M. Moe, *The Organization of Interests: Incentives and the Internal Dynamics of Political Interest Groups* (University of Chicago Press, 1980); and Mancur Olson, Jr., *The Logic of Collective Action: Public Goods and the Theory of Groups* (Harvard University Press, 1965).

To form a politically relevant organization and to maintain group cohesion requires effort and expense, so that citizens are likely to concentrate on groups that matter most. In some cases, the organizing principle can be a ubiquitous policy issue of widespread national concern, such as national defense. But if government affects the income produced in a particular economic sector, people who derive income from that sector have reason to focus their collective political activity on these policies. This incentive is a point of commonality among diverse individuals who would not otherwise find common ground. Moreover, their commonality of interest is not bounded by the national objectives motivating government support for them. The welfare of a program's beneficiaries typically is maximized at a scale of the program that exceeds the size that cures a market failure or achieves some other national objective.

The implication is that in seeking to build support coalitions, political leaders will bias policy in favor of interests organized around commonalities of production—industries, regions, trade associations, unions. This policy bias will take the form of excessively generous support compared with the actual public objectives at stake. Well-organized groups with a common interest will be so favored because they can deliver political support—votes, volunteers, contributions—and can provide the information necessary to sustain policies that favor them. Moreover, because all major industries and localities are likely to be organized, the natural tendency of political leaders, in seeking electoral security, is to provide policy benefits to as many as possible. Hence structural policies are likely be too inclusive, covering more of the economy than can be justified by market failures.

The importance of the interest group model of economic policy hinges on the relative importance of political organizations representing producers compared with other effective political groups. In times of war or national economic emergency, the saliency of shared national policy objectives is stronger, and more likely to dominate narrow economic interests, than in times of general prosperity and relative freedom from the threat of war. Likewise, issues besides the overall state of the economy and national security sometimes become of great interest to large groups of citizens. Examples in both Japan and the United States are environmental policy in the late 1960s and energy policy in the mid- to late 1970s. If many citizens think general policy issues are more important in assessing government performance, the influence of narrow economic interests will be smaller. In Japan, the importance of recovery from the devastation of World War II was plausibly such an overriding concern. Once the majority of the Japanese electorate had found political leadership that ran the government effectively, economic recovery could form the basis of a stable political coalition that for two decades was comparatively free from the influence of specific economic interests. But once economic recovery was achieved, the coalition's survival required ever-increasing responsiveness to the narrow economic interests of its members.

The Effects of Political Institutions

The importance of political institutions is illustrated by the consequences of different legislative structures. If legislators are elected from geographic areas, they are more likely to represent support coalitions built around narrow economic interests, because a small geographic area is more likely to be economically specialized than is an entire nation. Consequently, a specific industry may be unimportant nationally but important in some localities and hence well represented in the national government. In turn, if legislatures are based on geographic representation and also decentralized into committees that control the agenda of the larger body, legislators can specialize in policies of great interest to a narrow constituency. Thus a decentralized legislature should be more responsive to demands for special favors than is a legislature in which the agenda is controlled by a strong executive (as in France) or a centralized national party (as in Great Britain).

In some respects, Japan and the United States have similar electoral institutions. Both legislatures are based on geographical districts and organized into committees with the power to initiate legislation. However, the Japanese and American political systems differ in several ways that are likely to have important consequences for structural policies. These differences reflect divergent histories in the evolution of democratic political institutions. Predemocratic Japan was centralized and hierarchical, with political and economic power concentrated in a landed aristocracy. Modernization brought forth a series of decentralizing and equalizing reforms, but in the political sphere the present structure—a single dominant parliament with weak local and regional governments—stands near the most centralized end of the spectrum of democratic forms of government. By contrast, the American system was constructed in an era of great skepticism about centralized authority. The U.S. Constitution left considerable power to state and local government.

Moreover, it diffused federal power by separating the executive and legislative branches, limiting legislative control over the judiciary, and separating the legislative branch into two coequal bodies with differing principles of representation.

The importance of differences in centralization of power is that they affect a nation's ability to develop a coherent, long-run structural policy. Specifically, coherency is less likely to emerge in the United States. If structural policies are essential to maximize long-term growth, Japan, therefore, is politically advantaged. If individual creativity and initiative, unconstrained by a strong central government, promote growth, the United States is advantaged.

Beyond centralization, the two nations have other institutional differences that may affect their structural policies. One is the postwar emergence in Japan of a strong central party;[7] however, this may have been the result of Japan's economic condition after World War II rather than any fundamental feature of the Japanese system. The rising importance of factions in the ruling Liberal Democratic party (LDP) since it secured power is evidence that a strong party system may be unstable and so may be disappearing as the nation's economic strength grows. Another difference is multimember Diet districts, usually electing three to five members each, compared with single-member districts in the U.S. House of Representatives and dual-member districts (states) in the U.S. Senate. Multimember districts make Diet constituencies larger than they would be if all members represented a different district. Hence Diet members represent a less specialized and homogeneous set of economic interests than they would if each was elected from a single-member district. Nevertheless, because the Diet is large, districts still tend to be relatively small, with approximately the same population, on average, as U.S. congressional districts. In addition, because Japan does not draw district boundaries strictly on the basis of population, some Diet districts are quite small, causing some interests (for example, agriculture) to be grossly overrepresented. Finally, multimember districts encourage the formation of multiple parties, each representing a different set of interests. Whereas factionalization of the LDP has helped to prevent this, in the long run the Japanese system may be one in which no party is dominant and governments tend to be unstable multiparty coalitions. In such a system, stable structural policies will be more difficult to sustain.

7. Junnosuke Masumi, *Sengo Seiji: 1945–1955* (Postwar politics: 1945–1955) (Tokyo: Tokyo Daigaku Shuppankai, 1983).

The United States has an independent executive with veto power over legislation. Because national offices are less likely to be influenced by narrow economic interests, the American president should provide a counter to the legislature's responsiveness to such interests. In addition, since the "one man, one vote" Supreme Court decisions of the 1960s, the size of House districts has become more equal, reducing the political power of agriculture; however, the Senate continues to overrepresent rural areas.

In both countries, structural policies require a coalition of several economic interests. In the absence of a salient national purpose, structural policies require support from numerous legislators whose constituencies are grounded in different industries. Other than agriculture and infrastructural sectors, few industries are so widespread that they are important in a large number of legislative districts. This has two consequences. First, it is difficult to focus support on one or a few key industries, other than ubiquitous ones like agriculture, energy, transportation, and communications. Second, if an industry is to be supported through infrastructural policies, the benefits must accrue to most firms in the industry. That is, a policy is not likely to succeed if it must pick a few winners and make losers out of most of the industry's participants. The implication is that structural policies are too inclusive, supporting some firms and industries in which support does not yield a high return. The tendency to avoid picking winners further constrains public decisions because officials want to avoid changing the structure of an industry. For example, if the government supports commercial R&D, the program is most attractive if all of an industry shares in the research and participates in the industry's future. By contrast, if technological realities require that the industry become more or less concentrated, existing firms are more likely to oppose the program, either because it unfairly must pick winners or because it will encourage entrants who threaten incumbents.

In any electoral system the frequency of elections also affects the efficacy of structural policies. The interval between elections determines the time horizon in which a party must take actions that respond to the preferences and interests of its support coalition. If, as in the United States, legislative elections are frequent, political actors have reason to seek programs that can deliver observable policy consequences relatively quickly. With respect to structural policies, frequent elections tend to focus attention on short-term changes in prices, employment, and profits, not long-term trends in productivity. For a year or two, the difference between rapid and slow technological progress is hardly observable to most citizens, or even to most participants in a target industry, but after a decade or longer, fast versus slow productivity growth is decisive in determining the health of the domestic economy.

In Japan, elections are less frequent and are called at irregular intervals by the ruling party. This encourages political leaders to adopt a somewhat longer time horizon and a greater tolerance for programs that are more uncertain about when payoffs will be realized. This gives Japan an advantage in undertaking policies that promote long-term economic growth.

The Role of the Bureaucracy

The nature of the bureaucracy also influences the performance of structural policies. Policy development and implementation require the work of professional civil servants. The bureaucracies involved in structural policies play an important part in identifying policy options.

An important determinant of the bureaucracy's role is its autonomy in designing and implementing programs. One factor affecting autonomy is the protection accorded civil servants from political interference and reprisal. Another is the depth of political appointments in the bureaucratic hierarchy. Still another is the formal role of agencies in initiating budgets and legislative proposals.

Much has been written about the relatively powerful role of the bureaucracy in Japan (and several European countries ranging from Great Britain to the Soviet Union) compared with its influence in the United States. Although we make no effort to disprove this view, there are good reasons to believe that national differences in the importance of the bureaucracy are overemphasized. First, even in the United States an extensive popular and academic literature emphasizes the significance of bureaucratic authority.[8] Second, generalizations about bureaucratic influence mask considerable variability among agencies and programs within each nation. If this variability is explainable by the same political forces, a focus on international average differences will overlook important factors affecting program performance. Third, the influence of

8. The argument is nicely summarized in Morris P. Fiorina, *Congress: Keystone of the Washington Establishment* (Yale University Press, 1977). See also William A. Niskanen, Jr., *Bureaucracy and Representative Government* (Chicago: Aldine, Atherton, 1971); and Aaron B. Wildavsky, *The Politics of the Budgetary Process* (Little, Brown, 1964).

bureaucrats, even when great, is always at the sufferance of elected political officials. Ultimately bureaucratic power rests on legislative actions, and bureaucratic discretion can be confined, shaped, and even eliminated by the legislature.

In Japan and the United States the role of the bureaucracy has substantial similarities. Both countries rely on an extensive professional civil service for running programs and performing analyses and evaluations. In both countries, budgetary and program proposals emanate from the agencies and then are independently evaluated by a separate budgetary agency that is also staffed primarily by professional civil servants.

Nevertheless, the two countries differ in important respects. The most important difference arises from the separation of legislative and executive power in the United States. High-level bureaucratic positions are part of the president's administration. Because the president and Congress have different constituencies (and are often controlled by different parties), a natural conflict arises between the two branches. Thus, in serving the president, the bureaucracy often is in conflict with Congress. This has several consequences.

First, Congress is less likely than the Diet to enact recommendations from the bureaucracy because Congress has less control over it. Second, Congress is likely to rely more on formal methods of control, such as legislative specificity, administrative procedural restraints, and judicial review, because it lacks some of the informal controls of a parliamentary system. Third, Congress has its own parallel bureaucracy for analyzing and proposing programs. Agencies such as the General Accounting Office, the Congressional Budget Office, the Congressional Research Service, the Office of Technology Assessment, and staffs of committees contain professionals whose tenure in office survives change in the political leadership of Congress.

The greater apparent influence of the bureaucracy in Japan reflects the fact that the ruling party in the Diet can serve to ameliorate political conflicts and provide coherent general policy directives for bureaucrats. The greater fragmentation of power in the United States lessens the apparent importance of the bureaucracy because policy is less coherent. This does not imply that each center of power, presidential or congressional, relies less on the bureaucracy for developing, implementing, and evaluating programs. It instead creates a fragmented bureaucracy that parallels the fragmentation of power.

Regardless of the relative autonomy of bureaus, political leaders in both countries design bureaucracies to achieve the political ends of those in power. The design problem for political leaders is, how can bureaucratic structures be best designed to achieve political ends? Political officials can vary the structure of government agencies in three important ways. Agencies can differ in the professional expertise of their staff, the scope of their missions, and the extent to which their responsibilities overlap with other agencies.

The importance of agency organization is that broader staff capabilities, more encompassing responsibilities, and more direct competition among agencies lead to less dominance by the organized interests that benefit from programs. The cause of this relationship is the role of information in forming and implementing policies. Effective structural policies depend on accurate information about future markets and technologies. Typically firms have the best information about these matters and can be expected to use this information strategically to achieve more favorable policies.

A bureaucracy can ameliorate the government's informational disadvantage. It can develop its own independent expertise, and it can be given a process that enables it to gather information by putting firms into conflict about the agency's policy decisions. Of course, agencies will not want to foment conflicts among constituencies; the preferred state is to keep them all happy. Indeed, government agencies with multiple responsibilities are often subdivided by constituency groups in order to minimize internal conflicts. For example, the U.S. Department of Energy, which subsidizes commercial R&D in energy, has offices for each major energy resource: coal, nuclear, solar. Thus broad authority does not create discretionary power unless the agency makes firms and industries compete for favorable policy decisions.

Another aspect of bureaucratic structure that influences performance is the extent to which agency decisions can be reviewed by courts. The use of judicial review is far more common in the United States than in other countries. Judicial interpretations of the constitutional principles of due process, equal protection, and separation of power cause few decisions to be beyond the reach of judicial review. Nevertheless, agencies differ substantially in the intensity, frequency, and substance of judicial review that their authorizing legislation requires.

Judicial review provides represented interests with a means for threatening to delay or reverse an agency's decision by appealing to the courts. If an agency cares about its policy and wants to implement it as soon as possible, it must anticipate the possibility of judicial review and, in so doing, objections by dissatisfied groups. Extensive judicial review, therefore, enhances the influence of represented groups, especially if the agency has relatively sparse resources for generating its own independent information and defending itself in court.[9]

Elected political officials establish the responsibilities, powers, structure, and administrative processes of implementing agencies. Presumably these officials take into account the effects of their decisions on the policy orientation of an agency. If so, the design of agencies should reflect the policy intent of elected political officials.[10] In comparing two programs, one can infer from the methods of implementation the extent to which political leaders were concerned about excessive influence by organized interest groups. Legislators can make policy especially responsive to organized interests by creating a monopoly agency with a narrow responsibility and too few resources to subject policy options to serious independent scrutiny.

In the postwar era, several developments have militated against allowing an agency to be the captive of a narrow interest. One is the overall effect of rising income, which, all else equal, increases citizens' demands for things that can be provided only with government's help, such as pure public goods or the correction of market failures. Thus membership in single-issue organizations, such as environmental organizations or consumer groups, grows with income, which in turn increases the representation of these interests in political, bureaucratic, and judicial processes. In addition, rapid technological progress in electronics has caused the cost of communications and information processing to drop precipitously. This reduces the cost of forming political organizations and so encourages more of them to come into existence.

As the interests that seek to influence a policy become more numerous, the apparent autonomy of a bureaucracy is likely to decline. Legislators are more likely to be called upon by a disaffected interest to reverse an agency's decision and are less likely to find political benefit in delegating authority to an agency that is closely aligned with a particular economic

9. See Roger G. Noll, "The Political Foundations of Regulatory Policy," in Mathew D. McCubbins and Terry Sullivan, eds., *Congress: Structure and Policy* (Cambridge University Press, 1987).

10. For further analysis of how political officials design agencies to achieve their political objectives, see Mathew D. McCubbins, Roger G. Noll, and Barry R. Weingast, "Administrative Procedures as Instruments of Political Control," *Journal of Law, Economics and Organization*, vol. 3 (Fall 1987), pp. 243–77, and "Structure and Process, Politics and Policy: Administrative Arrangements and the Political Control of Agencies," *Virginia Law Review*, vol. 75 (March 1989), pp. 431–82.

interest. This implies that the apparent power and autonomy of Japanese bureaucracy reflects the consensus in economic purpose and the single-party control of the government from 1950 until the 1980s. As Japan becomes less consensual, the demands on the bureaucracy will be more conflicting, causing political leaders to assert more direct control over policy.

Growth in the Demand for Government

As the size of government has grown, the incentive to participate in its decisions probably has increased. Interest group factors enter here as well. Government programs have an asymmetry that is especially relevant to structural policies. The asymmetry is that the political support for a program tends to be larger after it is established than before.[11] The reason is the way interest groups form around a policy issue. Before a program is established, some people who will benefit from it are unaware of this fact or are not effectively organized to support it. This includes not only the direct beneficiaries, but also people who will profit from the beneficiaries' incomes or who will become involved in implementing the program. Once a program is established and passes the threshold of detectability in these people's lives, they are more likely to become organized to support it. Consequently, programs once established are more likely to grow than to decline and can suffer a shortfall in actual performance without losing overall political support.

The performance shortfall a program can suffer and survive depends on how it is implemented. If implementation enfranchises performance-oriented groups as well as the program's beneficiaries, the performance shortfall that the program can survive will be less than if the implementing bureaucracy is structured to maximize dependence on the beneficiaries. The latter is most likely to be the case if the program's effect on the efficiency of the target industry was not its primary purpose, but was overshadowed by a straightforward desire to subsidize the beneficiaries. In both Japan and the United States, agricultural policy has this characteristic.

The preceding argument does not lead to the conclusion that government programs are, on balance, wasteful and excessively large. The

11. For more details, see Roger G. Noll and Bruce M. Owen, *The Political Economy of Deregulation: Interest Groups in the Regulatory Process* (Washington: American Enterprise Institute for Public Policy Research, 1983), chap. 3.

kinds of problems enunciated above can be expected to influence the enthusiasm of program supporters before a program is enacted, leading to two offsetting effects. First, political actors and their supporters will require greater expected performance to start a program than they would in the absence of ex post interest group problems. Second, some poorly performing programs will be retained after enactment because of these effects, but these will tend to be programs that have suffered bad luck or that were enacted initially because of strong interest group pressure so that performance was never a criterion for their political success.

Implications: Political Preconditions
for Structural Policies

The preceding is a sufficiently general statement of the political foundations of structural policy that it admits the possibility of almost all types of programs. One can imagine programs motivated solely by efficiency rationales, with implementing agencies that are structured to minimize capture by the organized beneficiaries. The policy debate about such a program would include a wide variety of influential political organizations representing the full spectrum of interests that are affected by it. The predictable characteristics of these programs are high political saliency and implementation that enfranchises conflicting sources of independent information in bureaucratic processes. One can also imagine agencies that are nothing more than conduits of the interests of a firm or industry, having been set up to provide subsidies or a favorable institutional environment, such as by promulgating cartelizing regulations. Agencies carrying out these programs would have narrow responsibilities, few resources for independent analysis, and procedures insulating them from interests other than the program's beneficiaries.

The latter type of program and implementing agency has probably become more difficult to maintain because of the growth of effective political organizations. Nonetheless, structural policies cannot necessarily be scaled back or eliminated just because they perform poorly. The performance standard for retaining them is lower than the standard for creation, owing to the asymmetry in interest group support for programs.

Structural policies will be more successful politically if they deliver benefits earlier rather than later and if they do not create losers among the targeted beneficiaries. These factors militate against long-term R&D policies that would fundamentally change an industry's underlying technology. They also work against programs that require contracts with only some firms in an industry. Hence structural policies are easier to implement for concentrated industries than for atomistically competitive ones; likewise, undoing a structural policy is easier if the policy is reallocating wealth among firms in the target industry.

The preceding analysis points to interesting similarities and differences between Japan and the United States.

—Because both countries are leading economic powers with high per capita GNP, both depend on being at the forefront of some rapidly developing technologies. Thus each country should exhibit considerable public concern over the international competitiveness of its high-wage industries and its ability to restructure its economy. Nevertheless, the richer resource base of the United States should cause it to exhibit less concern than Japan about these issues. Moreover, because Japanese elections are less frequent and timed flexibly, the time horizon of structural policies should be longer in Japan.

—Because legislatures in both countries are elected from geographically based constituencies and organized into specialized committees with the power to initiate programs, structural policies in both countries are likely to be substantially influenced by narrow economic interests. Both countries should face difficulty in scaling down failed or inefficient structural policies and pursuing policies that require picking winners in an industry.

—Because Japanese industrial markets are probably less competitive but certainly better coordinated through financial institutions and diversified trading combines, Japan is less likely to be forced to pick winners. This should make structural policy broader and more important in Japan.

—Because its political structure is more centralized, Japan should have a more coherent set of structural policies. Moreover, because multimember Diet districts should produce multiparty governments, Japan's structural policies are likely to be more inclusive. In the short run, the dominant party—the LDP—can use inclusiveness to fend off competing parties. In the long run, shifting multiparty coalitions should lead to an ever-widening range of industry-specific policies, each of which persists because of the asymmetry of support for structural policies before and after their enactment.

—Because the U.S. Constitution causes more judicial review, American structural policies should be more difficult and costly to implement and more influenced by organized interests. Thus judicial review leads to less flexible and less efficient structural policies and makes them less attractive politically.

—Because U.S. economic programs are more likely to be instruments of noneconomic international policies, U.S. structural policies are likely to produce a lower rate of economic growth than policies in Japan, which has less ambitious international objectives.

Structural Policies in
the United States

Roger G. Noll

THE United States does not have a coherent, comprehensive structural policy.[1] To the extent that the government engages in long-run economic planning, it undertakes this task in the Executive Office of the President with a staff of a few hundred professionals who work in several bureaus that oversee economic and budgetary policy. But nowhere is there a sizable group of people, having real authority, who make policy regarding the long-term pattern of economic development in the United States.

Nonetheless, the United States does have a structural policy by default. The government pursues many policies that together strongly influence the course of national development. What the country lacks is an institutionalized means of coordinating these programs in more than a cursory way and comprehensive coverage of all industries, localities, and technologies. Most of the components of American structural policy were initiated sequentially as separate, narrow policy initiatives in response to a salient national political issue or to requests for support from an industry or region. The result is a patchwork of policies intended to fix specific problems, rather than a systematic national development plan.

The absence of a comprehensive structural policy is not an accident, and it does not go unnoticed. Indeed, periodically it has been a contentious political issue. Several explanations have been offered for the American aversion to comprehensive economic planning, but one cause is the political structure of the nation as established by the Constitution. At the time of the American Revolution, the leading political figures were especially concerned that the centralization of power would open

1. Structural policies refer to domestic programs that are designed to subsidize or otherwise directly encourage specific industries or geographic areas. They include infrastructure investments, economic regulation, agricultural subsidies, support for research and development, and other forms of industrial policy.

the government to capture by either impassioned temporary majorities or coalitions of special interests. Their first attempt to organize a national government, through the Articles of Confederation, produced too weak a union to protect the mutual interests of the states. The second attempt, the Constitution, created a remarkably durable system that is nonetheless unusually fragmented and decentralized in comparison with other modern democracies. It reflects a political culture that is wary of government control of any important aspect of national life, including the economy. The constitutional impediments to coherent policies include the tripartite structure of the federal government, with its elaborate checks and balances, and the elevated status of state and local governments.

Nonetheless, as time passes, the number of structural programs tends to grow. More are created than are destroyed, and budget increases are usually larger than budget cuts. The pattern of programs that emerges is increasingly broad and complex.

Because American structural policies lack a coherent purpose or focus, any analysis of them necessarily lacks an overarching theme. Moreover, because these policies are generated by a variety of political and economic forces, a comprehensive treatment would require far more than one chapter. Hence the strategy of this essay is to discuss how a few structural policies have developed and changed. I will focus on policies that are important to the American economy and that provide a basis of comparison with other advanced industrialized societies such as Japan. I begin with a historical overview of several important structural policies and then discuss current policies concerning research and development, regulation, agriculture, and public infrastructural investments.

The Historical Development of Structural Policies

American structural policies constitute a mixed bag of unrelated programs, each of which was created soon after a national political issue first became salient. Some U.S. structural policies have their origins in periods of severe economic disruption in rural areas. In virtually all advanced industrialized economies, primary product industries have experienced a relative decline for more than a century. These industries—agriculture, forestry, mining, ranching—are almost exclusively rural. The United States has assisted primary product industries since the formation of the land grant colleges after the Civil War. Indeed,

232

ROGER G. NOLL

conflicts between rural interests and the owners of railroads and grain elevators gave rise to economic regulation in the 1870s. Then, in the first decade of the twentieth century, the Bureau of Reclamation was created to develop the nation's water resources in order to provide low-priced water for agriculture. And three major initiatives adopted during the Great Depression focused on rural areas: subsidies and marketing quotas to increase prices received by farmers, subsidies to develop utilities in rural areas, and federal regulatory policies to hold prices below costs for utilities and transportation in rural areas, offset by higher prices in larger cities (that is, cross-subsidization).

In addition to increasing rural subsidies, the Roosevelt administration proposed a rather comprehensive industrial policy, the National Recovery Act, which would have introduced systematic national planning in major industries. But the act was ruled unconstitutional by the Supreme Court. Even though the ideology of the Court soon changed so that the decision would surely have been reversed after 1940, neither the president nor Congress has since attempted to enact a comprehensive industrial policy.

World War II brought forth another category of structural policies— those created to encourage the development of defense-related industries. The United States has always favored domestic industries in military procurement, but a more broadly based policy to encourage other industries that supply manufacturers of military equipment arose out of the international tensions of the late 1930s, the subsequent war, and the postwar decision to bear most of the burden for national defense in the noncommunist world. Although this policy was designed to serve the technological requirements of the military, it had important commercial spillovers. Defense research and development (R&D) and procurement played an important role in the development of the American aerospace, communications, computer, and microelectronics industries. In all cases, national defense accounts for a declining share of the market for these industries; for the foreseeable future, however, defense is likely to continue to support their development and to be a strong force in shaping their technological progress.

Another set of structural policies emerged from the economic adjustment at the end of World War II. During the war years, the American economy became virtually nationalized. War-related production took first priority, and the greatly expanded demands on production in manufacturing, primary products, and transportation, in particular, led to government-financed investments. At the peak of the war effort, government officials and economists worried about the economic consequences of peace, fearing that the switch to a consumer-oriented economy could be achieved only after protracted economic dislocation.

Three postwar readjustment policies were important in shaping the future course of the economy. One was the decision to privatize virtually everything that had been nationalized or created de novo by the federal government during the war years. (The only important exception was government investments in nuclear energy, which were then seen as having exclusively military significance.) The second was to encourage construction through banking regulations, tax preferences, and federal home mortgage insurance, all of which led to a housing boom. The third important policy initiative was the Marshall Plan, whereby the United States agreed to finance a substantial part of the reconstruction of the countries devastated by the war. Because the United States and Canada were the only leading industrial countries with an undamaged manufacturing sector, rapid reconstruction in Europe and Japan increased the demand for U.S. products. Consequently, many war production industries experienced a milder adjustment than had been feared.

The most recent structural policies emerged in the wake of three more or less simultaneous events. The first was the end of the war in Vietnam, which, unlike the nation's past major conflicts, did not leave the government with a significant economic or military responsibility in the area of the hostilities. The second was the energy crisis, punctuated by the two OPEC-instigated oil shortages of 1973 and 1979. Largely because of its vast domestic energy reserves, the United States had developed under a regime of very low energy prices and so was among the most energy-intensive economies. Moreover, it was neither psychologically nor institutionally prepared to cope with significant economic dependence on other countries. Hence the energy shocks of the 1970s disrupted the U.S. economy. The third event was the completion of the redevelopment of the countries that were most devastated during World War II. The reemergence of these countries was accelerated by the shift of American economic resources to the war in Southeast Asia and the easier adaptation of these economies to the sharp increases in energy prices. But this reemergence was inevitable and even hastened by the proactive U.S. role in their postwar reconstruction.

The United States responded to the economic crises of the 1970s by easing economic regulatory policies and by dramatically increasing federal expenditures on energy-related R&D. The reduction of economic regulation, although it may have been inevitable, was hastened by stagflation. Meanwhile, the federal government greatly increased its involvement in the energy sector. It federalized some state regulatory powers and initiated a massive effort to develop new energy technologies.

A third response to the problems of the 1970s, although not analyzed in this chapter, was a noticeable change in American trade policy. Since the enactment of the Smoot-Hawley tariff, which was given much of the blame for turning an economic recession into the Great Depression, the United States had steadfastly reduced its trade barriers. But in the 1970s protectionist measures began to reemerge. Because of constraints imposed by the General Agreement on Trade and Tariffs, the government made extensive use of quotas, rather than tariffs, to control imports. Quotas have always been used, notably to protect domestic oil and sugar beets. But since the mid-1970s quota arrangements, formal and voluntary, have been used to protect such industries as textiles, automobiles, steel, and semiconductors.

During the 1980s structural programs in the United States underwent two further significant changes. First, the composition of direct governmental support for research and development reverted to the pattern that had prevailed before the early 1970s; that is, the government again focused mainly on basic research or on R&D related to national security (although perhaps with potentially important commercial spinoffs). Second, the composition of public investments changed. When a governmentally proclaimed plan to increase exports prompted agricultural production to expand but sales did not rise, subsidies to agriculture were vastly increased, while public investment in highways, airports, and water supply systems was substantially curtailed.

As the United States entered the 1990s, structural policies were not particularly salient in American politics. The U.S. economy had rebounded strongly from the deep recession of 1981–82, and unemployment had fallen to what most economists would regard as approximately full employment. During the 1988 elections only two structural issues emerged. One was the character of the recovery—how the new jobs compared with the jobs lost in the 1970s. The other was whether the changing patterns of trade might leave only the less attractive jobs in the United States and whether trade barriers ought to be used to prevent this from happening. In the end, these rather abstract issues did not capture the electorate's attention.

Among the most important problems in the 1990s is the decline of primary product industries: oil, mining, and agriculture. The oil and gas states of the Gulf Coast, which benefited from the energy shocks of the 1970s, were severely damaged by the low oil prices of the 1980s. Mining and agriculture have continued their secular decline.

The most immediate concern is the effect all of this has had on the American banking industry. Although there is considerable controversy about the magnitude of the problem, all parties agree that many financial institutions—especially savings and loan institutions in rural areas and in the Southwest—will require hundreds of billions of dollars to escape bankruptcy. One of the first challenges facing the Bush administration was how to deal with this problem in an era of already excessively large budget deficits. The federal budget will feel the impact of the decision to bail out the failing financial institutions at roughly the same time as the nation is expected to return to large agricultural surpluses and hence to greater crop supports, unless there is a major change in agricultural policies.

Despite the banking crisis and a mild economic downturn, structural policies were probably less salient in the United States in 1990 than they were five years earlier. They are unlikely to receive a great deal more attention unless the country falls into a major, protracted recession. Consequently, large new initiatives in structural policy are unlikely to spring forth.

Research and Development

The government has supported R&D in the United States for a very long time. In the nineteenth century, numerous public universities were established in the American tradition of combining research and education. Many of these institutions were created primarily to train technical personnel in engineering, medicine, agriculture, and mining and to engage in basic and applied research useful to the private sector. Both state and federal governments assisted in the formation of these institutions, the landmark federal program being the support for land grant colleges and associated programs in agricultural R&D. In addition, the federal government has intermittently subsidized the development of new commercial technologies, beginning with telegraphy in the 1830s and continuing with pending proposals to develop rocket planes (the "Orient Express") and new production methods in the manufacture of semiconductors (Sematech).

Since World War II, the federal government has supported three types of R&D. The smallest category consists of basic research projects, usually at universities, nonprofit research institutions, and government research laboratories. The largest category is military R&D geared toward developing either new weapons systems or specific technologies of interest to the military, such as specialized computers or telecommunications equipment. Although these projects can be commercially significant, they are not designed for commercial applications.

The third category consists of programs for the development of new nondefense technologies. Although international political concerns may spark these programs, as was the case with energy projects in the 1970s, the objective is to develop a technology that can be used in either governmental or private commercial enterprises. Projects in this category are more controversial and more unstable than the other two types.

The political basis of support for R&D is somewhat precarious. The products of R&D are usually harvested long after a project has been initiated, but the political system tends to focus on programs in which the time horizons for achieving progress comport with the frequency of elections. Also, the distributive politics of R&D expenditures can cut either way, depending on the likely consequences of a program with respect to the future structure of an industry. Yet R&D is essential to long-run economic growth and, in a nation that is a world military power, to national security, both of which are normally salient political issues in national elections.

Military R&D is perhaps the easiest to relate to national politics, as demonstrated by past political debates about missile gaps, warhead gaps, and the like. As President Dwight D. Eisenhower observed in his farewell address, defense R&D has substantial distributive momentum from the "military-industrial complex." Hence it is relatively stable in comparison with nondefense R&D. Nonetheless, in the early 1970s, the defense R&D budget fell, perhaps in response to the first successful negotiations with the Soviet Union concerning arms control and the public's growing dissatisfaction with the war in Vietnam. The composition of the federal R&D budget for the past three decades reveals that current-dollar budgets for defense R&D remained essentially flat from 1967 to 1974 (table 1). Corrected for inflation, the real budget actually declined precipitously. In constant dollars, the budgets for the three agencies that undertake defense R&D—the Department of Defense, the Department of Energy, and the National Aeronautics and Space Administration (NASA)—and for their predecessors declined by more than one-third during this period.[2] Defense R&D began to turn around in fiscal 1975, and since then nominal defense R&D expenditures have increased fourfold; even in constant dollars, the defense R&D budget has tripled. Whether this trend will be reversed as a result of the collapse of communist governments in eastern Europe is uncertain.

The budget for nondefense basic research exhibited a similar pattern. In constant dollars, expenditures in this category declined approximately 10 percent between 1967 and 1976 and then began to turn around in fiscal 1977. Since then federal support for nondefense basic research has increased by approximately 70 percent in constant dollars.[3] The greatest changes in federal support for R&D have taken place in applied R&D for nondefense purposes. These programs are directed at a specific application in the nondefense sector. In real terms, total expenditures in this category were half as large in the late 1980s as they were in late 1960s.

As is apparent in table 1, the composition of federal R&D has changed substantially since the 1960s. First, nondefense R&D dropped sharply in the late 1960s and early 1970s because of the cutbacks in the space program when NASA's Apollo and communications satellite programs ended. During this period, most other categories of nondefense R&D were stable or even increasing. Second, budgets in the late 1970s grew considerably, led by substantial increases in energy R&D. Then, in the 1980s, expenditures fell again, reflecting the Reagan policy that government should not participate in the development of new commercial technologies. In the last three years of the Reagan administration, ending with the fiscal 1989 budget, nondefense applied research and development turned around yet again. Since 1986 nondefense R&D has grown more rapidly than defense R&D. Moreover, the gap is widening: between fiscal 1988 and fiscal 1989, the total federal R&D budget grew by 4.6 percent, whereas defense R&D grew by only 1.2 percent (much less than the rate of inflation).[4]

2. National Science Board, *Science and Engineering Indicators—1987* (Government Printing Office, 1988), p. 245.

3. National Science Board, *Science and Engineering Indicators*, p. 265.

4. National Science Foundation, *Federal R&D Funding by Budget Function: Fiscal Years 1988–1990*, NSF 89-306 (1989), p. 2.

Table 1. Federal Research and Development, by Function, Fiscal Years 1961–90
Billions of dollars

	Federal R&D									Total federal R&D	Total R&D[c]
Year	Defense	Health	Space	General science	Energy	Resources[a]	Transportation	Agriculture	Other[b]		
1961	7.0	0.4	0.8	0.1	0.4	0.1	0.1	0.1	0.1	9.1	14.3
1962	7.2	0.6	1.4	0.2	0.4	0.1	0.1	0.1	0.1	10.3	15.4
1963	7.8	0.6	2.8	0.2	0.5	0.1	0.1	0.1	0.1	12.5	17.1
1964	7.8	0.7	4.2	0.3	0.6	0.1	0.1	0.1	0.2	14.2	18.9
1965	7.3	0.8	4.9	0.3	0.6	0.2	0.1	0.2	0.2	14.6	20.0
1966	7.5	0.9	5.0	0.4	0.6	0.2	0.3	0.2	0.3	15.3	21.8
1967	8.6	0.9	4.8	0.4	0.6	0.3	0.4	0.2	0.3	16.5	23.1
1968	8.3	1.0	4.3	0.4	0.7	0.3	0.3	0.2	0.3	15.9	24.6
1969	8.3	1.1	3.8	0.4	0.6	0.3	0.4	0.2	0.4	15.6	25.6
1970	8.0	1.1	3.6	0.5	0.6	0.3	0.5	0.2	0.5	15.3	26.1
1971	8.1	1.3	3.0	0.5	0.6	0.4	0.7	0.3	0.6	15.5	26.7
1972	8.9	1.5	2.9	0.6	0.6	0.5	0.6	0.3	0.6	16.5	28.5
1973	9.0	1.6	2.8	0.7	0.6	0.6	0.6	0.3	0.6	16.8	30.7
1974	9.0	2.1	2.7	0.7	0.8	0.5	0.7	0.3	0.6	17.4	32.9
1975	9.7	2.2	2.8	0.8	1.4	0.6	0.6	0.3	0.6	19.0	35.2
1976	10.4	2.4	3.1	0.9	1.6	0.7	0.6	0.4	0.6	20.8	39.0

1977	11.9	2.6	2.8	1.0	2.6	0.8	0.7	0.5	0.7	23.5	42.8
1978	12.9	3.0	2.9	1.1	3.1	0.9	0.8	0.5	0.8	26.0	48.1
1979	13.8	3.4	3.1	1.1	3.5	1.0	0.8	0.6	1.0	28.2	54.9
1980	14.9	3.7	2.7	1.2	3.6	1.0	0.9	0.6	1.1	29.7	62.6
1981	18.4	3.9	3.1	1.3	3.5	1.1	0.9	0.7	0.9	33.7	71.9
1982	22.1	3.9	2.6	1.4	3.0	1.0	0.8	0.7	0.7	36.1	80.0
1983	24.9	4.3	2.1	1.5	2.6	1.0	0.9	0.7	0.7	38.8	89.1
1984	29.3	4.8	2.3	1.7	2.6	1.0	1.0	0.8	0.8	44.2	101.1
1985	33.7	5.4	2.7	1.9	2.4	1.1	1.0	0.8	0.8	49.9	113.7
1986	36.9	5.6	2.9	1.9	2.3	1.1	0.9	0.8	0.9	53.2	119.9
1987	39.2	6.6	3.4	2.0	2.1	1.1	0.9	0.8	1.0	57.1	127.3
1988	40.1	7.1	3.7	2.2	2.1	1.2	0.9	0.9	1.0	59.1	135.2
1989[d]	40.6	7.7	4.6	2.4	2.4	1.2	1.0	0.9	1.0	61.8	142.0
1990[d]	44.3	8.2	6.1	2.7	2.3	1.1	1.1	0.9	1.0	67.8	150.0

Sources: National Science Foundation, *Federal R&D Funding by Budget Function: Fiscal Years 1988–1990*, NSF 89-306 (1989), p. 108–110; and National Science Foundation, *National Patterns of R&D Resources: 1990*, NSF 90-316 (1990), p. 43. Numbers have been rounded.

a. Includes environment.
b. Includes all research related to social services and international affairs.
c. Total R&D for calendar year.
d. Estimates.

Agriculture and Health

Only two categories of nondefense R&D have remained relatively unaffected by the budgetary cycles since the 1960s: agriculture and health. Both grew substantially even during the lean budgets of the Reagan administration. By the end of the Reagan era, the agricultural research budget had increased approximately fourfold and the health budget eightfold since the last budgets of the Johnson administration.

These programs are undertaken in university, nonprofit, and federal facilities and both can easily be divided into small projects and spread across numerous contractors in virtually all parts of the country. Hence the emphasis in contracting is on the research enterprise or the users of the research products, rather than on picking winners among institutions. However, the political bases of these two categories of programs are obviously quite different in that they have quite different user constituencies. Agriculture, as the nation's largest industry, is well organized and geographically concentrated so that it is influential in a large number (though less than a majority) of congressional districts. Thus the politics of agricultural R&D is essentially a reflection of the more general politics of support for rural interests across all fronts. In all policy areas examined in this chapter—R&D, regulation, and infrastructural support—agriculture is a main beneficiary of federal programs. However, unlike some other cases, the economic rationale for federal support of agricultural R&D is fairly strong. The program has generated benefits that substantially exceed its costs.[5] On all relevant grounds—ubiquitous contractors, relatively nonconflictual contracting and consequences, a well-organized beneficiary group, good economic performance—the stability of agricultural R&D is easily explainable and seems likely to continue.

In contrast, continued support for health R&D depends on whether medical care remains a national political issue. Since the 1960s the United States appears to have become especially susceptible to undertaking expensive but popular programs in health care. Since the war on cancer was launched in the 1960s, health R&D has been an important component of this program. Health care appears to be one issue, besides the state of the economy and national security, that persistently commands the electorate's attention. Distributive politics does not appear to play a significant role here.

    5. See R. E. Evenson, "Agriculture," in Richard R. Nelson, ed., *Government and Technological Progress: Cross-Industry Analysis* (Pergamon Press, 1982), pp. 233–82, and the references therein.

The popularity of health R&D among the electorate is something of a puzzle. Much of the research supported by the federal government is very basic, and its benefits are only achievable over a very long period of time and are usually difficult to measure. Whatever the reason for this support, it has prompted the United States to make an enormous investment in the biological sciences. If new biomedical technology turns out to be one of the great technological frontiers of the next century, the United States is likely to be well positioned to exploit it.

Energy and Space

At the opposite extreme from agriculture and health in terms of budgetary stability are the programs concerned with energy and space R&D. The primary components of the space budget are space science (including exploration), space transportation systems (such as the space shuttle), and space communications systems (including commercial communications satellites). All three have been on a budgetary roller coaster since NASA was created in the late 1950s. Likewise, the energy R&D budget, the primary purpose of which is to advance energy conversion technologies, experienced a boom after the energy price shock of 1973, a bust with the arrival of the Reagan administration, and then a new, more modest boom in the late Reagan and early Bush years. All of these trends are apparent in table 1.

Much of NASA's R&D budget has always been oriented toward the agency's primary mission, the advancement of space science and the exploration of the solar system. In the 1960s, owing in part to the competition between the United States and the Soviet Union in space science, these programs were popular politically. But by the early 1970s support for these programs had waned, and space research had to be geared toward producing tangible economic benefits. Although NASA had always maintained programs in communications and remote sensing for such things as weather forecasting and crop assessment, these applications became an increasingly important justification for the agency's budget.

The communications satellite and space shuttle programs illustrate some of the difficulties the federal government has encountered in undertaking commercially significant R&D projects.[6] In the late 1950s the

6. For more details, see Linda R. Cohen and Roger G. Noll, "Applications Technology Satellite Program," and Jeffrey S. Banks, "The Space Shuttle," both in Cohen and Noll, *The Technology Pork Barrel* (Brookings, forthcoming).

Department of Defense supported R&D for communications satellites for its own needs. Eventually NASA assumed responsibility for one of these projects, the geosynchronous satellite being developed by the Hughes Aircraft Corporation. The program was a success and ushered in the commercial use of communications satellites. Through the 1960s NASA generated a string of innovations in communications satellites that were quickly adopted by commercial users. The program also gave the United States a substantial lead in satellite technology.

The program made economic sense on three counts. First, it encompassed a considerable amount of work on defense communications, which made plausible the argument that the government could more effectively organize a program to spill over these developments to the private sector. Second, to develop satellite technology required expensive experiments. The commercial risks of these experiments were large, yet the benefits of a successful demonstration of the technology would be shared by the entire industry, not just the innovating firm. Third, the user group was telephone utilities, most of which are governmentally owned and the rest of which were then regulated. Thus government officials might insist on some sort of cost-plus pricing for satellites and thereby prevent private developers from capturing a return on the risks that they were bearing.

In 1974 the program was summarily killed, even though nothing had transpired to change its technological or economic justification. It was canceled because the primary industrial constituencies of the program— satellite manufacturers and telephone utilities—had turned against it. The manufacturers had become disgruntled because the program could not be subcontracted among them and so each new contract created a technological advantage for one firm in the industry. Thus, between the early 1960s and the early 1970s, the industry evolved from a Hughes monopoly to a competitive structure in which several firms were capable of undertaking the next developmental step. The firms that lost the contract competition in 1972 for the next generation of satellites lobbied Congress to have the decision reversed. Meanwhile, the telephone companies became dissatisfied because NASA satellites, once launched for test purposes, became a government-owned telephone utility. Although NASA desperately tried to find ways to organize the use of its satellite capacity that would not infringe on the business of the utilities, the latter strongly opposed further NASA launches as an unfair intrusion of the government on private industry.

Opposition within the industry proved to be a fatal blow to the program. Moreover, the private sector did not pick up the canceled project or any other significant satellite R&D. Consequently, over the next decade, while other nations continued to do relevant research, the United States lost its lead in this technology. Recognizing the effect that the cancellation had had on the performance of the U.S. industry, the government tried to restart the program in the mid-1980s. Some projects were actually begun, including an extended version of the previously canceled project. But conflict among the industrial players again emerged, and in 1989 the Bush administration canceled the program.

The story of the space shuttle is in almost every way exactly the opposite of the saga of communications satellites. Although NASA wanted a new launch vehicle for manned spaceflight in order to pursue its primary mission, the space shuttle sprang from mostly economic concerns. The purpose was to lower substantially the costs of launches and thereby to pave the way for a wide array of new commercial uses of space. The most important benefit of the space shuttle—accounting for nearly half its expected net economic return—was to be its capability to repair malfunctioning satellites. Because nearly all satellites are in a geosynchronous orbit, these benefits could not be captured unless a vehicle was available to take astronauts from the low orbit of a space shuttle to the high orbit of most satellites. This vehicle was named the space tug.

For a number of reasons, NASA's initial benefit-cost analysis was highly optimistic about the costs, number of launches, and capabilities of the shuttle. Thus the proposal appeared to provide substantial benefits in excess of costs and on this basis was adopted—despite relatively little evidence of support from contractors. In 1977 the program began to run into trouble. First, the capabilities of the shuttle were going to be considerably less than initially planned. The most important disappointment was that the space tug had to be scrapped because it was technologically infeasible. Second, costs began climbing. But by this time, contractor support had become politically important, and poor economic performance could not override distributive politics within Congress to kill or scale back the program. Consequently the United States came to rely on the space shuttle as its only launch vehicle for everything from secret defense missions to communications satellites to space science. And, because the vehicle was expensive and unreliable, this decision (like the earlier decision about satellites) cost the United States its lead in launch technology and in numerous technologies that depend on a reliable launch capability.

The *Challenger* disaster of January 1986 brought home the magnitude of the policy mistake regarding the space shuttle. Afterward, production and R&D on other types of launch vehicles were resumed, and the United States is building a portfolio of technological alternatives that are more efficient and reliable and that in the early 1990s should enable the nation to recover the ground it has lost. But the inertia of the shuttle program is still an important political fact of life, as revealed by the decision to replace the *Challenger* at a cost that cannot come close to being justified on the basis of the benefits it will produce.

The lesson from these examples is that the fate of commercial R&D projects depends largely on the politics of support or opposition that develops around them in the contracting and utilizing industries. Distributive politics can force good programs to be canceled and poor ones to be continued, even when such decisions undermine an industry in which the nation is a technological leader.

In energy, the most important historical development was the rapid rise and fall of a serious federal effort to develop new energy technologies in response to the OPEC-related events of 1973–79. Before 1973 the federal goverment played a relatively small role in energy R&D, except for the support it provided for the development of commercial nuclear power technologies in the 1950s and early 1960s. In the late 1960s the federal energy R&D program consisted of a few small projects, the most notable of which were for breeder reactors and synthetic fuels.

The breeder program arose from the expectation in the 1960s that commercial nuclear power would be the technology of choice for generating electricity for decades to come. But a massive investment in nuclear power would have strained the production capability for reactor fuel, and so breeders became the favored alternative because they produce more fuel than they use. When breeders became controversial because of their possible use in the proliferation of nuclear weapons, as well as concerns about safety, the federal government sought to develop the technology, in part to retain control over them for purposes of national security. By 1969 the government believed that it was time to demonstrate the commercial feasibility of the technology and proposed some demonstration projects, the first of which was to be the Clinch River Breeder Reactor.

The early synthetic fuels program had a far different political rationale.

Its purpose was to explore the possibility of developing new coal-using technologies that would reverse the economic decline of coal mining in Kentucky, Pennsylvania, and West Virginia. Not only was coal losing its market share to other energy sources, but new deposits were being worked in other parts of the country. Hence R&D on synthetic fuels was primarily a regional development program for eastern coal areas. The technological obstacle that the program had to overcome was that the physical and chemical composition of eastern coal made it especially difficult to convert to liquid fuels, such as gasoline or methane. Until the energy shock of 1973, the program had limped along with a small budget and no progress.

A third, even smaller, program, in solar energy, also was initiated in the early 1970s by the National Science Foundation. Initially the program consisted primarily of evaluations of alternative ways to exploit solar energy, motivated by the conservationist belief that sunlight, being a renewable resource, could cope with the ultimate Malthusian end to advanced, industrialized society and could do so in an environmentally benign way. Compared with the other programs, the solar energy projects were almost invisible and had a much less secure political base because they lacked both an industrial and a geographic constituency.

When the oil shocks from OPEC began in 1973, these three programs stood waiting in the wings.[7] Energy immediately became politically salient, and congressional leaders as well as government agencies began a mad scramble to respond. Within a few years, energy R&D had grown sixfold, from $0.6 billion in 1973 to $3.6 billion in 1980, with proposals on the table for still larger budgets.

Because the breeder reactor was regarded as ready for commercial demonstration before the energy crisis hit, it was the first program to experience a sharp increase in expenditures. From the beginning, nearly all of this increase took the form of a massive cost overrun. Initially expected to take only a few years and a few hundred million dollars, most to be paid by industry, the program quickly became a multibillion-dollar project financed almost entirely by the government. Even so, had its economic premise been correct—namely, that the demand for electricity would continue to grow exponentially and would be satisfied

7. For complete histories, see Cohen and Noll, "Synthetic Fuels from Coal," and "The Clinch River Breeder Reactor," and William M. Pegram, "The Photovoltaics Commercialization Program," all in Cohen and Noll, *Technology Pork Barrel*.

by virtually exclusive reliance on nuclear power—the program would
have been well worth the cost. By the mid-1970s, however, that premise
could not reasonably be accepted. New orders for nuclear plants came
to an abrupt halt in 1976, and electricity demand stopped growing. At
the same time, the expected date at which commercial breeders were to
become economically desirable, assuming that they worked, had leaped
forward from 1985 (the estimate in 1970) to beyond 2020 (the estimate in
1980). But the program could not be killed just by bad news.

In light of its poor programmatic performance and declining economic
benefits, President Jimmy Carter tried to put an end to the program in
each year of his presidency but failed to persuade his fellow Democrats
in Congress, largely for two reasons. One was distributive politics: by
this time, the program was allocating several hundred million dollars a
year to contractors, and their representatives in Congress fought to save
the program despite its performance. Second, in the general enthusiasm
for energy R&D in the 1970s, an "energy logroll" emerged, whereby
advocates of all programs agreed more or less to share the growing budget
among all technologies. During this period, attempts in committees or
on the floor of Congress to kill any specific program or to advantage one
approach almost always went down in defeat.

Eventually the program succumbed. In 1983 President Ronald Reagan
tried to save the breeder by eliminating most of the other energy projects
from the budget, but he merely succeeded in undoing its coalitional
support. Meanwhile, the price of oil fell, and the nation's dependence
on OPEC diminished as new resources at home and abroad were brought
into production.

The other technologies were in an earlier stage of development
when the energy crisis arrived, and so were not regarded as ready for
commercial demonstration. But by 1979, after another shock from OPEC
following the revolution in Iran, the quest for demonstrations began.
Then, during the last two years of the Carter administration, expenditures
on energy R&D rose dramatically, and authorizations for future projects
jumped even more. For example, the Synthetic Fuels Corporation,
created in 1980, was initially expected to spend $100 billion on developing
coal and oil shale technologies. But the big-ticket phase—construction
of demonstration facilities that could produce commercially significant
quantities of energy—had not begun before Reagan took office and,
roughly simultaneously, oil and other energy prices began to drop. For
the most part, such programs had not become sufficiently important to

large contractors, geographic areas, or targeted beneficiaries to develop a distributive political constituency. Hence, with a hostile president and a weakened economic rationale, the plans for numerous demonstrations could be scaled back without incurring great political cost. Energy had ceased to be salient, and the future beneficiaries of the projects—contractors, workers who would be employed at the projects, coal miners who would be added to employment in the coal industry—had not yet emerged as a political force to retain them.

As a result, the current-dollar budget for energy R&D was cut by 40 percent between 1980 and 1987. All but two demonstrations were canceled, and predemonstration research was scaled back. But the cuts never restored the constant-dollar budget to its level before the energy crisis, and in the waning years of the Reagan administration the coal program staged a comeback. In fiscal 1989 the government began a five-year commitment to share in the cost of demonstrating new "clean coal" technologies, which constitute the most successful outgrowth of the old synthetic fuels program.[8] By early 1989 the program had approved twenty-nine demonstration projects, expected to cost $2.3 billion in federal funds, for the purpose of commercializing new technologies that burn coal more efficiently while reducing emissions that contribute to acid rain.

Transportation

Transportation R&D is another important federal program, 90 percent of which consists of air transport projects.[9] About two-thirds of the total goes for research in aeronautics. The second largest component supports the activities of the Federal Aviation Administration in air traffic control and safety. The only other significant program is research on highway materials, construction, and safety. The last two programs are easy to justify because highways, air traffic control, and aviation safety are federal functions, so the government is simply supporting research to advance its own capabilities.

The aeronautics program is primarily concerned with developing new technologies for commercial application. Although one part of this program is devoted to in-flight control and guidance, which is related to

8. NSF, *Federal R&D Funding by Budget Function: Fiscal Years 1987–1989*, p. 59, and *1988–1990*, p. 62.

9. NSF, *Federal R&D Funding, 1987–1989*, p. 78ff.

safety, most of it deals with advanced designs for engines and airframes. The aeronautics program has a long history, going back well before World War II.[10] Commercial air transport also benefits from military R&D in aeronautics, which is part of the defense R&D budget. Although for several decades military aircraft development has been oriented toward technological capabilities of little or no commercial appeal (such as extremely high speeds and altitudes and low detectability), specific components developed for the military may have commercial application. In either case, the aeronautics program has traditionally not supported the development and demonstration of new aircraft.

One exception to this generalization was the abortive American supersonic transport (SST) program.[11] Initially proposed by the Kennedy administration, the SST was a response to the parallel commitments in Europe and the Soviet Union to develop the "next generation" of aircraft. The SST would fly at supersonic speeds, thereby vastly cutting travel times. After five years of research, the federal government decided to develop a prototype-demonstration model of the aircraft, and in 1966 serious money began to flow into the project. Unfortunately, soon after the contracts were let, it became apparent that the winning design was technologically infeasible and that the plane would perform far below the standards set forth in the initial plans. After more than a year of redesigning and reevaluating the project, the commitment to build the aircraft was reaffirmed.

The original political rationale for the SST program is easy to understand. The economic calculations appeared to be quite good, even though the aircraft industry was unwilling to tackle the project on its own. Of course, in hindsight this reluctance should have been a serious warning; in the 1960s the three most important American manufacturers of commercial aircraft—Boeing, Douglas, and Lockheed—had shown no such hesitation about undertaking other comparably expensive development programs for wide-bodied aircraft and efficient short-haul jets. Nonetheless, had the initial projections about the demand for the SST proved accurate, the program would have generated net economic benefits. Note, too, that the relevant industries—aircraft and airlines—

10. For details, see David C. Mowery and Nathan Rosenberg, "The Commercial Aircraft Industry," in Nelson, ed., *Government and Technological Progress*, pp. 101–61.
11. For details, see Susan A. Edelman, "The American Supersonic Transport," in Cohen and Noll, *Technology Pork Barrel*.

supported the project. Most aircraft manufacturers competed for all or part of the program. Airlines supported the project politically and then later placed firm orders for delivery.

By the end of the Johnson administration, the project had lost support from almost everyone but the contractors. The problems with the program that had become apparent in 1967 undermined its economic rationale, and public support for aerospace ventures was on the wane. The airlines, too, had become more wary, and orders for the craft began to soften. Despite mounting controversy, the project continued through the first two years of the Nixon administration. Then, in late 1970, a new issue emerged: the possibility that the SST would cause environmental problems, especially ozone depletion. Although the environmental argument subsequently proved to be vastly overblown (the SST would have had relatively little effect in comparison with other causes of ozone depletion), the issue arose just when environmental concerns were capturing the government's attention: the Clean Air Act was passed in 1970 and the Clean Water Restoration Act in 1972. In the spring of 1971, the budget for the SST was eliminated from the appropriations bill, and the program died.

The most interesting aspect of the SST story is the politics of the project's demise. When the technological bad news of 1967 arrived, the popularity of the program declined, but not enough to kill it. Between 1968, when it was restarted, and 1971, when it was killed, its fundamental economic and technological characteristics were not substantially altered. All that changed was that environmental issues had begun to be politically significant, and the aircraft caused a relatively minor environmental problem. Again, once the contracts were signed, the distributive politics of the program managed to keep it alive despite the certainty of bad performance—until it ran afoul of the environmental movement. It took bad performance plus environmental problems to overcome the distributive politics.

Recently the federal government initiated two new projects like the SST: an advanced high-speed transport and the national aerospace plane (or "Orient Express"). The first is really a revived SST, using recent advances in aircraft materials and jet engine design. The second, even more ambitious, is aimed at building a plane that will fly into orbit and cut intercontinental flights to an hour or two. Like the SST, both planes would be much more expensive to build than other commercial aircraft and would succeed only if the added costs to passengers were regarded as justified by the greater speed. In fiscal 1988, about $174 million was spent on this program; in 1989, the budget rose to $262 million.[12] As yet, no commitment has been made to build either plane; however, these decisions are probably only a few years away.

Microelectronics

Although, as already mentioned, military R&D concentrates on products used almost exclusively by the military, it has numerous commercial spinoffs, particularly in communications and microelectronics. Recent examples are the programs in large-scale integration and the $500 million subsidy to initiate Sematech, the industry consortium established to undertake research in the manufacture of semiconductor devices. The Department of Defense budget for advanced technology development, which includes the strategic defense initiative and the transatmospheric aircraft, also allocated more than $1.5 billion in fiscal 1989 to materials research, electronics, and other items related to microelectronics and computing. Comparable sums are also spent in the intelligence and communications R&D program on such things as advanced signal processing and communications satellites. Thus, through the military budget, the scope of federal support for technologies with potential commercial applications in the information/microelectronics sector is comparable in size to federal support for R&D in energy or health and exceeds that for commercial transportation.

The justification for defense involvement in microelectronics, computers, and communications is that these are essential inputs to modern military operations and weapons. As long as voters regard defense as a significant national political issue, and as long as the United States bears an especially high share of the burden of defense expenditures among advanced industrialized democracies, the Department of Defense will continue to push for the development of technology in these areas. The interesting policy question is whether these programs should support only domestic capabilities. The stated justification is security: the United States can best control the diffusion of technologies with military significance if it keeps them inside its borders. But perhaps equally important is a perception of political equity. If the United States is going to pay for most of the defense of Europe and Japan, its own companies

12. Although some of this budget is in NASA, most of it is in the Department of Defense. See NSF, *Federal R&D Funding, 1987–1989*, pp. 14, 79.

should receive most of the technical spinoffs of that effort. If the latter is an important consideration in current practice, it is difficult to see why this form of federal support for new commercial technologies would change very much, unless the costs of defense were more equally shared.

Implications

The lesson to be learned from the postwar history of federal R&D policy is that it is here to stay. The Reagan revolution has not killed federal support for commercially relevant R&D; on the contrary, many of these programs grew during Reagan's second term.

A second lesson is that a program's performance has little bearing on its political success. The popularity of a program usually depends on other factors, such as the pattern of support and opposition from industry and the extent to which the program is associated with an electorally significant national political issue, such as space competition with the Russians in the 1960s, the energy crisis of the 1970s, or the enduring concern over medical care and national security.

Together, these two lessons suggest an interesting puzzle concerning policy development in the United States. Although R&D receives considerable support within the federal establishment, the composition of the national R&D budget changes substantially and relatively rapidly because of political factors. Indeed, it changes faster than the speed with which major new technologies can be developed and brought to effective commercial use. The result is surely an enormous waste of the nation's R&D resources as they are shifted from sector to sector, often before worthy projects are completed—but often long after the handwriting is on the wall for poorly performing projects. The key policy question here is whether a more rational approach to national R&D can be institutionalized in the United States, or whether policy inconsistency is an unavoidable consequence of American governmental institutions and political attitudes.

The government appears to be embarking on several projects that, in the words of the sage of the national pastime, Yogi Berra, seem to be déjà vu all over again. Specifically, such endeavors as the Orient Express and Sematech appear perilously similar to predecessors such as the SST, the space shuttle, and the Synthetic Fuels Corporation. Sematech even has a cost-sharing arrangement for demonstrations of new facilities that is patterned after the Clinch River Breeder Reactor program. Will cost overruns be followed by a massive increase in federal contributions because of the difficulty of shutting down a mistake?

These problems aside, the core of the U.S. R&D effort remains undisturbed by the political swings of the postwar era. Basic research, along with commercially oriented, fundamental work to broaden the technological base of many industries, has grown steadily and has been relatively unaffected by the budgetary swings that have affected commercial demonstration programs. In medical technology, microelectronics, aeronautics, and agriculture, for example, the contribution of the federal government to advancing the technological base has been consistent and relatively generous.

Regulatory Policy

In the mid-1970s the U.S. government embarked on a program of extensive deregulation of basic infrastructural industries. In no case has regulation been completely eliminated; however, in every case controls on prices and on the entry and exit of firms have been greatly relaxed. In some industries, such as airlines and stock brokerage, regulation now plays a minor role.

The deregulation movement of the 1970s is also something of a puzzle, for it does not seem consistent with the analysis of the politics of structural policy discussed above. The movement toward deregulation began in approximately 1975, soon after the ink was dry on George Stigler's famous paper explaining that economic regulation is the inexorable result of the intersection of the supply and demand for use of the coercive power of the state for private gain.[13] Regulated industries have generally opposed deregulation, and in most cases the organized political support for it was weak or nonexistent. Economic deregulation was initiated mainly by executive branch officials and regulatory commissioners during the presidencies of Gerald Ford, Jimmy Carter, and Ronald Reagan. Congress only reluctantly went along, either acting to slow the pace of change or failing to find a consensus on which to respond. And, even though these three presidents advocated less regulation, sometimes their appointed officials went too fast for them as well. For example, the Ford White House stalled the deregulation of cable television, and near the end of the antitrust case that broke up the American Telephone and

13. George J. Stigler, "The Theory of Economic Regulation," *Bell Journal of Economics and Management Science*, vol. 2 (Spring 1971), pp. 3–21.

Telegraph Company (AT&T) the Reagan White House opposed the relief that was sought (and ultimately obtained) by Assistant Attorney General for Antitrust William Baxter.[14]

Nonetheless, there were good economic and political reasons to reform regulatory policy in the 1970s. Before 1970, U.S. dominance in the world economy obscured the costs of inefficient policies. Industrialization during World War II caused the United States to dominate the world economy for a quarter of a century thereafter. Although the rebuilding of Europe and Japan slowly eroded this dominance, American industry remained highly successful until the major recession of 1970 and the first oil crisis of 1973. At that point, structural rigidities and inefficiencies became more hazardous to the health of the national economy.

Infrastructural industries are important to economic development everywhere, but especially in a large country with a relatively low population density like the United States. Long distance transportation and communications integrate the national economy. They permit firms to serve large, nationwide markets for goods and services, which in turn attract industries that are competitive and yet have large enough firms to exploit economies of scale and integration.

From the end of World War II until the early 1970s, the central problem for U.S. economic policy was demand management: in other words, the challenge was to maintain full employment without causing significant inflation. In the early 1970s, the problem became stagflation—meaning that unemployment and excess capacity coexisted with politically unacceptable rates of inflation. And, because advances in productivity had been substantially greater before 1970 than after, rising real wages gave way to stagnant or falling real wages. Infrastructural industries are a natural place to look for causes of low productivity growth because they are important inputs to production processes throughout the economy. And, when such industries began to attract attention in the anti-inflation policies of the Nixon-Ford administration, waiting in the wings was a rich literature on the economics of regulated industries.

The basic message of this research was that regulated industries were inefficient and that regulation served more to protect inefficient suppliers

14. On cable, see Paul W. MacAvoy, ed., *Deregulation of Cable Television: Ford Administration Papers on Regulatory Reform* (Washington: American Enterprise Institute for Public Policy Research, 1977). On the AT&T case, see Peter Temin with Louis Galambos, *The Fall of the Bell System: A Study in Prices and Politics* (New York: Cambridge University Press, 1987).

than to protect consumers from price gouging. Most of the literature dealt with traditional cost-and-demand analysis, ending in estimates of the economic loss due to regulation. Often these estimates were in the billions of dollars for a particular industry. Some of the literature described new technologies and explained how regulation created perverse incentives that led firms to pursue the wrong types of technological change.

When stagflation emerged as a salient political issue, White House officials found in regulation a potentially important "whip inflation now" strategy. Moreover, although the research on regulation had no more ideological content than the utilitarian foundations of normative economics, it fit nicely into the antigovernmental, antibureaucratic rhetoric of conservative politicians. First Gerald Ford, perhaps in reaction to the challenge thrown out by Ronald Reagan, and then Jimmy Carter and Reagan as nominees and presidents, adopted strong positions against regulation.

The details of deregulation differ greatly from one sector to another, but a number of commonalities deserve emphasis. First, all the debates about reforming regulation have been concerned in large measure with economic efficiency. The research findings that regulated firms have high costs and are otherwise inefficient were an important part of the justification for reform. Second, to the extent that a political "smoking gun" opened the door to deregulation, it took the form of a frustrated entrant or potential entrant into a regulated industry, typically a firm that could offer a convincing case that all it wanted to do was charge a lower price or provide a better service. Yet byzantine regulatory procedures and anticompetitive acts by regulated firms prevented or retarded entry. For example, the first competitor in long distance telecommunications, MCI, was organized in the early 1960s but was not granted a license to provide service until 1969, and then spent another fifteen years obtaining technically equivalent access to its customers through local telephone companies. Similarly, World Airways, which proposed a $100 transcontinental air fare, had its application for a license to serve pending before the Civil Aeronautics Board (CAB) without response for a decade.

The American deregulation movement was not so much a commitment to eliminate price controls as it was a decision to let competition emerge. In many cases incumbent firms were, and still are, prevented from behaving as aggressively toward competitors as they would like. The purpose was to create viable competitors. Deregulation is a late stage of the regulatory reform process that normally takes place only after an industry has become relatively competitive.

Deregulation remains largely confined to the federal government, not the states. Most industries that were deregulated at the federal level were not deregulated as extensively by the states. For public utilities, like telephones and electricity, differences might be expected to emerge, because the case for natural monopoly in local utility distribution systems is stronger than for the national and regional segments of these industries. But there is more to the issue than this; even in markets where competition is feasible, states have been reluctant to deregulate. One explanation is that the salient policy issue—stagflation—was more relevant in national politics than in the states; however, states, in competing for industries that use utilities, might be expected to pursue greater efficiency in regulated industries as a means of obtaining a competitive edge. Generally, however, this has not led states to begin to deregulate, although there are exceptions.

Telecommunications

The events leading to telecommunications deregulation were primarily technological: the development of the computer industry in the 1950s and 1960s, which put increasing demands on the telecommunications system, and the development of technologies such as microwave transmission and satellites by firms outside the industry.

SATELLITES. AT&T, an important participant in satellite R&D, launched the first communications satellite; however, it pursued an inferior technology and quickly lost the market to Hughes's geosynchronous satellite. The federal government created a separate company, Comsat, to exploit satellite technology in international markets, and several other companies sought to enter the domestic satellite communications business. The Federal Communications Commission (FCC) did not permit the latter to enter until the early 1970s, when it adopted its "open skies" policy. Meanwhile, NASA, which supported satellite R&D, pursued a procompetitive policy by developing satellite production capabilities in several firms and by demonstrating commercial uses of satellites for a variety of users other than regulated telephone companies. While NASA's policy killed its own program, it also helped build the foundation for competition and deregulation in telecommunications.

CUSTOMER EQUIPMENT. Until the 1970s, only telephone companies could own equipment that was connected to the telephone network. Computers presented the first successful challenge to this policy. In the 1960s, customers wanted to use telephone lines to access computers. A decade earlier, AT&T had settled a government antitrust suit by forswearing participation in the computer industry. Hence computers had to be a competitively supplied exception to the prohibition against "foreign attachments" to the telephone network. About the same time, the Carterfone was introduced, which was a new technology for wireless telephones. AT&T, supported by the FCC, prohibited its customers from using Carterfone; however, the courts overturned the prohibition. Eventually, being unable to sustain the notion that customers needed to be protected against buying "inferior" and "dangerous" equipment from someone other than telephone companies, the FCC in the 1970s replaced the prohibition on foreign attachments with a simple testing and licensing procedure and deregulated customer telephone equipment.

LONG DISTANCE. During the 1960s, AT&T's R&D branch sought to expand transmission capacity and to develop new services, such as switched video ("picture phone"). But it left two largely unoccupied niches: very inexpensive service of lower quality than AT&T's network and high-speed, extra-high-quality service oriented toward computers. In the 1960s some firms proposed to occupy both niches. MCI proposed to offer private telephone lines at very low cost (and with very cheap investments compared with AT&T) between St. Louis and Chicago. When the FCC permitted this entry, on the grounds that MCI was offering something new, a flood of other applications was released, including requests from MCI to construct a national network, from Southern Pacific Railroad to sell services on the company's private system along its right of way, and from Datran to build an elaborate computer network. Having previously decided to allow MCI to enter, the FCC shortly let in the rest.

The most cataclysmic event in the industry was the divestiture of AT&T. The rationale for the antitrust case is not easily summarized and is beyond the scope of this chapter.[15] But the basic idea was to separate competitive, or at least potentially competitive, services from the regulated monopoly. The second category contains local telephone

15. For a complete description and analysis, see Roger G. Noll and Bruce M. Owen, "The Anticompetitive Uses of Regulation: U.S. v. AT&T," in John E. Kwoka, Jr., and Lawrence J. White, eds., The Antitrust Revolution (Scott, Foresman, 1989), pp. 290–337.

service, which is regulated by the states. The first category includes almost everything else: equipment manufacturing, long distance, and information services. The reasoning behind this objective was that the competitive components remained largely monopolized by AT&T only because AT&T used its control of the local monopoly to favor its own services and equipment. Behind this reasoning was the belief that AT&T was probably not a natural monopoly anywhere except perhaps in local service, but that in any case it was inefficient. In the absence of vertical integration into local service, it would lose its market share to more efficient competitors. Moreover, if it did, federal regulation could be substantially relaxed, if not eliminated.

Divestiture has had most of the results that were predicted by the government's theory of the antitrust case.[16] Since divestiture, AT&T has reduced employment and lowered prices. It has lost nearly all of the market for customer equipment and about a third of its market share in equipment sold to telephone companies. In long distance, its market share has fallen from slightly below 100 percent to about 70 percent and continues to drop at about 4 percentage points a year. Postdivestiture events indicate that local telephone companies and their customers used AT&T equipment largely because of the vertical integration of the company. Since divestiture, the procurement of equipment and services by local telephone companies has been more diversified, and AT&T has successfully embarked on an ambitious plan to cut costs and improve its products.

Some of the consequences of divestiture and deregulation have sparked political opposition. First, competition has forced regulators to change the structure of telephone prices, eliminating the circumstances that allow prices to be far above costs (since such prices attract entry and cause the regulated firm to lose business) and raising prices that are far below costs (since the first action leaves less revenues for subsidizing the latter). In general, nominal prices for all telecommunications services and equipment fell drastically during the 1980s; however, a notable exception was the monthly charge for basic access to the telephone

16. For details on the effects of divestiture, see Peter W. Huber, *The Geodesic Network: 1987 Report on Competition in the Telephone Industry* (Department of Justice, Antitrust Division, 1987); and Roger G. Noll and Bruce M. Owen, "U.S. v. AT&T: An Interim Assessment," in Stephen P. Bradley and Jerry A. Hausman, eds., *Future Competition in Telecommunications* (Harvard Business School Press, 1989), pp. 141–92.

system, paid by residences and small businesses. In rural areas, these prices are unambiguously still below the average cost of service, but in urban areas residences are now probably paying close to the average cost, and small businesses are probably paying more than it costs to service them.[17] Customers who make no use of the telephone except for ordinary calls in the local network are worse off because of deregulation of the interstate part of the system. Hence telephone pricing is politically controversial.

Second, wages in the telecommunications industry have been adversely affected by competition.[18] One of the major beneficiaries of the regulated monopoly in telecommunications was the Communications Workers of America. Hence deregulation is controversial among political leaders who represent union constituencies.

Third, one effect of divestiture has been to open the equipment market to international competition. Simple customer equipment is now almost completely the province of foreign manufacturers, and inroads have been made in virtually all parts of the equipment industry. Before divestiture, AT&T kept the production of telecommunications equipment in the United States.

Despite these drawbacks, the move toward deregulation probably will continue because its original economic rationale has proven to be correct. Falling prices for sophisticated communications equipment and services are important to information-intensive industries, including such high-tech jewels as computers, microelectronics, and information services. To date the effect of divestiture has been a bonanza for firms that make intensive use of communications systems. The advantage of divestiture is that the most intensive users can be provided with very sophisticated networks without having to reengineer the network for everyone. In the long run, this could be a disadvantage if enhanced capabilities are economically warranted for all residences and businesses. But for now, the effect of divestiture is beneficial for a set of industries that are very important to the future of the U.S. economy.

17. For details about the changes in prices since divestiture, see Roger G. Noll and Susan R. Smart, "The Political Economics of State Responses to Divestiture and Federal Deregulation in Telecommunications," in Barry Cole, ed., *After the Breakup: Assessing the New Post AT&T Divestiture Era* (Columbia University Press, forthcoming).

18. See James H. Peoples, Jr., "Wage Outcomes Following the Divestiture of AT&T," *Information Economics and Policy* (forthcoming).

Transportation

Before the wave of deregulation that began in the 1970s, the most extensively researched area of economic regulation was transportation.[19] The findings of this work constituted a bill of particulars against economic regulation. First, regulation caused transportation firms to be inefficient because of the way regulators granted route awards and made entry-exit decisions. Second, by failing to set prices in proportion to costs, regulation misallocated business among customers and firms and thereby caused further inefficiency. Third, regulation distorted technological progress, encouraging too rapid adoption of new technologies in some cases (for example, jet aircraft in short-haul, low-density service) and too slow adoption in others (for example, unit trains and truck-rail piggybacking).[20]

Most of these problems were a natural outgrowth of the political forces acting upon regulatory agencies.[21] For the most part, citizens do not focus on mundane matters of transportation regulation when evaluating politicians, and so most of the political attention to regulatory policy comes from organized interests with atypically great stakes in the regulated sector. In surface transportation—rails, trucks, barges—such interests include the companies providing the service, a few organized users of the service (such as agriculture), and, when service to a community is at stake, the local government representing citizens who might lose service. In the airline industry, no user groups are particularly well organized except, again, communities that might lose service. As a result, regulation in transportation protected regulated companies from price competition, skewed the price structure in favor of well-organized user groups, and ensured that service to the least profitable communities was continued. Not surprisingly, this policy did not yield an efficient

19. For a survey of this research, see Paul L. Joskow and Roger G. Noll, "Regulation in Theory and Practice: An Overview," in Gary Fromm, ed., *Studies in Public Regulation* (MIT Press, 1981), pp. 1–65.

20. See Aaron J. Gellman, "Surface Freight Transportation," in William M. Capron, ed., *Technological Change in Regulated Industries* (Brookings, 1971), pp. 166–96; and George C. Eads, "Competition in the Domestic Trunk Airline Industry: Too Much or Too Little?" in Almarin Phillips, ed., *Promoting Competition in Regulated Markets* (Brookings, 1975), pp. 13–54.

21. For a detailed discussion of the politics of regulation, see Roger G. Noll, "Economic Perspectives on the Politics of Regulation," in Richard Schmalensee and Robert D. Willig, eds., *The Handbook of Industrial Organization*, vol. 2 (North Holland, 1989), pp. 1254–87.

route structure, and cartelization combined with cross-subsidization did not produce efficient pricing. Moreover, because these industries were reasonably competitive by nature, cartelized prices simply caused the domain of competition to shift to services, thereby distorting the choice of technology as well as other factors affecting service quality.

The last effect probably benefited the U.S. aircraft industry in the 1960s but turned against it in the 1970s. Service competition led American carriers to adopt jet aircraft more quickly than was economically justifiable, especially for short-haul service.[22] But the principal advantage of wide-bodied aircraft was lower costs per seat. The absence of price competition stood in the way of using these planes to gain added business through lower prices. As events later confirmed, the demand for air travel is price elastic, so that lower prices through deregulation substantially increased travel, which in turn justified more extensive use of high-capacity, low-cost aircraft.

In surface transportation, the inability to engage in intermodal price competition militated against all kinds of investments by railroads, including investments in new technologies.[23] Regulators established very low rail prices for bulk commodities, responding to agriculture and coal interests where transportation can be a relatively large fraction of the delivered costs of products. Moreover, prohibitions against multimodal transportation companies, as well as irrational pricing rules, prevented mixed-mode shipping from achieving its rightful share of the market.

The horror stories of transportation regulation came to public light in the mid-1970s. Senator Edward Kennedy, a Democrat with presidential aspirations who was looking for a probusiness policy initiative, held well-publicized hearings on airline regulation that revealed dubious acts by the Civil Aeronautics Board to prevent new airlines from entering the industry and to orchestrate cartel agreements. Nevertheless, in both air and surface transport, deregulation was led by the regulatory agencies that bore the brunt of the criticism. Disgruntled staff produced internal studies critical of their agencies.[24] Beginning in the Ford administration and proceeding at a quickened pace during the Carter presidency, appointees to regulatory commissions were selected on the basis of

22. See George C. Eads, *The Local Service Airline Experiment* (Brookings, 1972).
23. Paul W. MacAvoy and James Sloss, *Regulation of Transport Innovation: The ICC and Unit Coal Trains to the East Coast* (Random House, 1967).
24. See Martha Derthick and Paul J. Quirk, *The Politics of Deregulation* (Brookings, 1985).

their commitment to relax regulatory controls. Both the CAB and the Interstate Commerce Commission came perilously close to deregulating faster than Congress would tolerate; nonetheless, Congress eventually passed legislation substantially deregulating transportation in 1978 (air) and 1980 (surface). This legislation secured the administrative deregulation that had already taken place in both agencies.

The experience in transportation, like that in telecommunications, illustrates the importance of leadership in the White House and the agencies for bringing forth change in structural policies. Because the president is elected from a national constituency, distributive politics are normally a weaker force in executive policymaking than in Congress. Here presidents concerned with stagflation aggressively pursued regulatory reform through the appointment process. Congress, caught in the conflict between distributive politics and overall national economic policy, could not lead or otherwise act on its own, but it did go along with the direction of policy advocated by the executive branch.

Deregulation in transportation has turned out as predicted. First, prices in general have fallen dramatically.[25] Between 1976 and 1982, prices fell 25 percent for full truckloads, 14 percent for less than full truckloads, and 9 percent for rail shipments. In 1983 air fares were about 40 percent lower than the CAB formula prices abandoned in the late 1970s. A bonus from deregulation, combined with relaxation of the postal monopoly, is the rapid growth of package air express, which now provides guaranteed overnight delivery of mail and small packages throughout the United States at reasonable prices.

The costs of transportation deregulation have fallen on three groups. First, unionized labor has been hurt substantially, especially in trucks and airlines.[26] Average compensation per employee in trucking alone fell 14 percent between 1977 and 1982. Second, deregulation has harmed some companies and forced several into bankruptcy. Profits of trunk airlines, for example, turned negative in early 1979 and remained negative until early 1983. Roughly the same pattern occurred in trucking; however, railroads have on balance improved their profitability since deregulation.

25. For details about the initial impact of deregulation, see Elizabeth E. Bailey, "Deregulation: Causes and Consequences," *Science*, vol. 234 (December 5, 1986), pp. 1211–16.

26. In addition to Bailey, "Deregulation," see Nancy L. Rose, "Labor Rent Sharing and Regulation: Evidence from the Trucking Industry," *Journal of Political Economy*, vol. 95 (December 1987), pp. 1146–78; and Thomas Gale Moore, "U.S. Airline Deregulation: Its Effects on Passengers, Capital, and Labor," *Journal of Law and Economics*, vol. 29 (April 1986), pp. 1–28.

Third, not all customer groups have shared in lower prices. In general, because of the policies pursued during the era of regulation, since deregulation prices have been higher and service quality has been lower in rural areas. In addition, very wealthy travelers and business travelers whose trips are paid by others have had to endure more crowded planes and greater flight delays due to the increased volume of traffic. Nonetheless, the net economic impact of economic deregulation has been in the range of $10 billion a year in efficiency gains. This has not only reduced business costs and consumer prices, but has made further integration of the national economy more attractive.

Although changes in service to small communities were expected to be the most important political issue surrounding deregulation, two other issues have attained greater significance. One is safety. Airline disasters and near-misses are characteristically tied to deregulation, as, to a lesser extent, are highway accidents involving trucks. The crux of the argument is that deregulation puts greater financial pressure on transportation companies, which leads them to relax standards for maintenance and safe working conditions. In reality, there is no theoretical reason to believe that deregulation reduces the incentives for safe operations, and as an empirical matter safety does not appear to have been adversely affected by deregulation. By all measures, commercial airline service was safer in the deregulated 1980s than it was in the regulated 1970s.[27] For the most part, this issue is a red herring.

The second public issue associated with deregulation pertains to flight delays. This allegation has more substance. Deregulation has brought lower prices, which have greatly increased ticket sales. As a result, passenger-miles flown have about doubled since deregulation. Because the capacities of airports and the air traffic control system have not increased correspondingly, flight delays are more likely. Part of the problem is a misallocation of scarce prime-time landing, take-off, and gate assignments at major airports. Airports and the Federal Aviation Administration have refused to reserve the use of busy airports for commercial flights and to use auctions or landing fees as a means of peak-load pricing for airlines. In addition, as will be discussed below, federal expenditures on new transportation capacity have not kept pace with the growth of demand, thereby increasing congestion.

A classic mistake of distributive politics has further undermined the

27. See Jonathan D. Ogur, Curtis Wagner, and Michael G. Vita, *The Deregulated Airline Industry: A Review of the Evidence* (Federal Trade Commission, Bureau of Economics, 1988).

benefits of airline deregulation. Mergers in the airline industry became the province of the Department of Transportation, an agency attuned to the political demands of the transportation sector, rather than either the Department of Justice or the Federal Trade Commission, the agencies that normally have jurisdiction over antitrust matters and are more likely to pursue a vigorous procompetitive policy. As a result, several mergers that were opposed by antitrust authorities were nonetheless approved by the Department of Transportation, and service to several large cities has become all but monopolized by a single carrier, such as USAir in Pittsburgh and TWA in St. Louis. Limited airport capacity precludes extensive entry into these cities. Not surprisingly, service to these cities is more expensive than service in more competitive markets. It is puzzling that as an advocate of deregulation the Reagan administration created an uncertain future for continued free competition in the airline business by allowing some key cities to have their service monopolized through mergers.

Energy

Among the advanced industrialized societies, the United States has arguably experienced the greatest difficulty in adjusting to the swings in energy prices since the early 1970s. To some extent, this reflects the conflicted domestic politics of energy. Alone among the leading industrialized societies, the United States is an important producer of all major energy sources. Hence the rapid rise and fall of energy prices divides the country according to whether local economies are primarily users or suppliers of energy. Moreover, as a large, wealthy economy that relies less on international trade in energy than other advanced nations, the United States found it feasible to respond to political pressures to cushion the distributional effects of price changes through regulation. Indeed, while deregulation was beginning in communications and transportation in the mid-1970s, energy regulation was actually increasing, as the Federal Energy Administration was created to implement a complicated system of price controls on oil and petroleum products. Although the system was complex, inefficient, and fraught with problems, some of which are still the subject of litigation over allegations of excessive prices, the program achieved its objectives. Americans faced slowly increasing prices, rather than abrupt price shocks, during the 1970s.

Price regulation of both oil and natural gas had two principal effects.

It encouraged wasteful uses of fuel during a period of high prices and intermittent domestic and world shortages. And it discouraged further exploration and exploitation of new sources of oil and gas, because of the expectation that regulated prices, not market prices, would be imposed on the discoverer. This further contributed to shortages, higher prices, and greater inefficiency. Considerable research in the early 1970s demonstrated that natural gas regulation created these problems.[28] Subsequent research on oil price regulation in the late 1970s generated similar results.[29] As a result of this information and growing dissatisfaction with the performance of the domestic oil and gas industries, oil and gas have been deregulated.

The gas story is especially interesting, for the Natural Gas Policy Act of 1980 set up the most confusing and complicated regulatory process ever invented. It separated sources of gas by vintage, depth, and other factors into a bewildering array of categories, deregulating only new discoveries and some new production from the more costly old sources. Meanwhile, gas utilities continued to base prices on average cost and thus were forced to contract for very expensive gas in order to satisfy orders at the lower average price. But deregulation of new sources soon brought substantial new production at lower prices, and gas utilities were stuck with contracts to buy more expensive gas. Meanwhile, oil deregulation and the collapse of OPEC caused oil production to rise and prices to fall. Gas utilities had to follow oil price cuts to retain industrial customers, yet were obligated to buy expensive gas, rather than cheaper new-production gas. The result was the "gas bubble"—the strange combination of low-price gas going unsold, high-price gas being purchased, and gas utilities losing business when, with freedom to buy, sell, and price as they wanted, many customers could have been retained. Eventually large industrial customers were permitted to rent transportation capacity from pipelines and buy their own gas; gas utilities responded by abrogating their contracts. As a result, there is an endless dispute before federal and state regulators and in the courts over who owes what to whom. But, fortunately for the economy, oil and gas suppliers are all but deregulated at the production end, and—for the first time since about 1960—there is some semblance of rational allocation of these fuels. This benefited consumers in the late 1980s, when oil and gas prices were very

28. Paul W. MacAvoy and Robert S. Pindyck, *The Economics of the National Gas Shortage (1960–1980)* (American Elsevier, 1975).
29. Joseph P. Kalt, *The Economics and Politics of Oil Price Regulation: Federal Policy in the Post-Embargo Era* (MIT Press, 1981).

low. Of course, when prices increased in 1990, because of another disruption of supply from the politically volatile Middle East, consumers experienced more rapid price increases than they did under similar circumstances in the 1970s.

The other domain of economic regulation is electricity, and here the United States is undergoing a protracted shift toward far less regulation than in the past.[30] The entering wedge was the Public Utility Regulatory Policy Act of 1978, which was designed for an entirely different purpose: to encourage exotic new methods of generating electricity, such as industrial cogeneration, solar energy, and geothermal energy. The law defined a number of technologies as candidates to become "qualified facilities," which meant that local electric utilities would be required to buy their electricity at prices based on the costs of other ways to increase capacity. States were given considerable latitude in deciding how to price these sales to utilities, and many set the prices relatively generously, in part because they wanted to encourage the use of renewable energy resources and more efficient use of energy in industry, and in part simply because long-term contract prices were based on the unusually high energy prices of the early 1980s. In any event, this led to the development of a new industry consisting of largely unregulated businesses using new technologies to generate electricity for sale to regulated utilities.

By restricting these sales to exotic generation facilities and adopting arbitrary rules for pricing, the program obviously opened the door to inefficiency. But the primary benefit was that regulators, utilities, and the new entrants came to realize that an unregulated market for wholesale electricity might be feasible. This perception was further encouraged by another experiment born of necessity. In the late 1970s, new generation facilities became especially expensive for utilities, and rate regulation proved to be sufficiently inflexible during periods of inflation that utilities could not expect to recover all of their costs and a reasonable profit on their own new generation equipment. Meanwhile, because of a virtual standstill in the growth of electricity demand, only some utilities needed more electricity; others had excess capacity. As a result, utilities began to buy and sell power from each other.

In response to these developments, a largely unregulated market for electricity has emerged among generators and utility retailers. The

30. For an excellent analysis of the evolution of the electricity industry, see Paul L. Joskow, "Regulatory Failure, Regulatory Reform, and Structural Change in the Electrical Power Industry," *Brookings Papers on Economic Activity: Microeconomics* (1989), pp. 125–99.

266

details of how this market operates, who will be permitted to participate in it, how integrated utilities will be required to separate generation from distribution, and what procedures will be followed for expanding transmission capabilities to facilitate the market are all in a state of flux. The importance of deregulating generation and the extent to which it will be done remain uncertain; however, the chances are reasonably good that in the 1990s much of the electricity generated will be deregulated and largely competitive. The implications for the economy are generally positive. First, on balance, electricity generation should become more efficient and prices lower, which will benefit consumers directly in their energy use and indirectly through lower product prices. Second, a deregulated, competitive generation sector should improve the efficiency with which new technologies are adopted. It will give appropriate signals about the costs that need to be beaten by a new technology and will eliminate barriers caused by regulation (including the lethargy of regulated firms in adopting cost-reducing innovations, especially if owned by someone else). The question that remains is whether suppliers of facilities for generating electricity will respond with sufficient R&D and product innovation to make an observable improvement in the rate of technical progress. Because the federal government has also substantially reduced support for the development of new generation technologies, other than clean coal and the distant prospect of fusion, the net effect of changes in both regulatory and R&D policy may be no significant improvement.

The political factors entering into the regulatory changes of the 1980s seem most influenced by the horrendous inefficiencies created by the policies of the 1970s. No doubt the loss of interest in new capacity by electric utilities, because of the nature of economic regulation in times of rising costs, facilitated the deregulation of generation. The move to undermine the complexities of gas pricing also precipitated a crisis in that byzantine collection of regulations. And, until Iraq invaded Kuwait in 1990, energy policy had all but disappeared from the political agenda. Even after the 1990 crisis began, real oil prices were lower than in 1979–80, and energy was generally abundant. At the end of 1990, therefore, political leaders faced little threat from responding to entreaties from the energy sector to eliminate the more bizarre and inefficient aspects of regulation. The pertinent political question is whether these developments can survive the next, inevitable round of energy price increases when they arrive, or whether extensive energy regulation is a permanent cyclical phenomenon that will predictably be reimposed whenever prices rise again.[31]

Conclusion

Economic deregulation in the United States has generally been successful. Prices have fallen, and the process has thus far encouraged technological progress. In most cases, the academic contention that many of the regulated industries could be workably competitive is borne out by their performance in the 1980s. Nonetheless, the victory is not complete.

Congress has recently threatened to reimpose regulation. Bills rolling back deregulation in all sectors are regularly introduced, and proponents of regulation, primarily the losers under deregulation, still fiercely fight to restore the status quo ante. In part, these moves are symbolic, but the chances of reversal are not zero. In each case, but especially in communications and airlines, the Reagan administration sowed the seeds of reregulation by ill-advised policies. In telecommunications, the Federal Communications Commission was openly confrontational with Congress, thereby reducing the credibility of the portion of its program that represents a completely sensible furtherance of the goal of eventual deregulation. The administration further lost credibility by proposing, only three years after divestiture, that the Bell operating companies be permitted to reenter competitive markets in manufacturing, long distance, and information services. Obviously, this was tantamount to a policy reversal that calls into question the wisdom of the 1984 divestiture of AT&T and the deregulatory actions surrounding it. In airlines, merger policies and cutbacks in expenditures for safety regulation, airport construction, and the air traffic control system have created controversy about deregulation that was unnecessary and easily avoided.

Most likely, deregulation policies will endure, and the U.S. economy will reap the benefits in consumer welfare and international competitiveness in industries that are closely linked to these sectors. But poor presidential leadership and distributive politics just might undo some part of the deregulation effort. The outcome depends greatly on the political leadership of the Bush administration and key members of Congress during the early 1990s.

31. For further elaboration of this view, see M. Elizabeth Sanders, *The Regulation of Natural Gas: Policy and Politics, 1938–1978* (Temple University Press, 1981).

Sectoral Subsidies and Infrastructural Investment

In comparison with other countries, the United States has nationalized relatively few infrastructural industries and has generally avoided direct subsidies to specific industries and geographic areas. Nonetheless, some important programs do provide direct financial support of this type, particularly for agriculture, water resource development, and the transportation infrastructure.[32]

An important aspect of each category is its great emphasis on rural areas. Agriculture is the only industry in which subsidies constitute a large fraction of income, and obviously it is rural in character. Water resource development provides nearly all of its benefits to rural areas, in the form of irrigation, flood control, and recreational industries. The focus of transportation investments has been construction in rural areas. The rural orientation of subsidy programs stems from the politics of the federal government. First, agriculture, although comprising a very large number of small firms, has been effectively organized since the formation of the National Grange in the mid-nineteenth century. Second, until quite recently rural areas were substantially overrepresented in the House of Representatives and still are in the Senate.

Rural overrepresentation arose from the structure of Congress as determined by the Constitution. Because each state is accorded two senators, whether it is highly urbanized New York or largely rural and sparsely populated North Dakota, rural industries such as agriculture, forestry, and mining are significant constituencies for far more senators than their economic size would otherwise dictate. In the House, states are accorded members on the basis of population, but state legislatures draw the geographic boundaries of congressional districts. These boundaries originally were drawn when the nation was primarily rural. As cities became more important, state legislatures tended to retain historical district boundaries, for to change them to reflect the shifting distribution of the population would have required state legislators to undermine the political power of their constituencies and their own chances for reelection. As a result, the process of drawing district lines can best be characterized as a bipartisan incumbents' gerrymander.[33]

32. The United States has also occasionally pursued regional and urban development programs, especially in the mid-1960s, but these have generally been small and short-lived, and so are not analyzed here.

33. See Bruce E. Cain, *The Reapportionment Puzzle* (University of California Press, 1984).

The overrepresentation of rural interests persisted until a series of Supreme Court decisions in the 1960s required states to equalize districts by population for all state and federal legislative offices except the U.S. Senate. The result was a vast reduction in rural representation—and thus the influence of rural interests—in the House and in state legislatures.[34] This change is expected to reduce subsidies and infrastructural investments in rural areas; however, at least in some cases expenditures might be reallocated rather than reduced. Another important change in the underlying politics of these programs is the roughly simultaneous rise to prominence of the environmental movement and the consequent increase in environmental consciousness in the formation of rural development activities.

The most common form of subsidy is for investment, the most notable exception being price supports for several important agricultural commodities. Until the 1970s investment programs faced little opposition. Members of Congress developed a norm that let all members share in investment programs, giving each the prospect of bringing home projects to constituents.[35] Because a project provided visible local benefits that loomed large in comparison with a district's tax share of the costs, constituents tended to reward legislators who succeeded in bringing home the bacon, even if the overall benefits and costs of the nationwide program were unfavorable.[36]

Around 1970 environmentalists began to oppose many public investment projects, with considerable success. The same political muscle that led to the passage of strong environmental legislation, such as the Clean Air and Clean Water Restoration acts, and that killed the SST also caused the passage of the National Environmental Policy Act in 1969, which called for an environmental review of every significant investment involving federal resources (whether financial support or federal land). This in turn caused environmental consequences to be explicitly taken into account in evaluating projects. The courts interpreted these requirements strictly and stood ready to prevent projects for which cursory or obviously inaccurate environmental assessments had been done. Consequently, agencies were forced to institutionalize serious environ-

34. See Mathew McCubbins and Thomas Schwartz, "The Politics of Derustication," Discussion Paper, Stanford University Center for Economic Policy Research, 1984.

35. See Barry R. Weingast, "A Rational Choice Perspective on Congressional Norms," *American Journal of Political Science,* vol. 23 (May 1979), pp. 245–62.

36. See Barry R. Weingast, Kenneth Shepsle, and Christopher Johnson, "The Political Economy of Benefits and Costs: A Neoclassical Approach to Distributive Politics," *Journal of Political Economy,* vol. 89 (August 1981), pp. 642–64.

mental analysis in their decisionmaking processes, thereby enfranchising environmentalists at all stages of project design and evaluation.[37]

The consequences of the approximately simultaneous changes in congressional districting and environmental politics worked against the use of investment strategies for structural policy. The first change affected rural areas, the second affected the entire nation. Consequently, such policies became less politically attractive to legislators.

Agriculture

The federal government subsidizes agriculture in several ways. One is agricultural R&D, as discussed above. Another is infrastructural investments, as discussed below. Here the focus is on three other types of subsidies: crop supports, production limitations, and farm loans.

The object of agricultural policy has always been to make agriculture more profitable, rather than, as political rhetoric often contends, to help out low-income small farmers. Direct subsidies are available for several important agricultural commodities, whereby the federal government establishes a target price, lends money to farmers on the basis of that price, and then either forgives whatever part of the loan represents the shortfall in the actual price or takes delivery of the crop in lieu of repayment. Virtually all of the commodity support funds go to a handful of crops: corn, wheat, soybeans, rice, cotton, tobacco, and milk.[38]

The magnitude of the commodity support program varies greatly, depending on conditions in the world market. For example, expenditures on commodity support programs were $19.9 billion in fiscal 1987, but $9.6 billion in fiscal 1988.[39] This particular drop was caused by a domestic drought; however, low prices and new import restrictions in other nations can cause low prices in the United States (by causing a glut in domestic markets when the expectations for international sales are unrealized). The recent history of commodity support (figure 1) reveals a volatile downward trend in real expenditures during the 1970s, as would be expected from the decline of rural representation in Congress.

37. See Serge Taylor, *Making Bureaucrats Think: The Environmental Impact Statement Strategy of Administrative Reform* (Stanford University Press, 1984).

38. For a description of commodity support programs, see the annual reports of the Congressional Budget Office, *The Outlook for Farm Commodity Program Spending* (various years).

39. See CBO, *Outlook: Fiscal Years 1988–1993* (1988), p. 2, and *Fiscal Years 1989–1994* (1989), p. 3.

Figure 1. Commodity Credit Corporation Outlays, Fiscal Years 1962–93[a]

Billions of dollars

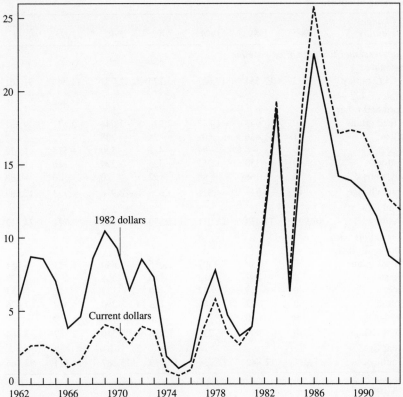

Source: Congressional Budget Office, *The Outlook for Farm Commodity Program Spending, Fiscal Years 1988–1993* (1988), p. 4.

a. Data beyond mid-1987 are projected.

But expenditures skyrocketed from 1982 to 1986. Two factors caused this jump. One was the deep domestic and worldwide recession of 1981–82. The other was unrealized expectations about exports. As part of the reaction against the involvement of the Soviet Union in Afghanistan, President Carter ordered a boycott of wheat sales to the USSR. Not only did sales decline, but other countries began to express concern that the United States would use its agricultural exports as a means of gaining political leverage. In 1980 Ronald Reagan campaigned vigorously against the wheat boycott and promised that agricultural exports would never again be used for political purposes. Upon election, his administration encouraged farmers to expand production and to expect a permanent

Table 2. Changes in Commodity Credit Corporation Outlays Resulting from Higher and Lower Export Paths, Fiscal Years 1988–93
Millions of dollars

Change in outlay	1988	1989	1990	1991	1992	1993	Six-year total
Congressional Budget Office baseline							
Estimated CCC outlay	17,032	17,351	17,022	15,275	12,777	11,844	91,301
High export path							
Corn and other feed grains	0	−943	−1,887	−2,210	−2,044	−2,677	−9,761
Wheat	−41	−1,436	−1,609	24	−208	−772	−4,042
Rice	0	−8	−94	−422	−520	−578	−1,622
Cotton	0	−358	−353	−325	−224	−116	−1,376
Soybeans	0	−168	−68	−92	20	20	−288
Total change	−41	−2,913	−4,011	−3,025	−2,976	−4,123	−17,089
Total CCC outlay	16,991	14,438	13,011	12,250	9,801	7,721	74,212
Low export path							
Corn and other feed grains	0	138	507	1,055	1,840	1,511	5,051
Wheat	0	287	112	116	308	270	1,093
Rice	0	43	47	70	72	12	244
Cotton	0	23	66	223	290	474	1,076
Soybeans	0	0	0	0	0	0	0
Total change	0	491	732	1,464	2,510	2,267	7,464
Total CCC outlays	17,032	17,842	17,754	16,739	15,287	14,111	98,765

Source: Congressional Budget Office, *The Outlook for Farm Commodity Program Spending, Fiscal Years 1988–1993* (1988), p. 79.

and massive increase in export sales. Unfortunately, these sales did not materialize. The result was a massive obligation by the government in commodity subsidization programs.

The continuing dependence of agricultural programs on exports is shown in table 2, which traces the expected size of commodity support programs under three possibilities: business as usual, a substantial relaxation of trade barriers against American agricultural goods, and a further tightening of these barriers. In the early 1990s, the United States has approximately $25 billion in federal expenditures riding on the outcome of its trade negotiations with its principal trading partners.

The estimates in table 2 should not be taken too seriously, for they presume no change in commodity support programs for the period in question, and hence no responsiveness of federal budget outlays to the cost of the program. In reality, the chances for change in legislation are higher if the costs of the existing program escalate. Not only is there likely to be a federal counterpart to a price elasticity of demand for commodity support programs, but, as argued above, the agricultural constituency grows weaker with time. Reapportionment after the 1990 census should further erode support for these programs. Nonetheless, the scale of support for agriculture is likely to be influenced significantly by conditions in the world market. At domestic target prices, American agricultural products are still competitive in the rest of the world; hence success by the federal government in negotiating freer trade in agriculture is likely to prove important not just to the balance of trade, but also to the federal budget deficit.

Most subsidized production in agriculture takes place through programs other than direct price supports. Production controls are applied to a wide variety of products, the mechanism being to create marketing authorities that set acreage limits or production quotas for the domestic market. By restricting supply, these policies drive up prices. In some cases, production surpluses can be sold internationally at unsubsidized prices, as is the case with citrus fruit, where international sales are potentially significant. In others, production or acreage controls apply to all production and so limit the international competitiveness of American agriculture. In essence, these programs effectively cartelize agricultural marketing. As a result, the subsidies do not appear in the budget and so are almost invisible politically. Although research has produced cost estimates for a few of these programs, their cumulative economic effect remains unknown. But because of their invisibility, they are unlikely to be repealed in the near future, despite the declining political influence of agriculture.

Capital market subsidization of agriculture has taken the form of indirect subsidies channeled through the regulations imposed on financial institutions. Historically, financial institutions were subject to regulatory restrictions on their investment portfolios, which in many cases limited their operations to a single state or to the community in which they were located. This had the effect of targeting savings in agricultural areas for investment where the savings are made. In addition, the federal government insures deposits and bails out failing institutions. This cushions deposits in the financial sector from downside risks, thereby lowering the lending rate. Because rural banks are more prone to fail, the effect of this policy is to subsidize credit for agriculture.

Most of the biases in favor of rural interests in financial regulations were eliminated through bank deregulation. Like other regulatory re-

forms, financial deregulation may reflect the declining political representation of agriculture. In any case, this indirect source of support for rural
interests is likely to continue to decline through the 1990s.

The conclusion from this discussion is twofold. Support for American
agriculture is on the downward slope, but is still strongly affected by
international market conditions. American agriculture might well end
up relatively free of direct subsidies in a decade or so—except in
occasional years of world food glut. But this will depend on whether
world markets become more open than they are now. If they do, the
existing support programs, if unchanged, will shrink in nominal terms to
where they were two decades ago and in real terms to a fraction of those
levels. If world markets do not open, two conflicting influences will
probably be more or less offsetting: an increasing domestic agricultural
crisis and a decreasing willingness to pay, given any fixed level of farm
problems. The program that is most costly to Americans, production
controls, will probably remain. The last program, indirect loan subsidies,
is likely to disappear.

Water Resources

In the 1950s the federal government embarked on a massive effort to
develop U.S. water resources, especially in the arid western half of the
country. Because most of the United States is too arid to support
highly productive agriculture without irrigation, America's strength
in agriculture depends on water resource projects. Although water
development projects help all interests in states with projects, nearly all
of the benefit flows to rural communities. For example, in highly
urbanized California, 85 percent of the water from various state and
federal water projects is used by agriculture. Moreover, water is sold
much more cheaply to farmers than to urban water systems, with the
price to farmers generally a few dollars per acre-foot and the price in
cities as much as $200 per acre-foot. Finally, in times of shortage, high-
priced urban use is the residual claimant. In California during 1988, when
precipitation was approximately 60 percent of normal, nearly all of the
cutback in supply was allocated to urban users.

As a consequence of the political factors discussed above—redistrict-
ing of the House of Representatives and rising environmentalism—
federal expenditures on water resource development have declined more
or less steadily since the late 1960s (figure 2). Only to a slight degree has
the decline in federal expenditures been offset by the states. The overall

Figure 2. Federal Spending for Water Resources, by Purpose, Fiscal Years 1965–84[a]

Billions of 1984 dollars

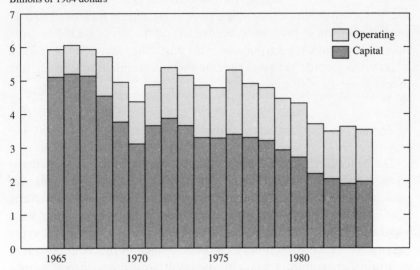

Source: Congressional Budget Office, *The Federal Budget for Public Works Infrastructure* (1985), p. 70.
a. Excludes federal spending for research and development by all agencies and spending under the Mississippi River and Tributaries Account by the Army Corps of Engineers.

pattern of support from all levels of government has essentially been a steady decline for twenty years.

The decline in water investment has been beneficial to the overall performance of the American economy, but in ways that for the most part have not yet been substantially felt. Whereas federal water projects provide water for agriculture, with two exceptions the implicit subsidy contained therein is not particularly important to the U.S. position in the world industry. Most American agricultural production of commodities in world trade is not irrigated. The exceptions are cotton and rice in the West. Rice production in the Sacramento Delta has access to vast quantities of water, for it is located in the floodplain of the runoff from the Sierra Nevada range. Western cotton, however, is highly dependent on irrigation, being a major agricultural product of arid land in Arizona and California. Citrus production in the Southwest is also dependent on irrigation; however, orchards are less water-intensive than many other crops and might actually expand if water allocation were rationalized. Finally, some animal feed stocks in the West are irrigated; however, this is not a large fraction of total production.

More than likely, the reduction in federal support for water projects will have little effect on agricultural production in arid regions for decades.[40] It will slow or stop further conversion of land to agricultural use, but it will continue to supply existing agricultural regions. And a far smaller investment program is needed to add resources for urban areas than the one that has been pursued in the past. The main effect of rational water pricing would be to shift the composition of agricultural production to less water-intensive crops.

Transportation Infrastructure

The American transportation system has long been regarded as almost exclusively a governmental responsibility. The nation's rail network was built in response to land grants to railroads. As a reward for building lines in the western two-thirds of the nation, rails were given wide swathes of federal land along the right-of-way. Eventually—largely because of the construction of railroads—much of this land proved to be in prime agricultural areas or in growing urban centers. In this century, highways and the air transport infrastructure have been built with federal subsidies. Waterways have also been maintained and developed as part of the water resource programs discussed above.

An interesting feature of the infrastructural program in transportation is that it is financed in large measure by user fees. Gasoline taxes feed the highway trust fund,[41] and ticket taxes, fuel taxes, user fees, and the waybill tax finance investments in airports and air traffic control.[42] Yet, for the most part, these fees are not calculated for the purpose of creating proper incentives for users or a rational calculus for determining the scale of investments. Only in the case of highways are such fees calculated both to return expenditures and to be based—more or less— on use; however, even in this case the allocation of funds is not closely tied to the allocation of use, and fees across user classes do not reflect the costs of serving them.

Figure 3 contains recent historical information about the distribution of various infrastructural investments. As is apparent, three parts of

40. Eventually the nation will need to worry about siltation of reservoirs and the substantial reductions in storage capacity that it will cause; however, this is a concern of the next century.

41. See Congressional Budget Office, *Federal Policies for Infrastructure Management* (1986), chap. 5.

42. See Congressional Budget Office, *The Status of the Airport and Airway Trust Fund* (1988).

Figure 3. Federal Spending for Infrastructure, by Area, Selected Fiscal Years, 1968–84

Billions of 1984 dollars

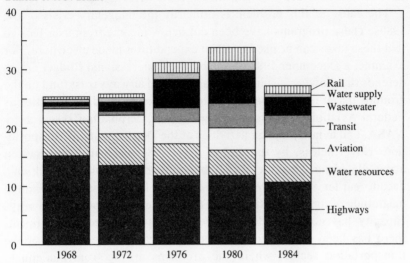

Source: CBO, *Federal Budget for Public Works Infrastructure,* p. 6.

the infrastructural program grew in the 1970s: rails, wastewater, and "transit," which refers to urban transportation systems. The first reflects the bankruptcy and nationalization of passenger service (Amtrak) and eastern freight service (Conrail), and so is a transfer from private to public responsibility. In the 1990s these expenditures will fall because of reprivatization of Conrail and some passenger service.

Wastewater and transit are primarily urban programs that are popular with environmentalists and so reflect the political shifts that occurred around 1970. Urban transit investments generally have been uneconomic, and their popularity has waned. Wastewater management has also declined, in part because of the large one-time expenditures necessary to respond to the 1972 Clean Water Restoration Act and subsequent legislation regarding water pollution.

The stabilization of air transportation investments and the decline in highway investments have proved more controversial. Transportation deregulation has substantially increased the use of these investments, as discussed earlier. Yet investments have not kept pace with demand. The result has been a decline in the ratio of capital to use and visible deterioration. In the case of highways, surface quality has suffered because of inadequate repair and maintenance as well as increased traffic congestion. As for the airways system, flight delays have increased, as have reported incidents of near-misses for aircraft in flight.[43]

The cause of this problem is primarily the budgetary crisis of the 1980s. These programs have been cut below income from user fees so that these taxes can be used to offset expenditures made elsewhere. For example, a December 1988 report by the Congressional Budget Office defends the growing surplus in the airport and airways trust fund on the grounds that it is more than offset by such general budget activities as Federal Aviation Administration operations, aeronautics research by NASA, and aviation policy activities at the Department of Transportation. Nevertheless, by the end of fiscal 1988, the trust fund had an accumulated surplus of nearly $10 billion, compared with $3.3 billion a decade earlier when deregulation began.[44] Regardless of the actual magnitude of the net subsidy of air transportation, airport and airways capacity has not expanded to keep pace with usage. As a result, there has been something of a backlash against deregulation of the transportation sector, where the problems arising from inadequate infrastructure are attributed to deregulation, rather than to the failure to match the infrastructural investment to increasing demand.

To some degree, political pressure from the affected industries can offset this in the long run, but their response is mitigated to the extent that some relevant industrial players (such as unions) want reregulation. Moreover, part of the political basis for these programs lies in rural areas and so is declining in importance. Thus the ultimate outcome remains uncertain, as does the realization of the full benefits of deregulation.

Implications for the Future

The historical practice of structural policies in the United States provides considerable insight into how and why such policies are likely to evolve. Structural policies are adopted as responses to relatively narrowly defined issues that achieve political salience. Because of the fragmented nature of the American political system and the general aversion to centralized planning that is manifest in this structure, long-term national economic development is not the driving force in establishing structural policies. Instead, three factors intermix to influence the selection of structural policies: economic efficiency, as

43. See Congressional Budget Office, *The Federal Budget for Public Works Infrastructure* (1985), chaps. 2, 3.

44. CBO, *Status of the Airport and Airway Trust Fund*, pp. ix–xi, 12–13.

revealed by opportunities for the government to pursue specific policies with significant economic payoffs; nationwide political controversy, usually surrounding a national crisis, but sometimes reflecting the ever-relevant issues of national security and health care; and distributive politics, driven by the specific geographic and sectoral interests that stand to gain or to lose from the policy.

Whereas the tug of war between economic efficiency and distributive politics has been much noticed, the importance of salient national political issues has received less attention. The unusually large U.S. commitment to national defense has led to strong governmental support for defense-related aspects of high-technology industries. In addition, the environmental movement has had a large effect on the selection of public infrastructural investments and energy projects. It also was a critical element in the defeat of the American SST.

Although all categories of infrastructural policy are subject to cyclical swings in popularity, they vary considerably in their degree of stability. Historically, R&D budgets for defense, agriculture, and health care have been more stable than for others; however, support for agriculture (and rural interests generally) has declined since the courts required more uniform representation of the population in the House of Representatives. Nonetheless, the good track record of agricultural R&D is likely to keep it going. Other commercial R&D projects have proven to be the most volatile, in part because of the variance in the total budget for such activities, but more importantly because of the tendency for individual projects to experience sharp rises and falls in popularity.

In the 1990s, if history is a guide, the United States will continue to support defense-related R&D, basic research, and R&D related to agriculture and health care. More than likely, the increased demands on transportation infrastructure because of deregulation will produce greater expenditures on these programs. The deregulation of infrastructural sectors is also likely to survive, thereby further encouraging competition in industries that are inputs to much of the rest of the economy, especially to high-technology sectors. Here the U.S. policy is likely to remain more liberal than that of its principal trading partners. Hence, if competition leads to faster productivity growth and lower prices in electricity, telecommunications, and transportation, the U.S. industries that are intensive users of the services of these sectors should experience a gradual improvement in their international competitive position.

U.S. structural policies also provide some clues to the type of economic controversies that may arise between the United States and Japan in the future. Agricultural import policies in Japan will grow in importance as the United States tries to reduce its trade and federal deficits through lower subsidies and greater sales in agriculture. Increased exports are politically a very easy way to reduce federal expenditures and so the United States is sure to want to pursue them with increasing vigor. Similarly, deregulation in energy, transportation, and telecommunications, if it succeeds in making these sectors substantially more efficient, will encourage U.S. politicians to push for relaxed trade barriers in services and technologies from these industries. Finally, the desire to retain strong domestic industries in areas related to national defense will also be a continuing cause for concern in the United States, regardless of future developments. If these industries grow more competitive, the United States will have both economic and national security reasons to want to see them prosper on the world market. If these industries become less competitive, it will seek to protect them against foreign displacement, again for national security reasons. To some degree, conflicts arising from defense policies can be reduced through greater burden sharing of defense expenditures; however, even this will be a point of contention in the domestic political environment, given the strong distributive effects that create political support for a large national defense program.

Structural Policies in Japan

Haruo Shimada

JAPAN HAS COHERENT and systematic structural poli-
cies. The national government has played a critical role in formulating
and implementing those policies, but its role has changed with each stage
of industrialization.

Early in the twentieth century, the government took the initiative in
developing key industries and constructing an infrastructure to facilitate
industrialization. To foster modern industries and strengthen its military
power, the government took an active part in introducing advanced
technologies, setting up modern industrial plants and military arsenals,
constructing transportation, communication, and irrigation systems,
and developing educational systems and training centers.[1] As industrialization proceeded, the rapidly growing private sector began to take risks
and initiatives. But the development of military production in the
1930s led the government to strengthen its control of private industrial
activities. Until the country's defeat in World War II in 1945, it dominated
all spheres of economic activity.[2]

The reconstruction of Japan's economy after the war called for
government action. The political system was "democratized." Government's new role was to work with the private sector, guiding, regulating,
and controlling it in the pursuit of efficient allocation of limited resources.
As the Japanese economy grew, the government shifted its role to one
of indicating the direction in which industrialization should move.
However, in this switch to indicative and indirect control, the govern-

---

1. William Wirt Lockwood, *The Economic Development of Japan: Growth and
Structural Change, 1868–1938* (Princeton University Press, 1954); and Kazushi Ohkawa
and Henry Rosovsky, *Japanese Economic Growth: Trend Acceleration in the Twentieth
Century* (Stanford University Press, 1973).
2. For a useful review of wartime control experiences, see Takafusa Nakamura,
Showa Keizaishi (Economic history of the Showa era) (Tokyo: Iwanami Shoten, 1986).

ment did not give up all of its initiative. It continues to have a strong influence through its structural policies.[3]

Japan's economic power and high nominal income in the 1980s have prompted both the international community and the Japanese people to make new demands on the government. Because of its substantial and persistent trade imbalances, Japan is constantly urged to open its domestic market to international competition. Japan's structural imbalances have become increasingly apparent—between the nation's prosperity and the low quality of life of urban workers, between Japan's nominal income and its domestic purchasing power, between high labor productivity and long working hours, between excessively concentrated Tokyo and depressed regions, and between different social classes' assets. Consequently, the people have begun to question the legitimacy of the political system.

Major structural reform of the economy, the society, and the political system is needed. Such reform would have to reorganize the conventional structure of political power. But while frustrated people may want political change, they may resist rapid changes in their own vested rights. At any rate, the postwar success of the Japanese economy now poses a serious new question of how to distribute the fruits of success. This paper investigates the political implications of structural change in research and development and industrial policy, in policies toward low-productivity sectors such as agriculture, and in regional development and land policies.

Industrialization and Government Initiative

At the end of World War II, Japan's political and economic system was radically restructured. More than 80 percent of the farmland owned by large landlords was given to peasants. The large financial clans that had dominated economic activity were dissolved, allowing markets to become more competitive. Educational reform opened opportunities for children of all social and economic backgrounds. And enactment of basic labor laws gave power to workers in their relations with management.

To help reconstruct the Japanese economy, the Diet enacted a series

3. Policy changes by the Ministry of International Trade and Industry in the postwar period are described by Toshimasa Tsuruta, "Japan's Industrial Policy," in Lester C. Thurow, ed., *The Management Challenge: Japanese View* (MIT Press, 1985), pp. 160–90.

of laws empowering the government to allocate resources preferentially—for example, toward such basic industries as coal mining, electric power, and iron and steel.[4] Later, to help develop strategically important industries, ranging from shipbuilding and machinery to computers, banks were allowed to provide them with "over loans" vouchsafed by the central bank. The government provided favorable tax treatment to foster export-oriented industries and to help industries introduce advanced foreign technologies.

By the end of the 1950s, the Japanese economy was growing vigorously. From 1958 to 1973, the annual rate of real economic growth averaged 10.4 percent. During this period, government spending on agriculture, communications, and the industrial infrastructure grew substantially, and the mode and role of government intervention gradually changed.[5]

The shifting involvement of government emerged in continuing revisions of formal long-term economic plans.[6] These plans were an amalgam of policy measures formulated by extragovernmental advisory committees. The main object of the committees was to obtain agreement on new policy proposals before plans were submitted for parliamentary consideration.

The Japanese economy kept growing through the two oil crises and the structural adjustment in the latter half of the 1970s. The long-term growth rate, however, apparently slowed. Many corporations altered their investment plans, reducing the demand for basic industries. Some industries faced stiff competition from newly industrialized countries. Government provided a package of assistance to help structurally depressed industries reduce their productive capacities, restructure their corporate activities, and protect workers' jobs and assist job leavers.[7]

Slower economic growth, reduced tax revenues, and growing government expenditures very quickly resulted in a large budgetary deficit.

4. The postwar government strategy of reconstructing the economy by focusing on basic industries is well explained by Yutuka Kosai, *Kōdo Seichō no Jidai: Gendai Nihon Keizaishi Nōto* (The era of rapid economic growth) (Tokyo: Nihon Hyōronsha, 1981).
5. For a discussion of the shift from the "Japan, Inc." model to the market-oriented model in the process of postwar economic development, see Tsuruta, "Japan's Industrial Policy."
6. The history of the government's economic plans is reviewed by Saburo Okita, "Economic Planning in Japan," in Thurow, ed., *Management Challenge*, pp. 191–217.
7. Sueo Sekiguchi, "An Overview of Adjustment Assistance Policies in Japan," paper prepared for the Japan Center for Economic Research–Rand Corporation Conference on Industrial Adjustment, March 18–19, 1989, Tokyo.

Partly to solve the deficit problem, the government undertook an administrative reform. The Rinchō committee was organized in 1980 to investigate the causes of inefficiency, abuses of power, and excessive regulation in the public administration system.[8] The committee concentrated its effort on deregulation. By the 1980s, most industrial activities had become tightly controlled by government regulation. The Rinchō committee, during its three-year existence, made 253 recommendations for regulatory reform. These included relaxing regulation of major airline companies and of interest rates for large deposits in financial intermediaries. Most of the committee's proposals were subsequently implemented.

Rather than relaxing pressure for reform, the committee's success gave impetus to the formation in 1983 of yet another organization, popularly known as the Council for Administrative Reform. Between 1985 and 1987 council recommendations led to modifications in 258 regulations. Despite these changes, the Japanese economy remains highly regulated. Extensive price regulation, such as the price support system for agriculture, has immediate effects upon prices, as do quantity regulations, such as restrictions on imports and controls on entry in wholesale and retail trade. While many obstacles still exist, considerable deregulation has taken place in the financial sector by liberalizing external capital transactions and deregulating interest rates for certain funds. Liberalization is also proceeding in agriculture, for example, in promoting free transactions of rice and relaxing regulations against the transfer of farmland. Relaxation of regulations against entry of large-scale retailers is being promoted, which will have significant effects on the distribution industry.

Another area of major structural change in government regulations was the privatization of major corporations that were either partially or totally public. Prime examples include the Japanese National Railways in 1987, Nippon Telegraph and Telephone Corporation (NTT) in 1985, and Japan Air Lines in 1987. The national railway system had accumulated a large deficit, which adversely affected national fiscal policy and made reform more difficult. Its privatization helped to revitalize the corporation. NTT did not have similar problems, and in privatizing NTT,

8. A concise review and summary of activities and proposals prepared by the Rinchō (Ad Hoc Council for Administrative Reform) may be found in Rinji Gyōsei Kaikaku Suishin Shingikai Jimushitsu (Office of Promotion, Council for Administrative Reform), *Kisei Kanwa* (Deregulation) (Tokyo: Gyōsei, 1988).

the government earned substantial revenue, which helped restore fiscal balance.

Much remains to be done to make the Japanese market more open and flexible. From September 1985 to September 1986, the value of the yen appreciated almost 60 percent against the dollar. Export-oriented companies struggled to preserve the pace of their exports by cutting costs, squeezing profits, and restraining wage increases. Alert companies, realizing that the trade environment had changed, started to shift production to the domestic market. Their strategy was facilitated by the drastically increased price of land. The Economic Planning Agency estimated that the Japanese economy benefited from a windfall of almost ¥30 trillion in saving from 1985 through 1987, enabling industries to import oil and raw industrial materials at low prices.[9] Corporations with urban land were able to restructure their production lines and sales toward the domestic market because banks were willing to give them loans. The increased value of land also stimulated consumption by land-rich people. When the Japanese labor market recorded the postwar peak of unemployment in early 1987, increased private investment was beginning to pay off in higher consumption, which helped to stimulate demand, economic growth, and employment.

Structural Distortions

Although the economy managed to realize a miraculous recovery, three serious structural distortions grew to grave proportions. They were the gap between high nominal income and low standards of living, increased wealth differentials in terms of real estate and financial assets, and the differential allocation of economic resources between Tokyo and other regions.

The nominal income of Japanese people rose sharply in dollar terms after the sizable realignment of exchange rates in late 1985. Although the average wage of Japanese manufacturing workers was still about 20

9. According to the EPA estimate, ¥18.28 trillion accrued from the reduced yen price of oil, and 11.17 trillion was due to other imports. Economic Planning Agency, Bureau of Prices, unpublished data, January 29, 1988; quoted by Miyohei Shinohara, "Kaiho taisei ka no chingin, bukka" (Wages and prices under an open economic system), in Tokeii Kenkyukai, *Kaiho Taiseka no Rodo Seisansei, Chingin, Bukka no Arikata ni Kansuru Kenkyu* (Studies on labor productivity: wages and prices under an open economic system) (Tokyo, 1990).

percent lower than that of their U.S. counterparts in 1986, it surpassed the American wage level by about 10 percent in 1988. But because the purchasing power of the yen increased only marginally, its increased value did little to help Japanese workers. In industries such as agriculture, distribution, construction, and personal services, response to the change in exchange rates was particularly sluggish, in sharp contrast with the swift adjustment in modern manufacturing industries such as automobiles and electronics. Both low productivity and government policies held back the sluggish industries. The concentration of public and private resources in highly efficient industrial sectors is responsible for a gap between the nominal income of people and their real standard of living, as is the failure to invest in sectors directly related to consumers' living conditions.

Although enrichment of the quality of working life and reduction of working hours have been advocated by government agencies and trade unions, a large gap remains between targets and reality.[10] One of the reasons Japanese workers work much longer hours than workers of other advanced countries of comparable labor productivity may well be the exceptionally high costs of living in Japan.

Values of both financial and land assets rose so rapidly in the last two decades that the aggregate value of land in Japan is nearly five times the gross national product. Indeed, the annual growth in nominal wealth has exceeded nominal GNP. For example, in 1987, when GNP was ¥345.5 trillion, financial assets increased by ¥382 trillion and land assets grew by ¥374 trillion.

Most of the increase in land assets occurred around Tokyo. Wealth differentials widened abruptly between those who were able to enjoy capital gains by holding land assets in and around Tokyo and those who could not. Many high-income people invested in rental apartments as a means of evading inheritance taxes.[11] The enormous asset differentials

10. The Japanese government set the target of reducing annual average working hours per worker from 2,100 hours to 1,800 hours by the end of 1992 in its five-year economic plan of 1987–92 and other official statements. Organized labor, as represented by the dominant labor confederation, Rengo, aims at achieving the same goal by 1993. However, actual hours worked have shown only a marginal decline, if any, in recent years. The average was 2,111 in 1987 and 1988 and 2,088 in 1989. Ministry of Labor, *Monthly Labor Survey*.

11. Takao Komine points out, on the basis of his analysis of the data of asset holding and capital gains obtained from General Affairs Agency, *Chockiku Dōkō Chōsa* (Survey of savings), that richer families who have high-valued real estate in the greater Tokyo area also tend to have a greater amount of high-yielding financial assets. Takao Komine, *Kabuka, Chika Hendō to Nihon Keizai: Shisan Infure no Keizaigaku* (Stock and land

that were created in this way may well have serious long-term economic, social, and political repercussions.[12]

The rapid increase of land prices per se may have been triggered by such monetary factors as the accumulation of liquidity and very low market interest rates, but this phenomenon would not have occurred if economic resources and opportunities were not concentrated in Tokyo. Tokyo is not only the capital of Japan but also the center of the country's economic, monetary, industrial, commercial, educational, cultural, and international institutions. Despite the concentration of functions and resources there, the development of the infrastructure and systematic city planning—particularly in housing, commuter networks, and utilization of urban space—have lagged. For instance, the tax system works against, rather than for, effective and efficient utilization of land.[13]

The concentration of resources in Tokyo has worked against development of rural areas, especially those far away from Tokyo. Unemployment rates in remote areas like Hokkaido, Shikoku, and Kyushu are two or three times as high as those in more prosperous areas like North Kanto and Tokai.[14] While the natural environment and amenities of life in remote areas may be superior to those in Tokyo, rural areas lack business and employment opportunities. People and resources are underutilized, and in some areas land prices are declining. Distorted allocation of resources enlarges regional differences.

All these structural imbalances have caused dissatisfaction and frustration. The government, with the support of the dominant Liberal

price fluctuations in the Japanese economy) (Tokyo: Toyo Keizai Shinpōsha, 1989), especially chap. 1.

12. Likely long-term effects would include the discouragement of saving incentives due to prohibitively expensive houses and land; work incentives because of large, unsurmountable asset differentials between those who have land and those who do not; and entrepreneurship for small new businesses because of banks' biases in favor of those who have land as collateral. Haruo Shimada, "Tochi to Kinyu ga Nihon o Yugameru (Japan is distorted by land and financing systems), *Bungei Shunju,* August 1989, pp. 194–208, trans. as "Asset Inflation and the Strained Social Fabric," *Japan Echo,* vol. 18, special issue (1990), pp. 13–20.

13. This is because extremely low property tax rates encourage holding land, high sales tax rates discourage sale of land, and low inheritance taxes on land encourage inheritance in the form of land rather than other types of assets.

14. In mid-1988, for instance, unemployment rates in Hokkaido, Shikoku, and Kyushu were all 3.2 percent, and the ratio of job openings to applicants was 0.60, 1.12, and 0.83, respectively. At the same time, unemployment rates in Kanto and Tokai were 2.1 and 1.6 percent, and the ratio of job openings to applicants was 1.68 and 2.13 percent, respectively. This pattern of regional differentials has been quite persistent regardless of macroeconomic fluctuations. Economic Planning Agency, *Chiiki Keizai Dōkō* (Survey of regional economies), 1990.

Democratic party (LDP), has been promoting policies to modernize low-productivity industries such as agriculture, distribution, and construction. Markets in these sectors must be opened for international competition, and prices must be reduced if the standard of living is to be improved. Measures to prepare for the aging of society are also important. One such measure was introduced in the form of a broad indirect tax, the consumption tax. Not surprisingly, such policies have been extremely unpopular because they oblige people to sacrifice some of the privileges they have been enjoying. Popular resentment has undermined the political dominance of the ruling party, which suffered substantial losses in the upper house election in 1989.

Research and Development and Industrial Policy

Japan's remarkable growth in the postwar period initially depended on adapting the latest technologies from advanced countries. Eventually Japanese industries became as advanced technologically as their foreign competitors, and so they gradually increased their efforts to promote research.

One feature of Japanese research and development (R&D) that differs conspicuously from that of other advanced countries is the government's relatively small share of total R&D expenditures. Japan's government spends about a half or a third as much as other major advanced countries (see figure 1). Yet the Japanese government takes a strong role in providing information, organizing projects, and directing the allocation of resources. Another characteristic of Japan's R&D activities in the last decade is the remarkable growth of expenditures by the private sector. As shown in figure 2, private-sector expenditures have increased at a much higher rate than in other advanced countries since the end of the 1970s. Much of this increase is due to government policy.

In the early phases of Japan's industrialization, the government initiated and developed modern industries such as textiles, iron and steel, machinery, and shipbuilding. The government set up pilot plants and established military arsenals, brought in foreign engineers and workers, and sent Japanese students to advanced nations to study. As private industries developed their own capabilities, the government's role was dwarfed. But its influence continued to be felt in the development of an advanced educational system and research institutions. And in the prewar era, it played a central and leading role in the development of

Figure 1. Government Share of Research and Development Expenditures in Selected Countries, Fiscal Years 1965–85[a]

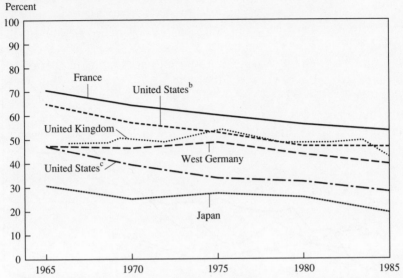

Source: Ministry of International Trade and Industry, *Sangyō Gijyutsu no Dōkō to Kadai* (Trends and issues of industrial technology) (Tokyo: Government Printing Office, 1988), p. 63.

a. Data for Japan are for natural sciences only; for all other countries, data for social sciences are included as well.

b. Total government R&D expenditures, including defense.

c. Excludes expenditures for defense.

military industries and research.[15] After World War II, the government was stripped of its military leadership and left to concentrate its energies on reconstruction of the economy. The single most important objective was to fill the technology gap.

The era from the end of the war to the mid-1960s saw vigorous introduction of advanced foreign technologies. Royalties for foreign know-how constituted about 20 percent of expenditures on technology in the private sector during this period.[16] The Japanese government, suffering from a shortage of foreign exchange, rationed opportunities for adopting foreign technology. Under the Foreign Capital Law of 1950, proposals were judged for their usefulness in stimulating corporate

15. A detailed analysis of the government's role in Japan's prewar industrialization may be found in Solomon B. Levine and Hisashi Kawada, *Human Resources in Japanese Industrial Development* (Princeton University Press, 1980).

16. Ryuhei Wakasugi, *Gijyutsu Kakushin to Kenkyū Kaihatsu no Keizai Bunseki* (Economic analysis of technological innovation and R&D) (Tokyo: Toyo Keizai Shinpōsha, 1986), p. 9.

Figure 2. Private-Sector Research and Development Expenditures as a Share of GNP in Selected Countries, Fiscal Years 1965–85ᵃ

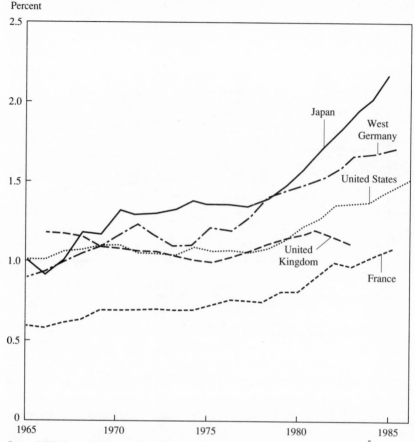

Source: MITI, *Sangyō Gijyutsu no Dōkō to Kadai,* 1988, p. 56.
a. Includes private corporations, research institutions, and universities.

growth and enhancing international competitiveness. A positive list identified useful technologies that the government would support. These criteria were relaxed in 1959, when the Ministry of International Trade and Industry (MITI) switched to a negative list that specified undesirable categories of technologies. In 1968 the government dropped this regulation, freeing the introduction of foreign technologies. With each relaxation, the number of contracts for new technologies increased, which suggests how effective the regulation was.[17]

17. The number of contracts for technology introduction allowed by the Japanese government increased from around 100 a year during the 1950s to 300–600 following

The positive list prepared by MITI in 1950 specified thirty-three technologies designated as useful to Japan's industrialization, including mainly technologies in the iron and steel, chemical, and machinery industries. The revised list of 1959 added basic chemicals and heavy industries. This regulatory policy necessarily had a bias in favor of existing companies. The system tended to help major companies expand their productive capacities. Although this policy led to an oligopolistic market structure, it also permitted the exploitation of scale economies and thereby contributed to productivity growth.

Hand in hand with the introduction of foreign technologies, Japanese companies began investing in R&D. The high correlation between the rate of change of technology introduction and R&D expenditures suggests that Japanese corporations used foreign know-how not only in their operations but also as a stimulus to new ideas. The introduction of foreign technologies played a critical role for Japan's industrialization during this period. Foreign technologies were relatively accessible, they involved much fewer risks than developing new technologies, and they stimulated domestic R&D activities.

Between the mid-1960s and the mid-1970s, the Japanese economy enjoyed rapid growth—on average, more than 10 percent annually in real terms. Expenditures on R&D increased substantially along with investment in productive equipment.[18] In the 1970s the emphasis in R&D shifted from steel, chemical, and machinery industries to such industries as electric appliances, electronics, and automobiles. And new research programs were started at the government's initiative in atomic energy and space.

Beginning in the mid-1970s, R&D in so-called high-tech industries accelerated. Automobiles and electric appliances still claimed a large proportion of R&D, but increasingly greater expenditures went to the electronics, computer, communications, and pharmaceutical industries, and for good reason. In these high-tech industries, R&D represents a larger proportion of total costs than in other industries. In addition, the tempo of technological innovation in these industries is rapid and product cycles tend to be short.

---

the relaxation of admission criteria in 1959 and to more than 1,000 after the liberalization of technology introduction in 1968. Wakasugi, *Gijyutsu Kakushin*, p. 10.

18. Total R&D expenditures increased from ¥0.42 trillion (of which ¥0.16 trillion was borne by the government) in 1965 to ¥1.21 trillion (¥0.37 trillion) in 1970 and ¥2.61 trillion (¥0.88 trillion) in 1975. General Affairs Agency, Bureau of Statistics, *Kagaku Gijyutsu Kenkyū Chōsa Hōkoku* (Survey of science and technology research), respective years.

In the 1980s, Japanese high-tech industries began to compete with those of other technologically advanced countries. In fact, the export of technologies from Japan began increasing rapidly.[19] The value of technology imports is still much greater than that of exports, but in the near future Japan expects to become a net technology-exporting country.

The Government and R&D Associations

Theoretically, the government's role in research and development is to supply public goods or services to supplement the market. The classic case of market failure consists of too little investment when investors cannot fully recoup money spent on R&D. But excessive investment also can cause the market to function badly: for instance, lucrative opportunities to invest in a new commodity close to commercialization often lead to excessive investment. In principle, government intervention can correct these problems; however, bureaucratic rules, political constraints, and insufficient information all limit the government's ability to supply public goods or services.

In Japan about half of R&D expenditures by the government have financed research institutes and special R&D organizations. Less than 20 percent of government expenditures on national, public, and private (nonprofit) research organizations has been in basic research; the rest has supported applied and development research.[20] Both private and public research organizations work closely with private industries. The major functions of these research organizations are to promote new technologies that are advocated by technical experts, to act as leader or coordinator of collaborative projects, and to test the outcome of development projects.

In contrast, R&D organizations with the special legal status of public nonprofit organizations have carried out well-defined public objectives. Groups such as the Japan Atomic Energy Research Institute, the Power Reactor and Nuclear Fuel Development Corporation, and the Space Development Organization have been allocated increasingly greater R&D budgets. All of these research institutes and special organizations

19. The value of technology exports from Japan increased from ¥66 billion in 1975 to ¥160 billion in 1980 and ¥185 billion in 1982, while technology imports increased from ¥169 billion to ¥239 billion and ¥282 billion in the same years. General Affairs Agency, *Kagaku Gijyutsu Kenkyū Chōsa Hōkoku*, respective years.
20. Wakasugi, *Gijyutsu Kakushin*, p. 117.

supplement R&D activities of the private sector rather than compete with them. Also, since government makes few R&D grants to private corporations, government programs do not overwhelm private investment.[21]

The government does provide assistance for private R&D through taxation, subsidies, and loans. It has offered a special high depreciation rate since 1952 for testing and research equipment, and since 1958 for commercialization of new technologies. Testing and research expenditures have been exempt from taxation since 1966. Custom duties on important imported machines were exempted from taxes in 1951, and royalty payments were reduced on important foreign technology in 1953. In 1956 a special tax exemption was enacted for overseas income accruing from new technologies.[22]

The government offers subsidies for R&D in important mining and manufacturing technologies and for technology improvement generally. Since 1961 it has offered R&D grants for next-generation industrial technology, and since 1966 for large-scale manufacturing technologies. It began providing subsidies in 1967 for the development of cargo planes for the private sector and in 1972 for the development of computers. Since 1973 it has subsidized R&D on energy technologies.[23]

Public funds are loaned at relatively low interest rates to encourage private-sector R&D. The Japan Development Bank began offering loans in 1951 for commercialization of new technologies and in 1964 for development of heavy machines. Since 1970 a comprehensive system of loans for commercialization of national technologies has been available.

The Japanese government's policies to assist R&D stress close consultation and collaboration with the private sector. Subsidies are granted and joint R&D activities are organized by carefully taking into account the expressed needs of private corporations. The government rarely organizes major R&D projects independently from the private sector. Careful consultation and coordination with the private sector minimize the "crowding-out effect" of the government's projects. Most of the government-initiated or -assisted projects are of the kind that private corporations or industries would have eventually launched anyway, and they thus supplement, encourage, and speed private efforts,

21. Wakasugi, *Gijyutsu Kakushin*, pp. 123–24.
22. Tax exemptions amounted to ¥13.3 billion in 1965, ¥19.1 billion in 1970, ¥33.0 billion in 1975, and ¥38.0 billion in 1980. Wakasugi, *Gijyutsu Kakushin*, pp. 124–25.
23. Wakasugi, *Gijyutsu Kakushin*, pp. 125–26.

rather than substitute for private activity. However, government R&D policies are so closely geared to the needs of business that projects not serving the narrow economic objectives of the private sector have not been adequately developed.

Joint R&D Associations

Joint R&D associations, organized by the government, play an important role in promoting R&D in Japanese industry. This unusual element, modeled on a European idea, was introduced in the early 1960s. Most of the first dozen associations were engaged in promoting basic research. One, comprising three major electronics companies that sought to develop large-scale computers for commercial use, has been a model for subsequent associations.[24] Most of the early groups that attempted to promote basic research encountered problems of competition among members, shortages of researchers, and an unclear scheme for outcomes and burdens.

A new wave of joint associations, led by government rather than by private companies, began in the 1970s. The new groups mostly aimed at developing technologies in frontiers such as computers, information processing, and aircraft, where Japan had been attempting to catch up with the United States and needed to develop its own technologies to compete. In the 1980s many of these groups shifted their focus to new technologies such as fine ceramics, biotechnology, and new materials.

Most joint associations have fewer than a dozen members, coming from different industries to encourage cross-fertilization of technical knowledge. Most rely on member companies for research facilities, staff, and other resources, but their financing combines government subsidies with contributions from members. Member companies are assigned topics and report the outcomes to the association. The joint associations' offices coordinate the R&D and are often managed by former government officials. The associations enjoy tax exemptions, favorable depreciation rules, and above all easy access to government R&D subsidies.

The associations have chosen to do research largely in the application and commercialization of new ideas, but in the 1980s they began to conduct basic research for the next generation of technologies.

24. The three companies were Nippon Electric Corporation, Fujitsu, and Oki Electric Company.

Expenditures for basic research—usually less costly than applied research—have been increasing as importation of new ideas and technologies from the United States has become increasingly difficult.

One of the merits of this joint collaborative approach is that it internalizes the externality of R&D outcomes. One of the market failures in promoting R&D is deficient investment, because investors cannot be sure if they can recoup the cost of investment when new ideas are developed. Joint associations provide a broad range of possibilities for profitably exploiting new knowledge. That benefit is balanced against the risk that narrow membership or high entry barriers will stifle competition. And narrow membership, while useful for R&D on specific commodities, may not be useful for basic research on ideas shared broadly in the society. So far the joint associations seem not to have limited market competition because member companies have worked hard to develop their own commodities by utilizing ideas developed by their associations and have competed fiercely in the market.

R&D in the Semiconductor Industry

The semiconductor industry is one of the high-tech industries where the effects of various policies and organizational arrangements on technological innovation can be observed.[25] This industry has been heavily dependent on foreign technology since the introduction of integrated circuit (IC) technology in 1962. In the 1970s many Japanese companies contracted with companies in the United States to expand their knowledge of semiconductors, and by the 1980s those contracts encompassed the IC system as a whole.

While the Japanese semiconductor industry has been heavily dependent on foreign technology, it has vigorously pursued its own R&D.[26] Undoubtedly, the rapid pace of technological change has required substantial R&D, and the rapid expansion of demand has enabled the industry to set aside such lavish funds.

The introduction of foreign advanced technology and vigorous R&D mutually reinforced and effectively promoted technological innovation

25. This section draws upon a detailed analysis by Wakasugi, *Gijyutsu Kakushin*, chap. 15.

26. The semiconductor industry spent as much as 15 to 20 percent of total sales on R&D during the 1970s and early 1980s, while the manufacturing industry as a whole spent only 1 to 2 percent of its sales on R&D for the same period. Wakasugi, *Gijyutsu Kakushin*, p. 169.

in the Japanese semiconductor industry. The first major breakthroughs in technology in the early 1970s were made by U.S. companies. Japanese companies, absorbing these technologies, participated in the race to develop more advanced commodities and in 1976 commercialized the next stage simultaneously with American companies. By 1978 Japanese companies were ahead of their foreign competitors, producing commodities of greater capacity or higher quality at lower costs. A further step in 1980 gave Japanese companies dominance in this niche of the world market.

Government assistance played a vital role in this process of development. In the extraordinary measures adopted between 1957 and 1971 for promoting the electronics industry, the government set forth guidelines and development plans for each branch of the electronics industry. Measures for promotion of designated electronics and machinery industries were followed in 1971–78, and of designated machinery and information industries in 1978–85.

The government did not directly finance R&D but provided subsidies for large-scale R&D projects to develop supercomputers (1966–72), advanced ICs (1972–74), the very large-scale IC (1976–80), an optical measurement-control system (1979–87), a rapid computing system for natural sciences (1981-89), and the next-generation industrial base (1989–91). The government subsidized an especially large proportion of R&D in the semiconductor industry in the late 1970s.

The vigorous R&D efforts of high-tech industries, assisted by government subsidies and coordination, stimulated investment in productive facilities. To implement new technologies required new investments in large-scale production facilities. While this enhanced the industry's international competitiveness, it inevitably led to an oligopolistic market structure.

Innovation and Government Policy

The government has acted as a starter or catalyst for R&D activities. From the viewpoint of cost effectiveness, government expenditure has been highly efficient in stimulating such activities. This helps to explain the seeming contradiction between government's powerful role and its small expenditures.

While policymakers have become increasingly aware of the government's responsibility to promote basic scientific research to benefit the general public, policy has not yet encouraged genuine public goods or services. Recent developments may, however, encourage the Japanese government to assume a much broader role.

Structural Policies for Low-Productivity Industries

A large segment of the Japanese economy, including agriculture, distribution, construction, and various kinds of personal services, consists of low-productivity industries. These industries are made up mostly of small family-owned businesses that are organized by intermediaries into a complex industrial structure. The community of small family businesses is often an important source of support for politicians who represent their interests. And competition in these industries is often regulated by government intervention and other institutional arrangements. Because of low labor productivity, prices in these industries tend to be high. High costs and prices became conspicuous in the mid-1980s when the appreciation of the Japanese yen caused the gap between domestic and world prices to increase.

The productivity gap between these industries and Japan's export-oriented manufacturing industries also increased as the latter strove to improve productivity. Growing price differentials have brought mounting pressure from overseas for Japan to open its markets in these industries. Japanese consumers, workers, government planners, and employers in modern industrial sectors have demanded that these industries reduce their prices. To do so would require rationalizing and modernizing the low-productivity industries. The competitive menace of opening markets to international competition may stimulate the drive for rationalization, but it may also stimulate fear and resentment, which could trigger political repercussions.

Protecting and Rationalizing Agriculture

Agriculture is a major example of an industry with very high prices, low labor productivity, and strong government protection. Import restraints and protection are applied mainly to primary staples, such as rice and wheat, and to a few foods, but not to crops, such as corn and beans, that are used for livestock feed or industrial materials. In fact, Japan ranks next to the Soviet Union in imports of the latter types of produce.

The high degree of protection for food reflects the peculiar history of

Japanese agriculture, which has evolved around rice production.[27] A
staple food control system, established in 1942, put every aspect of rice
distribution completely under government control. Under this system,
the government determines a producer's price (buying price for the
government) and a consumer's price (selling price for the government).

Agricultural policy after World War II emphasized land reform, which
was essentially completed with enactment of the Agricultural Land Act
of 1952. After the Japanese government's first reform plan was rejected
by the Supreme Commander for the Allied Powers, a second plan,
formulated in 1946 under the guidance of the Allied Powers' General
Headquarters, forced landlords to sell their land in excess of three
hectares (or in Hokkaido, twelve hectares) to the national government.
By 1948, with about 90 percent of planned purchases completed, the
proportion of arable land that was rented had been reduced from nearly
half before the war to about 9 percent. The proportion of purely tenant
farmers fell to 5 percent of all farmers.

The Agricultural Land Act of 1952, aimed at improving agricultural
productivity, stressed ownership by those who farm the land. The law
regulates the transfer of ownership, limits land owned for rental, sets
rental rates, and protects tenants. Farmers can own relatively small plots
of land, and tenants are protected by low fixed rents and a system of
rights. For some time after enactment of the law, self-employed farmers
worked hard to increase their output, but eventually the system began
to work against modernization of agricultural production.

Improvement of farmland has long been an important policy objective
and a major item in Japan's budget. As early as 1923, the national
government subsidized half the cost of major irrigation improvement
projects conducted by prefectural governments. In the postwar era,
direct subsidies and favorable loans were used to finance improvements
of fields, roads, and the like as communal projects.

Agricultural associations and agricultural committees, fostered by the
government, play important roles in implementing agricultural policies.
The associations (or *nōkyō*), in accordance with the Agricultural Association Law of 1947, are organized by village, town, city, prefecture, region,
and nation. They are cooperatives that seek to allocate resources
optimally and profitably among member farmers; they also act as
government agents in implementing the staple food control system and

27. A concise and systematic review of the history of agricultural policy in Japan
may be found in Masakatsu Akino and others, *Gendai Nōgyō Keizaigaku* (Modern
agricultural economics) (Tokyo: Tokyo Daigaku Shuppankai, 1978).

as bargaining agents for farmers, notably in conflicts with the government over the producer's price of rice.

The agricultural committees, also organized at the local, prefectural, and national level, were established to combine the roles of three preexisting organizations that were charged with land reform, adjustment of demand and supply, and technical guidance. They supervise control of agricultural land and formulate local agricultural plans.

The agricultural system worked well immediately after World War II in stimulating incentives of small self-employed farmers and increasing rice production; however, from the beginning of the 1960s to the mid-1970s, serious structural problems emerged in Japanese agriculture. In many industrialized countries and regions, as agricultural production increased, the disparity between agriculture and the nonagricultural industrial sector—particularly in income—began to grow. European countries adopted structural policies designed to modernize and improve agricultural conditions.[28] In Japan, agricultural production grew, the prices of overseas produce increased relative to domestic prices, and farmers' income declined compared with incomes of urban industrial workers. Agricultural laborers' productivity was low and stagnant, the number of part-time farmers rapidly increased, and most farms continued to be small-scale.[29] The policy formulated to increase rice production and encourage small self-employed farmers soon lost its purpose. Increased supplies of staple food in the world market, coupled with the rapid growth of Japan's industrial income, reversed the price differential between Japanese and overseas produce. Japanese farmers would have to increase their productivity to survive in the world economy. Ironically, the very strategy of land reform designed to stimulate production now limited Japan's international competitiveness. Agricultural associations and interest groups insisted on increasing subsidies and enhancing protection. In contrast, financial and industrial circles warned of the danger of such measures and advocated rationalization of agriculture and modification of protection against agricultural imports.

A government investigation committee issued a report in 1961 that underlined three critical changes affecting Japanese agriculture: eco-

28. Around the late 1950s, many European countries also adopted basic agricultural laws, including West Germany (1955), Holland (1957), the United Kingdom (1957), France (1960), and Italy (1960). Akino and others, *Gendai Nōgyō Keizaigaku*, p. 48.

29. These problems were identified as serious symptoms of the dualistic structure of the Japanese economy for the first time in Economic Planning Agency, *Keizai Hakusho* (White paper on the economy) (1957).

nomic growth, changes in employment structure, and changes in terms of trade. Following the report, the Agricultural Basic Law was enacted in 1961. It stressed two objectives: improvement of productivity and reduction of income differentials between farmers and urban industrial workers. It recommended a production policy that included regular announcements of predicted demand and supply of principal produce, enrichment of the infrastructure to encourage production of items expected to grow in demand, and assistance in introducing new technologies. It outlined a pricing and distribution policy that encompassed stabilization of prices, rationalization of distribution, promotion of industrial processing of produce, and importation of foreign produce. And it called for a structural improvement policy to foster viable and well-managed farms, encourage cooperative management, and promote the transfer of rental land to farmers. The law, however, remains an expression of basic ideas rather than a policy measure.

LAND REGULATION. The Agricultural Land Act of 1952 encouraged farmers to own their own farmland but restricted them to small plots. Tenants were highly protected and their rents were fixed at low rates. These regulations made it difficult to accumulate large farms and thus take advantage of economies of scale. It was not easy to modify this land policy because small farmers now had a strong vested interest in the system of land ownership. After minor modifications in 1962, the law was revised in 1970 to relax the limit on the size of farmland and employment, relax the restriction on owning land for rental, abolish rent control, and relax restrictions on renting and loaning farmland. Policy planners sought to encourage contract farming and farming on rented land and to facilitate large-scale farming and a more efficient use of land resources. The Agricultural Land Utilization Promotion Law enacted in 1975 permits short-term rentals and authorizes new projects to promote the efficient use of farmland.

STAPLE FOOD CONTROL SYSTEM. The system of complete control of rice distribution established during World War II served the purpose of allocating food for a nearly starving population. Both producer's and consumer's prices were intentionally set at low levels (which sometimes yielded surpluses rather than deficits), and a strict rationing system was adopted. In the 1950s, when prices of imported staples were higher than domestic prices, producers were given subsidies. Direct control of nonrice staples was relaxed or lifted gradually during this period.

In 1955 a reserved purchase system was introduced under which the government bought rice unlimitedly at a given purchase (producer's) price. With this system, government control was somewhat weakened. As import prices fell below domestic prices, the staple food control special account yielded surpluses for imported staples; they were combined with the deficits associated with domestic staples and administrative expenditures to yield modest deficits.

The situation changed substantially in the 1960s. In 1960, the producer's price of rice was adjusted to provide farmers a reasonable income. As the standard of living rose in the 1960s, the producer's rice price had to be raised to keep pace, even though it was already much higher than the world market price. However, the government did not increase the consumer's price of rice commensurately. With high producer's prices, which stimulated rice production, and declining demand, excess supplies became chronic. Together, the high producer's price, low consumer's price, excess supplies, and growing storage and administrative costs for the control system resulted in a massive deficit in the staple food control special account.

To deal with this critical situation, the rice distribution system was deregulated in 1969. In 1971 an upper limit was set on government rice purchases. This modest measure put a brake on an uncontrollable accumulation of deficits. The lifting of price controls, based on a World War II ordinance, was a belated move to reduce the degree of direct control and to tolerate elements of market competition. But the control system was so deeply entrenched in Japanese agricultural policies and so closely tied with the interests of powerful groups—most notably the nōkyō—that it was impossible to get rid of the heavy burdens imposed by the system.

MAKING FARMING VIABLE. The major reforms of the 1960s and early 1970s sought to modernize farm management and improve productivity by encouraging large-scale farming and introducing competitive elements. The single most important objective was to make Japanese agriculture viable. It became obvious in the 1960s that Japanese agriculture should no longer rely on traditional small-scale self-employed farmers, rigid regulation of land use, and strict control of the distribution of staples. The reforms of the 1970s were intended to prepare a more flexible and competitive market environment for farm management.

Despite the objective of encouraging larger farms and full-time farm households, one of the conspicuous developments has been a remarkable increase in part-time farmers. From 1960 to 1985 the share of farmers for whom farming is the primary job was reduced by 44 percent, and farmers for whom farming is a secondary job increased by 77 percent.[30] The breakdown by the types of agricultural households is even more striking. Over the same twenty-five years, households devoted fully to agriculture were reduced from more than 2 million to 0.6 million. Agricultural households whose head has a nonagricultural job as a secondary job—primary part-time households—have also declined by a wide margin. In contrast, secondary part-time households—whose head has a nonagricultural job as a primary occupation—have been increasing. While full-time and primary part-time farm households declined by 71 percent and 66 percent, respectively, over the past twenty-five years, secondary part-time farm households increased by 64 percent. Now two-thirds of agricultural households are secondary part-time households, for whom agriculture is only a marginal source of family income.

These trends provide eloquent evidence that one of the primary objectives of structural improvement of agricultural policy, fostering viable full-time agricultural households, did not succeed. Small self-employed farmers were increasingly attracted by lucrative nonagricultural job opportunities and left farming largely to aged parents and wives. As a consequence, an increasingly larger proportion of households is relying on nonagricultural incomes and making little effort to improve agricultural productivity.

Agricultural reform had also aimed at encouraging large-scale farming by concentrating the use of farmland, but the 1962 amendment to the Agricultural Land Act failed here as well. Policymakers supposed that as farmers shifted to industrial occupations and left their villages, the price of farmland would fall and the remaining farmers could purchase land and increase their scale of farming. During the period of rapid economic growth in the 1960s, younger sons and daughters did move to urban industrial areas, but farming households almost never broke up. Moreover, prices of farmland started to increase with the increase of urban land prices.[31] The imputed rate of return to farmland dropped dramatically from 10 percent in the 1950s to 0.6 percent in 1980. This incredible decline discouraged farmers from purchasing new land and discouraged farm owners from selling because they expected rapid appreciation in land values. The strong protection of tenants and rigid

30. Yujiro Hayami, *Nōgyō Keizairon* (Agricultural economics) (Tokyo: Iwanami, 1986), p. 191.
31. Hayami, *Nōgyō Keizairon*, p. 196.

rent control also interfered with the development of large-scale farming. Rents were too low to provide a reasonable income to owners, and once land was rented to tenants, it was difficult to get rid of them.

Japanese agriculture seems to be at an interesting and difficult crossroads, with a promising possibility of growth in the number of viable, resourceful farmers. Large full-time and well-managed farming households have begun to introduce new technology and capital equipment in their farming and to rationalize their management.

The Agricultural Land Utilization Promotion Law of 1975 and other related laws of 1980 exempted rental contracts from regulation, and land renting is increasing. Nevertheless, by the mid-1980s only 7.5 percent of farmland was rented. Another trend is in the differences between small-scale part-time farmers who have their own land and large-scale and vigorous full-time farmers. As part-time farming households grow older, they should be willing to rent their land to tenants willing to pay enough to supplant the farmer's agricultural income. For secondary part-time households, farming income constitutes only a marginal proportion of their family income.

In contrast, full-time, large-scale farmers are interested in economies of scale. If they can accumulate enough farmland, their modernized agricultural businesses may well enhance international competitiveness.[32] Unfortunately, communities seldom coordinate the renting of farmland; rented lots of land are scattered and consequently interfere with the economy of mechanization. The tendency of retired workers to hold on to their small pieces of land also hinders the development of large-scale farming. And the satiation of demand for certain products, shifts of demand for other items, and increased imports squeeze expected rates of return and discourage investment for modernization.

The plan to open part of the domestic agricultural market to external competition, announced by the LDP government in 1988, offered encouragement to resourceful farmers to modernize their operations in order

32. Hayami proposes the following scenario as a possible course of enhancing international competitiveness of Japanese agriculture during the coming decade. During the 1990s, the number of agricultural households that have a full-time male farmer under age 60 will decline from 900,000 to 400,000 due to aging of the population. If part-time farming households would agree to lend a large part of their land to these remaining full-time farming households, the full-time farmer would have twelve to twenty hectares for cultivation, on average, depending on the type of lending arrangement. Given their current land productivity, these full-time farmers would certainly be able to compete well internationally. Hayami, *Nōgyō Keizairon*, pp. 210–12.

to build international competitiveness.[33] But the announcement seems to have been at least partly responsible for the lessening of political support for the LDP in many agricultural areas.[34]

Reform in Distribution and Construction

The Japanese retail distribution industry consists mostly of small family shops. Likewise, the number of wholesalers relative to the population is much greater than in countries such as the United States. Wholesalers constitute a complex, multi-tiered system of distribution that allegedly serves to spread the risks of market fluctuations. However, the system imposes high prices on the consumer, adding margins throughout the distribution network. The construction industry also contains a large number of small contractors, again organized in a complex, multi-tiered contracting system.

Like the agricultural associations that regulate agriculture, institutions and organizations exist to oversee the functioning of small, mostly family-owned businesses. Industries are often regulated and protected by the government. Entry of large-scale retail shops, for example, is restricted by legislation. In construction, close cooperation between the government and general contractors facilitates smooth and efficient contracting among insiders while it precludes bidding from outsiders.

These institutions and practices have a long history and thus cannot be changed overnight. Furthermore, the industries provide massive employment opportunities. In the mid-1980s, while about 4 million jobs were in agriculture, there were 15 million in distribution, 5 million in construction, and 10 million in other services. The employment absorption of these low-productivity industries is huge compared with the relatively efficient manufacturing sector, with only 13 million work-

33. In 1988 the Takeshita administration committed itself to some major programs of liberalization of agricultural trade. One was the bilateral agreement that was reached in May between Japan and the United States—that Japan would gradually liberalize the import of beef and oranges over five years—and the other was the decision made in December by the General Agreement on Tariffs and Trade, in response to the appeal of the United States, to liberalize the import of twelve items such as cornstarch, tomato juice, peanuts, milk products, and beans.

34. Masayuki Fukuoka predicted as early as a year in advance a major loss by the LDP in the upper house election in the summer of 1989 due to increased dissatisfaction and frustration among farmers who opposed the series of agricultural liberalization measures adopted by the Takeshita administration. Masayuki Fukuoka, "Jiminto ō yurugasu Nōsanbutsu Jiyūka" (LDP shaken by liberalization of agricultural trade) *Ekonomisuto*, July 12, 1988, pp. 44–50.

ers. Drastic structural change and rationalization of these industries may throw a large number of people out of jobs.

Mounting pressure from other countries to open Japanese markets to international competition and from inside Japan to reduce the prices of products and services will inevitably bring about substantial structural change in these industries. Perhaps the most important strategy for them is to rationalize their structure and increase their productivity. One way would be to streamline their production process to minimize waste, increase efficiency, and reduce costs. Another would be to develop products and services geared to the needs of customers in specific parts of the market. Innovativeness and vigorous entrepreneurship are a mandatory part of the process. While some businesses will succeed, others will fail, but this competitive menace is a driving force for innovation and modernization. Opening markets to international competition is an important lever to innovation.

If the move toward opening markets and liberalizing trade is too hasty, it could have a disruptive effect on domestic sales of industrial goods, stir up resentment against change, and even destabilize the political system. One of the reasons the LDP has been losing support in agricultural communities in recent years may be the hasty, ad hoc way it has introduced foreign products, lowered the government's purchasing price of rice, reduced farmland, and encouraged business conversion. While the objectives of the policies may be economically legitimate, their introduction may trigger resistance among those who are directly affected and the policies may fail politically if they are not carefully initiated.

Tokyo and Regional Development

Since 1985 prices of land in major urban centers, particularly in and around Tokyo, have risen remarkably—in some business areas in Tokyo by several hundred percent and in a few neighboring prefectures by more than 100 percent. The dramatic increases of land prices in the Tokyo region have begun to spill over into other areas of Japan, but increases have been much more moderate elsewhere.[35] The concentration of

35. Official land prices in Tokyo commercial districts rose an average of 48.2 percent in 1986 and 61.1 percent in 1987, while in Osaka comparable land prices increased by 13.2 percent in 1986 and 37.2 percent in 1987. Other major metropolitan areas such as Nagoya lag still further. Economic Planning Agency, *Keizai Hakusho* (White paper on the economy), 1989, pp. 280–82, 592.

resources and economic opportunities in Tokyo suggests that other regions are relatively deprived, causing a mismatch between the labor force and employment opportunities. The concentration of resources in Tokyo offers economic payoffs, but in the long run it can cause a misallocation of resources that slows the growth of the Japanese economy.

The rapid rise of land prices is in part the result of low interest rates and an easy money supply.[36] But the critical factor is the extraordinary concentration of money, people, information, and functions (corporations, government, international transactions, and educational institutions) in Tokyo. The distribution of economic opportunity and welfare is wildly distorted. Those whose land and related real estate are revalued benefit from price increases, but those who have no land assets are affected adversely.

Since the mid-1980s, Japanese monetary authorities have kept reducing interest rates to stimulate private investment. This was aimed at increasing Japanese domestic demand and encouraging investment in U.S. financial assets in order to help finance U.S. government deficits. Even though long-term interest rates were markedly higher in the United States, Japanese corporate investors grew increasingly cautious about investing in U.S. financial assets for fear of capital losses as the value of the dollar declined. Large amounts of funds accumulated as investors searched for outlets with reasonably high and certain returns. Urban land, particularly around Tokyo, and corporate stocks turned out to be profitable outlets.

Bank loans for investment in land increased disproportionately. Total bank loans grew by 7 percent in 1980, 10 percent in 1985, 9 percent in 1986, and 9.5 percent in 1987, while real estate loans increased by 5 percent, 23 percent, 35 percent, and 17 percent.[37] This generous financing of speculative purchases of land was stimulated by the excessive concentration of resources and functions in Tokyo. Most major corporate headquarters, the national Diet, government offices, the Bank of Japan, foreign companies, universities, major commercial banks, and other financial intermediaries are all based in Tokyo. Nearly 30 million people

36. A recent research report by the Bank of Japan analyzes that an easy money policy, adopted in 1986 to stimulate macroeconomic activity, was partially responsible for boosting land prices. "Backgrounds and Impacts of Recent Increases of Land Prices in Japan," in Bank of Japan, Bureau of Research and Statistics, *Chōsa Geppō*, April 1990, pp. 34–85.

37. Bank of Japan, Bureau of Research and Statistics, *Keizai Tōkei Geppō* (Monthly review of economic statistics), 1988.

live in the greater Tokyo metropolitan area, about 31 percent of the nation's population. The metropolitan area accounts for more than a third of the nation's industrial shipments, 45 percent of wholesale sales, 80 percent of security exchanges, more than two-thirds of stock exchanges, more than a third of all employees, 46 percent of all college students, and 60 percent of information industry workers.

Excessive concentration of economic activity could have been avoided or mitigated if public policy had been used to maintain a balance between demand and supply of land and housing. The unresolved problem in Japan is the tax system, which, in effect, limits the supply of land by encouraging owners to expect increases in prices. Owners are discouraged from selling land by the low property tax, especially the low rate on agricultural land located in urban areas. Moreover, the high tax rate on income from the sale of land discourages sales. Owners are encouraged to hold on to inherited land because its estimated taxable value is lower than that of other financial assets. All these features of the tax system limit land supplies relative to demand, which tends to inflate the price of land.

Japan also has not engaged in comprehensive urban planning and has engaged in perverse land use regulation. Restrictions on building size and the utilization of air and underground space limit the effective utilization of urban land. The need for more public and private housing has hardly been addressed. No major investments, public or private, have been made for the last two decades in a commuter network to link Tokyo to other areas. As a consequence, people who work in Tokyo are forced to live in densely populated suburbs and to suffer from both congestion and high land prices.

Social and Economic Problems

The increase in land prices around Tokyo has had some positive effects on both investment and consumption. Companies used land as collateral to borrow funds to invest in other businesses, and many of these corporations were instrumental in propelling the restructuring that was geared toward the domestic market. The increase in land prices was also considered at least partially responsible for boosting consumption in 1987.[38] Increased land values also increased the income from property

38. Consumption increased markedly in 1987 due largely to a sizable increase in consumption by the nonwage earner category of households, which consists largely of self-employed people. This suggests that the self-employed, who tend to be able to enjoy the benefits of increased asset prices, including land, more than wage earners,

308   HARUO SHIMADA

taxes, which helped to restore the nation's fiscal balance much sooner than planned. These favorable effects helped cause much faster economic growth than had been anticipated. The increased wealth due to higher land prices also stimulated Japanese direct investment in foreign financial assets, real estate, and productive facilities.

The increase in land prices had serious negative effects as well. In the three years from 1986 through 1988, the official average price of residential land in Tokyo rose by 167 percent, and of apartment houses by 205 percent.[39] The increase in Tokyo asset values increased the differentials between those who own real estate in Tokyo and those who do not; between those who acquired land or houses before the mid-1980s and those who did not; and between those who have enough assets to engage in financial maneuvering and those who do not. As a result, wealth differentials between rich and poor increased.[40]

Widening wealth differentials may have adverse economic effects. Workers may be discouraged from working hard because their earnings will do little to fill the gap between themselves and land- or asset-rich people. This could seriously erode the positive ethic of Japanese workers, which has contributed to the powerful performance of Japanese industry. Saving may also be affected as people realize they may never be able to purchase a house with their earned income. They may choose to rent a house and consume their income rather than save it. If this behavior becomes prevalent and the rate of saving is reduced, it will suppress the long-term investment capacity of the Japanese economy.

Prohibitively high prices of urban land also make it difficult for government to expand the public infrastructure. As the average age of society rises, the savings ratio of the Japanese economy is expected to decline while the need to enrich the public infrastructure for an older populace is growing. But budgets will be consumed simply to appropriate land, and little will be left to build facilities.

---

spent more, thanks to the "wealth effect." See General Affairs Agency, Bureau of Statistics, *Household Income and Expenditure Survey*, 1987.

39. Data for land prices from National Land Agency, *Chika Kōji* (Official land prices) (Tokyo: Kensetsusho Tochi Kantei Iinkai), respective years; and prices of apartment houses from Japanese Association of High-rise Residences, *Kōsōjūtaku Kyōkyūdōkō Chōsa* (Survey on prices of high-rise residences), respective years.

40. Tachibanaki suggests on the basis of his analysis of the distribution of assets such as land, houses, and stocks that holding of different types of assets and income level are highly correlated and consequently tend to enlarge differentials between those who have greater wealth and those who do not. Toshiaki Tachibanaki, "Fluctuations of Asset Prices and Inequality of Asset Distribution," in *Nihon Keizai Kenkyū* (Journal of Japanese Economic Research), March 1989.

Land prices also make it difficult for small entrepreneurs to open offices or run plants in urban areas. Moreover, the tendency of banks to rely more on collateral values of land than on the evaluation of ordinary business activities in making loans makes it increasingly difficult for small-scale creative entrepreneurs to start businesses. Meanwhile, small business owners who have land may be tempted to quit their businesses and develop their real estate by building apartment houses, office buildings, or parking lots. The decline of small business, which has been a source of Japan's economic vigor, could well erode the vitality of the economy.

With the disproportionate concentration of resources and economic opportunities in Tokyo, remote regions such as Hokkaido, Shikoku, and Kyushu tend to be left behind and suffer from a relatively slack labor market. With economic expansion, beginning in 1987, the demand-supply balance in these regional labor markets became tighter; however, the cause was not the creation of good job opportunities, but the limited supply of labor. The mobile young labor force has already moved to the major urban centers around Tokyo. The middle-aged and older labor force has been less willing to move because of increased transfer incomes and high housing costs.

Because land is a market commodity, its price is bound to be determined by the balance of demand and supply. Thus efforts to control land prices must rely on control of either demand or supply of land.

Perhaps the most effective and desirable policy to minimize concentration in Tokyo would be to develop regions remote from Tokyo. Prime Minister Noboru Takeshita proposed to reduce demand by decentralizing the location of government offices. Another idea was to move the Diet out of Tokyo or to build a new capital.[41] The Fourth National Land Development Plan advocated the development of regional core cities to mitigate excessive concentration in Tokyo and bring about a more balanced development of the Japanese archipelago. Kansai International

---

41. Under the leadership of Takeshita, each of the government agencies identified in 1988 one or several of its branch offices or facilities to be moved out of the Tokyo metropolitan area. However, the identified facilities are mostly small and are not likely to have a major effect on land prices. Several committees, both administrative and private, proposed ideas for either building a new capital city or shifting political and government functions out of Tokyo. For a review of such discussions, see Kazuo Yawata, *"Tokyo Shūchū" ga Nihon o Horobosu* (Singular concentration in Tokyo will destroy Japan) (Tokyo: Kodansha, 1987); and Shakai Keizai Kokumin Kaigi (National Congress on Social and Economic Issues), *Task Force Report on Building New Capital City*, 1990.

Airport and Kansai Science and Research City are steps in that direction. In early 1989 Prime Minister Takeshita offered to provide ¥100 million to each municipality to use to promote ideas for re-creating their *furusato*, or homeland. Standing in the way of proposals of this kind has been the strong centralized system of national administration. Some experts thus advocate introduction of a federal system, breaking Japan into several broad states, with prefectural governments having much greater administrative discretion than they now enjoy.

To increase the supply of land, some large lots owned by the national or municipal governments and other public organizations might be sold. Land once used by the national railways as locomotive fields could be sold for construction of houses and offices.

A substantial amount of urban land is underutilized, but could be converted to more efficient use by policy changes. Property tax rates should be based on best use, rather than current use, to discourage inefficient and speculative holdings. The income tax on land sales should be reduced, and the inheritance tax on land assets increased to encourage earlier sales and development. The Tenants Law should be modified to remove the excessive protection of tenants' rights. Relaxation of these rights might encourage landowners to offer more rental housing.

A novel proposal by Yukio Noguchi and others would provide landowners with permanent payments equal to the rent on their land in exchange for letting investors develop their land more intensively.[42]

Policy Response and the Political Process

About a year after the dramatic increase in land prices in Tokyo began, the Japanese government organized a committee of the Council for Administrative Reform to recommend how to attack the problem. The seven-member committee consisted of the former president of the Japan Association of Employers' Organizations, two members from financial circles, two from labor unions, and two representing the public. Their remedies, sent to the Nakasone cabinet on October 12, 1987, were adopted by the government on October 16. The government's "Outline for Emergent Remedies for Land Problems" called for control and regulation of land transactions. It also recommended disposal of some of the land owned by the old national railways and the national government,

42. Yukio Noguchi, *Tochi no Keizaigaku* (Economics of land) (Tokyo: Nihon Keizai Shinbunsha, 1989).

consideration of tax reform, and promotion of urban renovation measures and development of housing and residential areas.

The 1987 amendment to the National Land Utilization and Planning Law introduced some changes in the income tax, reducing the tax rate for those who sell land for housing development projects. This measure is supposed to increase supplies of residential land. To facilitate acquisition of newly supplied land, the 1987 amendment reduced acquisition taxes, enlarged exemptions for those who sell land, and deferred taxes for those who sell their houses to move to other houses.

Taxes on land were increased moderately for those with relatively large lots. Tax rates equivalent to those on residential land were applied to farmland within cities. To discourage speculative transactions, corporate income taxes were increased on profits obtained from selling the land. And to stabilize housing conditions for small landowners living on their land, the fixed property tax rate and the inheritance tax were reduced.

Unfortunately, the modifications of the tax system have done little to resolve the problem of abnormally high land prices. The modifications are too moderate to have an impact on demand-supply balances of urban land. For example, the revised tax rate for farmland is now applied uniformly to a broader area of major city districts than before, but the amount of farmland was reduced by only 1.7 percent in 1985 and 2.4 percent in 1986 for the entire country, and 2.7 percent and 1.7 percent in the same years for the three major cities: Tokyo, Osaka, and Nagoya.

Some measures offset each other. Property taxes, for instance, were increased to encourage new supplies of land, while official property valuations were reduced to mitigate tax burdens on ordinary citizens. Thus the official average land price in a Tokyo district increased 276 percent from 1985 to 1988, while the standard taxable land price was raised only 50 percent. This kind of tax policy obviously discourages landowners from selling land and contradicts the objective of increasing land supplies.

In "regulated areas," transfers of land would have to be sanctioned by the government regulatory agency, and in "areas under surveillance" prefectural regulatory agencies would examine the purpose and content of land transactions. Earlier in 1987 the National Land Utilization and Planning Law had been amended to regulate land transactions that were obviously for speculative purposes.

By early 1988, Tokyo, seven prefectures, and nine major cities had adopted the system of surveillance areas, which is applicable when drastic increases in land prices are observed or are likely to occur. Many groups, including financial circles and labor unions, supported these measures. Real estate handlers may have been an exception, as were neoclassical economists who believe that land prices increase not because of speculative transactions or excessive bidding but because of shortages of land relative to demand.

Regulation of financial intermediaries also increased. Financial agencies had taken advantage of higher land prices to increase their profits, some using dummy organizations to finance real estate handlers. Loans for real estate from financial intermediaries increased by 13.6 percent in 1984, 23.3 percent in 1985, and 30.1 percent in 1986. The increases from major city banks were even more impressive—8.7 percent, 34.0 percent, and 49.3 percent. In December 1987 the chief of the Bank Bureau in the Ministry of Finance issued a special notice that banks should refrain from financing apparently speculative transactions. In response to the administrative warning and social criticism, banks and other financial intermediaries announced self-regulation in the summer of 1988.

Proposals to sell national railways and government land were not successful. Only once in 1985 and three times in 1986 was nationally owned land in Tokyo released, and it was sold for another public use. None of the land could be resold to private purchasers for ten years.

The Council for Administrative Reform's committee on land problems submitted its final report to the new prime minister, Noboru Takeshita, on June 15, 1988, and on June 28 his cabinet announced the "Outline of Comprehensive Land Policies." It emphasized policies to disperse the various administrative, political, economic, and other functions concentrated in Tokyo. Its proposals were statements of principle rather than substantive policies.

To promote development of residential areas, it recommended large-scale development programs for the Tokyo Bay Shore areas, conversion of farmland within the Tokyo area for residential use, reclamation of unused plant sites and other unused land, and utilization of above- and underground spaces. It also recommended developing new residential areas from unused spaces, modifying space restrictions on buildings, promoting public housing programs, encouraging employee housing programs, enriching financial aid programs for those planning to buy houses, and revising land and house renting laws.

Relatively concrete policy measures were suggested for formation of appropriate land prices. The report supported continued intensified control and regulation of land transactions. It called for development of market information systems, improvement of the real estate licensing system and the official land price system, and reconsideration of evaluation of the real estate and inheritance taxes.

The Tax System and Regional Development

To correct the inefficiencies of land use, a major and systematic revision of the tax system is mandatory. The property tax must be increased, the income tax on land sales decreased, and protection of tenants' rights against landlords relaxed. These revisions, aimed at creating new supplies of land, would help to dampen the inflationary pressure of land prices or reduce those prices. Politically, these revisions are hard to sell, for at first sight they appear to benefit the rich and harm the poor, quite the contrary of their intended economic effect.

An equally important need is for a comprehensive regional development policy. The greatest obstacle is the national government's strong control of local governments. The need to foster local initiatives is stressed repeatedly, but the concentration of power and authority in the national government makes it almost impossible to prepare an environment conducive to regional development.

Politics and Structural Changes

Historically, Japan has had fairly systematic and cohesive structural policies designed to promote industrial development. When fostering a strong military force and developing modern industries were primary goals of the nation, the national government exercised strong central control. This power, reinforced during wartime, has continued during the postwar period, even under the democratized political regime. After the war, the aim of reconstructing Japan's economy secured a national consensus. Government was essential in determining the most effective allocation of limited resources. With industrial development, the nature of governmental control gradually became more indirect. The relationship between government agencies, politicians, and industries became increasingly institutionalized, and decisions affecting different branches of government and industry became increasingly difficult to make. Since the mid-1970s the government has used indirect control extensively in reallocating resources for industrial adjustment and restructuring. This industrial policy has also depended on well-developed relationships among government agencies, politicians, and business for each industrial sector.

During the postwar industrialization, strategically important companies were given preferential treatment. These corporations, many of them export-oriented, were given favorable loans, special tax treatment, and guidance so that they could quickly and effectively develop international competitiveness. A peculiarly Japanese industrial culture emerged, emphasizing labor-management cooperation and hard work for corporate survival.[43] This culture has been highly instrumental in organizing employees and fostering a common goal of corporate growth. Furthermore, it has focused labor's attention on corporate production activities and away from social issues and living conditions.

The successful industrialization process, promoted by both government assistance and vigorous corporate efforts, has left some serious imbalances. These are most notable in the allocation of resources for industrial purposes rather than for improving the quality of life. When Japan was catching up, this distorted resource allocation did not attract much social attention. As the economy achieved high manufacturing productivity and nominal income, the Japanese grew increasingly aware that their living conditions were far behind those of other countries of comparable industrial productivity.[44]

Many of the reasons for the gap lie in the failure to enrich the infrastructure supporting the quality of life. While industrial sites, transportation, and communication were well developed, urban planning, housing projects, resort facilities, commuter transportation systems, and other elements that enrich people's lives lagged behind. Moreover, the tax system, the legal system, the school system, and other social and institutional systems have not been developed to improve living conditions. This bias in policy emphasis and resource

43. Haruo Shimada, "Japan's Industrial Culture and Labor Management Relations," in Henry Rosovsky and Hugh Patrick, eds., *The Political Economy of Japan,* vol. 3: *Culture and Economy* (Stanford University Press, forthcoming).
44. For example, Japan's largest labor confederation, Rengo, has increasingly emphasized the need to improve the quality of workers' life as well as that of the population at large. See, for example, *Rengō Hakusho: Shunki Seikatsu Tōsō no Shiryō to Kaisetsu* (White paper of the Japanese trade union confederation: data and analysis of the spring offensive for improving the quality of life) (Tokyo: Rengō Headquarters, 1988, 1989, 1990).

allocation seems to be responsible for the gap between Japan's industrial capacity and its quality of life.[45]

Reform of the Political System

While the legacy of a strong central government remains pervasive, the relationship among the government, politics, and private-sector activities has changed. The postwar institutional reform in Japan was similar to a democratic socialist revolution. The financial clans were dissolved and antimonopoly laws were introduced to ensure that the Japanese economy would never again be dominated by a handful of major capitalists, that instead there would be competitive markets and many small producers. Through land reform, tenant farmers were given their own small pieces of land. The size of land transfers was strictly restrained so that farmland would not again be owned by a small number of large landlords. Through educational reform, opportunities for higher education were distributed equally among various classes and groups of people in the society. Similarly, labor unions were legally recognized and labor laws enacted so that workers could obtain countervailing power against the power of employers.

This series of laws and institutional reforms served their purposes well in the early postwar period. Competitive markets were created. Small farmers with greater incentives worked harder, causing a marked increase in agricultural production. The greater numbers of young people who went to high school provided excellent material for the industrial work force. Labor unions grew to be powerful social groups that supported the Socialist and Communist parties with both money and human resources. Indeed, in the late 1940s, with the backing of organized labor, the Socialists led the government in coalition with other parties under the leadership of Tetsu Katayama. Although this Socialist government was short-lived and relinquished power to the conservative Liberal party led by Shigeru Yoshida, the Socialists, with the support of organized labor, were a political power for a decade after the war.

45. The official policy platform for the 1990s of the Ministry of International Trade and Industry (commonly known as MITI's *Vision for the 1990s*), which is subtitled "Creation of Human Value and Virtue in a Global Era," admits openly for the first time in the series of these visions published over the last few decades that the lopsided concentration of resources on production has deterred improvement of people's quality of life and advocates forcefully promoting enrichment of the quality of life.

The conservative parties developed their broad political roots and influences in confrontation with socialists. They secured increasingly broad support among farmers, small producers, shopowners, and salaried-workers, in addition to their traditional, relatively wealthier supporters. Their political power was not unchallenged, however. One of the most critical crises for the conservative parties came in 1955, when left- and right-wing socialists merged to form the new unified Japan Socialist party (JSP). For fear of losing their political dominance, the two major conservative parties, the Liberal party and the Democratic party, merged to form the Liberal Democratic party in the same year.[46] The LDP underwent another crisis in 1960, when political and social turmoil mounted as opposition forces criticized the ratification of the U.S.-Japan Security Pact.

To perpetuate its political dominance, the LDP adopted many laws during the 1950s and 1960s that protected the economic rights of small farmers, small shopowners, small producers, and ordinary citizens. It also introduced policies favoring specific industrial or interest groups. These developments reflected the emergence of strong coalitions of interest groups, politicians, and government branches that formed the basis of the political economy. For example, the price support system for rice was promoted by a joint political committee of agricultural associations that claimed to represent the interest of farmers, politicians who were members of the agricultural committees of the Diet, and the office in charge of the Ministry of Agriculture, Forestry and Fisheries.[47] The system is run through a delicate balance of power among *habatsu* (the political factions) and strictly institutionalized rules of promotion. The appointment of Diet members to various functional roles and posts is carefully defined and administered. Internal practices and rules are so complicated and institutionalized that the party seems to be a highly secluded, self-contained organization.

The Socialist party has steadily lost its share in the Diet over the last

46. The two-party political system established in 1955 characterized the basic nature of Japanese politics, at least through the next few decades. Masumi named the system "the 1955 system." See Junnosuke Masumi, *Sengo Seiji: 1945–1955* (Postwar politics: 1945–1955) (Tokyo: Tokyo Daigaku Shuppankai, 1983).

47. Politicians who intervene between a specific industry and the relevant government agency, as members of the Diet House committee of policy issues directly pertaining to the industry, are named *zoku* (tribe) politicians by Takashi Inoguchi and Tomoaki Iwai, *"Zokugiin" no Kenkyū: Jimintō Seiken o Gyūjiru Shuyaku-tachi* (A study of "zoku" representatives: main actors controlling Japanese politics) (Tokyo: Nihon Keizai Shinbunsha, 1987).

few decades. It has relied largely on the support of the left-wing segment of organized labor, which has also lost its share in the labor movement. The party is often criticized for having lost touch with the reality of the political economy and for adhering to outdated principles such as nonrecognition of South Korea and Japan's self-defense force. While party leaders, particularly of right-wing groups, have at times attempted reforms, the party has been regularly losing its seats in the Diet.

Structural Change and Political Response

Since the mid-1970s, with slower economic growth, fiscal burdens have accumulated and restoration of fiscal balance has become the prime target of the nation's economic policy. Vigorous increases in Japanese exports triggered trade conflicts with importing countries, most notably the United States. Intensified trade conflicts aggravated external pressures for Japan to open its domestic markets to international competition.

Shortly after taking office in 1982, the Nakasone cabinet began serious efforts to remove some of the regulations on financial intermediaries, interest rates on certain types of deposits, and data communication networking. Subsequent cabinets attempted to deregulate rice distribution, interest rates on other types of deposits, and more of the activities of financial intermediaries. In the distribution industry, there have been attempts to relax regulations against the entry of large-scale retailers, and in agriculture, attempts to liberalize imports of citrus fruits, beef, and other items. Other cabinets have tried to open admission to foreign contractors in the construction industry.[48]

In an effort to reform the tax system and find new sources of revenue, several successive LDP governments tried to introduce a broad indirect tax (see Muramatsu and Mabuchi's chapter in this volume). The Ohira government tried to introduce a general consumption tax and lost the election in May 1980. The Nakasone government attempted to introduce a 5 percent value-added tax, breaking the prime minister's public promise, and failed. It had to withdraw the tax proposal from Diet consideration in April 1987. The Takeshita government proposed a 3 percent consumption tax in 1988, which was finally approved in April 1989.

After more and more LDP politicians and faction leaders were found to have received bribes from the Recruit Cosmos Company in the form

48. Rinji Gyōsei Kaikaku, *Kisei Kanwa.*

of stocks before their sale on the market, Naboru Takeshita was eventually obliged to resign as prime minister in April 1989. Sosuke Uno, his successor, was found to have been involved in a sex scandal and quickly lost popularity. Uno's leadership was severely criticized during the campaign for the 1989 upper house election, in which the main public focus was on the new consumption tax. The result was a miserable defeat for the LDP and a remarkable victory for the Socialist party.[49] The LDP lost its majority position, and opposition parties, combined together, gained the majority in the upper house.

Beyond the Recruit scandal and Uno's sex scandal, the landslide defeat had deeper causes, including resentment against the consumption tax and dissatisfaction with agricultural policies. The LDP had carried out measures to promote structural changes for both international and domestic reasons. With the remarkable increase in Japan's income relative to the rest of the world, Japan must open its domestic markets by liberalizing trade practices and institutions. With Japan's rapidly aging population, the tax system, which relies mostly on income taxes, will have to bear an ever-increasing burden of social costs.

The introduction of a broad indirect tax to cope with the latter problem was perhaps inevitable. At the time the new tax was introduced, inflationary pressure was minimal, and dramatic increases in land values had enriched tax revenue, which provided funds for large-scale income tax reductions to offset increased consumption tax burdens. However, the LDP and the government introduced the new tax too hastily, in an insensitive and arrogant fashion. Without allowing time for parliamentary debate and public examination of the new policy proposal, the law was passed unilaterally, taking advantage of the LDP's overwhelming majority in the Diet.

Of course, the LDP alone was not responsible for neglecting debates; its opponents—most notably the Japan Socialist party—kept rejecting a parliamentary debate. Because the procedures for managing Diet sessions are based on the unanimous agreement of all parties, opposition parties often reject parliamentary debate as a bargaining tactic. Consequently, time is spent in behind-the-scenes bargaining rather than open parliamentary debate. Such uncooperative attitudes on the part of opposition parties are understandable, for it is likely that a proposed bill will be passed in any case. In effect, critical decisions are made not in

49. The Liberal Democratic party dropped from 142 seats to 109, while the Japan Socialist party increased from 42 to 66. As a result, the LDP no longer holds a majority of the 252 seats in the upper house.

the Diet, but by a closed circle of the LDP's powerful faction leaders. Therefore the decisionmaking process is closed to the public. With barely any possibility of opposition parties' obtaining the prime minister's office, the office has passed among LDP leaders, depending on the power balance among the party's factions. The public, shut out from critical information about decisionmaking processes and from opportunities to have any influence by altering the parties in power, has become apathetic, while a sense of powerlessness, alienation, and frustration has been accumulating.

Public frustration and dissatisfaction are rooted in the structural inequities of Japanese economy and society. For instance, while the aggregate value of financial assets was almost five times Japan's gross national product in the mid-1970s, these assets had grown to more than seven times GNP by 1987.[50]

The Japanese public is growing more aware of the ironical disparity between their high nominal income and their low quality of life. The prices of consumption goods and services and of land and houses in major urban areas are extremely high. To pay for goods and houses, Japanese urban workers are forced to work much longer hours than their Western counterparts.

The Recruit scandal revealed that some LDP politicians (and others) were increasing their assets through behind-the-scenes manipulations of stocks that were unavailable to the public. Coming on top of the public's frustrations and uneasiness, and the hasty, unilateral introduction of the consumption tax—which to the public appeared to hit helpless and relatively poor people—the scandal triggered an explosion of anti-LDP sentiment. The Japan Socialist party used the frustrations and dissatisfaction with the LDP, promising to abolish the consumption tax, slow down the liberalization of agricultural trade, and continue regulating the entry of large-scale retail shops. Housewives, to whom the nuisance of the consumption tax was most visible, applauded the Socialists' promise. Farmers, who had been irritated by government reductions of the purchasing price of rice, government guidelines to reduce farmland, and recommendations to convert to other produce and activities, now decided to look to the JSP rather than the LDP. Small shopowners, who had feared entry of large-scale retailers into the community, shifted to support the Socialists.

50. In 1975, for instance, the estimated value of aggregate financial assets, including corporate stocks, was ¥699 trillion and GNP was ¥148 trillion; by 1987 the comparable figures had increased to ¥2,557 and ¥345 trillion, respectively.

In addition to the JSP's victory in the 1989 elections, independent candidates supported by labor unions were remarkably successful. Eleven out of twelve candidates whose support was organized by Rengo (the Japan Private Sector Trade Union Congress) were elected. After the election, they formed a registered political group, the Rengo-Upper House. This success by Rengo-assisted candidates may reflect the unanswered frustrations and unfulfilled desires of the silent working masses.

With the remarkable victory of the Japan Socialist party and the appreciable success of candidates assisted by Rengo, the possibility of a coalition government by parties formerly opposed to each other began to attract attention. Would a coalition government led chiefly by the JSP be a realistic and reliable alternative to the LDP? I believe there are two important prerequisites.

First, a positive, not negative, policy package is needed. Opposition parties, particularly the JSP, have criticized and opposed LDP policies, but they have not proposed their own policy packages. Indeed, it is questionable whether the JSP's public promises would serve the long-term interests of wage earners. I believe they would contradict those interests. For example, to rely primarily on income taxes and reject a large-scale indirect tax, such as a consumption tax, would inevitably increase the burdens of wage earners relative to other social groups. Their entire income is taxable, unlike that of self-employed entrepreneurs and large asset owners who have a variety of measures to evade taxes. Slowing down the liberalization of agricultural trade would also retard improvement of the standard of living of urban wage earners as competitive forces in agriculture weaken. Continued regulation of entry of large-scale retail shops acts against the interest of working people as consumers, preserving inefficient segments of the distribution sector and keeping consumer prices high. What the opposition parties need to propose is a program that will bring about a better life for people than the LDP's policies brought them.

The other prerequisite is a strong coalition of opposition parties. It is not easy for these parties—each with its own ideology, commitments, and background—to form a coalition. However, they will not be able to capture power if they fail to do so. Disparities and confrontations are particularly serious in the spheres of defense and foreign policy; the outdated, stubborn position of the extreme left of the JSP is well known. The opposition parties need a coalition organized around a commonly agreed and realistic strategy for pursuing world peace. These are difficult challenges the opposition will have to tackle if they are serious in their pursuit of power.

While the political parties try to reformulate their strategies, people's concern about inequities and structural deficiencies in the Japanese political economy is apparently increasing. To tackle the increasing asset differentials, the cleavage between nominal income and the quality of life, and the gap between Tokyo and the rest of Japan, a major restructuring of the Japanese economy is needed. Low-productivity sectors such as agriculture, distribution, construction, and various services have to be modernized; their markets have to be opened to stimulate competition and modernization; and working hours need to be shortened so that employment opportunities can be shared among the redundant workers who will emerge in the process of modernization and rationalization. These measures will require major redistribution of income and employment opportunities, as well as of assets and property among different social and economic groups. Such restructuring will also require people to change occupations and activities through retraining and entrepreneurial changes.

These changes and challenges are hard to swallow. Voters tend to pursue their own vested interests. As the party in power, the LDP attempted to promote various measures for needed structural reform. When these measures were perceived as having an adverse effect on the immediate interests of the people, opposition parties such as the JSP were able to make gains by opposing such policies.

After more than forty years of a unilateral and relatively stable political system with de facto one-party dominance by the Liberal Democratic party, under which Japan was able to mobilize its resources quite efficiently toward the goal of enriching the productive capacity of the economy, the Japanese public seems to be beginning to question the validity of that system. Whether their choice results in a life of better quality, improves economic efficiency, and promotes desirable restructuring of the political economy remains to be seen.

Part V
Conclusion

The Primacy of Politics
in Economic Policy

Samuel Kernell

COMPARATIVE ANALYSES of American and Japanese
politics typically stress each country's distinctiveness so much that they
end up describing each one as a special or deviant case. Observers
portray policymaking in Japan as regulated by cultural prescriptions and
dominated by some unelected elite. In a recent popular introduction to
Japan's politics, Karel van Wolferen intones, "The Japanese are rarely
allowed to forget the existence of socio-political arrangements that are
infinitely stronger than any kind of might the individual could ever bring
to bear on them." Instead, a "System" run by and for economic elites
rules Japan. Dismissing the relevance of conventional political analysis,
he adds that the average citizen has "only a dim notion that ideally one
should have recourse to democratic processes."[1]

Public policy in the United States, by contrast, is depicted as little
more than the by-product of a pluralist free-for-all in which no one's
policy preferences are maximized. In his best-selling critique of American economic policy, Lester C. Thurow identifies the chief culprit as
America's political parties:

> Our problems arise because, in a very real sense, we do not have
> political parties. A political party is a group that can force its elected
> members to vote for that party's solutions to society's problems. . . .
> We have a system where each elected official is his own party and is
> free to establish his own party platform. . . . This means a splintering

The author wishes to thank Gary W. Cox, Gary C. Jacobson, Mathew D. McCubbins,
Gregory W. Noble, Bert A. Rockman, Frances M. Rosenbluth, and R. Kent Weaver
for their comments on an earlier version of this essay.
    1. Karel van Wolferen, *The Enigma of Japanese Power: People and Politics in a
Stateless Nation* (Knopf, 1989), pp. 43–44.

of power that makes it impossible to hold anyone responsible for failure.[2]

With the first author describing a system so orderly as to be undemocratic and the second one so disorderly as to be incoherent, these typical descriptions set policymaking in Japan and the United States poles apart. As a result, the absorbing peculiarities of each country's politics frustrate comparative analysis.

Before considering how the preceding essays break with conventional wisdom, I should note that many of the familiar observations about these two countries' politics reappear in this volume. Japan's powerful bureaucracy, headed by the Ministry of International Trade and Industry (MITI) coordinating industrial and trade policy and the Ministry of Finance (MOF) overseeing the full spectrum of government finance and expenditures, appears no less authoritative than it is typically represented to be. Similarly, many of the peculiar features of American national politics—a fragmented bureaucracy, a decentralized legislature, and a weak party system—are once again said to account for American economic policy.

These essays also accept much of the conventional comparisons of public policy. Japan's economic policies exhibit greater coherence and capacity for long-term planning. Even if its role is largely that of a broker, MITI has greater influence over private investment and trade policies than does the assortment of U.S. institutions that occupy this policy domain. The thousand or so cartels and the many government-sponsored research and development consortia do add up to an industrial policy. The closest the United States comes to such an enterprise, Roger Noll maintains, is in the procurement policies of the Pentagon.

Although the authors acknowledge that these overall differences exist, the message of their essays is that the differences are not so pronounced as generally represented. The forces of particularism appear as powerful in Japan as they do in the United States. Eisuke Sakakibara dismisses the notion of rational, synoptic planning at the outset. While conceding MITI its due, he argues that its influence has been overstated and that its domain is unrepresentative of economic policymaking in Japan. The Japanese miracle has occurred in the sectors of the economy where the government has remained relatively uninvolved.

2. Lester C. Thurow, *The Zero-Sum Society: Distribution and the Possibilities for Economic Change* (Basic Books, 1980), p. 212.

Basically, Japan's economic policies, like those in other countries, function to redress grievances of economically suffering constituencies. Frequently, such policies redistribute income from wealthy to poor regions. Hence Sakakibara describes the mostly rural public works programs as one of the central and most expensive policy concerns of the national government. Such policies may also subsidize inefficient sectors of the economy. Haruo Shimada points out that many Japanese politicians and bureaucrats, like those in most modern industrial democracies, are singularly absorbed in protecting agriculture.

These essays retain the image of policymaking in America as a whirligig of politics, but they also identify underlying sources of coordination and a measure of policy coherence. The twentieth century presidency has been sufficiently strengthened beyond its original constitutional mandate, John Chubb and Paul Peterson argue, to provide a potent active sponsor for nationally oriented policies. Even Congress, that sea of particularism, contains important elements of policy coordination. Where most observers see the budget deficit as evidence of a process spinning out of control, Mathew McCubbins sees recent budgetary politics as a logical product of divided party control of Congress and the presidency. By showing that even this seemingly intractable area of policy displays a measure of coordination, at least within party teams, McCubbins suggests that policymaking contains more investment in providing collective goods than is generally supposed.

Nowhere in these essays does the resemblance between Japanese and American policymaking show up more prominently than in the case studies of tax reform. In both instances, tax reform originated as a comprehensive policy to repair inequities and inefficiencies that had cropped up in the tax code over the years. Not surprisingly, given their national policy focus, both reforms received their strongest early push from the executive. The seed of tax reform in the United States was sown in the Treasury Department when Secretary Donald Regan interested President Ronald Reagan in the notion of a flat tax rate in 1984. In Japan, the Ministry of Finance was always interested in finding new sources of revenue, but only when the deficits began mounting did reform become politically compelling. After earlier false starts, the idea of a sales tax was rejuvenated by Prime Minister Yasuhiro Nakasone's Administrative Reform Council. Once introduced in each country's legislature, each reform proposal encountered stiff resistance from constituencies advantaged by current policies.

At this juncture, the legislative histories of the two cases diverge sharply. Tax reform in the United States quickly gained momentum and, despite dire predictions, sailed through Congress with its major provisions intact. Allen Schick describes the many shoals of economic interests on which tax reform could have foundered, but concludes that it succeeded largely because each political party's leadership realized the political gains to be had by the other if it failed to embrace the program enthusiastically. In Japan, as Michio Muramatsu and Masaru Mabuchi report, tax reform similarly embarked on its legislative odyssey with a strong push from the national executive, but soon stalled when it entered the legislature. After consuming several sessions of the Diet and contributing to the downfall of several Liberal Democratic party (LDP) prime ministers, a new tax law finally emerged, but it was so emasculated that even its early boosters hesitated to call it a reform. The politics of tax reform in Japan arguably resembles the image of America's discordant politics more closely than it does the calm progression toward consensus commonly ascribed to Japanese politics.

The Sources of Particularistic Economic Policy

These essays depict economic policy in both countries as generally responsive to organized constituencies, especially those who have suffered in the marketplace. Consequently, policy tends to be remedial. Rather than implementing some comprehensive strategy of growth, it offers protective cover to ailing and favored sectors of the economy through trade protection, sympathetic commercial regulation, and direct subsidy. And an economic constituency's association with the political parties offers at least as good a prediction of policy focus as any prescriptive economic theory.

This is not surprising news for anyone who has even a cursory familiarity with American politics. It is precisely the problem Lester Thurow complains of regarding U.S. economic policy. The Constitution's Framers succeeded, after all, in constructing a governmental system that assures easy access to society's competing "factions." The dispersion of authority among national institutions is reinforced by a federal structure that assigns important responsibilities and authority to the states. The biases of the governmental system are reinforced by political parties composed of locally oriented officeholders. While not altogether bereft of coordination and the potential for coherence, policymaking remains highly fragmented and responsive to local constituencies.

That organized constituencies would be so successful in shaping economic policy in Japan is less apparent. It flies in the face of the innumerable popular reports of comprehensive rational economic planning by an elite, most frequently found in the bureaucracy, that distances itself from the political fray and is thereby free to formulate policies that advance economic growth.[3] Others, such as van Wolferen, discern a cozy alliance of these bureaucrats with senior LDP leaders and big business representatives who promote their own, self-serving view of the public good. However much these interpretations differ over who constitutes the inner club, they agree in describing a top-down policymaking structure that offers few points of access to the parochial concerns of local interests.

Yet the essays in this volume describe a government of *zoku*, a policymaking process particularistic to its core. Organized and local interests are comfortably ensconced in the Diet. "Were it not for the particular patterns of LDP clientele support," concludes John Creighton Campbell in his authoritative analysis of Japanese budgeting, "the budget shares to rice price supports, to war widows' benefits, to certain kinds of public works . . . to doctors' fees, to the maintenance of many rural railroad lines, would doubtlessly be substantially lower."[4] Higher-level tiers of governmental and party organization—including the substantive ministries and the Policy Affairs Research Council—serve not as refuges for a ruling elite but as arenas where claims for relief are aggregated into public policy.

How could budgets and taxes, the central features of a nation's economic policy, be riddled with particularism while the more celebrated aspects of economic policy remain insulated from politics? How could Japan's fabled economic technocrats remain undistracted in their pursuit of economic growth? One answer proposes that the economic policy process in Japan is bifurcated. Politicians are given loose rein to play politics by larding public works budgets and subsidizing inefficient

3. Chalmers Johnson, *MITI and the Japanese Miracle: The Growth of Industrial Policy, 1925–1975* (Stanford University Press, 1982).

4. *Contemporary Japanese Budget Politics* (University of California Press, 1977), pp. 137–43.

industries in return for staying clear of the policies directed by MITI and the MOF that produce the national wealth to pay the bills.[5]

An alternative possibility is that policymaking is consistent across these realms. The policies that have been credited with Japan's extraordinary growth are just another face of the politics of particularism. After all, the economic growth proceeds through the coffers of the industries that stand to benefit most from collusive solutions to market dilemmas. With a conservative regime in place, it behooves different industries to have the bureaucracy broker and legitimize cartel agreements and police would-be free riders to share the costs of technological development and adhere to their allocated share of the market. The political forces and the governmental system that led to the emergence of economic protectionism for an inefficient agricultural sector may be fundamentally the same as those that yielded an aggressive, technologically sophisticated, export-driven consumer industry.

The special regard paid organized constituencies sets Japan and the United States apart from the industrial democracies that approximate responsible party government. And it provides the essential commonality for a comparative assessment of these two countries' economic policies. For each country's politics, particularistic economic policy raises questions: What are the institutional arrangements that foster this pervasive responsiveness to organized constituencies? Are there occasionally sufficient incentives and opportunities for politicians to withstand these pressures and to stake their political fortunes on some broader conception of the public interest?

The answers to these questions are to be found in the ways each country's political institutions reflect and in turn channel the behavior of ambitious politicians. Among the consequential variables are the array of interests in society and their competition for influence over policy, the ways politicians pursue their self-interest as they serve their constituents, and the institutional rules and procedures that transform the diverse preferences of politicians and their constituencies into collective decisions.

For American politics, with its large population of loosely tethered politicians, there would be no dispute with this emphasis on these actors as the central figures whose behavior needs to be accounted for. But for

5. Chalmers Johnson, "The Japanese Political Economy: A Crisis in Theory," *Ethics and International Affairs,* vol. 2 (1988), pp. 86–87.

Japan, where elected officeholders have typically assumed a more subordinate posture in relation to economic notables and above all, to powerful bureaucrats, such an emphasis may appear misplaced. A culture of deference and consensus has led many students of Japanese politics to eschew the kind of institutional analysis entertained here. The responsiveness of national economic policy to the preferences of local and well-organized constituencies suggests, nonetheless, that the politicians who can be expected to give local concerns their most sympathetic hearing—namely Diet members—must indeed have considerable say over policy.

I examine the competition between public goods and particularism in two main arenas: the political party, in both the electorate and the national legislature; and the national executive, which at the top encompasses either the prime minister or the president, and lower down the bureaucracy. The first discussion mostly concerns the distinction between "weak" and "strong" political parties, defined according to the extent to which they formulate national policy and sanction members' conformity to the collectivity's decisions. I argue that the particularism that is deeply entrenched in both countries' party systems is closely reflected in their national legislatures. The evidence is the similarly great devotion to constituent service shown by members of both the Diet and Congress.

By contrast, executive institutions are generally understood to be more insulated from parochial forces and therefore more likely to entertain a broader conception of the public interest. The institutional source of this insulation differs across parliamentary and presidential systems. Nonetheless, the prime minister and the president perform basically the same duty in representing their political party before a national electorate. The governing party's association with national policies is most likely to be founded on the actions and rhetoric of the national political executive. The bureaucracy's insulation from particularistic influences is rooted in its professional, nonelective status as well as its statutory mandate to promote general principles and apply universal criteria in its implementation of policy.

The Party System: The Roots of Particularism

At first glance, political parties in the United States and Japan appear about as different from one another as possible. How could one expect to find here a basis for similar economic policies? The distinguishing feature of America's party system is its firmly entrenched, highly competitive, two major parties. Throughout the country, Democrats and Republicans vie for partisan office at every level of government. Both have their successes, which create divided party control of government in both Washington and the state capitals. In Japan, five or six parties routinely win seats in the national legislature, but one, the Liberal Democratic party, dominates all the others. It has effectively controlled a majority of seats in the Diet's House of Representatives, and thus the cabinet and prime minister, every year since 1955, a modern record for uninterrupted control of government among postwar industrial democracies.

With the consolidation of the "progressive" and "conservative" parties in the mid-1950s, Japan's politics appeared headed toward two-party competition. However desirable this may have appeared to scholarly observers who embrace a Westminster model of parliamentary government, it lasted but a single election. In 1958, the Socialists were unable to muster much more than a third of the popular vote in the national elections. Soundly defeated and with little prospective profit from maintaining a facade of unity, the progressive factions splintered into separate parties over the next decade. The LDP's victory, conversely, justified the conservatives' consolidation strategy. Controlling the levers of policy, and gaining access to the largess of those who do business with the government, this new party was able to cement its confederational structure.

Whatever the dimension—whether in the number of parties, their competitiveness, or the ways elections are conducted—the Japanese and American party systems belong on different ends of the continuum. Yet it is here in the respective party systems one should expect to find the source of particularistic economic policy. From quite different paths, political rationality has led both countries' politicians to embrace broadly similar conceptions of representation. To understand how each reached this common ground, one needs a theory that encompasses politics in both countries.

A Rationale for Party Action

Politicians succeed at the ballot box to the degree they can deliver desired benefits to their constituency and gain credit for doing so. The first implies performance, whether in creating national policy or in providing local services, while the second implies communication to a mass electorate. Alone, the incumbent officeholder possesses too few resources to achieve sufficient levels of either to assure reelection. And the solitary challenger who can offer only promises is even more disadvantaged. Both require cooperation among similarly situated politicians. To solve this classic problem of collective action, politicians invented political parties.

Political parties address the former problem by creating a broad alliance of politicians whose authority spans the governmental system, and, in doing so, they contribute to solving the communication problem by giving policy content to the party label. Participation in a party team has its costs, however. The creation of a party program requires politicians at times to adopt policy positions that differ from the median preferences of their districts—a locally unpopular national policy or added taxes to pay for programs benefiting another constituency.

This trade-off of benefits and costs of party action implies a strategic relation of the politician to the political party. The politician engages in a continuing reassessment of whether to remain loyal or to try to do better by taking an independent course. Individual politicians will decide the matter differently according to the requirements of their constituency and their personal situation. For some, whose median voter is well aligned with party policy, the advantages of party action so outweigh independence that they will never seriously contemplate an alternative course. Others will find that the discrepancy between their party's and constituency's preferences pushes them to apostasy on most important issues. For this reason, many southern Democrats in Congress and urban Liberal Democrats in the Diet predictably stake out more independent postures on certain national issues.

Even when politicians agree that their individual success is closely tied to their party's fortunes, the party still may not be able to satisfy the collective needs of its members. This is because each politician will, if given the opportunity, attempt to reap the benefits of the party's collective effort while exempting his or her local constituency from the costs or sacrifice the policy requires. Consensus for the party's national economic program may therefore prove insufficient to achieve voluntary party loyalty. To solve this dilemma, party members entrust their leaders with the authority to enforce adherence to the party's collective position. Uncooperative members might be punished by having their favorite projects vetoed or by being denied staff and favorable committee assignments and, in extreme cases, even by being banned from the party ballot. Such sanctions allow party leaders to translate enthusiasm for a national policy into party action.

Politicians cede authority to their leaders in direct relation to what they perceive as the costs and benefits of a strong party. In a system where constituencies are highly diverse and conformity to a party program imposes unacceptable costs for too many of its members, the party's control will be limited in scope. Similarly, in a system where, by virtue of their office and the availability of outside resources, politicians can independently satisfy their constituency, members will have less need for party action than they would were their election wholly dependent on their party's provision of public goods. Thus the electorally optimal mix of local services and national policies will define the relations between leaders and followers. Where selective benefits to constituencies weigh heavily in elections and can be provided through simple mechanisms of reciprocity within or outside party channels, there is little need for strong party leadership.

From the reports provided in these essays, both American and Japanese politicians appear to have invested their careers in local service. If so, there will be evidence of this in both party structures and economic policy. This is not to suggest the party's provision of collective goods is inconsequential. National policies do matter and political parties are the chief mechanism by which they are achieved. It is simply the case that, in these two democracies, representation prescribes that politicians remain keenly attentive to the local median voter, reducing the extent to which political parties can afford to bid for votes with promises of collective goods. Understanding why requires a careful examination of each country's system of representation.

The Party in the Electorate

Electoral laws determining how votes are cast and representation is awarded play a generally underappreciated role in shaping the party system. Few principles in political science are backed by as much solid evidence as the one which holds that the greater the number of seats up for election in a given electoral district, the greater will be the number of political parties competing for those seats.[6] America's single-member

6. The definitive statements on this issue, which oddly omit reference to Japan's electoral system, are Douglas W. Rae, *The Political Consequences of Electoral Laws* (Yale University Press, 1967); and Rein Taagepera and Matthew Soberg Shugart, *Seats and Votes: The Effects and Determinants of Electoral Systems* (Yale University Press, 1989).

plurality districts have yielded two-party competition, while Japan's multimember districts have opened up elections and seats to a number of minor parties. Although these electoral arrangements define the general contour of the party system, other, partly derivative, rules governing how candidates are nominated for office also determine the role political parties will play both in elections and in the government.

THE ELECTORAL SYSTEM. Virtually all U.S. elections occur within single-member plurality districts. The reason this electoral system should lead to two-party competition is straightforward. With only a single seat available and a runoff election obviated by the plurality rule, the likelihood of a third party entering the race and winning the election is remote. Recognizing the prospect of wasting their vote, even citizens sympathetic with the platform of a third party will be disinclined to support it. Instead, the second most preferred candidate will be selected. The "wasted vote" dilemma prevents all but a few potential third party movements from ever bothering to field candidates.[7]

While the single-member plurality district accounts for the dominance of two-candidate races, it does not explain why the same two parties show up everywhere. A likely reason is the necessity of creating national alliances to compete in presidential elections. The few parties that have endured have done so by creating an attractive national ticket. Conversely, the quick demise of the Whig party on the eve of the Civil War appears to have been triggered by its failure to find a national standard-bearer mutually acceptable to its northern and southern factions. And the truncated third party movements that briefly enjoyed local and state hegemony never were able to withstand raids from one or both of the national parties.[8]

The need of America's parties to be both national in scope and yet able to appeal to numerous, highly diverse, local pluralities dampens their enthusiasm for ideological appeals. Instead, success comes from being associated with nationally attractive policies—economic growth and a clean environment are two favorites—while accommodating the diversity of political views to be found across the many local constituencies. In the American setting, the single-member plurality

7. Occasionally, a single party will become so dominant that even the second party, with only a remote chance of achieving a plurality, will be reduced to token opposition or even disappear altogether. Politicians still compete for office, but—as in the solid Democratic South during the first half of this century—they do so within the confines of the dominant party.

8. Richard M. Valelly, *Radicalism in the States: The Minnesota Farmer Labor Party and the American Political Economy* (University of Chicago Press, 1989).

system promotes localism, even in giving each politician an opportunity to tailor the party's national appeal to the local constituency.

The classic proportional representation systems found throughout Western Europe are about as different as imaginable from the single-member plurality system in their effects on the number and orientation of the political parties. They tend to maximize the number of parties contesting elections. Moreover, voters cast ballots for party lists of candidates, with the seats in the legislature awarded to the parties in proportion to their overall vote. Under this system, citizens can support a minor party without fear of wasting their votes as long as it can win the minimum number of votes necessary to gain a seat. Rather than having to appeal to the median voter, a party can afford to target its appeal to a narrower range of preferences and still expect to gain representation.

The inherent biases of proportional representation are relevant here because Japan's electoral procedures represent a hybrid of plurality vote and proportional representation; consequently, so does its party system. Its chief resemblance to proportional representation is found in the multimember districts. Nearly all of the the prefectures contain from three to five seats for the lower house of the Diet. Rather than endorsing a party list, however, the voter casts a single ballot for one of the competing candidates. As in plurality systems, the top vote getters win the seats, irrespective of the political parties' shares of the overall popular vote. Also similar is the likelihood of wasted votes. LDP supporters may not know which of several LDP candidates most needs their votes. "Progressive" voters confront a similar puzzle in trying to decide which opposition candidate stands the best chance of winning. Uncertainty by voters in deciding whom to support and by political parties in calculating how many candidates to field contributes to various possible election results, one being a winning candidate who is less preferred by the voters than is one of the losers.

While the effects of this unique, hybrid electoral system have not been fully explored, the evidence suggests that the design of Japan's party system closely reflects its inherent biases. The multimember district encourages minor parties to compete by lowering the vote threshold necessary to win representation. In a four-member prefecture, for example, a party need capture only 20 percent of the vote to be guaranteed a seat. Without having to approach a plurality, minor parties are not severely penalized for failing to appeal to the median voter.

Many, perhaps most, of the Japan Socialist party's Diet members are safely ensconced in office while remaining uncorrupted from having to work the political center. A serious attempt at becoming the majority party would require additional candidacies for Diet seats, thereby jeopardizing the safe seats of the opposition incumbents with the same vote dilution plaguing their LDP counterparts. "How lucky the LDP was to have the opposition it had," observes one close student of Japanese elections, adding, "It is not often that one finds a country in which the opposition parties . . . are so determined to remain deeply wedded to their traditional ideologies and basic support groups, to resist change."[9] The opposition's determination reflects no more than the iron logic of electoral rationality, and the LDP's luck rests more directly on the peculiar electoral system that keeps the opposition in place. The 1990 general election produced the best opportunity progressive parties have enjoyed since the early 1970s to make serious inroads into the LDP majority. What did they do? The Japan Socialist party (JSP) contested fewer seats than its leadership had advertised it would before the campaign. The united progressive front fielded so few candidates, in fact, that even had they all won, the alliance would still have fallen short of a majority in the Diet's House of Representatives. In the end, the opposition settled for modest gains.[10]

For the majority LDP, these features of the electoral system depreciate the value of the party's label by requiring its candidates to compete with one another. Over 90 percent of LDP candidates share the ballot with a fellow party candidate in general elections. Each seeks an advantage by differentiating his or her appeal in a variety of ways: offering local services, disassociating one's campaign from the party's unpopular policies, and denigrating fellow party members. This setting stimulates the emergence of candidate-centered, locally oriented cam-

9. Gerald L. Curtis, *Japan's Political Party System: Its Dynamics and Prospects* (Tokyo: Japan Foundation, 1983), p. 4.
10. The plurality features of this mixed system appear to favor the majority LDP. With relatively few seats in each district, an efficient distribution of the LDP vote across candidacies, combined with a fragmentation of opposition support, will sometimes allow the party to win a disproportionate share of seats. Even after correcting for the favorable malapportionment, the LDP gained 55.5 percent of the Diet seats in the 1980 general election with 47.8 percent of the popular vote. Arend Lijphart, Rafael Lopez Pintor, and Yasunori Sone, "The Limited Vote and the Single Nontransferable Vote: Lessons from the Japanese and Spanish Examples," in Bernard Grofman and Arend Lijphart, eds., *Electoral Laws and Their Political Consequences* (New York: Agathon Press, 1986), pp. 154–59.

paigns.[11] The party's record and promises tend to get lost in the resulting fray between candidates from the same party.

Politicians in these situations still need the kinds of services political parties provide—namely, the prospect of performance and the ability to communicate with a large constituency. But how can one LDP candidate working alone succeed at either or manage to gain a competitive edge over rivals? Consider what they need to offer local voters: "Should they want a new airport, they are assured that he has the best entrée . . . to the Transport Ministry and the Finance Ministry; if wider roads are needed, or a new bridge, then he has more friends at the Ministry of Construction than any other candidates. . . . The LDP politician compares his access to bureaucrats with that of his fellow LDP members."[12] In other settings, these are the kinds of benefits competing political parties offer. With the party neutralized, and yet unable to provide these services alone, individual LDP politicians associate themselves with one of the half dozen or so factions (*habatsu*) that have dominated the party since its inception.

Each faction is organized around a senior leader who brokers the flow of resources to his members' constituencies in return for support in some future bid for prime minister. Factions are so prominent a part of the political landscape that newspapers and political almanacs commonly label LDP politicians by their factional associations. Successful politicians' strength in their constituencies rests on the comparative advantage of their faction's claim to control the policies of the ministries that administer locally important programs. The centrality of intraparty competition to LDP politics can be seen in its "blood feuds."

> Under the present middle-sized election district system, several candidates from the same party must stand and fight in the same election district. Both the candidates and their campaign workers

---

11. When asked the main reason for their vote, the percentage of respondents identifying party decreased across prefectures as the number of candidates from the party increased—from half of the responses with one party candidate to less than 10 percent when the party listed five candidates. Conversely, the percentage of respondents giving the candidate as the main reason for their vote increased from 36 to 89 percent. Thomas R. Rochon, "Electoral Systems and the Basis of the Vote: the Case of Japan," in John Creighton Campbell, ed., *Parties, Candidates, and Voters in Japan: Six Quantitative Studies* (University of Michigan, Center for Japanese Studies, 1981), p. 8.

12. Van Wolferen, *Enigma of Japanese Power*, p. 57.

keep their hands off the domains of the opposition parties . . . but aim at the domains of the candidates of the same party. These . . . so-called election blood feuds . . . can be observed in each district throughout the nation. Because of them, the election battles are becoming fiercer, are requiring increasing amounts of money, are giving rise to the development of factions within the parties, and are preventing party unity.[13]

"We are always too busy fighting among ourselves. Look at the men from the same electoral districts. They're terrible," complained one veteran Diet member. "They can't even talk pleasantly to each other in the Diet. That's because there is usually a serious war between them. . . . Everybody has had this terrible experience."[14] The results of the 1990 elections for the lower house portend continued incivilities. Of the thirty-nine defeated Diet members, twenty-three were replaced by an LDP politician from another faction. The highly factionalized LDP reflects the logic of an electoral system that forces candidates from the same party to differentiate their appeals.

The electoral systems of Japan and the United States create less hospitable settings for national campaigns waged on the party's national platform than those systems that place little premium on the quality of individual candidacies. In the United States, the critical importance of local pluralities discourages the major parties from formulating highly programmatic positions on national issues. For a candidate to rely exclusively on party policies would be risky. If the policies are popular, this strategy would attract a general election opponent who would adopt similar positions on national issues and then bid for votes with promises of local goods and services. In Japan, party-based campaigns make even less sense for LDP candidates, since their nearest rivals share the label. Bids for support must necessarily be founded upon a personal or factional appeal. As different as these countries' electoral and resulting party systems are, they similarly reward a politician's parochialism while depreciating the electoral value of the party's national program.

13. Tsuchiya Shozo, "Senkyo Seido no Kaisei Mondai ni Tsuite" (Concerning the reform problem of the electoral system), *Shinseikei*, no. 190 (August 1, 1966), p. 10, quoted in Nathaniel B. Thayer, *How the Conservatives Rule Japan* (Princeton University Press, 1969), pp. 118–19.

14. Senkyo Seido Shingikai, *Dai-niji Senkyo Seido Shingikai Giji Sokkiroku* (Transcript of proceedings of the Second Election System Deliberation Commission), 1963, pp. 230–31, quoted in Thayer, *How the Conservatives Rule Japan*, p. 119.

THE NOMINATION AND CAMPAIGN. The formal rules and established practices by which candidates are recruited and campaign for
office necessarily conform to the basic requirements of the electoral
system. Not surprisingly, then, in both Japan and the United States they
reinforce candidate-centered elections.

The nominating primary is an American invention adopted at the turn
of the century to thwart the influence of local political machines on
elections. It removed control over party nominations from local party
organizations and lodged it instead with the voters in a primary election.
From state to state, present-day primary laws vary in the extent to which
they permit political parties to participate in the selection process. Some
states, for example, permit party conventions to endorse candidates,
while others strictly ban any party participation in the nomination phase
of the election. Many states restrict primary voting to citizens registered
as party members, while others open the election to all voters. Everywhere, an aspiring candidate can qualify to run in the primary by filing
a short petition of registered voters with election officials. Whatever its
particular provisions, the direct primary reform has thoroughly achieved
its goal of emasculating political parties. If political parties are the losers,
the winners are incumbent officeholders. Since 1980 only about 5 percent
of House incumbents who have sought renomination have lost.

Recent reforms in the ways elections are financed and conducted have
further served to increase the independence of politicians from their
political parties. Campaign finance reform in the 1970s was designed to
open up fundraising to public scrutiny and to clarify the procedures and
legal limits of contributions from businesses, unions, and other groups.
The reforms clarified these matters so well that many organizations that
had previously shied away from contributing to candidates for fear of
breaking ambiguous state and federal laws could now safely join in.
From 1976 until 1988, the number of political action committees grew
from 992 to 4,268. Their donations to congressional candidates increased
over this period from $22.6 million to $151.3 million. Over 80 percent of
these funds go to incumbents.[15]

Another equally dramatic trend liberating representatives from their

15. Harold W. Stanley and Richard G. Niemi, *Vital Statistics on American Politics,*
2d ed. (Washington: CQ Press, 1990), pp. 160, 163. Meanwhile, the political parties are
severely restricted in the financial support they can provide to any candidate for the
general election races. While increases in allowable party donations are limited to
inflation, the available PAC money and campaign expenditures have grown at a far
greater rate. As a consequence, the share of an adequately financed campaign
underwritten by the political party has dwindled in each election.

dependence on party-based resources is expansion of office staffs. Between 1957 and 1987, the number of employees on House members' office payrolls increased from 2,441 to 7,584.[16] Those more concerned about the next election have tended to concentrate this growth in servicing increased casework from their district offices. No matter where they are located, virtually all staff members play an active role in what has typically become a permanent reelection campaign. In addition, a more generous travel allowance, a more liberal use of franking privileges for constituency mailings, and other perquisites of office have made the modern member of Congress as self-sufficient as any politician could reasonably hope.

When it comes to conducting elections, Japan's political parties appear to be in the driver's seat, especially when compared with America's parties. A central party apparatus within the LDP, headed by the party's president (who by virtue of this office is also the prime minister) and including the secretary-general and members of the Election Policy Committee, endorses candidates and endows campaigns. But, at least with respect to the majority LDP, appearances are deceiving. These prerogatives are more form than fact and do not purchase the party much leverage with its politicians.

There is clear evidence in the election returns that the prime minister's personal participation in the party's central funding of campaigns gives his faction an advantage in the election, but for the most part the party leadership's discretion is tightly circumscribed by both factional competition and the fact that meaningful endorsements are made in the prefectures rather than in Tokyo. Party endorsements are directed less toward resolving "blood feuds" and more toward keeping the ballot from becoming congested with too many Liberal Democratic candidates, which could badly split the vote and cause a *tomodaore*, or "going down together."[17]

For races where the party endorsement mechanism matters most— that is, where a marginal shift in the party vote will win or lose a seat— factions in place will be the most diligent in defending their turf, while

16. Norman J. Ornstein, Thomas E. Mann, and Michael J. Malbin, *Vital Statistics on Congress, 1989–1990* (Washington: Congressional Quarterly, 1990), p. 132.

17. The ideological and organizational barriers to the coordination of candidacies across several opposition parties allow the conjecture that opposition candidacies will be less efficiently distributed for maximizing votes than will those of the LDP, which has the easier task of coordinating nonideological factions. This probably gives the LDP greater leeway in tolerating factional competition than if it were contending with a single dominant opposition party.

those on the outside will vigorously press their claims in party councils for an opportunity to run a candidate. Because the LDP does not issue its endorsements until near the election, it is feasible for candidates to run as factionally sponsored independents. They start out knowing that the more impressive their early campaign, the better their chance of winning the party's blessing. The traditional modus operandi for resolving endorsement disputes involves factional negotiation. In recent years, competition for endorsement has become so fierce at times that automatic criteria have been adopted to allow party committees to escape having to make controversial decisions that would be difficult to enforce. The chief criterion appears to be seniority, a favorite of incumbents everywhere. But there are no guarantees that party councils will resolve conflicts. Candidates denied the party's endorsement sometimes run anyway as independents with the faction's support. They show up at the Diet, rejoin the party, and pledge their fealty to the sponsoring faction.

Another reason the party's leverage over its members is hollow is that it has no greater control over financing. The factions and candidates generally raise as much campaign money as the central party organization. Thus the two most valuable commodities the LDP has to offer a candidate—endorsements and funds—are awarded in ways that defer to the independence of politicians rather than induce or reward their conformity to some national program.

Not surprisingly, the Hobbesian world of Japanese elections yields some of the lowest victory margins and reelection rates for national legislators anywhere. In the 1986 elections, 20 percent of the LDP candidates who won did so by a margin of less than 10,000 votes, compared with about 7 percent of U.S. congressional candidates that year in comparably sized constituencies. In the 1983 elections, the incumbent reelection rate was 66 percent, and in 1990 it rose to 84 percent.[18] During these years, over 90 percent of the members of Congress were winning reelection.

The inherent complexities of Japan's electoral system require its politicians to cultivate the local constituency as if their careers depended upon it. In this regard, Japanese legislators surpass even their American counterparts, who are renowned for their dedication to district casework. Japan's Diet members are expected to represent constituents in tax

18. Kent E. Calder, *Crisis and Compensation: Public Policy and Political Stability* (Princeton University Press, 1988), pp. 66–70. The average total for a winning candidate for the Diet's House of Representatives was about 110,000 votes in 1983.

disputes with the government, assist them in securing pensions or loans for their small businesses, gain school admission for their children, and, after graduation, help them find employment. Beyond serving as an intermediary with the government, the Diet member is expected to be the community's most generous benefactor. The Diet member, or a senior aide, attends village festivals, weddings, and funerals. Beyond casework for individual constituents, the representative serves as the main agent in Tokyo for local governmental and private organizations.

Many of these duties resemble the district responsibilities of members of Congress. But because two or more incumbents are bidding for the same vote within the district, Japanese constituency service soars beyond the high standards of American politicians. Diet members sponsor social and recreational events—travel, golf tournaments, flower-arranging shows, and cooking schools. Those they do not originate, they are expected to underwrite with donations. These activities are organized under the auspices of their support groups (*koenkai*), huge social clubs with up to tens of thousands of members. Prime Minister Nakasone's *koenkai* was reputed to be capable of turning out 65,000 votes for him without campaigning.[19] By one estimate, about a third of all LDP voters belong to one of these organizations.[20]

All this requires an extensive network of offices and staff, and of course it costs a great deal of money. And, unlike members of Congress, Diet members are not entitled to government-paid staff. The need to maintain these *koenkai,* as a Diet member must, is the best explanation for the pervasive use of money for almost every transaction politicians make with organized constituencies and frequently even with one another in the Diet. That the careers of so many of Japan's prime ministers are marked by financial scandal reflects the effort required to rise in Japanese politics.[21]

Local support groups have their origins in the early postwar era, but for many years they were not the potent electoral weapons they are today. With a large campaign chest, a retired senior bureaucrat once could have reasonably expected to secure an LDP seat by buying into local political machines. The rise of these personal support organizations,

19. Thayer, *How the Conservatives Rule Japan,* pp. 92–98.

20. Gerald L. Curtis, *Election Campaigning, Japanese Style* (Columbia University Press, 1971), p. 136; and Calder, *Crisis and Compensation,* pp. 64–66.

21. More than one Diet member reported in interviews that one of the first decisions made in organizing a campaign was to agree on who among the campaign aides would be the "fall guy" if violations of campaign finance laws were uncovered.

however, has increased the ante so much that fewer senior bureaucrats, who might be expected to embrace a more national view of economic policy, are finding their way into the Diet. And increasingly those who do make the transfer are being lured away from a bureaucratic career by a headless *koenkai* searching for a new leader who has marketable prospects of bringing projects to the constituency.[22] Vacant seats increasingly go to politicians who have had extensive experience running these support organizations as local prefecture politicians or as staff of the incumbent Diet member.[23] Moreover, the labor and capital invested in creating a strong federation of *koenkai* have introduced a new level of political inheritance to Japanese politics. In the 1990 elections, 40 percent of the LDP candidates were supported by a political organization created by their fathers.[24]

The Party in the Legislature

The electoral and political circumstances that structure relations between representatives and their constituencies differ greatly between the United States and Japan, yet their effects are remarkably similar. The individual politician, and not the political party, assumes primary responsibility for satisfying the citizenry's demands and adapting the party's appeal to win constituents' support. Politics in both countries follows former House Speaker Tip O'Neill's favorite verity: "All politics is local."

Localism in politics translates into particularism in policies—policies that distribute benefits to specific constituencies. Facing elections as self-reliant entrepreneurs, politicians in both countries need to be able to claim credit for distributing goods and services to their districts. These benefits may flow from some larger, encompassing policy, perhaps even one truly directed toward some national purpose. Both countries' tax reforms had their inspirations in the requirements of the national

22. A typical instance of this practice occurred in the First Nagano District in 1983, when a *koenkai* forced the retirement of its aging Diet member and recruited a bureaucrat as its LDP standard-bearer. This and other examples were identified by Michio Muramatsu in personal communication.

23. Haruhiro Fukui, "The Liberal Democratic Party Revisited: Continuity and Change in the Party's Structure and Performance," *Journal of Japanese Studies,* vol. 10 (Summer 1984), pp. 393–95.

24. Karl Schoenberger, "Winds of Change Ruffling Japan's 'Windless' Election Campaign," *Los Angeles Times,* February 17, 1990, p. A12.

economy. Yet each contained dozens of provisions with specific benefits or considerations for particular constituencies.

The citizenry also wants its leaders to solve national problems, and the political parties are judged by their performance in this realm. Public opinion polls in both countries report great dissatisfaction with public policy generally and with the manner in which special interests frequently appear to prevail over the national welfare. To the extent the public holds its leaders accountable, its politicians are restrained from sacrificing economic policy at the trough of the pork barrel. Without the necessity of pursuing these collective goals, economic policy would become little more than the aggregation of many local interests.

Observers of Japanese politics, especially foreigners, are sometimes inclined to find more ideology and coherence in that country's policies than the case studies in the preceding essays suggest. The conservative thrust of Japan's economic policies has been characterized by such phrases as "parent-hearted [paternalistic] politics" and "corporatism without labor."[25] While these portrayals accurately characterize the policy bias of a nation where the conservative party has ruled for a generation, their implication that ideology is the motivational force of Japanese politics is misguided. The actions and policies of Japan's politicians who constitute the Liberal Democratic party, like those of their American counterparts, can be strictly accounted for by their desire to win elections, which in turn requires them to adapt to the disparate policy preferences of their constituencies. Nathaniel Thayer cautiously offers this oblique definition of the ideological disposition of the LDP: "The conservatives are not Marxists, but their ranks include just about every other shade in the political spectrum."[26] The powerful pull of localism, set against the need to provide collective goods, has yielded a class of highly pragmatic politicians in both countries.

Earlier I described party leadership as a function of the needs of its members. Politicians seeking a steady flow of distributive benefits and pragmatic approaches to national issues clearly require political parties to achieve their goals, but not the muscular kind that formulate national policy and proceed to implement it. In strong party systems, such as Great

25. Jun-ichi Kyoguku, *Nihonjin to Seiji* (The Japanese and politics) (Tokyo: Tokyo Daigaku Shuppan Kai, 1986); and T. J. Pempel and Keiichi Tsunekawa, "Corporatism without Labor? The Japanese Anomaly," in Philippe C. Schmitter and Gerhard Lehmbruch, eds., *Trends toward Corporatist Intermediation* (Sage, 1979), pp. 231–70.
26. *How the Conservatives Rule Japan*, p. xiii.

Britain's, the annual party conference is attended by representatives of core constituencies who have a large voice in the formulation of party policy. In addition to selecting leaders, these conferences create party platforms and oblige party members in government to support them. The electoral fortunes of individual members of Parliament are closely bound to the electorate's assessment of the party's success in fulfilling its national policy commitments.[27]

Because electoral fortunes in Japan and the United States are more closely associated with the representation of local interests, their politicians have fashioned their parties to perform more as service organizations. They collect individual members' preferences and package them into policy. This responsiveness is best achieved by keeping control of the legislative party machinery within the legislature. Accordingly, national party conferences in both countries do little beyond nominating the party's candidate to head the government. The two major parties in America meet every four years in the summer before the presidential election to select a nominee. They also engage in an exercise of crafting a policy platform on which no candidate need stand.[28] Members of Congress do not control these conventions; in fact, in recent years most have not even attended. Since no one else controls them either, and they do little of consequence except ratify the results of the state-level presidential nominating caucuses and primaries, the national conventions do not intrude into the affairs of the party's legislative leaders.

Japan's Liberal Democratic party meets annually. Every second year it elects the party's senior officials, including the president, who becomes the prime minister. From all reports, there is no pretense of transacting real business at the off-year convention. Unlike American presidential conventions, these meetings are run by the party and factional leaders of the legislature. In this candidate-centered parliamentary system without federalism, it is understandable that "Diet members . . . dominate the party organization and policymaking."[29] Neither country's

27. The circumscribed capacity of the individual member of Parliament to serve the district with casework and locally targeted policies is described in Bruce E. Cain, John Ferejohn, and Morris Fiorina, *The Personal Vote: Constituency Service and Electoral Independence* (Harvard University Press, 1987).

28. The Democratic party flirted briefly during the 1970s with midterm conventions, but all that they did was deliberate national policy, which proved such a source of mischief for those politicians who had to represent the party before local constituencies that they were shortly abandoned.

29. Fukui, "The Liberal Democratic Party Revisited," p. 432.

legislative parties are controlled by politicians who take a national view of public policy and seek to exact ideological conformity from party members.

Just as the overall decentralization of the political parties within the districts and prefectures gives candidates full discretion to stake out locally attractive issue positions, so too the internal decentralization of the legislative party gives its individual members the flexibility to concentrate their attention on policies and legislative posts that best serve their constituencies. Within Congress, legislative assignments flow from the party caucus. Here leaders are elected, the appointments they make to committees and party offices ratified, and occasionally, positions on issues voted upon. The main resources available to party leaders to promote the party's program and to encourage loyalty are control over the institution's procedures and the filling of vacancies on the all-important standing committees.

The distribution of legislative offices shows both the limitation of party leadership in a decentralized setting and the subtlety of its employment. The House of Representatives and the Senate contain dozens of powerful offices among the standing and party committees and within the leadership organization. One of the principal benefits of party membership and loyalty is the opportunity to gain control over one of these policy levers. Party leaders play the role of broker—making initial appointments to these posts, enforcing institutional norms among members who have been delegated important party responsibilities for policy, and preparing the way for the recommendations of these committees to receive final consideration by the full legislature.

In a historic revolt against the Speaker of the House of Representatives in 1910, the members stripped away party leaders' authority to select committee chairmen and to reassign members to different committees. In place of leadership discretion, they installed an automatic rule of seniority, which remains the standard method of selecting chairs today. Once on a committee, a member cannot be removed without some serious violation of caucus or chamber rules, and, with few exceptions, the majority party member with the longest continuous service on a committee serves as its chair.[30]

30. Since the 1970s, various institutional reforms have weakened the seniority rule. In 1971 House Democrats instituted secret ballot elections for committee chairmen. In 1975 House Democrats (a large proportion of whom were newly elected in the wake of Watergate) took advantage of the rule change and ousted three senior committee

Unable to reconstitute committees, party leaders rely heavily on their one unrestricted prerogative: the authority to fill vacancies. This provides a circuitous means for correcting committee proposals that diverge from the median preference of the party membership.[31] If a committee begins to appear too liberal, a conservative member might be appointed to fill the next vacancy. This is not the kind of leadership empowered to issue authoritative pronouncements of party policy.[32] Although it does not give the leadership sanctions against uncooperative members, this indirect method of enforcing party policy through committee appointments is nonetheless vital for allowing the party to strike a balance between giving members the latitude to be good local representatives while keeping the party directed toward producing electorally attractive national policies.

Many of the same features of a decentralized legislative party can be found within the Diet. In order to avoid damaging conflict and the opposition's obstructionist tactics (such as the famous dilatory "cow walks" on floor votes), the LDP surrendered much of its control over committee and floor proceedings in the lower house during the early 1970s, when it controlled a bare majority. The rules allocating committee seats require the LDP to relinquish control over some committees during periods when it holds a narrow majority within the chamber.

The LDP's limited control of Diet committees helps explain the emergence of a parallel party organization called the Policy Affairs Research Council (PARC) as the major legislative apparatus for allowing party members to influence policies important to their constituencies. Twenty years ago, few bureaucrats mentioned clearance with this organization as an important activity for ministry success; today, few ministers would dare broach a major initiative without having it fully vetted before this organization.[33] Commensurate with PARC's growing

chairmen. Although violations of the seniority rule have been infrequent since then, the revision reduced the autonomy of chairs and made them more responsive to the party.

31. Gary W. Cox and Mathew D. McCubbins, *Parties and Government in the House of Representatives* (University of California Press, forthcoming).

32. If these leaders take public positions at all, they are more likely to be in the form of a "trial balloon" they can easily disown if the proposal meets with disfavor.

33. This view that the PARC system has emerged as the functional equivalent of the American committee system is also argued by John Creighton Campbell, who writes, "The relationship between a ministry and its corresponding PARC division is not dissimilar to that between an American executive department or bureau and a Congressional legislative committee." *Contemporary Japanese Budget Politics*, p. 125. However, the institution's and party's division of labor are not the same. The Diet's

control over policy, the status of the PARC chairman has risen to perhaps second only to that of the prime minister. And seats on PARC's leadership committee, the Policy Deliberation Commission, have emerged as some of the most sought-after plums in factional negotiations.

The base of PARC is seventeen standing divisions (*bukai*), their jurisdictions coinciding with those of individual government ministries. These divisions amount to de facto committees of the Diet. One indicator of this is that the Liberal Democrats on a particular standing committee automatically serve on its counterpart division. Membership also includes LDP Diet members whose prefectures give them a special interest in a division's business and others whose past service in the cabinet or in some other party capacity makes them especially suited to monitor a ministry's affairs. Ministry officials do all they can to cultivate the goodwill of their division, for it contains the Diet members who must be accommodated.

This important organization will also be discussed below in examining legislative-bureaucratic relations. The important point here is that, in the Diet as in Congress, the governing party has created offices to give its members selective control over the policies most important for their reelection. Moreover, the proliferation of offices creates an important resource for leaders to cultivate cooperation.

There is little evidence, however, that the LDP's leaders have been any more successful than their congressional counterparts in exploiting their control over offices to enforce party discipline against the pull of local interests. The limitation of central party authority that has been achieved within Congress by formally curtailing leaders' prerogatives to select committee chairmen and reassign members is achieved within the LDP by the competition among factions. Factional leaders negotiate appointments to committees, PARC's divisions, the cabinet, and other leadership positions. Typically, ministerial posts are awarded in approximate proportion to the faction's size.[34] Offices that confer upon their occupants an opportunity to advance their faction's interests, such as the party presidency and cabinet ministries, are subject to frequent

committees are arenas where politicians from all parties interrogate government representatives about new programs for their districts, lodge constituency complaints with bureaucrats summoned before them, and joust with one another as they create a record for the next election.

34. Michael Leiserson, "Factions and Coalitions in One-Party Japan: An Interpretation Based on the Theory of Games," *American Political Science Review*, vol. 62 (September 1968), pp. 770–87.

rotation to prevent any one faction from long having the upper hand. The average tenure of a cabinet minister is about one year. Of the nine prime ministers since Eisaku Sato's departure in 1972, only Nakasone managed to stay in office for more than a single two-year term.

Because the welfare of each faction member is dependent upon the resourcefulness of the leader in negotiations and in raising campaign financing, factional leadership is personal and merit-based. And because this leadership position is a valued stepping-stone to the party presidency, succession conflicts are commonplace. Occasionally they cannot be resolved and a faction will split apart, a subset of its members forming a new one or individually melding into one of the other factions. In these informal groups, there must be a premium on loyalty, or the leader could be easily undercut by other factions' secret side payments to his faction's members.[35]

The discipline and conformity factions instill are not wasted on making policy, for the faction is a primitive genus of political organization. Its function is the strict exchange of tangible benefits: the leaders supply the followers with financing and party offices, and followers supply leaders with a base for their political advancement. Devoid of ideology, the closest these organizations come to making policy is their efforts to "colonize" a ministry in order to gain a favorable flow of programs to their members.

Given the tendencies of American and Japanese politicians to concentrate on particularistic rather than national policy, how do members of these countries' legislatures ever bring themselves to enact national economic policies, especially when they impose costs on local constituencies? The tax reform cases do offer two instances of economic policy emerging as something more than the aggregation of special interests. Where are the selective incentives and institutional mechanisms for prompting these politicians to resolve these and other national economic issues?

Part of the answer, I have argued, lies in the prerogatives and responsibilities party members vest in their legislative leaders to arrive at and enforce collective decisions. When national policy imposes costs on a member's local constituency, leaders can offer the potential defector special consideration on future legislation or a coveted legislative assignment when a vacancy arises. They can also shield vulnerable

35. There are a number of instances in which a party presidency was won when a wealthier faction purchased a sufficient number of "secret ballots" from members of an adversary faction. See Thayer, *How the Conservatives Rule Japan*, pp. 163–64.

members from unpopular actions through specific procedural mechanisms such as closed votes, agenda control, and minimal majority votes to enact policy.[36] But, all said, the pull of localism limits the scope of legislative leadership, and frequently the resources available to these leaders will be insufficient to pass national policy.

The governing party extends into the executive, which is where politicians largely delegate responsibility for addressing national policies. In parliaments, such consignment is straightforward, since this, after all, is where the party leaders reside. The role of the American president in formulating his party's national policy is more complicated and less certain. The Constitution's Framers, bent on frustrating party action, created an office that is elected directly and separately from the legislature and endowed it with independent authority. Unlike parliamentary executives, presidents are not the creatures of their legislative party. But the office's insulation from parochial pressures and its national duties give these politicians impressive credentials for assuming responsibility for defining and achieving the party's national policy goals. In return, they require, and can claim, a measure of loyalty. With such reciprocity, presidential systems occasionally accomplish the levels of party action taken for granted in parliamentary governments.

Over the postwar era, many students of comparative politics have discerned a shift of power in industrial democracies from legislatures to executives. Nonpolitical reasons are commonly cited for this phenomenon: the emergence of the welfare state, the demands of a more interdependent international order, and the growing importance of specialized information.[37] While these may all be true, they do not diminish the political reason for reliance on executives: they provide the wherewithal for elevating national priorities over parochial interests.

The Rationale for Executive Leadership

The postwar rise of executive leadership has been a prominent theme in the literature of both Japanese and American politics. Japan's dramatic

36. A recent illustration of the role of political parties in providing a collective mechanism for its members can be found in the LDP rule that its Diet members could not report their vote on the controversial tax bill in 1989. By exempting them from the potential grief of confessing their vote before hostile constituents, this rule made it easier for members to support the legislation. This example was brought to my attention by Gregory Noble in personal communication.

37. Michel Crozier, Samuel P. Huntington, and Joji Watanuki, *The Crisis of Democracy: Report on the Governability of Democracies to the Trilateral Commission* (New York University Press, 1975).

352   SAMUEL KERNELL

economic growth since the war has been widely cited as an instance of political evolution toward executive policymaking. The nation has realized its full potential by virtue of the extraordinary talents and statecraft of an elite cadre of civil servants who staff MITI and the MOF. "Their primary concern was the advancement of the wealth and power of Japan as a nation rather than the promotion of an environment in which particular interests would flourish," writes Clyde V. Prestowitz. "The ministries could take this approach," he explains, "because they were run by autocrats whose writ was law."[38] This is the dominant view of Japanese economic policymaking. I shall return for a closer look below. The office of the prime minister also has its admirers who, although less fulsome in their praise, find its occupant occasionally entertaining a national vision of economic policy.[39]

In the United States, the executive is largely synonymous with the presidency. Since President Theodore Roosevelt described the office as "the bully pulpit," the president has emerged as the nation's chief problem solver. The American bureaucracy, by comparison, occupies a less exalted position. The word *bureaucrat* is mostly synonymous with a career civil servant, someone less involved in making policy than in implementing it under the close supervision of the president, Congress, the courts, and even the interested public.

Despite the common claim in both countries of executive ascendance, one must regard this assertion circumspectly, whether addressing the national political executive or the bureaucracy. The sheer size and activity of modern executive institutions give the appearance of control, but whether reality fully matches it is another matter. As one student of the American presidency has observed, "In form all Presidents are leaders nowadays. In fact this guarantees no more than that they will be clerks."[40] The same assertion can be made, although it rarely is, about the role of Japan's bureaucracy.

The rationale for a prominent bureaucracy in Japan and a strong political executive in the United States can be found in these countries' constitutions. In the parliamentary formula, the prime minister and the cabinet are agents of the legislature, and in practice they are recruited

38. Clyde V. Prestowitz, Jr., *Trading Places: How We Are Giving Our Future to Japan and How to Reclaim It* (Basic Books, 1989), pp. 227–28.
39. An example of this genre is Michio Muramatsu, "In Search of National Identity: The Politics and Policies of the Nakasone Administration," *Journal of Japanese Studies,* vol. 13 (Summer 1987), pp. 307–42.
40. Richard E. Neustadt, *Presidential Power and the Modern Presidents: The Politics of Leadership from Roosevelt to Reagan* (Free Press, 1990), p. 7.

from the legislature. These actors are delegated the responsibility for developing policy proposals that are in accord with the median preferences of those who selected them—the majority party or coalition within the legislature. The governing party is able to use its consolidated power to harness the bureaucracy's expertise to formulate and implement its policy preferences. The prime minister and cabinet's failure to follow the preferences of the legislative majority will cause the "government's" defeat, which might result in national elections or its immediate replacement by a new government team.[41] Aside from his prerogative to dissolve the legislature and call elections, the prime minister does not enjoy independent constitutional authority. Because the legislature is controlled by the majority party, this provision generally constitutes no special asset for his leadership. It is used in consultation with other leaders to schedule elections at the most propitious moment for the party.[42]

In presidential systems, the separation of powers between legislature and executive can be decisive in determining which party's policy preferences will prevail. Although the legislature retains the ultimate authority to enact public law, the American president is guaranteed a substantial independent role. This includes the power to appoint federal officers (with Senate confirmation), a large measure of control over the military and the nation's foreign affairs, and a veto over legislation passed by Congress. The last is especially important. By requiring two-thirds majorities in both chambers of Congress to override a presidential veto, the Constitution preserves a strong legislative role for the president in policymaking.

Perhaps more important than the separation of powers in reducing the prospect of unified government in presidential systems is the way elections are scheduled and constituencies stacked. Representation in

41. Many parliamentary systems are bicameral, as is the Diet with its House of Councillors and House of Representatives. The upper chamber does not participate in the selection of the government, and typically its authority is limited to oversight and the employment of dilatory tactics to oppose legislation a majority of its members find objectionable. The absence of a firm majority in the upper chamber is a distinct possibility, since election to that body follows a different electoral calendar.

42. Only if the legislature were composed of minor parties unable to form a majority coalition, thereby necessitating a "minority government," might this become an instrument of executive power. Such a situation did, in fact, arise in Japan during the 1920s. It was an era of numerous weak political parties and minority governments. A favorite ploy of prime ministers was to threaten to dissolve the legislature and call for elections if it did not accede to their legislative proposals. Prime ministers frequently delivered on their threats, and election-weary legislatures slowly began to acquiesce.

the House of Representatives divides the nation into 435 separate constituencies and in the Senate into 50; and the presidency keeps it whole. And with respect to the electoral calendar, the entire House faces the voters every two years, one-third of the Senate is elected every two years, and the presidency is on a four-year cycle. One implication of these differences, which perhaps most distinguish presidential from parliamentary systems, is that different parties may control the executive and legislative branches. Indeed, in recent years divided party control has become the norm. By the 1992 elections, Republicans will have controlled the presidency and Democrats one or both chambers of Congress for twenty-six of the preceding thirty-eight years.[43]

Beyond divided party control, these constitutional prescriptions introduce another source of tension into institutional relations. Elected nationally, presidents are liberated from the narrow confines of local constituencies and instead rewarded for addressing public policy from a national perspective. Moreover, the electoral college gives voters in populous urban states a disproportionate influence in electing the president, while the Senate is inherently malapportioned in favor of voters from small rural states.[44] Some observers have described American politics as governed by a four-party system: Democrats and Republicans, subdivided into presidential and congressional wings. As one important result of this institutional competition for power, these actors are sometimes more concerned with insulating the bureaucracy from the influence of the other branch than with empowering it to achieve policy goals.

Presidents and Prime Ministers

Unlike legislators in these two countries, who are similar in their ties to local and organized constituencies, Japan's prime minister and the U.S. president have very different policy orientations. The former remains rooted in the obligations of particularism and derives his power

43. See Gary W. Cox and Samuel Kernell, eds., *The Causes and Consequences of Divided Government in the United States* (Westview Press, 1991).

44. Votes in the electoral college are apportioned to each state according to its number of senators and representatives, while each state receives two seats in the Senate, regardless of population. To put these structural biases in perspective, a senator from California represents over 25 million constituents while a senator from neighboring Nevada represents fewer than 1 million constituents. In presidential elections, the bias toward populous states is reflected in the fact that California has 8.74 percent of the votes in the electoral college while Nevada has only 0.74 percent (1984 census figures).

from success in this endeavor. The latter, conversely, is sufficiently liberated from his party to rest his political fortunes on national problem solving. Yet these same constitutional features weaken his ties to other politicians, particularly those in the legislature, whose cooperation he needs. The results typically are Japanese prime ministers short on vision and American presidents short on power. Leaders are the products of the systems that select them. These differences are most apparent in the ways prime ministers and presidents are recruited and in the resources they have for national leadership once they are in office.

RECRUITMENT. In the United States, reforms over the past two decades in the selection of delegates to presidential nominating conventions and in federal campaign financing have severed selection of the president from control by the political parties. Candidates for the nomination must create their own campaign organizations to compete in numerous state primaries and caucuses. After satisfying modest fundraising requirements, the candidates qualify for federal matching funds. The organizational and financial resources that party and constituent organizations once supplied candidates have been replaced by organizations of personal loyalists, television campaigns, and federal financing.

These and related reforms have inspired nationally unknown candidates to enter and stay in the race. Others who once could lay claim to the party's nomination—by virtue of their service to the party or proven leadership in Washington—now find their assets of far less value under the reformed selection system.

Consider the plight of congressional leaders who aspire to the presidency. While their counterparts in parliamentary systems provide the near-exclusive pool from which prime ministers are drawn, they find the road to the White House a bumpy one. A presidential bid takes enormous amounts of time for travel and public speaking in primary and caucus states, time away from the performance of one's duties in the legislature. In winning election as House majority leader in 1989, Richard Gephardt had to pledge to his Democratic colleagues that he would not seek the 1992 presidential nomination. Another problem is that running Congress requires the continuous, diligent brokerage of party members' disparate preferences. The leader's job to discover the policy mix that will produce majority support involves endless efforts at compromise, logrolling, playing down contentious provisions of legislation, and the many other methods of mediation that sometimes yield public laws. The problem from the vantage of those with presidential aspirations, of course, is that success in this endeavor best proceeds quietly, away from public view. It also discourages the development of a strong record on national policy issues.

This was Lyndon Johnson's dilemma as Senate majority leader during the 1950s. Arguably the most powerful Senate leader of the twentieth century, his policy leadership was nonetheless tightly confined by a powerful bloc of southern Democrats. He could ill afford to take prominent positions on many national and popular Democratic issues for fear of alienating these senators, who were prepared to bring the chamber's business to a standstill, if necessary, to prevent passage of legislation they opposed. Johnson had to stand aside, until it was too late, and watch his colleagues—John Kennedy, Stuart Symington, and Hubert Humphrey, among others—compete for the 1960 presidential nomination. In the end, Johnson became president probably the only way he could, by being selected as a ticket-balancing running mate of a nationally attractive colleague who was not viewed as a product of the Senate.

Given the way presidents are recruited in America, the politicians who are most likely to win the nomination will have staked out clear positions on national issues. But their views may not be rooted in the ideology or commitments of their political party. Therefore party resources may not be available to help them realize their policy goals. I have stressed the separation of presidential recruitment from legislative leadership in the United States because it stands in stark contrast with the recruitment of the Japanese prime minister, who succeeds to the office by virtue of his talents in playing the legislative game. As a consequence, the Japanese executive's power depends almost exclusively on party support.

A Japanese politician's successful bid to become party president, and thus prime minister, depends on the candidate's ability to satisfy his supporters' voracious appetites for distributive policy and financing. Because many of the resources flow to members through their factions, the penultimate office to that of prime minister is the factional leader, or his designee. Factional leaders succeed to the degree they can furnish local resources and their faction prospers. Over the years, politicians skilled in the arts of "colonizing" ministries will secure a formidable claim to the party presidency and with it the office of prime minister. The entire logic of the faction leader's entrepreneurship is based upon this ultimate payoff.

Unquestionably, the most talented and powerful politician of his generation was Kakuei Tanaka, a man who fully matched Lyndon Johnson's legislative prowess. By assembling the largest faction since the formation of the Liberal Democratic party, Tanaka had amassed enormous personal influence within the party by the time illness forced his retirement from public life in the early 1980s. Like Lyndon Johnson, he came to the capital representing a poor prefecture desperately in need of public works. Also similar to LBJ, he advanced swiftly in the legislature by skillfully nursing district projects through the bureaucracy and assiduously raising campaign funds for his LDP colleagues. With his comparatively youthful promotion to faction head, Tanaka's formidable talents were formally recognized by his Diet colleagues.

Unlike Johnson, however, Tanaka found his legislative work led directly to his elevation to the prime minister's office in 1972. Such is the beauty of a parliamentary system, where leadership in one arena is rewarded with advancement to the other. Even after his formal resignation in 1976 from the party in the wake of the Lockheed bribe scandal, which occurred during his tenure as prime minster, Tanaka remained the leader of the largest and still-growing LDP faction. In the 1980s, no aspiring party politician, whatever his factional affiliation, could expect to advance to prime minister without Tanaka's endorsement.[45]

While American politicians have to decide fairly early whether to advance their careers by working diligently within their current institutions or by using their office as a base for seeking higher office, the continuity of upward mobility presents no similar point of decision for Japanese politicians. One need not be an American-styled political entrepreneur who engages in self-promotion by cultivating broader constituencies with promises to solve national problems.

Clearly, the party membership has a stake in cultivating leaders who have a more expansive view of public policy, if for no other reason than to solve its own collective action problems. Yet with factional leadership providing the chief stepping-stone, there is little in the recruitment of prime ministers that grooms politicians for national

45. Kent E. Calder, "Kanyro vs. Shomin: Contrasting Dynamics of Conservative Leadership in Postwar Japan," in Terry Edward MacDougall, ed., *Political Leadership in Contemporary Japan* (University of Michigan, Center for Japanese Studies, 1982), pp. 1–28; and Chalmers Johnson, "Tanaka Kakuei, Structural Corruption, and the Advent of Machine Politics in Japan," *Journal of Japanese Studies*, vol. 12 (Winter 1986), pp. 1–28.

358 SAMUEL KERNELL

policy leadership. Advancement does proceed slowly, while aspirants to leadership invariably hold important policy posts within the Diet and on the Policy Affairs Research Council. Moreover, most preside, albeit briefly, over MITI or the MOF, as well as various clientele ministries. So a prime minister will enter office generally familiar with the preferences of his colleagues and the policies and organization of the ministries. As helpful as this service may be in dealing with a headstrong bureaucracy, it does not in itself inspire the prime minister to adopt a national perspective.

Once a leader is in office, the demands of his faction intensify, not relax. During his brief, typically two-year, stint in office, the prime minister must energetically advance his faction's interest by making cabinet appointments, promoting bureaucrats associated with the faction (in the vernacular, "laying pipes"), securing his faction's financial base with outside groups, and gaining the party's endorsements for his followers in attractive prefectures. It is the exceptional politician who can achieve these immediate goals and still retain a perspective that allows him to address national issues. Former Prime Minister Zenko Suzuki represented the view ingrained in the recruitment system when he described the prime minister's work as "the response to problems as they arise and the slow and deliberate adjustment of interest relationships." For the prime minister to exercise policy leadership is "the height of arrogance."[46]

Thus American presidents, by virtue of their recruitment, are strong on national vision but possess few political assets beyond those granted by the Constitution. Japanese prime ministers, conversely, retain the political associations necessary for influence but remain bound to the parochial interests of core constituencies.

NATIONAL LEADERSHIP. During the nineteenth century American presidents spent far more time making patronage appointments than formulating public policy. They simply were not expected to lead the nation, except perhaps during foreign crises. During the early twentieth century, as issues began to move up the federal ladder to Washington with increasing frequency, the American people started turning to presidents for solutions. Some incumbents did not measure up to the challenge, but others saw in these rising demands new opportunities

46. Interview in *Asahi Shimbun*, cited in Muramatsu, "In Search of National Identity," p. 311.

for leadership. The Progressive presidents, Theodore Roosevelt and Woodrow Wilson, paved the way for the emergence of the fully conceived activist presidency under Franklin Roosevelt. The problem these men, and all who have followed, encountered is that the Constitution dealt them a weak hand with which to meet such expectations for their performance.

For one, the resources of a party system, rooted in localism, are not sufficient to bridge the gulf between the president's national mandate and Congress's constituency-oriented mandate. The different policy planes on which presidents and members of Congress labor occasionally lead to impasse, but typically do not prevent agreement. Most national policies have distributional consequences. What is good for the nation generally will be good for many congressional districts. The Pentagon gets its new strategic weapons system; the various congressional districts receive contracts and installations.[47] And when disagreements arise, a policy solution is arrived at through compromise. The variety of forms mutual adjustment may take is well represented in the American political lexicon: logrolling, horse trading, splitting the difference, back scratching. Hardly a political relation exists in Washington that is not based on reciprocity, hardly a policy enacted that has not accumulated a history rich in exchange and compromise.

At the center of this pluralist bazaar is the president, who more than any other politician is "the human embodiment of a bargaining society."[48] Normally, national economic policy originates with a presidential initiative. As the proposal wends its way through Congress, the bureaucracy, and perhaps even the federal judiciary, and is amended each step of the way, it may continue to carry a presidential association. Whether the policy remains the president's in more than name only depends on his skills as a bargainer.

Because U.S. economic policy reflects the fragmented political process more than the preferences of any particular actor or party team, comprehensive, future-oriented policy gives way to incremental, present-oriented adjustments to the status quo. This is, of course,

47. Political, probably more than military, prudence has inspired the navy to locate its aircraft carrier bases in as many congressional districts as possible. As a result, no facility services more than one ship. Hedrick Smith, *The Power Game: How Washington Works* (Random House, 1988).

48. Robert A. Dahl and Charles E. Lindblom, *Politics, Economics, and Welfare: Planning and Politico-Economic Systems Resolved into Basic Social Processes* (Harper, 1953), p. 333.

precisely the criticism of those who decry America's inability to formulate a comprehensive industrial policy.[49]

Students of the modern presidency have discerned an increasing
tendency for presidents to rely less exclusively upon bargaining for their
policy leadership and more on unilateral methods. A full examination of
these trends lies beyond the scope of this essay. The causes are to be
found in the increasing incidence of divided party control, which makes
bargaining more costly; in the erosion of the power of the leaders with
whom presidents have traditionally transacted business, which makes
bargaining less efficient; and in the opportunity presidents now have to
build national constituencies through television.[50] Instead, presidents
rely increasingly upon centralized administration and the cultivation of
public opinion for their leadership in Washington.

"The President needs help," warned Louis Brownlow in the opening
paragraph of his 1937 report on strengthening the presidency. The
reforms this proposal set in motion have created a presidential bureaucracy with its layers of organization, standard operating procedures, and
professional personnel. The Executive Office of the President houses a
dozen or so presidential agencies. The first to be installed in this new
institutional niche, and still the most important, was the Bureau of the
Budget (renamed the Office of Management and Budget in 1970). This
modern agency houses some 600 professionals and more than a dozen
presidential appointees whose mission is to monitor and revise the
budgetary and programmatic requests of the line departments and to
oversee their implementation of policy. Other Executive Office agencies
include the National Security Council, the Council of Economic Advisers, and the Office of the U.S. Trade Representative. The president's
personal staff in the White House similarly grew at an average annual
rate of about 5 percent until the Watergate era. What began as a personal
entourage of several dozen assistants and clerks detailed from other
agencies is today a small bureaucracy of more than 500 budgeted staff.[51]

49. Some see in the absence of central planning the genius of the American political
system. The argument is analogous to that in behalf of the "hidden hand" in the
economic marketplace. The most forceful statement of this view is David Braybrooke
and Charles E. Lindblom, *A Strategy of Decision: Policy Evaluation as a Social Process*
(Free Press, 1963).

50. See Samuel Kernell, *Going Public: New Strategies of Presidential Leadership*
(Washington: CQ Press, 1986).

51. Terry M. Moe, "The Politicized Presidency," in John E. Chubb and Paul E.
Peterson, eds., *The New Direction in American Politics* (Brookings, 1985), pp. 235–71;
and Samuel Kernell, "The Evolution of the White House Staff," in John E. Chubb

Because the centralization of administration is one of the prominent postwar trends in presidential leadership, much of the staff work within the White House is directed to overseeing appointments and performance of political executives and the implementation of programs throughout the executive branch. Because direct communication to the nation is also an important aspect of modern leadership, about a third of the staff is routinely involved in feeding information to the press, analyzing public opinion polls, preparing presidential travel, and writing speeches. Whether these strategies and institutional resources are adequate for the president in satisfying the demands for his leadership remains questionable. All that is apparent is that presidents have sought greater independence in the formulation of national policy.

As discussed above, little in the recruitment of Japan's prime minister inspires its occupants to champion national policy over distributive, selective benefits. Nor do the institutional assets of the prime minister's office provide its incumbents with much opportunity to break the mold. Occasionally, however, unusual circumstances present a politician who tests the capacity of the office for a different kind of leadership. Such an instance can be found in the election of Yasuhiro Nakasone as prime minister in 1982. During his nearly six-year tenure, he sought to break out of the confines of his office and govern, in his words, as a "presidential-styled prime minister." He even advocated reforming Japan's constitution to allow direct popular election of the prime minister.

Why he alone among Japan's prime ministers chose this approach must stem in part from his personal makeup. By local standards, Nakasone had always been regarded as something of a gadfly. There is also a compelling strategic rationale in the way he was initially elected. According to one veteran observer, few would have guessed early in his career that he would ever become prime minister. Representing a small faction, Nakasone reached office as a dark-horse candidate after the front-runners refused to yield to their principal adversary. According to one informant, Nakasone realized his good fortune was unlikely to be repeated, and the only way he could survive the next party presidency election two years later was to be so popular in the country that the party leaders could not deny him renomination.[52] Nakasone followed a course

and Paul E. Peterson, eds., *Can the Government Govern?* (Brookings, 1989), pp. 185–237.

52. According to a senior member in the Prime Minister's Office, "Nakasone knew he did not have strong support from the LDP, and he had to appeal to the people directly." Interview with Hiroshi Fukuda, November 12, 1988, Tokyo.

of political communication and centralized administration that resembles in quality, if not quantity, the favored practices of recent American presidents. In doing so, he offers a comparison case for discerning the structural differences in the prime ministry and the presidency.

Rhetoric was an important part of his leadership strategy, as was the favorable media coverage generated by attending heads-of-state summits. Although the volume of his public activities has not been measured precisely, observers agree that Nakasone increased his personal visibility with the Japanese public well above that of anyone else who has occupied the office. Under Nakasone, the prime minister's Public Relations Office, which had traditionally functioned more as a nonpartisan information agency, found itself drawn into the prime minister's leadership strategy. When asked how her work differed under Nakasone, the head of this agency responded, "Nakasone was very interested in the twenty or so surveys we conducted each year; about half originated from his requests. He had one of his assistants work with us closely. . . . The ministries paid a lot more attention to us when he was around. Things were more fun.''[53]

Nakasone's unprecedented efforts at political communications were more than matched by his dedication in gaining administrative control over the ministries. Again, there is a strategic rationale for his actions, rooted in his precarious political circumstance. Fulfilling national policy commitments, such as tax reform and upgrading Japan's role in international affairs, was an important component of his strategy, and it required the cooperation of the ministries. There was a practical political payoff as well: the stronger his control over ministry appointments and programs, the more successful his faction would be in attracting new members.[54]

In 1981 Nakasone, then director of the Administrative Management Agency, had commissioned the Second Ad Hoc Administrative Reform Council to offer suggestions to streamline government and make it more responsive to national needs. In an effort to prevent the bureaucracy's vested interests from corrupting the council's recommendations, Nakasone enlisted the participation of scholars and outside policy experts. They interpreted their mandate broadly, and from their recommendations came an agenda of future LDP economic policies, including

53. Interview with Mariko Bando, November 16, 1988, Tokyo.
54. By this narrow measure, he succeeded. Nakasone's faction grew from forty-six to sixty-seven Diet members between 1975 and 1985. Hans H. Baerwald, *Party Politics in Japan* (Allen and Unwin, 1986), p. 27.

privatization of the railways and the tax reform described in this volume by Muramatsu and Mabuchi.

Close observers generally credit Nakasone with some success in his efforts to strengthen the prime minister's administrative control over the ministries. He created a Prime Minister's Agency and charged it with overseeing policy disputes between ministries. As a former private secretary explained, "In the past when two ministers disagreed, nothing happened. Mr. Nakasone wanted those stalemates to come to him for final resolution."[55] Seeking to break the parochial bonds of party and bureaucracy, Nakasone sought leadership in the same manner as modern American presidents—through direct appeals to the public and centralized administration.

Parliamentary systems, with their cabinet governments, are noted for their collegialism. The prime minister presides over cabinet sessions of the ruling party or coalition, primus inter pares. But in Japan it is hardly collegialism founded on common party purpose. Rather, the factional competition for seats in the Diet and services to the prefectures extends all the way to the top. In the present political setting, the party places little value in a strong prime minister who addresses national problems. Such an incumbent's success poses a political threat to the other factional leaders. In 1986, when Nakasone proposed calling elections for the upper and lower houses of the Diet on the same day because it improved the LDP's prospects of success, his proposal was vehemently opposed by the other factional leaders waiting their turn. They feared a run-up of the LDP vote would assure Nakasone's reelection as party president.[56]

With Noboru Takeshita's succession to office in November 1987, the prime minister's leadership style returned predictably to diplomacy among factions and ministries. Some of Nakasone's management innovations remained in place, however, and increasing trade tensions with the United States required greater personal leadership by the prime minister in formulating economic policy. Nonetheless, the job remains rooted in a domestic milieu of factions and localism. This can be seen in the rapid cycling of leaders in and out of the office and the hollow platforms on which they are elevated. The fundamental paradox of the office,

55. Another innovation was the External Affairs Office, similarly created to "be sure that ministry disagreements were adjudicated and did not become a political liability." Initially, the Foreign Affairs Ministry opposed its formation but relented when Nakasone agreed to appoint as its head someone from that ministry. Interview with Kimio Fujita, November 14, 1988, Tokyo.

56. Baerwald, *Party Politics in Japan*, pp. 174–75.

described in the pre-Nakasone era, remains relevant today: "When you have prevailed in the struggles for power and won the ultimate position of the premiership, you find yourself in a position to be overtaken rather than to overtake others."[57]

The Bureaucracy

In the United States, political control of the bureaucracy has meant different things at different times. In the nineteenth century, the president's party controlled an enormous patronage pool of several hundred thousand jobs, from secretary of state to fourth class postmaster. In a series of reforms straddling the turn of the century, a merit system was introduced to civil service to insulate the bureaucracy from partisan influences. In order to guarantee the kind of job security that would frustrate a future administration's attempt to return to a patronage system, the reformers relegated the civil service to comparatively low-level operations. Policy discretion, to the degree present, remained in the hands of a class of political executives appointed by the president, confirmed by the Senate, and subject to removal by the president at any time.

Nowadays, several thousand of these political transients enter office with each new administration, and, once there, they serve about two years on average. Valued more for their loyalty to the president than their policy expertise or familiarity with the bureaucracy they administer, these actors are more appropriately regarded as members of the current president's team than as members of the bureaucracy.[58] Moreover, congressional committees have played an active role in overseeing the actions of the bureaucracy and guiding its policies through law, budget stipulations, and informal clearance procedures. In the United States, unlike in Japan, few look to the bureaucracy as an authoritative source of policy guidance.

In Japan, by comparison, where the bureaucracy's independence and authority have been conceded by virtually all who study the country's political economy, few bother to look elsewhere. In this pristine,

57. Jun-ichi Kyoguku, "The Common Sense of the Public and of the Political Establishment," *Japan Echo*, vol. 2 (Spring 1975), p. 18.
58. This classification belongs to Hugh Heclo, who aptly summed up the predicament of these transient politicians in their dealings with careerists in the bureaucracy and Congress as "poor credit risks in a well-established credit market." *A Government of Strangers: Executive Politics in Washington* (Brookings, 1977), p. 194.

politically hermetic setting, national economic policy is said to be conceived and implemented. Chalmers Johnson, who established Japan's bureaucracy as a research field for a generation of scholars with his book *MITI and the Japanese Miracle,* champions this interpretation:

> Politicians reign but do not rule; the actual decision makers are an elite bureaucracy of economic technocrats; the system works by serving those interests that are necessary to perpetuate it . . . but it otherwise excludes parochial interest[s] that would deflect it from developmental goals; and since the bureaucrats are guided by principles of economic rationality and *raison d'etat,* they ultimately serve national economic interests and are legitimized by popular nationalism.[59]

Some subsequent studies give the LDP a marginally greater role in overseeing ongoing management of economic growth. Others have detected the presence of more assertive politicians in recent years than Johnson's characterization allows.[60] But few have challenged the dominant role of the bureaucracy the way Sakakibara does in his essay. Before conceding that Japan's self-interested, ambitious politicians have somehow managed to remain uninvolved in formulating vital policies, one needs to reconsider the issue of bureaucratic primacy.

There are several problems with assertions of bureaucratic primacy as they now stand. Foremost among them, the industrial development policies described in Shimada's essay are not divorced from the economic interests that have actively supported the LDP. Rather, they are consistent with the kinds of policies one would expect from thirty-five years of this conservative party's hegemony. The policies simply do not in themselves favor a case for either bureaucratic or political primacy. Similarly, direct evidence of the level of political involvement in postwar industrial policymaking is subject to alternative interpretations.

Consider briefly the evidence Johnson marshals in *MITI and the Japanese Miracle.* He dates the emergence of MITI's ascendancy around 1955, which is the same year that the two conservative parties—the

59. Johnson, "Japanese Political Economy," p. 87.
60. Scholars' arguments are creeping into the conveyed wisdom on the subject. See Clyde Haberman, "Japan's Politicians Eclipse Bureaucrats," *New York Times,* December 22, 1986, p. A3.

Liberals and the Democrats—merged and took firm control of the Diet.[61] Throughout the era, policy shifts in MITI's domain were either mandated by a minister or, if favored by MITI's leadership, at least required a party leader's endorsement. None appears to have been pro forma. For example, the Special Measures Law, which Johnson describes as "the single most important piece of proposed economic legislation since the early years of the occupation," did not have an easy passage. Originating within MITI, it gave the ministry authority to promote the consolidation of companies in overly competitive industries. After an early endorsement by PARC and introduction in the Diet in 1962, the legislation, with its relaxed antimonopoly clause and other provisions, became so controversial the LDP withdrew its support. This ministry's program languished "sponsorless" through several sessions of the Diet, never coming to a vote. Confronted with a "structural recession" in late 1964, MITI Minister Hajime Fukoda embraced most of the bill's provisions and directed MITI to implement them through administrative guidance. MITI's eventual success in gaining this redirection of policy has been commonly hailed as an example of bureaucratic primacy. Although this policy was subsequently undermined by industries (principally auto manufacturers) that refused to cooperate, the important point here is that this brainchild of the bureaucracy was not implemented until the politicians decided they needed it.[62]

If the public record of LDP intervention in MITI's affairs does not portray activist, adversarial politicians, making their careers by public demonstrations of mastery of the bureaucracy the way their U.S. counterparts do, neither does it confirm political abdication. Why, then,

61. George C. Eads and Kozo Yamamura emphasize the implicit importance of the conservatives' control of government: "The ability of the government to pursue the pro-growth strategy was substantially strengthened by the effective disenfranchisement of the Left." "The Future of Industrial Policy," in Kozo Yamamura and Yasukichi Yasuba, eds., *The Political Economy of Japan*, vol. 1: *The Domestic Transformation* (Stanford University Press, 1987), p. 432.

62. During the 1970s, MITI's difficulties mounted. In 1970, the "pollution Diet" enacted fourteen environmental bills containing language opposed by MITI. The next year, Kakuei Tanaka took over the ministry and immediately embraced a minority position that MITI should begin addressing the social dislocations and costs of rapid economic development. The favorable publicity his efforts generated helped propel him into the party's presidency and redirected MITI's mission. A price-fixing scandal in the oil industry, apparently orchestrated under a framework created by MITI, led to the passage in 1977 of a revision of the Antimonopoly Law, again over MITI's energetic opposition. This legislation, according to Johnson, "put the ministry on notice that administrative guidance must be used in the interest of the nation and the people." *MITI and the Japanese Miracle,* p. 301.

have the politicians who do, after all, hold constitutional authority, been considered as the backbenchers of economic policymaking?

The answer is to be found in false appearances. The bureaucracy may be acting simply as the agent of politicians who have given it a mandate to identify policies that achieve the party's objectives. Where the party leaders are confident the bureaucrats are responsibly pursuing stipulated economic objectives, they may leave delegation open-ended, allowing the ministries free rein to adapt policies to changing economic circumstances. Extensive delegation to the bureaucracy is not unique to Japan and does not constitute abdication. Similar stories of political-bureaucratic relations have been told for Western parliamentary democracies—particularly Great Britain and France.[63] With legislative and executive authority consolidated within the governing party, politicians in parliamentary systems expose themselves to fewer risks in delegating tasks to the bureaucracy than do politicians in the United States, where there is an ongoing competition among institutions for control.

The relation between political control and delegation suggests that the latter should be more extensively developed in Japan than elsewhere because of the unequaled dominance of the LDP during the postwar era. The opposition is chronically splintered and mired in a seemingly permanent minority status; its influence over policy is largely limited to dilatory tactics. LDP politicians do not have to chisel policy in public laws or construct other barriers against their dismemberment by some imagined future majority coalition. Nor do they have to worry about bureaucrats hedging compliance in anticipation of a dramatic change in regimes. Under these favorable circumstances, informal means of party control suffice. The irony of Japan's politics is that the bureaucrats are delegated such great discretion, which is what gives rise to the bureaucratic primacy argument, because the governing party monopolizes political power.

THE NATURE OF DELEGATION. Not much effort is required to recognize why politicians prefer to delegate decisions to the bureaucracy. They avoid work; they may even be able to displace blame for policies that prove unpopular; and the expertise and technical information available to the bureaucracy means better policy is likely to result. The

63. James Q. Wilson, *Bureaucracy: What Government Agencies Do and Why They Do It* (Basic Books, 1989), pp. 295–314. See also Richard Crossman, *The Diaries of a Cabinet Minister,* vol. 1 (Holt, Rinehart and Winston, 1975); and Ezra N. Suleiman, *Politics, Power, and Bureaucracy in France: The Administrative Elite* (Princeton University Press, 1974).

downside of delegation, of course, is the risk that the bureaucracy may fail to faithfully pursue the politicians' preferences. Bureaucrats may have their own, different notions about what constitutes good public policy, reflecting either their professional assessment or their organization's interest. Consequently, politicians must monitor bureaucrats and occasionally apply sanctions to discourage shirking and prevent policy from drifting from the governing party's preferences. These costs of delegation are reduced to the degree bureaucrats anticipate the reactions of politicians and adjust policy accordingly. In a dominant-party setting where political control is complete, the bureaucracy will have developed highly sensitive political antennae.

The anticipation of reactions is, of course, ubiquitous to politics. Elected officeholders engage in it with their constituents and with one another. Similarly, politicians and bureaucrats alike will anticipate outcomes and behave in ways that render the appearance of power. Japan's bureaucrats have an expression for this syndrome: *jishu kisei.* As vital as they are for delegation, anticipated reactions pose special problems for institutional analysis. Observed behavior will not always reflect the individual's sincere preferences. And such behavior can corrupt the temporal sequence of events and throw suspicion on statements of causality that are founded on detailed descriptions of the policy process.

Consider the following statement that could describe a transaction between a bureaucrat and an elected officeholder: Actor A proposes policy X to actor B, who accepts it, thereby allowing proposal X to become law. Which actor is controlling policy? There are several possible answers. It looks as if actor A is dictating policy to B, especially when this scene appears repeatedly. Alternatively, A and B could be jointly producing policy X. Each appreciates that his or her true preferences— say, policies Y and Z—are unattainable without the other party's cooperation, and the compromise position X has been discovered over time to be the most attractive available outcome.[64] Or, finally, the correct explanation might have B dictating policy to A. Actor A's anticipation of the undesirable results of failing to provide B with what he wants dictates the submission of proposal X.

The first and third explanations imply that these actors are in a hierarchical relation that is not evident in the simple transaction. Actor A may have a monopoly on information that forces B to acquiesce to A's

64. Robert Axelrod, *The Evolution of Cooperation* (Basic Books, 1984).

policy proposals, or conversely, B may control A's tenure in office, thereby inducing compliance. To appreciate where power lies, one needs to know more than the details of the well-observed but bounded transaction of A proposing X to B. Instead, causality—that is, control over policy—can be identified only within the structure of the overall relationship.

The critical importance of this distinction becomes quickly apparent in the following example from contemporary Japanese politics. One widely cited study reported that the share of the Diet's laws originating in the ministries was growing steadily. By the mid-1970s, over 90 percent of successful bills were drafted by the agencies. This led the researcher to conclude "the bureaucracy is seen as a driving force" in policymaking, and public policy is "a step further removed from popular control."[65] But ministry proposals are not normally introduced to the Diet without first being cleared with the executive board of PARC, which frequently follows the formal recommendation of its relevant division and informally clears policy with the relevant *zoku*. As often as not, legislation is commissioned by politicians, who do not hesitate to have the ministry redraft policy until acceptable proposals are ready for submission. The strengthening grip of LDP politicians over bureaucratic discretion is at least as reasonable an interpretation for the rise of ministry authorship as the one originally offered.[66]

In a world of anticipated responses, convergence, and other forms of strategic behavior, the traditional research techniques of "poking and soaking" cannot guarantee success. Careful observation of the transaction may well miss critical information about the structure of the relationship that conditions each actor's behavior. Similarly, interviewing the participants may fail to uncover the real reasons for their behavior. After all, the investigator must know which questions to ask, and this

65. T. J. Pempel, "The Bureaucratization of Policymaking in Postwar Japan," *American Journal of Political Science*, vol. 18 (November 1974), p. 664.

66. For a more successful analysis of the bureaucracy's influence, see John Campbell's insightful study of Japanese budgeting, *Contemporary Japanese Budget Politics*. While the observable political intervention in ministry budget decisions appears to be mostly concerned with the distribution of appropriations for specific constituency projects, Campbell suspects the LDP has been able to satisfy its policy commitments without closely supervising the budgetary process. Even without active political intervention in general budget allocations, the annual budgets clearly favor programs that are close to the heart of LDP politicians and not a reflection of the "forward-looking" sensibilities of the MOF bureaucrats. One reason, he offers, is the MOF's anticipation of LDP politicians' preferences.

presupposes an understanding of the structure of the relationship. Even then, informants may not fully appreciate the strategic rationale of their actions. Worse still, they may exploit appearances to claim more credit than is due.[67]

INFORMAL MECHANISMS OF POLITICAL CONTROL. Because a single conservative party has presided over Japan's parliamentary system for nearly four decades, it is likely that policy deliberations would migrate out of the Diet, where they are exposed to challenge by the opposition parties and the potential disruption of public view, and into less formal settings such as PARC, the coteries of the LDP's senior policy specialists (*zoku*), and the prime minister's office. This does not mean that the constitutional order has been corrupted or that policymaking has become less democratic.

It does mean, however, that descriptions of policymaking run the risk of overstating the role of the bureaucracy. The observation of one senior bureaucrat is cautionary: "Real decisions come from above, formal decisions from below."[68] Even if all the accumulated descriptive facts about the activities of the prestigious ministries—the MOF and MITI— in formulating policy are correct, there remains the essential question: who controls economic policy?

The fact of every bureaucrat's life is that there is a politician somewhere who can make or break his or her career. More than anything else, bureaucrats' ultimate dependency on elected officeholders provides party politicians with the lever they need to overcome their relative lack of information and expertise and to insist their preferences be followed. This is the Achilles' heel of a bureaucratic primacy argument, applied to Japan or anywhere else.

Those who credit the professionals in the bureaucracy with Japan's economic growth argue that bureaucrats insulate themselves from political pressure by a long-term strategy that begins with the recruitment of the best and brightest from Japan's premier Tokyo University and

67. The extraordinary claims of Shigeru Sahashi, the former vice-minister of MITI and one of the heroes of Johnson's book, contain suspicious examples of just such self-promotion. In his autobiography, Sahashi asserts that during his tenure the Diet was merely an "extension of the bureaucracy." It is easy to see why Sahashi is a favorite source for those arguing a case for bureaucratic primacy in Japan's policymaking. Chalmers Johnson, "Japan: Who Governs?" *Journal of Japanese Studies,* vol. 2 (Autumn 1975), pp. 10–12.

68. Yung H. Park, *Bureaucrats and Ministers in Contemporary Japanese Government* (Berkeley: University of California, Institute of East Asian Studies, 1986), p. 108.

continues with the careful inculcation of neophytes in the virtues of professionalism and organizational patriotism. Loyalties are cemented with the prospect of steady advancement up the organizational pyramid strictly according to standards of merit. The attrition of offices near the top leaves only the most capable in charge of the ministry.

Careers must be comparatively short in order to supply vacancies for the steadily advancing cohorts. This potential liability has been ingeniously turned into an advantage through arrangements that virtually guarantee the bureaucracy's fifty-year-old retirees an attractive position elsewhere in government, business, or politics. From their new offices they maintain close ties with their former colleagues and pay back their ministry by protecting it from interference. Japan's ministries have presumably pulled off the neat trick of insulating themselves from political intrusion through a strategy of penetrating the institutions with which they conduct business and including those that have formal control over them. Many leaders of industry, the trade and business associations, and the governing LDP have attained their lofty positions after a fulfilling career in the bureaucracy. Little wonder the ministries seem to run the country.

On its face, the sharp attrition of ministry positions and the intense competition for them make for a risky and uncertain career. At the upper rungs of the career ladder, losers do not just fail to advance; they also have to accept early retirement.[69] These circumstances would appear to promote self-serving behavior by these ambitious bureaucrats to the detriment of the ministry. As these professionals advance each step up the organization and the competition becomes increasingly intense, they gain marketable assets in their administrative discretion. While bartering such assets in the private market violates the law, and its discovery would be the surest way of ending a career and losing a prosperous retirement, the political market is more inviting. With the factions actively "laying pipes" in the ministries to gain access to distributive policies for their constituencies, these bureaucrats have ample opportunity to exchange favorable consideration for political sponsorship in the next round of promotions. This is well worth doing since LDP politicians everywhere—the cabinet ministers, the *zoku* members, even PARC's

69. Even the individual who reaches the pinnacle of professional service, the administrative vice-minister, faces the prospect of having to leave the organization soon with poor retirement benefits and take up a new career with some client he is currently regulating.

divisions—become involved in clearing promotions, especially at the level of bureau director and above.[70]

One senior bureaucrat in the Foreign Affairs Ministry has described the political circumstances in terms that belie the concept of ministry autonomy:

> It is through the faction that the bureaucrat seeks peace and security for himself. When he reaches the division chief level, he picks out a political boss and joins his faction "in anticipation of future gains." Before joining he must carefully determine which faction is most advantageous and offers most security to him. In short, at this point (of his career) he is taking one of his greatest risks as an elite bureaucrat. When he moves up to the bureau director class, he gets frantic; he must squash his rivals before he is thinned out. To achieve this, he must borrow the power of his political boss.[71]

The logic of factional association applies equally well to the ministry, which has its own political needs, including access to each of the factions. There is clear evidence that an individual's factional ties are an important consideration for promotion within the ministry. Herein lies an instance of anticipated reactions: the bureaucracy has so thoroughly accommodated the priorities of the long-standing governing party in its training and advancement practices that the LDP rarely has to undertake a major intervention. "Partisanization of the bureaucracy has proceeded to such an extent that basic bureaucratic values . . . [are] acceptable to the party," argues Yung Park. "The party has confidence . . . in the 'weeding out' processes and views the bureaucracy as a partisanized ally and even 'tool.' "[72] So much for the autonomous ministries whose members deliberate public policy free from political concerns.

Supervision of internal advancement is just one of the many ways LDP politicians exercise subtle control over the bureaucracy. Other equally effective informal methods include rewarding responsive senior bureaucrats with attractive positions after they retire, encouraging ministry rivalries to bring policy disputes to the political leaders for

70. Among the most frequently cited Japanese statements on the political ties of Japan's bureaucrats is Michio Muramatsu, *Sengo Nihon no kanryōsei* (Japan's postwar bureaucracy) (Tokyo: Toyo Keizai Shinpōsha, 1981).
71. Quoted in Park, *Bureaucrats and Ministers,* p. 154.
72. *Bureaucrats and Ministers,* pp. 56–57.

resolution, and providing ready access to business firms wishing to appeal a ministry's regulatory action. As authoritative as the ministries and their leaders are, they lack the autonomy to shield their actions from the intrusion of political interests.

But if the bureaucracy is not as powerful as has been described, where among politicians is there a stake in growth-oriented economic policy? From the lowliest Diet member to the prime minister, LDP politicians have been presented here as preoccupied with providing particularistic goods to local and organized constituencies. There are several possibilities. First, because the LDP must periodically compete with the opposition parties in general elections that highlight national issues, each of the party's candidates finds it attractive for the party to address national problems, even at the expense of locally powerful constituencies. In the early 1970s, as the LDP's popular support dropped to dangerously low levels, reflecting in part general dissatisfaction with the country's polluted environment, the party leadership finally responded aggressively by passing a spate of strong and highly visible clean air legislation. Moreover, it directed a reluctant MITI to revise many of its regulations that subordinated environmental considerations to economic growth.

Other acclaimed national economic policies can be reconciled with the LDP's particularistic urges because they also address the needs of one of the party's core constituencies. Consider the thousand or so production and pricing cartels MITI instituted during the late 1950s and 1960s. One would be hard pressed to identify a more favorable regulatory environment for the profitability and rapid growth of the participating firms. With the cartel arrangements assuring market shares and dampening price competition, industries were virtually guaranteed high profits and low risks from expanding their productive capacity. Similarly, the bulk of MITI's administrative guidance decrees, which have over the years given it such an aura of autonomy and control, may represent little more than the codification of LDP-endorsed "implicit understandings" among the affected businesses.[73] These policies, which have been widely

73. Hiroshi Iyori, cited in Kozo Yamamura, "Success that Soured: Administrative Guidance and Cartels in Japan," in Kozo Yamamura, ed., *Policy and Trade Issues of the Japanese Economy: American and Japanese Perspectives* (University of Washington Press, 1982), p. 84. Similarly, John O. Haley argues, "There has been a misplaced emphasis on administrative guidance as a means used by the government 'to encourage private firms to take actions that [it] deems useful or necessary.' A more accurate description would stress the extent to which government policies reflected the needs and demands of those being 'guided.' " "Administrative Guidance vs. Formal Regulation: Resolving the Paradox of Industrial Policy," in Gary Saxonhouse and Kozo Yamamura,

acclaimed and imitated for yielding Japan's economic miracle, can be reasonably viewed as the fruits of the political process described in this essay.

Conclusion: The Palm Springs Rendezvous

At a time when the relationship between the United States and Japan was "as bad as I've ever seen it," in the opinion of one former State Department official, Prime Minister Toshiki Kaifu and President George Bush convened a hastily arranged summit in Palm Springs, California, in early March 1990.[74] These two heads of state took a dip in the pool and played a little golf to convey to photographers and the world their warm mutual regard and the cooperative spirit with which they would seek to resolve a quickly developing crisis in their countries' relations. President Bush faced a congressionally mandated deadline: he either had to declare that substantial progress had been made toward opening Japan's markets or he had to invoke trade sanctions. And yet, after more than a year of negotiations, the administration had almost nothing to show for its effort. If anything, each side's position appeared to have hardened. Despite the urgency, not much was resolved at the meeting. As it ended, Prime Minister Kaifu pledged before the television cameras to increase his country's purchase of American goods, and both men stood shoulder to shoulder to reiterate the familiar platitudes about the two countries' special relationship. Every informed observer recognized that months of negotiations with uncertain prospects lay ahead.[75]

Some correspondents covering the summit were clearly disappointed that they had no dramatic breakthrough to report. A superficial reading of each leader's circumstance might have given rise to inflated expectations. President Bush was basking in the highest job approval ratings the polls had ever bestowed on a president this far into his term. And Prime Minister Kaifu's party had just staved off a major defeat in the national elections, retaining firm control of the lower house of the Diet. Yet neither

eds., *Law and Trade Issues of the Japanese Economy: American and Japanese Perspectives* (University of Washington Press, 1986), pp. 107–08.

74. Bill Jaretski, "Can They Douse the Flames?" *Business Week,* March 12, 1990, p. 36.

75. Lower-level trade talks continued into summer with some significant concessions won in opening the Japanese market to American lumber products, supercomputers, and satellite technology. Remaining to be implemented were general agreements to alter Japan's retail trade laws and long-standing subcontract relations within Japan's manufacturing sector that made it difficult for outside firms to enter the market.

leader appeared able to capitalize on these favorable circumstances. Despite appearances, neither was in a position to bring new initiatives to Palm Springs. The reason, of course, is that each side's economic policies that caused the current crisis are rooted in domestic politics that stretch far beyond either leader's sphere of control.

Consider President Bush's predicament at the summit. He arrived in office greeted by a Democratic Congress that had grown suspicious of Republican commitment to redress the trade imbalance. Five months into the new president's term, Congress strengthened the trade law to give itself a larger role in formulating policy and monitoring the administration's performance. Among other provisions, it instructed the U.S. trade representative to report to Congress countries engaging in discriminatory trade practices and to undertake negotiations to remove such practices. If, after eighteen months, no progress were achieved, retaliatory sanctions were mandated. In giving the trade representative these responsibilities, Congress circumvented the traditional trade departments—principally, Commerce and State—and empowered an agency more beholden to Congress and therefore more sympathetic with its point of view.[76] As U.S. Trade Representative Carla Hills explained to reporters on leaving a Senate Finance Committee hearing one afternoon, she "consult[s] with Congress on everything . . . particularly when Congress has an interest."[77] The law that gave President Bush a headache at the summit was the brainchild of Congress's Democratic leadership.

Divided party control of the government is one reason for the tension between this president and Congress over trade. In recent years, Democrats have been more sensitive to the loss of jobs in industries, such as the automobile industry, whose work forces are important constituencies of the party. But there is also an institutional basis for the two branches' different level of concern over trade. Although no one has accused recent presidents of outright callousness toward the unemployment and lost business posed by U.S. trade relations with Japan, it is fair to say that nationally elected presidents need not be preoccupied

76. An example of the trade representative's responsiveness to congressional pressure is the reformulation of the joint production of Japan's next-generation fighter aircraft. See Prestowitz, *Trading Places*, pp. 39–64.

77. Ronald D. Elving, "Hills Vows Not To Keep Congress in the Dark on Soviet Talks," *Congressional Quarterly Weekly Report*, February 10, 1990, p. 381. To this end, USTR Hills conducts monthly closed-door briefings of the Senate Finance and House Ways and Means committees. Explained one of her staff, "The main message of the trade act is that Congress expects to be treated as a full partner in the trade process." Bruce Stokes, "Off and Running," *National Journal*, June 17, 1989, p. 1566.

with issues affecting narrow constituencies to the same extent as their representatives in Congress. Senator Max Baucus of Montana, who led the legislative charge to stiffen the administration's resolve, represents a state where the lumber industry is in a depression. With the prospect of a serious challenge in the fall of 1990, he understandably sought to impress constituents with his efforts to force Japan to relax its import barriers to finished lumber. As the Constitution's Framers fully intended, Congress is the representative branch. It is the natural home for the sponsorship of the particular concerns of local constituencies.

Moreover, the president is the one individual who has a political stake in a large variety of national policies, some of which work at cross-purposes. This has meant that trade issues must take a back seat at times to other pressing national concerns. American intransigence on the trade front could damage Bush's efforts to have Japan assume a greater role in financing economic reforms in Eastern Europe. After all, a month before the summit, Prime Minister Kaifu had visited that region and unveiled a new financial assistance package, only to return home to press criticism. On his arrival at the summit, when Kaifu announced that the agenda of discussions with Bush included their "global partnership," he was not simply blowing smoke over the trade impasse. For the Bush administration, if no one else, Kaifu's rhetoric had bite.[78]

As much as he might have liked to help the president out of his predicament, Prime Minister Kaifu was scarcely in a position to be of assistance. Indeed, he had ample cause to cry on the president's shoulder. Although he had avoided a feared election disaster, his political situation remained highly precarious. The peculiar sequence of events that had landed this unlikely figure in the prime minister's office also put him in a weak position. A host of senior faction leaders stood well ahead of him for this post, but in one way or another all were implicated in the Recruit bribery scandal and forced to disqualify themselves from consideration. Prime Minister Noboru Takeshita was forced to resign in April 1989. His successor, Sosuke Uno, resigned after only three months because of exposure of an extramarital affair with a geisha and the LDP's stinging defeat in the May 1989 elections for the Diet's upper house.

78. Another issue that has at times directly interfered with pressing Japan on trade is the two countries' security relations. The U.S. presence in the Pacific and its costs are directly tied to Japan's contribution to complementing these military forces and offsetting the financial costs. The most recent case in point was the administration's vacillating policy toward Japan's decision to build its own FSX warplane. See Prestowitz, *Trading Places*, pp. 13–58.

Finally, the party patriarchs turned to this comparatively young, untainted, improbable figure. Everyone assumed Kaifu would be easily controllable and easily replaced once the public's displeasure over the scandals subsided. The prime minister's weak position was not lost on the Bush administration. Shortly after the summit, Secretary of State James Baker conferred in Washington with former prime minister Takeshita, who still presided over the LDP's largest faction and had backed Kaifu's election.

In addition, it is reasonable to wonder whether even Kaifu's more resourceful predecessors would have been in a much better position to respond to U.S. demands. The factional politics of the LDP limit the national executive's political clout in lining up party support and mobilizing the bureaucracy behind his initiatives.[79] Other factional leaders may, at times, find their own political advancement in the incumbent prime minister's failure. As the LDP struggled in the aftermath of the summit to formulate a response, it labored under its own variety of divided government.

The limitations of weak national leadership are compounded by the LDP's dependence on core constituencies, which deters it from formulating policies that impose short-term costs. The special difficulty LDP politicians have in dealing with their constituencies extends beyond the color of money to the fundamental relationship between the representative and the local constituency, made especially strong in this instance by the electoral system.

American negotiators hammered at precisely the policies that had served the LDP's core constituencies so well. One concerned revising the Large-Scale Retail Store Law, which allows local shopowners to postpone the opening of supermarkets for up to ten years. This practice has long been blamed for Japan's high consumer prices and the failure of foreign goods to penetrate Japan's domestic market. But to draw the support of the large numbers of these shopowners, Kaifu had campaigned within the month that the LDP would not allow any change in this law. Not content with promises, their associations subsequently staged a mass demonstration.

Even more threatening was Bush's effort to have Kaifu dismantle long-established arrangements, called *keiretsu,* whereby a set of businesses within an industry privately work out agreements for the purchase and distribution of goods. For many foreign firms, breaking into these

79. See Sam Jameson, "Japan's Ruling Party Balks on Trade Proposal," *Los Angeles Times,* March 17, 1990, p. D2.

378 SAMUEL KERNELL

informal networks has proven an insurmountable hurdle. But this practice is pervasive and strikes at another core constituency of the LDP. By one estimate, businesses so engaged had invested $200 million in the recent LDP campaign. "If you change these practices, the LDP government cannot survive," proffered one trade negotiator.[80] No wonder, as the newspaper *Asahi Shimbun* charged, the party is attempting "to get through . . . with the minimum possible reforms in order to protect vested interests at home."[81]

When asked by a correspondent about the likely outcome of negotiations on these and other summit issues, Chalmers Johnson declared, "They are doomed, because Japan will not change voluntarily. To suggest otherwise is self-delusion."[82] Perhaps "cannot" would be more accurate, for it is less a question of will than of means. The leaders who matter are not the reportedly disinterested bureaucrats but the politicians who rose to their stations by virtue of their superior performance in the service of particularism. In the process of upward advancement, they become bound by and accustomed to the many lilliputian threads of political commitment.

The dissimilar predicaments of Bush and Kaifu notwithstanding, the trade friction that periodically brings discord to these countries' relations is found not, as many observers claim, in their differentness. What strains the countries' bilateral relations is not a failure to communicate, rooted in national character or civic culture, but a conflict of interests that are well represented in each country's politics and reflected in its economic policy.

The causes of these leaders' predicaments run parallel. The inability of Bush and Kaifu to find an easy solution to the trade impasse springs from the responsiveness of each country's politicians to appeals from local and organized constituencies. When the pressure mounts, those few politicians who are entrusted by party or sufficiently insulated by the constitution to assume a national perspective find themselves, in the absence of a broader agreement, unable to move policy beyond the pressures of democracy.

80. Steven R. Weisman, "Trade Talks Fail to Produce Gains for U.S. or Japan," *New York Times*, March 16, 1990, p. D2. For the political constraints posed by Japanese interest groups on these trade negotiations, see Sam Jameson, "Interest Groups: Strong Silent Partner at Bush-Kaifu Talks," *Los Angeles Times*, March 3, 1990, p. A8.
81. Sam Jameson, "Kaifu Will Try to Convince Bush that Trade Progress Is Being Made," *Los Angeles Times*, March 1, 1990, p. A8.
82. Weisman, "Trade Talks Fail to Produce Gains."

Contributors

JOHN E. CHUBB
Senior Fellow
Brookings Governmental Studies
Program

SAMUEL KERNELL
Professor of Political Science
Coordinator, American Political
Institutions Project
University of California, San Diego

MASARU MABUCHI
Associate Professor of Law
Osaka University

MATHEW D. MCCUBBINS
Professor of Political Science
University of California, San Diego

MICHIO MURAMATSU
Professor of Law
Kyoto University

YUKIO NOGUCHI
Professor of Economics
Hitotsubashi University

ROGER G. NOLL
Morris M. Doyle
Centennial Professor in
Public Policy
Stanford University

PAUL E. PETERSON
Henry Lee Shattuck Professor of
Government
Director, Center for American
Political Studies
Harvard University

EISUKE SAKAKIBARA
Director General
Tokai Local Finance Bureau
Ministry of Finance

ALLEN SCHICK
Professor of Public Policy
Director, Bureau of
Governmental Research
University of Maryland

HARUO SHIMADA
Professor of Economics
Keio University

Index